Asia's
Orthographic
Dilemma

漢字

ASIA'S ORTHOGRAPHIC DILEMMA

Wm. C. Hannas

With a Foreword by John DeFrancis

University of Hawai'i Press, Honolulu

for Thu

with love and appreciation

02 01 00 99 98 97   5 4 3 2 1

Library of Congress Cataloging-in-Publication Data
Hannas, Wm. C., 1946–
     Asia's orthographic dilemma / Wm. C. Hannas ; with a foreword by
John DeFrancis.
          p.   cm.
     Includes bibliographical references and index.
     ISBN 0–8248–1842–3 (cloth : alk. paper). — ISBN 0–8248–1892–X
(pbk. : alk. paper)
     1. Chinese characters—East Asia. 2. Chinese language—Writing.
I. Title.
PL1171.H34   1996
495—dc21   96–44397
                                                                                  CIP

Frontispiece illustration: Calligraphy by Catherine Yu.

Book design by Kenneth Miyamoto

Contents

Foreword

THIS STUDY OF the use of Chinese characters in the writing systems of China, Korea, Japan, and Vietnam is, amazingly, the product of a single scholar who may well be the only person to have ever achieved command over all four of the languages involved, not to mention a few others that have helped him gain access to additional material and to the thought of other scholars. Such a unique linguistic endowment has provided a solid basis for a comparative study that is both incisive and comprehensive.

In relating the character-based writing systems to the languages they represent, the author cuts through a great deal of mythology about their commonality to reveal how difficult and ill-suited each one is in comparison to systems of writing founded on simple alphabetic principles. He further shows how the impact of alphabetic systems is undermining the hegemony of the character base of the traditional systems of writing. Arguing that the Asian cultures based on these systems are therefore in crisis, he builds a particularly strong case for the conclusion that the intractable incompatability between characters and computers will be a primary factor in the eventual demise of the former.

To a considerable extent the turmoil in the writing systems of three of the countries (that of Vietnam has in the main been resolved) is going on largely unnoticed. This is due in part to the fact that the technical aspects involved make understanding difficult while aiding the perpetuation of myths and misunderstandings about Asian writing, both within these countries and among foreign observers.

Such myths and misunderstandings, compounded in the case of China by pseudo-scientific claims for the superiority of the "ideographic" characters and their impending global replacement of the inferior alphabetic systems of the West, have led to a situation where advocating reform, or even questioning the ability of character-based writing to satisfy modern needs, is met either by deliberate or unthinking inattention, by reflexive cultural defensiveness, or, again especially in the case of China, by venomous xenophobic attack against native proponents of reform and their Western supporters.

This is a deplorable situation. While the problems involved are complex, they are by no means of mere academic interest but of such critical importance to the cultural and overall future of the countries involved as to warrant conscientious consideration. They are extensively discussed in this book.

In the author's own often trenchant and occasionally memorable phrasing, here are a few of his main observations that merit particular attention:

1. It is not, as many argue, that the characters are intrinsically well suited to Chinese, but that they generated this "suitability" themselves by forcing the language into their own characteristic mold.

2. Linguistically speaking, the only good thing that can be said about Chinese characters is that they help solve problems which their own use has created.

3. Reform of character-based writing is basically a zero-sum game, where changes introduced in one area lead to problems in another, until the whole effort falls apart because of the shortsightedness of reformers who cannot perceive that there is *no solution* within the context defined.

4. Our position here is not that East Asians lack creativity, but that they achieved their intellectual greatness *in spite of* the character-based writing system.

5. Under pressure to absorb international vocabulary, encouraged by new technological venues, and facilitated by English language bilingualism, the alphabet is taking its place alongside traditional orthographies in more and more applications.

6. Viewed globally and historically, it is clear that characters are on their last legs.

Not everyone will agree with these conclusions. I too have reservations, particularly as regards the last item. I agree in the case of Korea, but am less sure in the case of Japan and even less sure in the case of China. It seems to me that while China's need to access the global information highway is forcing it to make practical use of pinyin, which reformers are promoting not as a replacement for characters but as part of digraphia, that is, a two-script policy of indefinitely long duration, opposition to alphabetic writing is so strong that it will in all likelihood severely retard the advance of pinyin even as a secondary system of writing.

My own assessment of the Chinese situation at the end of the twentieth century is that it bears some analogy with that of Italy at the end of the thirteenth century, when Dante began to promote Italian in place of Latin in some areas of usage, primarily poetry. Although Italian early became established in "practical use," as in commercial transactions, it was slow to make progress in academic areas. As late as the sixteenth century the amount written in Italian was still less than what was written in Latin. The latter was not completely relegated to an antiquarian status until well into the eighteenth century, almost five hundred years after Dante's limited initiative.

Perhaps the Chinese situation, like the Italian, can be charted on a coordinate system with the proportion of pinyin (or Italian) usage on the vertical axis and time on the horizontal axis. Over time will the line representing pinyin usage remain utterly flat, barely above zero, as it is at present? Will its trajectory rise steeply in the next few decades, as the author seems to expect? Or will it rise slowly, taking generations, perhaps centuries, to approach the halfway mark and then either level off indefinitely or continue to climb until it nears the hundred percent mark?

It is impossible, of course, to provide definitive answers to these questions now. But this book offers background information and stimulating analysis for thinking about them. In the years to come it will help readers plot the trajectory of that problematic line.

JOHN DeFRANCIS

Acknowledgments

I WISH TO THANK a few people who helped make this book possible.

My debt to Professor John DeFrancis is enormous. I was introduced to his work on East Asian writing reform early in my academic career and have been trying in vain to catch up ever since. To him I owe the inspiration for this volume. Professor DeFrancis also took time from his busy publishing schedule to review each of my chapters and offer badly needed criticism.

Professor Victor H. Mair also reviewed my earliest drafts. His advice, counsel, and constant encouragement were indispensable. It is one of life's ironies that, although we have long held similar views on the issues this book raises, our collaboration came about quite by accident. I am very lucky indeed.

Professor Michael McCaskey was always supportive. Dr. Pham Van Hai provided important materials for the Vietnamese segment of this book. Steve Zaveloff shared his broad knowledge of Japanese language and culture. Valery Chou and Helen Wang taught me Shanghainese and in the process something about China. Lee Mei-hsien offered many helpful thoughts on problems I had with various parts of the book. I am grateful to Professor Catherine Yu for her friendship and for the calligraphy that graces the frontispiece.

Thanks of a special sort are due to Patricia Hazelbarth and Lyle Horton for accommodating my erratic schedule and for supporting me in many other ways.

Finally, hats off to the unknown officer in the U.S. Navy's Bureau of Personnel, who years ago sent an unwilling recruit off to East Asia instead of to the stateside tour which he had requested.

Part 1 HISTORY AND STRUCTURE OF WRITING IN EAST ASIA

1. Chinese

AMONG EAST ASIA'S cultural artifacts nothing stands out as so peculiarly Asian as the unique system of writing shared by China, Japan, Korea, and until recently Vietnam. To the Westerner coming to grips with this economically dynamic region of the world, Chinese characters are at once the area's most salient unifying feature and the most impenetrable aspect of the culture. To East Asians, the characters are much more. As the dominant form of writing, the system forms the basis of their culture and their civilization, the Sinitic terms for which are, literally, "transformed by writing" and "enlightenment through writing."[1] To both groups of people, Chinese characters are also the source of countless myths, which refuse to disappear no matter what linguists say about them.

One source of these myths is confusion about the Chinese "language" itself. Accordingly, this study begins with a review of the language that gave rise to the writing: its typology, characteristics, and some myths of its own perpetrated by scholars who should know better—and by others with a political agenda who *do* know better. I shall then discuss the development of writing in China. Unlike many studies that view Chinese characters in isolation, my emphasis here and in subsequent chapters will be on the close relationship between written and spoken Chinese. Functionally and diachronically, it is impossible to describe the writing system without reference to the language it represents. It must also be understood that the dependency works both ways—that the language evolved in large measure under the influence of the system used to write it.

Spoken Chinese

"Chinese" means many things, and we can avoid much confusion by defining the term at the outset. When used here in a linguistic sense, unless otherwise identified, for example, as "Chinese characters" or "Chinese writing," or understood as such in context, the term "Chinese" always refers to language that is, was, or can be spoken. Linguists understand language to be a conventional body of abstract relationships that depends primarily on speech for its concrete realization and on a phonological component for much of its internal structure and functioning. Chinese writing, in other words, is not the language. It is a system for representing statements generated by the language.

Arguably, the conventions for writing Chinese can be included in an expanded definition of "Chinese," much as the protocols for producing speech from an abstract phonological component are. In this configuration, statements are represented visually through the application of one set of rules or verbally through another set. The mechanisms for writing are located somewhere in the literate user's psyche. Moreover, there is solid empirical evidence that linguistic elements can be accessed from visible stimuli without the intervention of phonology. There is, nonetheless, a qualitative difference between the two subsystems, speech and writing. Absent writing, language can still function. Phonology, in contrast, must exist for language to work, even if only as a code for short-term memory and as the basis for the phonemes and graphemes used in the language's representation. While Chinese writing is formally separable from language, the phonological precursors leading to Chinese speech are not.

There is another reason why we can distinguish writing from language (keeping in mind that all writing is based on language), while retaining speech as an integral part of the latter. Speech results from the application of rules to phonological units that have their origin within the linguistic apparatus of each user. Although the configuration of these units and the types of rules applied may vary from one individual and language to the next, the basic parameters of the process are fixed. Their steps and order apply generally, and hence are considered a part of language. This is not so with writing. Where writing maps onto language is a matter of convention. Although the present convention for writing Chinese is to represent the language's syllables and morphemes (basic units of meaningful sound), there is no reason why statements in Chinese cannot be expressed visibly through different conventions that are keyed to other levels, such as morphophonemes (phonemes that belong to the same morpheme) or phonemes, without changing the substance of what is communicated. There is no need for Chinese language to have the particular written representation people have given it, or for that matter to have any written representation at all.

Chinese language is not writing. This narrows our definition considerably, but there are other ambiguities surrounding the term "Chinese" that need to be resolved before we can understand the relationship between Chinese and Chinese characters. This first one is, if Chinese is not writing, what about the language that is written? Most contemporary texts reflect a language that is similar enough in its essentials to spoken Chinese to be considered a representation of the latter. By and large, reforms undertaken in the early part of the century have produced stylistic conventions for written Chinese that retain a large measure of phonetic intelligibility, so that most parts of many texts written today can be understood when read aloud to native speakers who have some knowledge of the subject addressed. This was not always so. Character texts composed two millennia ago in the Han dynasty, or in a style imitative of that era's grammar, cannot be understood by literate Chinese today even as written (not to mention if read aloud) unless they are trained in classical Chinese.[2] We have no more basis for considering both the language of these texts and the modern idiom "Chinese" than we have, say, for calling modern English and some attested variety of early Germanic both "English."

Those who have never read classical Chinese or who have a stake in one or more aspects of the Chinese myth can be fooled by Chinese characters into believing that the languages represented are one and the same. Whereas no one would equate modern English with Latin on the basis of their shared use of the Roman alphabet, the use of the same type of writing system for modern Chinese and its earlier states leads many to assert that the characters offer a unique bridge that unites "the language" through all time. From there it is a short step to the claim that "Chinese" is one of the world's oldest living languages, if not the single oldest. In fact, neither claim is valid.

Although the writing *system* has remained the same, many of its units—like the written morphemes of any language—are unique to a particular era, a particular part of China, or both. Many are not used in modern Chinese, and today's readers often have no clue of what they meant or sounded like. The fact that these units were written and recorded in dictionaries, however, and the fact that their pronunciations cannot be pinned down to a given era on the basis of their physical structure allow Chinese and students of Chinese to imagine that the inventory of symbols is cumulative and that, once created, the character is always part or potentially part of a user's repertoire. To a distressing degree this is true. Highly educated Chinese tend to reach back into the history of the written language to resurrect obsolete morphemes that are still listed in large dictionaries and hence technically still available. While effective as a means of demonstrating erudition, such usages have no currency among the body of users, most of whom have no idea what such a character is supposed to mean and will not even bother to look it up. The practice is equivalent to the use of Latin by modern English writers. In both cases we are dealing with entirely different languages.

Not only are many of the characters used in classical Chinese obsolete or obscure, others had meanings entirely different from those given to the characters by modern users. The extent of these differences can be gauged by the fact that non-Asian students of classical Chinese often learn more quickly than native Chinese fluent in the modern idiom, since the former are not encumbered by false associations between meaning and symbol—

which are, in fact, neologisms. The matter is no different with respect to grammar, which cannot be masked by the characters. Not only must classical grammar be studied deliberately for a modern reader to make sense of a classical text, students must learn many different sets of conventions for the different periods the "language" was in use. To summarize, just as Chinese language is not Chinese writing, so are texts written by Chinese in Chinese characters not necessarily "Chinese," if the term is to refer to a language comprehensible to modern speakers.

Our definition of "Chinese" has important implications for understanding the nature, functioning, and utility of the character writing system, as will become evident in later chapters. There are also social and political dimensions to the problem. We have seen that the "language" that was written and spoken historically in much of the area that constitutes present-day China was not uniform through time. What was spoken in China 3,500 years ago had little in common with what was used there two thousand years ago and shared almost nothing with the Chinese spoken in the sixth century A.D., from which point most of the modern descendants of the earlier language began to develop (Forrest 1973:220). Still it is all characterized as "Chinese." There are two ways to handle this discrepancy. We can reject the unqualified use of the term for historical periods and insist that it be distinguished with adjectives such as "old," "ancient," "archaic," and "proto," which describe more or less coherent states defined by records or reconstructions. This approach is taken by linguists, who find no more substance in the self-serving claim that "Chinese is the world's oldest living language," than in the idea that English, Russian, or Korean is. All human languages spoken today, unless they are the products of invention, can be traced back successively to genetic antecedents, making each as old as the next. If Chinese is unique in this respect, I would like to know how.

A second approach to the terminological difficulty is to follow common usage and accept the word "Chinese" as a generic label that encompasses the languages spoken today and ancestrally. This approach makes sense, because it accommodates the historical facts while clearing a path for solution of a more grievous misconception concerning the structure of Chinese as it is currently spoken. Not only is Chinese not a language for all times, it is not a "language" at all. Rather, it is a branch of the Sino-Tibetan language family (Mair 1991a: 4). Depending on the criteria, there are seven or eight—or as many as several hundred—mutually unintelligible varieties of modern Chinese, which in any other context would be considered languages in their own right, but which Chinese people (especially Mandarin speakers) and governments call "dialects" of a single Chinese "language." To most linguists, the claim is utter nonsense.

How this myth came about will be treated in detail later in the book. Meanwhile, here are the facts: modern Chinese is made up of a half dozen or more major languages, each with several of its own dialects. The "northern" variety known as Mandarin is the official norm sanctioned by all present Chinese governments and is spoken natively by some 70 percent of China's Han population living in the country's northern and central provinces. Mandarin is defined by at least four major regional dialects whose differences compare with American, Australian, and British English, and by an overlay of social dialects that also vary significantly.

Although Mandarin is the primary Chinese language in terms of government recognition and number of speakers, it is not the language most Westerners associate with Chinese, nor is it the language used natively by the most mobile segment of China's population. For more than a century, Cantonese was the Chinese language heard most commonly in overseas immigrant communities. With some fifty million speakers, it is still the undisputed language of choice in China's southern provinces and in Hong Kong. Farther up the coast, across the Taiwan Strait, and in large areas of Southeast Asia, there are many million more speakers of another "nonstandard" variety—Min—for whom Mandarin is as foreign as Spanish is to someone from France. Continuing northward to the coastal city of Shanghai and surrounding regions, one enters the Wu area of eighty million speakers, who without bilingual training cannot communicate with speakers of any other major group. Farther inland are tens of millions of Xiang, Gan, and Hakka speakers, to mention only the major languages. In terms of vocabulary, pronunciation, grammar, history, and mutual intelligibility, the Chinese languages are at least as distinct from one another as the individual Romance languages.

"Chinese," then, refers to a branch of spoken languages that, like all other languages, have histories that can in theory be traced to a common protoform. The progenitor of modern Chinese is believed to have existed until the second half of the first millennium A.D. The structure of earlier stages is hypothesized on the basis of written records, whose exploitation is complicated by the character writing system, which gives an idea of sound categories but no hint of the sounds themselves. It is not certain how closely the texts reflect the language or languages spoken, particularly for periods before the Han dynasty. One school of thought argues that a richer system of phonological contrasts enabled ancient Chinese speakers to understand the terse, monosyllabic texts handed down to us; in other words, they wrote the same language they spoke. Another school maintains, more plausibly, that pre-Han texts had very little in common with what was spoken anywhere in China. This latter thesis is supported by traditional comparative methodology based on dialects of spoken Chinese languages and on comparisons made between the individual languages' reconstructed protoforms.

The best analyses use the comparative method in conjunction with written records, including poetry and attested foreign borrowings. One fact that is emerging from these studies is that the spoken language never was "monosyllabic," certainly not now and not as far back as our methods allow us to reconstruct. Although one can argue, as I shall later, that Chinese *morphology* is highly monosyllabic, words commonly consist of two or more syllables that historically were often single morphemes as well. Examples include foreign borrowings into Chinese, including many that entered the language at an early period. More recent borrowings, known as "round trip" or "repatriated" words because they were coined in other East Asian countries with Sinitic morphemes, are almost all bisyllabic—the most common format for nonbasic Chinese terms, that is, the overwhelming majority of current lexical items.

With respect to everyday, basic vocabulary, however, Chinese does share with English a preference for single-syllable words, unlike the bisyllabic format used in Altaic and Semitic languages. It also has in common with English the same basic subject-verb-object (SVO) order. While some phrase structures are different, most notably the use in Chinese of long clauses in apposition to the noun being modified, where English uses the relative clause, professional translators are often surprised at how closely the two languages mirror each other. These correspondences may not be entirely coincidental. Recent scholarship has uncovered hundreds of cognate early Chinese and Indo-European terms (Chang 1988; Bauer 1994), many of which are basic and cannot be explained away as the result of cultural contact. More important, Chang's research on the evolution of Chinese tones from syllable finals shows detailed phonetic correspondences between the languages' reconstructed protoforms, the correspondence with Germanic being particularly close. The possibility of a genetic relationship between Chinese and European languages is not as far-fetched as it seemed a decade or two ago (Mair 1990, 1995). It certainly brings Chinese a lot closer to the Western experience and helps dispel notions of its uniqueness.

Next to Chinese writing, which strictly speaking is not part of the language, the feature most commonly associated by Westerners with Chinese is phonemic tone. All Chinese languages incorporate in their syllables tonal contours, which speakers use along with other phonemic contrasts to distinguish one syllable from the next. The tones number from three to nine or more, depending on the particular language and dialect and on how the tones are counted. Tonal distinctions are (or were) more the rule than the exception in East and Southeast Asia, and are noteworthy in the present context only inasmuch as they tend to be ignored in some of the less sophisticated arguments which suggest that Chinese cannot be written phonetically because it lacks sufficient contrasts. Tones also tend to give Chinese an unwarranted exotic flair, particularly languages with a large number of tones like Cantonese and Min. In fact, many of these tonal contrasts are determined by the syllable's segmental phonology and are no harder to master than the suprasegmentals (pitch, stress, juncture, etc.) of English.

Development of Writing in the West

Chinese characters are unique among writing systems used today. They look different, and, on the surface at least, they are different. Whereas casual observation of texts written in other languages shows a repetition of a limited number of discrete signs, you can scan several lines of a Chinese character text and find very few repeats. Further inspection shows that, unlike words written in phonetic alphabets, the characters do not decompose feature by feature according to the sounds they represent. They cannot even be consistently relied on to give the same pronunciation, because many characters have multiple readings. Furthermore, characters with manifestly different shapes may have identical pronunciations. Some symbols seem to resemble pictures. Yet the meanings ascribed to them generally have no connection with what they appear to represent. When asked what a particular character means, an informant will respond with no words or many words, some semantically related, others with no apparent semantic relationship. Indeed, the terms "letter" and "word" are irrelevant to what these symbols are all about.

These differences between Chinese character–based writing and scripts based on the alphabetic principle belie the fact that both types share conceptually identical origins. This is to say, alphabetic writing did not begin as such. It will be useful, accordingly, to precede our discussion of the evolution of Chinese writing with a review of the origins of Western alphabetic writing.[3] The purpose of this brief exercise is twofold: to demonstrate that Chinese writing, like the language itself, is less of an anomaly than many imagine and to show that the differences that do exist can be better understood not as features of an "alternative" form of writing, but rather as the arrested development of a universal process.

In the second half of the fourth millennium B.C., the Sumerians in lower Mesopotamia were using an advanced form of pictographic writing whose symbols had precisely as little in common with the alphabet as Chinese characters do today. Their cuneiform ("wedge-shaped") symbols were originally icons of natural phenomena, signs that bear a physical resemblance to the object represented. Their connection with language was established through two techniques. On the one hand, the symbols that originally had as their meanings the occurrence of specific objects came to stand for occurrences of the objects generally. This generalization cleared the path for the symbols to represent whole classes of phenomena or "the *meaning* of the word naming" the phenomena (Jensen 1970:51). Thus a symbol's primary referent became not an isolated event, as in pictures, but a unit of meaning corresponding to that delineated by a word in natural language—although the primary linkage was with the named concept, not with the name per se and even less with the name's phonetic characteristics. This judgment is supported by the practice in the early stages of the script's development of using a given symbol for a multitude of distinct values based on semantic congruity. This practice, in turn, put pressure on the system to evolve a set of graphic "determinatives" whereby certain symbols, taken as more basic than others, were affixed to ambiguous graphs to delineate the meanings of the latter (Sampson 1985:55).

The identification of symbol with word (i.e., with an existing association of meaning and sound) describes the "logographic" principle, the first of two devices used by the Sumerians to link their written signs with natural language. The second technique derives from difficulties encountered in using the above principle to depict relational concepts, such as function words in the language's grammar, and from the need to render personal names (Gelb 1962:194). Neither requirement could be satisfied, in a practical sense, by symbols associated with the concepts of a language through physical iconicity. Something more was needed. Meanwhile, as the symbols' referents were moving from specific events to generalized abstractions, the pictographic forms themselves also were becoming more abstract. Depicting every detail of an iconic symbol was not economical, especially after "literate" users had become familiar with the convention.

As the tie between referent and icon became more tenuous, so did the psychological bond linking the referent to a word's semantic component. Primary linkage thus began to shift to the phonetic attributes of words, at which point nothing prevented these symbols from standing for different, semantically unrelated concepts bearing the same sounds, for example, the symbol for "hand" (Sumerian *su*) for the syllable *su*. In this fashion, a full syllabary was able to develop alongside the logographic use of the cuneiform symbols, the two together making up the world's first "genuine writing system . . . used for extended texts," which could record "all lexical and grammatical elements" of the spoken language (Sampson 1985:49–50). Ultimately the system evolved into what DeFrancis describes as "a primarily syllabic system of writing with some secondary and non-essential word signs hung over from a pictographic past" (DeFrancis 1995:13).

Significantly, the same processes governed the evolution of Egyptian "hieroglyphs," which, while perhaps owing something to the Sumerians conceptually, developed independently of the latter, as attested by the earliest examples. By 2700 B.C. written Egyptian was using symbols that could represent (1) "the original object or action pictured," (2) "another word suggested by the picture," or (3) "a word or part of a word having the same (or nearly the same) consonants" appearing in the same order (Hodge 1973:477). As the hieroglyphs became more cursive in form and more closely identified with the sounds of the corresponding words, constraints on the use of these symbols for homonyms disappeared. By 1500 B.C., twenty-four hieroglyphs were being used for the most common syllables of spoken Egyptian, alongside the logographic hieroglyphs, which were never fully replaced.

Neither the Sumerians nor the Egyptians were able to make a full transition to the phonetic use of their respective symbols in disregard of the semantic values originally assigned. This transition was accomplished only by other peoples who borrowed these symbols for their own languages, who had no use for the semantic associations, wishing only to record sounds (Haas 1976:202). The Akkadians, for example, adopted the Sumerian cuneiform script sometime in the third millennium B.C. and made much greater use of the phonetic principle. The twenty-four hieroglyphs used by the Egyptians phonetically were, likewise, borrowed in the second millennium B.C. by Semitic peoples who used them for their sound values only.

The phonetic use of logographic symbols in Egyptian and Semitic was linked, initially, to the representation of entire syllables. This mapping works well only for languages with a small number of syllables. For languages with many syllables, such as Greek, pressure is put on the writing system to evolve into a one-sign-one-phoneme format, in other words, an alphabet. In Egyptian and Old Semitic this result was achieved by ignoring all elements of an indicated syllable except the initial consonant. There were also provisions for indicating vowels in Egyptian but the Greeks were the first to do so systematically. By adding vowel symbols to the syllabic signs borrowed from the West Semitic syllabary, the Greeks created the first true alphabet, the ancestor of those used in the West today.

Summarizing the above, the evolution of alphabetic writing systems can be characterized as a move toward increasing abstractness. Symbols evolved through the following stages: (1) picture of an object, (2) representation of that class of objects, (3) representation of the word for that class of objects, (4) increasing focus on the phonetic aspect of the word represented, (5) loss of the necessary identification of a symbol with a given word, and (6) fractionalization of concrete, naturally occurring syllabic units into abstract phonemes represented by letters.

Development of Writing in China

The development of character-based writing in China and its diffusion and metamorphosis throughout the other countries of East Asia show striking parallels with what I have described above. These similarities in part result from universal constraints on what can happen given the nature of language, the structure of the instruments used to express it, and evolutionary selection for efficiency. This last factor is still operating, and it need not occur incrementally. Reform of the character writing system, where effective, can be interpreted in a cosmic sense as the operation of impersonal evolutionary factors, that is, as part of a tendency for writing to become, like speech, less a concrete representation of the world (pictographs and onomatopoeia) and more an abstract tool for dealing with it. Practically speaking, however, individual users make the changes, and these users are often influenced by their knowledge of other societies and their writing systems.

The extent to which Chinese writing had its origin outside Chinese culture remains an open question. Gelb allowed that writing's "main principles . . . may have spread eastward [and] may have been the stimulus leading to the creation of the Chinese writing" (1962:195). Diringer reached the same conclusion: "The general conception of writing might perhaps have been borrowed, directly or indirectly, from the Sumerians, but not a single sign taken from the Sumerian system can be found. A dependence on Egyptian hieroglyphics is still more unlikely" (1968:66).[4] DeFrancis believes that the arguments advanced for both "independent invention" and "stimulus diffusion" are unconvincing; barring new evidence, he is inclined to credit the Chinese with the ingenuity to have "independently thought up somewhat similar solutions to somewhat similar problems" (1989:90).

Chinese tradition, for its part, holds that Chinese characters, the first writing of any sort to appear in East Asia, were invented by Cang Jie 倉頡, a historian employed by the legendary Yellow Emperor (2697–2597 B.C.). Cang allegedly was inspired by the "eight trigrams"—combinations of three broken or solid lines created by Fu Xi 伏羲 (2852–2737 B.C.) on the basis of patterns perceived within the hexagonal shapes of tortoise shells (Liu 1969:6). Some extant samples of what may have been a predecessor to Chinese writing were found on early bronzes, but they are too few and poorly understood to support a claim of genetic affinity. The earliest period for which records exist in quantity is 1400 to 1200 B.C. in the form of inscriptions on shells and animal bones used for divination and state inventories. From the hundred thousand or more pieces recovered, some three thousand different characters are distinguishable, showing a system that had already evolved well beyond the primitive picture-writing stage.

Chinese scholars beginning with Xu Shen (A.D. 30–124), author of the fifteen-volume dictionary *Shuōwén jiězì* (A.D. 100), classify all characters into six categories, a convention in use since Zhou times. Lacking particular data for the earliest periods, scholars interested in the formation of the characters infer a logical progression from one conceptual type to the next. The most basic type are the "pictograms" 象形, which are physical icons of natural phenomena such as ⛰ > 山 "mountain," ☉ > 日 "sun," and so forth, and the type most commonly thought of by Westerners. In fact, they constitute the smallest and least important part of the inventory. Moreover, as the samples to the right of the arrowhead indicate, these characters have lost whatever similarity they once had to their referents and are now purely conventional. A second type, the "simple indicative" 指示, represents abstract concepts such as position, number, and relationship by symbolism, without recourse to phonetics, such as 一 for "one," 二 for "two," 上

for "up," and 下 for "down." Some scholars continue to distinguish a third *zhuǎnzhù* 轉注 category, variously translated as "turn to explain" or "mutually explaining," which differs from the second only trivially through type or degree of abstraction. According to Creel, the class was "apparently intended to include characters evolved from a single parent form, which still approximate the original meaning" (1936:95–96). Karlgren explained it as allowing "the picture of a concrete object to symbolize an abstract idea intimately connected with or effectively suggested by the object in question" (1923:49). An example is 北 , which meant "two people standing back to back," then "turn one's back on," and finally its current meaning "north" (south is "front" to the Chinese).

A fourth category, "compound ideographic" or "compound indicative" 會意 , combines two or more existing characters on the basis of their semantic values into a single unit representing a word of corresponding meaning, for example, 日 "sun" and 月 "moon" become 明 "bright." This type was the final attempt to depict the words of the language on the basis of qualities possessed by (or attributed to) the referent. The immediate problem with this approach is that the morphemes of a language exceed the number of unique symbols that users are able to create and remember on the basis of physical design alone. As was the case in Sumerian and Egyptian, Chinese overcame this obstacle very early by creating a fifth class of characters based entirely on sound. Characters formed from one of the above principles were "borrowed" 假借 to represent homonyms or near homonyms, for example, *lai* "wheat" for *lai* "come." A sixth class of characters, known as "semantic-phonetic" or "phonetic compound" 形聲, is a hybrid category consisting of a "radical" or determinative that indicated in a general way a word's meaning and a "phonetic" element that gave the pronunciation. Although sound change and semantic evolution have seriously eroded these relationships, the outlines of the processes are still apparent, for example, in characters with the element 方: 坊 "district," 紡 "spin," 訪 "ask," 鈁 "kettle," and 枋 "board," all pronounced *fang*. The semantic elements (on the left for these characters) mean in isolation "soil," "silk," "speech," "metal," and "wood," respectively.

The distinction between categories 5 and 6 is clearer conceptually than it was in practice. On the one hand, it was probably common for existing characters to be identified first with homophonous words (category 5) and to be later supplied with identifying "radicals" (category 6). There was also a counterprocess observable historically: the wholesale elimination of characters representing specific morphemes and the accretion of these morphemes to other characters fully or partly homophonous. This phonetic borrowing differs from the process described for category 5 in that the morphemes newly assigned to existing characters already had their own unique characters, which dropped out of use as a result. The whole system of relationships between morphemes and characters appears to have been in a continuous state of flux, traces of which are evident even today in the optional use of determinatives for some morphemes and in multiple meanings, some unrelated, for many of the more common characters.

Complementing the attention to a word's phonetic properties was another tendency to rationalize the characters' shapes. As mentioned, the shell and bone inscriptions already evidence a degree of sophistication, not only in their relationships with the morphemes of the language but also in terms of their physical abstractness. With greater abstraction, however, came greater latitude in the manner in which characters could be depicted. By the early part of the Zhou dynasty (1100–722 B.C.), a given character had, on average, four different representations. This state of affairs prompted China's first known official attempt at writing reform (ca. 800 B.C.), in which certain of the competing forms were given court sanction, becoming known as "great seal" 大篆 characters.

A more thorough reform aimed at standardizing the characters' shapes and reducing their number occurred in 213 B.C. under the direction of Li Si, minister of the newly established Qin dynasty (221–206 B.C.). Li's list of 3,300 characters, known subsequently as "small seal" 小篆 characters, was a distillation of two processes designed to reinforce the link between the characters and contemporary pronunciation. Of the three-thousand-odd attested forms in use before the Qin, many single-element graphs passed through the reform unchanged. Since their structures give no indication of pronunciation, there was no reason to modify (or reject) the forms, because they could be read as whole units in any manner that the users agreed on. The contribution of this aspect of Li's reform was merely to sanction certain competing variants. The multielement graphs, however, were substantially affected. Hundreds disappeared altogether, probably because their indicated pronunciations had become obsolete. Those that were carried over, for their part, tended to retain clear "phonetic" elements despite structural modifications made to other parts (Barnard 1978:208).

Later styles also reflected this tendency toward simplification. The "clerical" or "official" script 隷書 style, also invented during the Qin dynasty, was a more practical, abridged refinement of the small seal characters, differing in style and number of strokes. With it, the curved strokes of Chinese characters "became rectangular, the round lines became square, the right angles thickened, the horizontal lines abbreviated and thinner" (Diringer 1968:70). The clerical characters yielded to the less stylized "standard" 楷書 characters in the Later Han dynasty (A.D. 25–221), an innovation that Karlgren attributed to a change in writing materials (1923:63). Although popular simplifications were made in great number over the centuries, "standard" characters remained the official style until recently. There are also cursive forms that evolved from the official styles: a "running script" 行書 from the clerical forms and the severely reduced "grass script" 草書.

As a result of these changes, the pictographic qualities that some of the original characters had were, for all practical purposes, lost entirely. Similarly, despite a pronounced tendency in Zhou times and later to create new characters on the "semantic phonetic" principle, sound change has made the system of phonetics very unreliable. The end point of the character writing system, as used by the Chinese, is a large set of conventional symbols that depend largely on the phonetic structure of Chinese language for their forms, but whose phonetic use, even today, is still considered exceptional.

Chinese Language and Chinese Writing

The relationship of Chinese characters to Chinese language will be treated in detail in a later chapter. My present goal is to deal with that relationship in a more modest way, while taking on the important task of dispelling the most widely entertained myth about Chinese writing, held even by some linguists and writing specialists, namely, that the writing is somehow independent of the language. Nothing could be further from the truth.

Although I have stated that Chinese writing is not the language, it *is* entirely dependent on the language on at least three levels: (1) Chinese characters identify the language's morphemes, that is, units of meaning peculiar to the language and designated by discrete sounds; at the same time, they also identify syllables and hence function typologically as a large syllabary (DeFrancis 1984a:111).[5] (2) Their implementation depends entirely on preexisting rules for ordering the morphemes into sequences, that is, on the grammar of natural language. Although the rules may vary somewhat according to whether the outcome is a written or a spoken string, there is no denying that the grammar governing their ordering is (or was) language based. (3) Finally, the forms of the characters—their physical structures—are also largely dependent on phonetic conventions established by the language.[6] This last dependency is what will concern us here.

Like Sumerian and Egyptian writing, Chinese characters probably originated as icons of natural phenomena. Unlike their counterparts in the Western systems, however, they failed to disappear from the inventory of symbols. Chinese today when they encounter these "pictographic," "indicative," or "compound ideographic" characters, however, do not (consciously at least) associate them with the physical universe. They treat them, like the other classes of characters, uniformly as symbols of morphemes and syllables. Moreover, the overwhelming majority of characters used today and throughout most historical periods were founded on principles that had nothing to do with pictures and everything to do with their relationship to the sounds of language. People explaining the system nonetheless usually focus on its historical residue, which is only slightly more relevant to a user of Chinese than the connection between Roman letter *A* and the head of an ox is to me.

Specialists, when they are not bamboozling the curious with tales of iconicity, do agree that functionally all Chinese characters relate in some way to sound and that structurally almost all were designed from their very beginning on the basis of their relationship to sound. Opinions differ only with respect to the origin of some classes of characters, which—it cannot be emphasized too strongly—has virtually no relevance to Chinese as users of the system. The question has occupied a fair amount of scholarly attention, however, particularly among earlier sinologists, and it was the focus of an interesting debate by Herrlee Creel (1936, 1938) and Peter Boodberg (1937, 1940) played out in the journal *T'oung Pao*. The debate has drawn notice both on its intrinsic merit and because it seems to crystallize the differences between two alternate ways of looking at language: from the top down through meaning and from the bottom up through sound.

Boodberg's position was that sound played the dominant role in the early formation of Chinese characters, as evidenced by the "borrowed sound" and "semantic-phonetic" classes, the latter accounting for 85 to 90 percent of the inventory by most estimates (Karlgren 1923:57). But whereas Karlgren was willing to admit more than a thousand of the so-called compound ideographic characters, the formation of which allegedly owed nothing to sound, Boodberg went a step further by maintaining that all complex characters were formed on phonetic principles (1937). Even the time-honored analysis of 好 "good" as originating from the combined sense of 女 "woman" and 子 "child" was shown by Boodberg to be a misinterpretation of a graph formed from the phonetic similarity of its two components. Creel's view was exactly the opposite:

> In constructing the character system [the Chinese used] the evolved element for the most part not phonetically, but to stand for the original object or to enter with other such elements into combinations of ideographic rather than phonetic nature. . . . Despite the fact that they knew and used the phonetic principle to a certain extent in their ancient writings, the Chinese on the whole rejected it, preferring to hold to the pictographic and ideographic principle. (1936:92)

Creel thus viewed the "borrowed sound" class of Chinese characters not as "characters borrowed to stand for homophonous spoken words which previously had no written form," but as "examples of simple semantic development into extended meanings, not phonetic loans at all" (1936:97). In any case, the outcome of this chicken-or-egg controversy is irrelevant since the characters of this class were borrowed (or were not borrowed) as wholes: their representation of sound was holistic and did not depend on the configuration of any part of the character.

Of greater interest to us is Creel's treatment of the "semantic-phonetic" class, where sound *is* conveyed, however imperfectly, by recurring components. Creel used two types of arguments to reduce the number of characters attributed to this class, one of which was flawed, the other possibly correct. The first involved a survey in which Creel randomly chose 592 characters from six different types of sources ranging from classic works to modern newspapers. Using Karlgren's *Analytic Dictionary of Chinese,* Creel found 237 or 56 percent of the nonrepeating characters to be "wholly ideographic" by Karlgren's own judgment, despite the latter's known phonetic bias (1936:110). The problem with this approach, however, is that in samples of fewer than several thousand characters, the percentage of "phonetic" characters would be low in any case. Nonphonetic characters of the sort Creel was seeking, historically the oldest, represent common words used necessarily in any discourse and as such occupy a disproportionately large part of a small sample. Since repeats are not counted, their effect would be felt less as the size of the sample increased. The "phonetic" characters, for their part, appear individually less often, but encompass a much larger part of the total lexicon—Karlgren's 90 percent.

Creel's second argument is more telling. He begins by noting that 7,697 or 82 percent of the 9,353 characters in *Shuōwén jiězì* were identified by its author as phonetic compounds by subtracting what the author believed to be the radical and calling the rest the character's "phonetic."

> But what if the sound of the character being analyzed was not all similar to the sound of the supposed phonetic? In this case, one took the supposititious phonetic and ranged over the whole field of Chinese characters, until he found a character satisfying two conditions, (1) containing the suppositious phonetic as one of its elements, and (2) being similar (not necessarily identical) in sound to the original character. . . . If one determines arbitrarily which is the ideographic element in a character, and puts down the remainder as phonetic, it very often means that everything which one does not understand goes into the record as phonetic. (1936:127–129)

As a result, "in a countless number of cases a series of variant forms of the same character is erroneously described as a series of compounds created on the phonetic principle" (ibid.: 146).

What happened instead was this: a word was written with a character. The word had, or acquired, a number of related meanings and ipso facto so did the character. Both word and character had one pronunciation (although variant pronunciations could arise for specific meanings of the word by application of early morphological conventions). At some point writers added "aphonic determinatives" (i.e., "radicals") to the character to distinguish the different meanings. Thus, strictly speaking, the new character forms are "compound ideographic," since both components were semantically motivated. This, I believe, was Creel's position.

An alternative analysis looks at the results of these processes. What one sees after the fact is a series of characters with the same or similar pronunciations, sharing one common element, with different meanings individually related to the "aphonic determinatives" assigned, looking for all the world like whole-cloth creations linked structurally by a fortuitous coincidence in sound. Semantic development of the basic word had proceeded so far that the original motivation of the reflexes is no longer apparent. Either way, I do not see that the above process necessarily precludes operation of the "phonetic" borrowing principle. Neither does Creel, who concedes that "it would be an exaggeration . . . to resolve every so-called 'phonetic series' in this manner" (1936:149).[7]

Whether sound (Boodberg) or "ideography" (Creel) was the dominant factor in the early formation of certain Chinese characters has no bearing on the fact that individual users perceive the characters both as sound symbols (holistically and, for many of the graphs, in terms of their major components) and as discrete units of linguistic meaning (morphemes). In this sense, they function much like the written words of any other writing system, although with far less precision, as will be shown later. Writing, in which basic units model sound, by connecting with language at a level higher than sound penetrates the human psyche on its own terms, develops a quasi-independent existence, and assumes a role not just as a passive instrument to convey language but, like speech, as an active force in shaping a language's development. Not surprisingly, the nature of the writing also figures into how the language is molded.

It is not my intent to argue for the primacy of writing over speech,

本报香港6月25日电 新华社记者**孙承斌**、本报记者**郑固固**、中央人民广播电台记者**李晚奇**报道：香港回归祖国倒计时一周年前夕，部分香港地区全国人大代表、全国政协委员今天聚集一堂，进行座谈，抒发迎接回归的喜悦心情，共商香港平稳过渡大计。

座谈会由新华社香港分社总编室、人民日报香港办事处、广播电影电视部香港记者站联合主办。全国政协副主席霍英东、新华社香港分社社长周南出席了会议。

Simplified Chinese characters used in the People's Republic of China.
(*Rénmín ribào*, 26 June 1996, p. 4)

much less over language itself, but rather to suggest that writing as an integral part of many languages nurtures language and causes the language to develop with and around it. The exact nature of the give-and-take, while interesting, is less important here than the fact that this active, two-sided relationship exists at all. Chinese writing has been intimately connected with Chinese language for at least three and a half thousand years. It is not, as many argue, that the characters are intrinsically well-suited to Chinese, but that they generated this "suitability" themselves by forcing the language into their own characteristic mold. For reform-minded people who would replace Chinese characters with a phonetic alphabet—which is where the system would have been headed, if the Chinese had not devised ways of living with it instead—this is both bad news and good news. The problem is, as reformers have discovered, one cannot simply graft a typologically different writing system onto existing linguistic conventions and expect the result to work. Corresponding changes need to take place in the language itself. The good news is that the language, having adapted once to the requirements of a particular writing system, demonstrated that it has the flexibility to adjust to a new form of representation if its users are sufficiently motivated.

Chinese Writing Reform

One measure of the utility of Chinese orthography is that people are always seeking ways to avoid it or get rid of it altogether. Westerners learning Chinese are taught that such-and-such is the proper way to write one character, something else is the correct form of another, and so on, as if the average Chinese actively cared about these conventions. Publishers, of course, honor formal conventions, and this adds to the illusion of stability. But then they are not actually *writing* Chinese characters; they are printing forms etched on lead blocks or their electronic equivalent. It makes no difference to printers how complex the character forms are. In fact, they have every reason to discourage innovation and work toward agreed standards. This is not so with the average user, whose priorities are simply to get one's thoughts written down with minimal effort, in a form that is communicable to oneself and one's proximate audience. If orthography gets in the way, it is ignored.

Popular contempt for the rules of writing is evidenced by innovative character forms designed from the bottom up, as it were, to simplify the average writer's task. For example, Ohara lists dozens of "incorrect" usages seen on mainland Chinese posters and signs, including, besides the usual simplifications based on phonetic substitution, creations that violate the one-character-one-syllable format, such as 白卜酒 (Mandarin) *báibùjiǔ* for 白葡萄酒 *báipútáojiǔ* "white wine," and 市廿會 *shìniànhuì* for 市革命委員會 *shì gémìng wěiyuánhuì* "city revolutionary committee" (1989:94). Non-Mandarin speakers take their own shortcuts, such as 王 (Shanghai) *wang* "king" for 黃 *wang* "yellow" (pronounced *huáng* in Mandarin) or 人門 (Shanghai) *ningmeng* (lit.) "person" and "door" for 檸檬 *níngméng* "lemon," not to mention hundreds of unique forms and usages devised popularly that have no application to Mandarin at all.

There is nothing new about this phenomenon. For at least two millennia, there have been two orthographies in China: the one formally sanctioned by lexicographers and the state, and a popular tradition used informally by people in their everyday lives. Occasionally, when the gap between prescribed and real usages gets too wide, popular forms are allowed to creep into the standard, which in no way diminishes the tendency of users to go on finding new ways to make a bad situation less painful. They can do this because, on the one hand, there is no discrete connection between the forms of the characters and their pronunciations; if there is a simpler, analogical way to make the same connection, why not use it? On the other hand, there is a measure of tolerance among Chinese for one another's mistakes, shortcuts, or innovations that would be inconceivable in an alphabetic culture, even one as imprecise as English. These observations are well supported by statistics. Surveys undertaken by mainland Chinese scholars before the "first batch" of simplified characters was introduced by the People's Republic of China in 1956 showed between 1,000 and 1,600 simplified or "vulgar" forms in use (Ohara 1989:96). This number equates to one-third or more of the inventory known to literate, educated speakers. Even after the official simplification reforms were enacted, Chinese continued to manufacture their own popular variants, evoking cries of alarm from the same people who had introduced the reforms.

At the opposite end of the spectrum, linguists and other scholars have been at the forefront of movements to simplify or replace Chinese character writing for more than a century. Research into character simplification became especially popular after the May 4 movement in 1919, in the form of scholarly works, proposals, and petitions by people such as Qian Xuantong (1887–1939) and Chen Guangyao (1906–1973/1974), who demonstrated the popular origins of simplified characters and advocated their formal acceptance as replacements for conventional forms. Qian in particular stressed the need to pattern the orthography on well-attested popular forms. In a proposal to the National Language Unification Preparatory Committee in 1922, Qian maintained that 70 to 80 percent of the popular forms dated from the Song (A.D. 960–1275) or Yuan (1276–1367) dynasties (Kaizuka and Ogawa 1981:356).[8] He further argued that these simplifications followed regular patterns, in other words, that both the forms and the mechanisms for producing them were established by tradition.[9]

A second school was represented by Chen Guangyao, who sought simplified forms for all characters in current use, even those with fewer than ten strokes (Barnes 1988–1989:147). Chen, too, claimed support from popular tradition as regards the means for simplifying characters, but, unlike the other group, he was willing to manufacture the simplified forms where precedents did not exist. Moreover, he ignored actual simplified characters in favor of his own to keep the corpus internally consistent (ibid.: 149). If Qian's school was the precursor of the People's Republic's "first batch" of simplified forms promulgated in 1956, which largely followed tradition, Chen's willingness to regularize changes throughout the inventory and, finally, to propose changes that were wholly without precedent characterized the government's next two attempts at simplification in 1964 and 1977.

Shanghai, meanwhile, seems to have had its own reform movement, separate from the two main currents described above. In 1935, Chen Wangdao and others began agitating for what they called "off-the-top-of-the-hand characters" *(shǒutóuzì)*. Whereas Qian Xuantong's and Chen Guangyao's programs aimed at reducing the number of strokes in characters, the model for the Shanghai-based movement was the "common" characters *(súzì)* used everyday by ordinary people, some of which had higher stroke counts than the orthodox forms they replaced (Kaizuka and Ogawa 1981:357). Some three hundred such characters (half of which were identical to simplified forms that Qian Xuantong was proposing) won the support of fifteen organizations and two hundred literary figures. Printing houses cast type for the forms, which began to appear in a number of the city's periodicals (Ohara 1989:102). Arising from the "mass language" *(dàzhòngyǔ)* movement, the *shǒutóuzì* tell us less about simplification per se and more about the essential arbitrariness of a writing system that is not keyed in some discrete fashion to speech. They illustrate my argument that beneath the facade of a standard character script for all time and all people is a morass of confusion, which cannot be satisfactorily addressed as long as the system is self-defining, with no *principled* attachment to a shared, extrinsic norm—the sounds of language.

The basic design for China's presently sanctioned orthography was worked out by the Chinese Committee on Writing Reform in 1954. The plan, ratified by the State Council on January 28, 1956, came in the form of three charts. The first two listed 230 and 285 simplified characters for immediate and gradual implementation, replacing 544 traditional characters (some of the new forms replaced two or more homophonous characters). The third chart identified 54 simplified components that could be used to replace parts of characters. The original goal was a total of about 1,700 simplified forms, but because of confusion over where the simplified components could be applied, a General List of 2,238 simplified characters (actually 2,236; there were two repeats) was issued in 1964. While the General List was a logical extension of the initial reform, it diverged in principle by sanctioning forms that had no precedent in common use, paving the way for a second attempt two decades later to simplify the characters even more radically. Outside China, Singapore adopted its own set of reforms, which followed the model of the People's Republic only in part. Taiwan continues to sanction the traditional forms only, with the result that materials published on one side of the Taiwan Strait are largely unintelligible on the other.

Another measure of the system's arbitrariness is the so-called *yìtǐzì* or "different form characters." Occupying a huge gray area between officially sanctioned standard forms and popular simplifications, these characters are said to represent alternate shapes of standard forms,[10] which have the sanction of printers and lexicographers, who often cannot decide among themselves which is the base form. In other cases "radicals" can be interchanged in some characters but not others (which says something about their usefulness as semantic indicators). According to Ding, there were 170 to 180 such pairs in common use prior to the reforms (1955:2–10). In December 1955, China's Ministry of Culture and Committee on Writing Reform jointly published a "First List of Adjustments to Different Form Characters," containing 810 sets including 1,865 characters, 1,055 of which were "abolished." This list was followed in October 1956 by a "Second List" with 595 sets of 1,360 characters, of which 766 lost sanction. In January 1957, the two lists were combined and republished as a "General List." These 1,821 redundant forms existed not because of a lack of standards, but because without a causal relationship with language there can be no genuine standard. It is not enough for a central authority to dictate standards, because the dynamics on which the standards are based constantly change. Thus in 1975 the Chinese government found it necessary to devise amendments to the earlier list of "different form characters," but they were never published because of criticism the government was taking for its second batch of simplified characters.

This "Second List" was published in *People's Daily* on December 20, 1977, in the form of two charts containing 248 and 605 characters. The first group was said to be already in wide use. The second group listed experimental forms, including those particular to occupations and geographical areas, some variants of existing forms introduced for trial usage, and wholly new creations. As with the 1956 reform, the present list identified 61 simplified components (21 characters from the first chart and 40 from the second) for use throughout the inventory, which amplified the reform's effects beyond the numbers given. There were three major differences between this and the earlier reforms: (1) the 1956 plan for the most part listed simplifications that had been in use for centuries, whereas the 1977 plan proposed forms in use for only twenty to thirty years; (2) the new plan eliminated 263 characters altogether by homophone substitution and dual readings for approved characters; (3) it also modified the structures of characters that were easily mispronounced through more consistent use of identifiable phonetic elements.

魯鎮的酒店的格局，是和別處不同的：都是當街一個曲尺形的大櫃臺，櫃裏面豫備着熱水，可以隨時溫酒。做工的人，傍午傍晚散了工，每每花四文銅錢，買一碗酒——這是二十多年前的事，現在每碗要漲到十文——靠櫃外站着，熱熱的喝了休息；倘肯多花一文，便可以買一碟鹽煮筍，或者茴香豆，做下酒物了，如果出到十幾文，那就能買一樣葷菜，但這些顧客，多是短衣幫，大抵沒有這樣闊綽。只有穿長衫的，纔踱進店面隔壁的房子裏，要酒要菜，慢慢地坐喝。

我從十二歲起，便在鎮口的咸亨酒店裏當夥計，掌櫃說，樣子太傻，怕侍候不了長衫主顧，就在外面做點事罷。外面的短衣主顧，雖然容易說話，但嘮嘮叨叨纏夾不清的也很不少。他們往往親眼看着黃酒從罈子裏舀出，看過壺子底裏有水沒有，又親看將壺子放在熱水裏，然後放心：在這嚴重監督之下，羼水也很爲難。所以過了幾天，掌櫃又說我幹不了這事。幸虧薦頭的情面大，辭退不得，便改爲專管溫酒的一種無聊職務了。

我從此便整天的站在櫃臺裏，專管我的職務。雖然沒有什麼失職，但總覺有些單調，有些無

Critics were quick to note the proximity of these changes in principle to phonetic writing, raising apprehension that the revisions were preparatory to replacement by an alphabet. Indeed, this seems to have been one motive of its sponsors in trying to reduce users' dependency on symbols keyed more on morphemes than on sound alone. There was also a consensus that too many distinctions had been removed, making the newer "simplified" forms more difficult to use than their predecessors. Finally, the simplifications were criticized for being ugly and lacking a mass base. Although most complaints focused on characters in the second group, by the end of 1978 publications that had been using the new simplifications on a trial basis had stopped using any from the plan.

For these reasons and because of the reemergence after China's Cultural Revolution (1966–1976) of a more conservative attitude toward "measures" generally, the new forms were allowed to disappear. On June 16, 1978, Zhou Youguang published an article in *Guāngmíng rìbào* calling for a "fifty- or one-hundred-year" moratorium on new simplifications. This was the last article on simplified characters that the newspaper carried; later articles focused on romanization and on popularizing Mandarin. In December 1985, the Committee on Writing Reform was renamed the "National Committee on Language and Script Work." Five months later, the reconstituted committee formally rescinded the second batch of simplified characters. In September 1986, it published a slightly revised update of the 1964 "General List" accompanied by an admonition that simplified forms not on the list should not be used. Reform of China's millennia-old character writing system had reached its logical limit.

The end of efforts by the People's Republic of China to rationalize its character writing system brought with it increased recognition that China's modernization would require a larger role for *pinyin*—China's phonetic alphabet. This was acknowledged in the 1980 inaugural issue of *Yǔwén xiàndàihuà*. The option of writing Chinese with an alphabet had been known to Chinese at least since the sixteenth century. Early phonetic systems designed by missionaries for proselytizing and bilingual instruction attracted the attention of Chinese toward the end of the nineteenth century, when the alphabet was considered as a means of facilitating literacy and arresting China's decline. In 1892, Lu Zhuanzhang (1854–1928), a native of Fujian province, published China's first (modern) attempt at an alphabetic system, which included fifty-five letters derived from Chinese and Western elements with diacritics for tone. Thirty-six of the symbols applied to Lu's Southern Min variety of Chinese; the remainder were created for the sounds of other Chinese languages. By 1911, when the Qing dynasty had fallen, a dozen or more indigenous phoneticization schemes had been propounded, one of which, created in 1900 by Wang Zhao (1895–1935), enjoyed considerable popularity.[11]

Most early Chinese reformers who devised phonetic systems were not

YIjyǒusānchInyán chíywe báhau, wǒ yichŕwán dzǎufàn wǒ jyou wàng

jùjádzai Běipíng de Jūnggwo Lùjyūn Dièrshrjyǒujyūnde Szlingbù dǎ dyàn-

hwà, syǎng chǐng tāmen gàusung wǒ yldyar gwānyu chyányltyan Lúgōuchyáu

shŕjyànde syángchíng (syángsylde chíngsying), yInwei wǒ tIngshwō Lúgōu-

chyáu nèiyldài shŕ Dièrshrjyǒujyūnde fángchyū. Èrshrjyǒujyūn Chíngbàu-

chù Chùjǎng dāying nèityān syàwu yldyǎnbàn jūng dzai tāde gūngshrfáng

jyàn wǒ. YInwei wǒ syInli hěn jíje syǎng jyàn ta, swóyl wǒ jyou jyǎn-

Romanized Chinese text. (*A Text of Chinese Military Terms*, by Pao-king Li.
New Haven: Far Eastern Publications, 1959, p. 10)

seeking the abolition of existing character writing, but saw their inventions as an aid to achieving literacy in the latter. This was and remains the purpose of China's "National Phonetic Alphabet," created in 1913 and still used in Taiwan to gloss characters for primary instruction. The system is part alphabet and part syllabary. Its symbols, whose shapes derive from Chinese characters, include twenty-one initial elements, three medials, thirteen finals, and provisions for indicating tone. Based entirely on the sounds of characters, the system is limited by design to serve as a supplemental notation.

The People's Republic's *pinyin* (lit. "joined sounds") alphabet is another breed altogether. Formally adopted in 1958, the system uses the letters of the Roman alphabet (minus *v,* whose sound is absent from standard Mandarin) plus diacritics for tone to indicate not the sounds of characters but the shapes of words. As such, it has the potential to become a full-fledged script. *Pinyin*'s present formal role as a "notation" belies the fact that it already enjoys de facto status as China's second writing system, with use in Braille, computer inputting, dictionary arrangement, elementary education, foreign language instruction, indexes of all types, international spelling of Chinese words, military communications, minority (non-Han) languages, product brand names and labels, road and railway signs, semaphore, sequencing printed materials, serial designations for machinery and equipment, sign language, standardizing pronunciations, and telegraphy. The only thing preventing *pinyin* from achieving full status as a recognized alternative writing system is a well-founded fear by Chinese traditionalists that, given a chance to compete on equal terms, the system would eventually marginalize the sphere of character usage to classical studies and decorative artifacts, as happened in Vietnam. If history is any guide, this will eventually happen, perhaps sooner than many realize.

2. Japanese

WESTERNERS UNTRAINED in East Asian languages have no difficulty distinguishing between materials printed in Chinese and in Japanese. Although both make use of Chinese characters, with the exception of an occasional *pinyin* word, Chinese write only in characters. A page of printed Chinese, accordingly, is either an orderly collection of symmetrical, neatly spaced symbols or an unrelieved block of marginally differentiated rectangles, depending on one's personal taste and vision. Although written Japanese uses the same or similar characters, they are islands (*many* islands) in a sea of patently different symbols that do repeat and that have structures that are individually much simpler. The former are the *kanji* ("Chinese characters"), the latter the phonetic *kana,* which make up the "mixed script" *(majiribun)* orthography of modern Japan.

As its appearance suggests, the complexity of the Japanese system derives not only—or even mainly—from the inherent difficulty of the characters. More formidable are the rules for relating Japanese writing to the language itself. I will describe some of these conventions below and explain how they came about as a function of the system's development through time.[1] As was the case with Chinese, it will become evident that Japanese writing, while based on language, shaped the language to its own requirements. The extent of these linguistic adaptations is apparent in the problems Japanese have encountered in more than a century of efforts to transform their writing into a serviceable artifact.

Chinese Characters and Japanese Language

If the suitability of Chinese characters to Chinese is more a function of what the former have *done* to the language than of any typological affinity Chinese has for this kind of representation, this is even truer of the relationship of Chinese characters to Japanese. There is nothing natural about the connection at all. To begin with, Chinese characters did not evolve from, or even with, Japanese, but were grafted onto it as a developed, structurally complete system. By the time the characters got to Japan, they were a fait accompli. There was none of the give-and-take between character shapes and the sounds of the language that happened with Chinese. All of the bending took place on the side of the language.

To make matters worse, there is no genetic relationship between Japanese and Chinese. Japanese and Korean both share characteristics with the presumed Altaic family of languages, which includes Mongolian and Manchu, but not Chinese or any language related to Chinese. The proximity of many Japanese words to Chinese is the result of borrowing, and although borrowing has had an enormous effect on the language, it in no way diminishes the typological differences between Japanese and the language that the characters grew up with. Chinese, like Vietnamese, is an "isolating" or "analytic" language with no (or little) inflection. Most of its morphemes have sounds that do not vary with their grammatical function. Japanese, a so-called agglutinative language, by contrast has inflected verbal and adjectival endings, which do not lend themselves to character representation. Moreover, the indigenous part of the Japanese lexicon is composed of morphemes that are predominantly polysyllabic. Since these words have to be accommodated too, the regular one-character-one-syllable pattern of Chinese gives way in Japanese to a system in which a character can represent as many syllables as there are in the word or some fraction of that number, depending on how the word is analyzed and represented, or even less than one syllable.

If this seems complex, I have only begun to describe it. As with English orthography, the greatest difficulty with Japanese writing is not learning the character set, but learning how the set maps onto the language. English spelling requires the user to remember as many as several dozen ways to represent a single phoneme. Many of these, however, can be generated by the application of rules, which, while numerous, do relate in a fairly predictable manner to what the native user already knows about the language, namely, its sounds. Although one cannot necessarily produce a correct spelling from a word's sound, the choices are constrained. Moving in the other direction, a literate English speaker can usually get enough information from a written word's spelling to match it with a word in his or her spoken repertoire the first time around and can generate a reasonably accurate pronunciation even if the word has never been encountered before in speech. As alphabetic systems go, this is about as bad as things get.

Japanese orthography shares with English the distinction of being the worst of its class, except that instead of being the worst of a good lot, it is the worst of a bad lot. I have already intimated in the discussion of Chinese some of the difficulties of learning and using a large character set whose symbols are only marginally coordinated with the language's sounds. These difficulties are already, in my view, unconscionable, and are enough to indict the system as it stands even when the mapping relationship with language is more or less consistent, as in Chinese. The problem with Japanese writing is that it inherits most of the intrinsic difficulties of the large character set and adds to them a myriad of mechanisms needed to make the character set represent the language. Although some of this complexity is historical residue that gets dealt with periodically by reforms, the bulk of it is part and parcel of the interface rules between Chinese writing and Japanese linguistic typology. Although no one would wish for it, it would have been far easier to write English, which is structurally similar to Chinese, with Chinese characters than to adapt this system to Japanese.

Let's look first at what literate Japanese users are faced with today, before addressing in the next section the historical roots of this complexity. I will begin with the simplest case, where Chinese characters are used to represent borrowed Sinitic words. Assuming the user has the fundamentals, that is, knowledge of the character and a proximate idea of what it represents in terms of the language, the first thing he or she must do is to decide which of several possible sound-meaning combinations the character in its present context indicates. This context may be overt—the presence or absence of phonetic *kana* symbols that are part of the word's representation; semi-overt, as, for example, when a second character appears adjacent to the character and helps delineate its role; or covert, when the character's function can be determined only from the meaning of the phrase or sentence. Since the character itself makes up part of that phrase's meaning, it is often a case of working one set of clues against the other until a plausible hypothesis of the constituents' individual and overall roles can be worked out. Of course, skilled readers of any system perform these mental gymnastics routinely as they skip around a page sampling text for clues to facilitate the decoding process. But the difference is that other readers do this as an adjunct to the basic processes, whereas Japanese readers are forced to extrapolate from context every time a character appears.

Sometimes no amount of context will suffice to identify the character's role, in which case the publisher may append to the side of the character small *kana* symbols called *furigana* to provide a pronunciation, which in combination with the larger symbol depicts the intended morpheme. This practice, common before the postwar reforms, seems to be enjoying a rebirth—with a new twist. Whereas previously the *furigana* would give the "reading" (pronunciation) of the character to help one determine its meaning, it is not uncommon nowadays to gloss unfamiliar characters or character combinations with *kana* for the corresponding *English* word, so that Japanese readers can use what knowledge they have of English and Chinese characters to get some idea of what is meant in Japanese! Think about this for a moment. Those of us who are used to the Japanese writing system and accustomed to its foibles tend to become inured to how absurd this whole thing has become. Some of us, perversely, begin to see beauty in these intricate mechanisms.[2] Others get so wrapped up in the orthographic meanderings that they imagine there is some redeeming pedagogical value in all of this, instead of seeing it for what it is: a hopeless mismatch, which requires glosses of glosses to work and which has wrecked the Japanese language to the extent that its users have been able to make it work.

How the manufacturers of the Lexus LS-400 and the world's finest microelectronics can live with a system like this is beyond comprehension, but the fact that there is such an enormous contradiction between Japanese society as a whole and its writing system gives some idea as to where the latter may be headed. But I am getting ahead of myself. Japanese readers need context to disambiguate Chinese characters for three reasons: (1) When, in the simplest of cases, the character represents a single Sinitic borrowing, its referent is a morpheme, which in Japanese is usually only a *part* of a word. Another character-morpheme is needed to complete it. (2) Unlike in Chinese, where a character is supposed to equate to only one morpheme, in Japanese multiple representation is the norm. These morphemes with differences in meaning are often related to different borrowed Sinitic *(on)* pronunciations, which depend on when and from what part of China the character and the word associated with it were introduced. You can stare at the character all day without figuring this out. (3) Finally, the character may not be representing a Sinitic borrowing at all, but an indigenous Japanese word (a *kun* pronunciation). Here is where the process really gets tricky.

Many Chinese characters in Japanese, besides designating one or more Sinitic borrowings, also stand in for a native Japanese word that is supposed to mean more or less the same thing in Japanese as the character does in Chinese. For example, the character 月, besides its two Sinitic readings of *getsu* "moon; month; Monday" and *gatsu* "month (of the year)," also represents the indigenous word *tsuki* "moon; month." Only context will tell you which of these morphemes is intended. One cannot use the characters in a straightforward fashion as a syllabary even in cases where two or more characters are joined together in what appears to be a Sinitic compound,[3] because there is no way to know in advance that the forms are not representing an indigenous compound word, such as 月見 *tsukimi* "viewing the moon" or 月掛 *tsukigake* "monthly installments." While this same dependence on context applies in principle to English orthography, there one can at least proceed with some assurance that the representation bears a resemblance to the pronunciation. One can do the same with characters in Chinese, using the symbols as a phonetic syllabary and taking into account variant pronunciations. In Japanese, the whole compound must be apprehended before the reader can even begin to decipher the pronunciations of the constituent characters and the meaning of the term as a whole.

And it gets worse. Chinese characters were introduced to Japan with the Sinitic sounds and meanings they represented. As described in the preceding chapter, most of these characters were created on phonetic principles, and this relationship was reinforced by the Qin dynasty reforms more than five hundred years before the characters came to Japan. Other characters with nonphonetic origins reappeared as components in compound phonetic characters, thereby acquiring a structural relationship to the sounds of Chinese themselves. Although the relationship was haphazard, inconsistent, and holistic, this link between the shapes of Chinese characters and the sounds of the language was and remains the system's only useful feature. Speakers of Chinese can depend on a character's shape perhaps two-thirds of the time to give some idea of the sound of the morpheme it represents (DeFrancis 1984:108). In conjunction with contextual clues this rough information makes reading somewhat less of a burden than it would be otherwise. The Chinese writer, in turn, who has to recall these forms from scratch, can make the connection between morpheme and symbol more easily when that link is supported by a rough correspondence in sound.

For Japanese *on* words (borrowed Sinitic vocabulary), the connection with sound is maintained, but it is even more haphazard, owing to the phonetic redaction that occurred when Chinese sounds were adapted to Japanese and the fact that the character pronunciations had various Chinese origins. Nevertheless, Japanese continue to use the phonetic relationship to good effect, as evidenced by sound-related errors in writing and various types of recall tests (Horodeck 1987; Matsunaga 1994). Unfortunately, this relationship only applies to Sinitic readings. When characters are used with *kun* readings to represent indigenous words, there is no motivated connection whatsoever between the shape of the character and its sound. Users have to remember that a certain shape relates (some of the time) to a certain word, with no help at all from phonetics, and virtually none from the character's so-called semantic component (if it has one and it can be identified). It is as rote as memorization gets.

Moreover, just as a character can have multiple *on* readings, it often has more than one *kun* reading, so that users must remember to associate these with the form as well—with no clue from the structure of the character to what any of these words sound like or which one is intended. If the word is a verb or an adjective, some hint can be found in the phonetic *kana* that follows to represent its conjugation. You run through the whole list of readings you can remember for the character until a word is found that does not conflict phonetically with the portion shown in *kana*, and if you are lucky you will come up with a single word. If the indigenous word is a noun, only context will help distinguish which one is meant.

Japanese cannot even count on the same indigenous word always to be written with the same character. The morpheme *mir* "see," normally written with the character 見 *(mi)* and one of the *kana* symbols that begins with *r* depending on the verb's syntactic function, can also be written 視 , 覽 , 觀 , or 診 , depending on its exact connotation. Some regard this variation as a positive feature, since it adds an element of specificity to a system sorely in need of it. A more credible evaluation would state that it is, at best, unnecessary, since all of these meanings are semantically related (unlike Sinitic homonyms in Japanese). One does not need a separate graph for each nuance of *miru* any more than one needs separate spellings of "to see" to figure out which of nine distinct meanings listed in *Webster's Third New International Dictionary* is intended when the word appears in English. Conversely, to the extent that the Japanese practice does fill a genuine need, it obviates and hence stands in the way of genuine changes to the spoken language, such as, in this case, the emergence of indigenous equivalents for "view," "observe," "examine," and so on.

Let me review what I have stated so far about the mapping relationship of Chinese characters to language. In Chinese, although the same sound can be represented by more than one character, characters are usually expected to have only one sound; in cases where the principle is violated, the sounds usually differ by tone or by one segment only, the latter generally being of the same phonetic class. The same is true of their representation of meaning. For better or for worse (in terms of the language's development), Chinese can generally depend on a linear relationship between sound, symbol, and meaning that imparts a measure of order and predictability to the orthography, bad as it is. The user of the orthography can find significant clues to a character's sound in Chinese from its structure. In Japanese, not only are the same sounds represented by many different characters, but single characters regularly represent several different sounds. Unlike in Chinese, many of these sounds are of various lengths and have no etymological relationship and hence no phonetic similarity to one another. Although some of a character's sounds may retain a marginal connection with its shape, other sounds had none to begin with.

Japanese, moreover, tend to play games with these relationships, letting two or more characters, each in one of its phonetic guises, represent a word phonetically without regard to the meaning of the characters individually, or they do the opposite: assign characters on the basis of their meanings to an etymologically unrelated term where none of the characters' individual pronunciations play any role at all in identifying the word's sound. These so-called *ateji* ("applied characters") were common before the postwar reforms, and enough of them seem to have slipped through to keep the principle alive. Some examples of *ateji* are given in Chapter 5. Another irregularity that deserves mention is the *okurigana* conventions, that is, rules for determining what part of a conjugated word is subsumed by the character and what part is represented by *kana*. Sometimes the *kana* is used for the last syllable of a word; for other words the domain extends over the last few syllables and into the root morpheme itself, depending on the word.

Looking at these various mapping relationships, it is evident that the congruency between sound and symbol in Japanese can be specified reliably at the word level only, with the individual rules leading up to this mapping of such limited scope as to be nearly useless for practical purposes. The Japanese "system," in other words, is the closest thing to logographic writing ever invented. How did it get this way?

Development of Writing in Japan

In China, the earliest records of character writing known to scholars show a system in essence already developed. We infer logically the course of its development, from iconic forms to symbols based mostly on sound, but we know virtually nothing about its origins. Lacking evidence to the contrary, we assume the characters were a Chinese creation and that their metamorphosis was an indigenous development occasioned in large part by the dynamics of the system's own requirements. These hypotheses await verification.

With Japanese we are on much firmer ground. According to *Kojiki* (Record of Ancient Matters, 712) and *Nihon shoki* (Chronicles of Japan, 720), Chinese books were first brought to Japan between the late third and early fifth centuries A.D. There is no evidence that the Japanese were using a script before then or, for that matter, that they considered "writing" a vehicle through which their own language could be expressed. In Japan the immediate problem was not how to write Japanese, but how to read Chinese texts in a way a Japanese could understand. As a consequence, two distinct practices emerged for writing in Chinese characters. The first of these, known as *kambun,* was based on conventions associated with this former requirement. The other arose from the need to record the indigenous elements of Japanese. Both practices made use of Chinese characters for their semantic and phonetic values, and both led ultimately to the same mixed script used to write Japanese today.

Kambun, literally "Chinese writing," refers to a genre of techniques for making Chinese texts read like Japanese, or for writing in a way imitative of Chinese. For a Japanese, neither of these tasks could be accomplished easily because of the two languages' different structures. As I have mentioned, Chinese is an isolating language. Its grammatical relations are identified in subject-verb-object (SVO) order and through the use of particles similar to English prepositions. Inflection plays no role in the grammar. Morphemes are typically one syllable in length and combine to form words without modification to their phonetic structures (tone excepted). Conversely, the basic structure of a transitive Japanese sentence is SOV, with the usual syntactic features associated with languages of this typology, including *post*positions, that is, grammar particles that appear *after* the words and phrases to which they apply. Word order was the first problem the Japanese faced in reading *kambun.* In order to read Japanese from a Chinese

私はその人を常に先生と呼んでいた。だから此所でもただ先生と書くだけで本名は打ち明けない。これは世間を憚かる遠慮というよりも、その方が私に取って自然だからである。私はその人の記憶を呼び起すごとに、すぐ「先生」と云いたくなる。筆を執っても心持は同じ事である。余所々々しい頭文字などはとても使う気にならない。

Japanese mixed character-*kana* text.
(From the novel *Kokoro*, by Natsume Soseki. Tokyo: Shinchosha, 1952, p. 7)

防衛庁は二十二日、一九九七年度予算の概算要求基準（シーリング）に関して、沖縄米軍基地の整理・縮小関連経費を除く従来の防衛関係費の伸び率として四・五％を要求することを決めた。二十三日の自民党国防関係三部会などを通じて与党に提示する。ただ、

Japanese character-*kana* newspaper text.
(*Asahi Shimbun,* 23 July 1996, p. 1)

(or Chinese-style) text, one had to treat the text as an inversion of the normal order, skipping back or ahead in search of the next clue to a sentence's meaning.

A second problem the Japanese faced in reading *kambun* was deciding which characters in a sentence should be read together, assuming, again, that the Japanese reader had no knowledge of Chinese and was interpreting what he or she saw as Japanese or something akin to it.[4] In Japanese, verbal inflections are expressed as a continuous series of morphemes, whereas in Chinese such morphemes are spread throughout the sentence; the reader had to reconstruct these sequences to make sense of the whole. A further complication arose from *kambun*'s practice of having one Chinese character stand "for two or more Japanese elements separated from each other by the demands of Japanese grammatical structure" (Miller 1967:114). Such problems were handled by writing small numbers next to or beneath individual characters to indicate the order in which the characters were to be read and by other signs showing which characters should be read with which others.

A third problem, which had an important effect on the development of the Japanese language itself, was deciding how the characters were to be read, since sound had to be assigned to the characters, if only as a mnemonic. There were two basic types of readings available for a given character, depending on whether the writer wanted it read with a borrowed Chinese "sound" (the literal meaning of the Japanese word *on*) or with the corresponding Japanese "explanation" *(kun)* of the character, that is, the sound of a semantically equivalent indigenous word. Distribution ideally was determined by whether the underlying element was a borrowed Chinese morpheme, in which case it would normally appear as part of a combination of two or more Chinese characters, or a native Japanese word, for which one character normally sufficed.

The assignment of "readings" to characters was more involved than the above outline suggests. Since the characters (and the words or morphemes they represented) came into Japanese at different times, the sounds of characters with the same "phonetic" element could vary depending on their pronunciation in Chinese at the time they were borrowed. Moreover, the readings tended to accumulate, so that a given character could have, in addition to one or more *kun* readings, several *on* sounds depending on which word or morpheme was represented. Two major sets of *on* readings are distinguished, including those based on Chinese of the fourth to sixth centuries *(go'on)*, as reflected in certain passages of the *Kojiki*, and the newer, Tang dynasty standard *(kan'on)* used in the *Nihon shoki*.[5] There are also *Tō'on* and *Sō'on* (Chinese Tang and Song) readings used mainly for Zen Buddhist terminology. In some cases, a mixture of two levels of *on* pronunciations found their way into the same word, for example, KAnai (wife, family) and the city kyōTO (uppercase = *kan'on;* lowercase = *go'on).*

The use of *kun* readings with Chinese characters was no less problematic, since no two indigenous Chinese and Japanese words shared exactly the same set of primary and derived meanings. In many cases, a Japanese word would be matched with several Chinese characters, each appropriate to a particular nuance. We have already noted the word *miru*, which currently uses five different characters corresponding to different usages of the Japanese word.[6] *Hakaru* today is represented by four characters according to the nuance. The opposite situation, where a polysemantic Chinese character is assigned a host of Japanese words to cover each of the character's meanings, was just as likely to occur. A notorious example is 生 (modern Mandarin *shēng*), for which Nelson (1962) gives fifteen *kun* readings.

The above applies to "content" words and the characters chosen to represent them. A fourth major problem with reading Japanese from Chinese texts or, as became the practice, disguising Japanese texts as Chinese,[7] was in locating suitable characters for the "function" or grammar words. Semantic equivalents for Japanese grammatical particles could sometimes be found, for example, Mandarin *zhī* 之 for Japanese *no* (the possessive particle), or *yú* 於 for *ni* (locative particle), although such matches were rarely possible. Instead, dots were used in various positions on a character's periphery to indicate Japanese particles and inflections. For example, □ meant "the Japanese particle *o* is to be appended to the reading of this character," □ meant "add the inflection *te*," and so forth. There were eight different conventions, known as *okototen*, each with its own following, governing their use in *kambun* by the twelfth century (Habein 1984:23).

One cannot help wondering to what extent the complexity involved in making a Chinese text interpretable as Japanese prepared the Japanese people psychologically for the intricacies of their own present-day writing system. Whatever effect *kambun* may have had on the linguistic sensibility of its users, there is no question of its effect on the Japanese language. When languages written with alphabetic systems "borrow" words from each other, it matters little whether the medium for the borrowing is the spoken or the written form of the language, since the alphabetic writing preserves an intelligible phonetic aspect. If there is enough phonetic information for the item to be understood in speech, the same is true when the item is written in a phonetic alphabet. Moreover, the items being borrowed invariably are *words*, stand-alone units that pretty much have to make sense in isolation. Only after a number of these foreign words are assimilated do users have enough material and enough command over them to begin analyzing the corpus into its constituent morphemes and recombining them into original words that are also phonetically intelligible because of the process and tradition that led to their formation.

In Japanese, none of these rules applied. Because of the large amount of graphic information expressed by individual Chinese characters, there was no absolute requirement that their sounds be sufficiently distinct from others in the language to be intelligible when spoken as long as the items were supported, directly or indirectly, by their written forms. Literate Chinese could, and did, use the single-syllable morphemes that the characters designated without concern over whether they would be intelligible phonetically. And this was before the "words" even got into Japanese. When the Chinese *kambun* texts came to Japan, character-literate Japanese adopted these new concepts into their own language in the same way they originally appeared—through a writing system that, while based on sound, provided no guarantee that the sound would make sense. Quite the contrary: because of the high level of graphic redundancy, users had every incentive to cut down wherever they could on the number of graphs written to convey an idea, reducing the serial (and hence phonetic) redundancy of a string even further. Morphemes, which may or may not be words, came to be used in written texts in place of whole words. Thanks to *kambun,* the whole corpus of Sinitic terms, which today accounts for more than half of the Japanese lexicon, never had to make any sense to a Japanese ear.

If the matter had ended there, the Japanese language would be no worse off today than Chinese. Despite the latter's direct and indirect dependency on characters to support much of its upper-level or "learned" vocabulary, the countervailing needs of Chinese users as speakers, on whose phonological habits the writing system was originally based, have preserved in the language enough phonetic intelligibility to make alphabetic writing an attractive option. Although ambiguities remain in some areas of vocabulary, they are being resolved as China's *pinyin* writing takes root and expands its conventions, and as the language adapts to the new system's requirements. For Japanese speakers, however, the same problems Chinese face are compounded by the fact that, when the Sinitic vocabulary was introduced to Japan, the attenuated, phonetically impoverished forms were further reduced in the process of adapting their sounds to Japanese phonology. Since distinctions are not added artificially to a borrowed word's sound, borrowing often results in words that are phonetically less distinct than they were in the original language. In Japanese (as we shall see in a later chapter) the number of syllables available to render the Sinitic borrowings was only a fraction of the number of Chinese syllables, so that this marginally intelligible set of sounds was further condensed, making discrimination through speech all the more tenuous. While the prospects for writing Japanese phonetically are far from hopeless—Japanese obviously do speak to one another—the language's greater dependency on the characters may help explain why Japanese have been willing to put up with the system despite its complexity.

Kambun, for all its adaptations, was still a system to make Chinese texts read like Japanese. It was not something Japanese could use to write and read their own language. Moreover, it could only partly accommodate the large number of Japanese grammar particles and morphological affixes.

Here the Japanese ran into the same problem the Sumerians and Egyptians had confronted trying to depict grammatical relations with semantic signs. Their solution was the same: to use the symbols phonetically, without regard for the original meanings. For example, in the sequence 好伎 , representing Japanese *yoki* ("good"), *yo* is an indigenous reading of the first character; the Japanese word and the Chinese character both mean "good." The second character, however, is used for its Japanese sound *ki*, to represent an attributive suffix in Japanese that is also pronounced *ki*. This innovation and the somewhat earlier phonetic use of characters for personal and place names (e.g., in the *Kojiki*) were already making possible the second major development of writing in Japan: the use of characters (and character-derived symbols) to write undisguised Japanese.

The evolution of the phonetic use of Chinese characters can be seen in the twenty volumes of the *Manyōshū*, a collection of 4,500 Japanese poems compiled before 759. Although both semantic and phonetic usages of the characters appear, the latter increased with time. There were two varieties: (1) The *kun* reading of a Chinese character (i.e., the sound of the equivalent Japanese word) was read off as such but interpreted phonetically, without regard to its lexical meaning, to represent Japanese grammar particles. For example, 庭 was read *niwa* for postpositions *ni* plus *wa*; the *kun* meaning "garden" is irrelevant. (2) Symbols could be used solely for their *on* readings, their semantic values again having no role, for example, 久 *(ku)* + 母 *(mo)* = *kumo* "cloud" (Habein 1984:12).[8] Characters used in this latter fashion became known as *manyōgana* from the name of the anthology plus *kana* (lit. "borrowed name," from *kari na > kanna > kana > -gana*).

Manyōgana developed in two directions. On the one hand, the inventory of symbols was reduced from the 480 found in the *Manyōshū* to the forty-eight basic *kana* used today.[9] Originally a given Japanese syllable-sound had several character representations. For example, there were at least nineteen different Chinese characters pronounced *ka* in Japanese used to represent that syllable. In every case popular usage settled on a stylized or abbreviated form of one character of the series. The process ultimately produced two equivalent sets of sixty-nine *kana* symbols. One of them, *hiragana*, developed from the "running" (Mand. *xíng*/Jap. *gyō*) and "grass" *(cǎo/sō)* styles of the characters used for these syllables. Habein believes they were first used for writing "poems, private letters and notes" (1984:25). The second set, *katakana*, was developed in the ninth century to assist in reading Chinese texts. Opinions differ on whether *katakana* arose, like *hiragana*, from cursive forms for character segments (Miller 1967:126), or from a part or side of the square *kaisho* (Mand. *kǎishū* "standard") forms (Sansom 1928:42; Thranhardt 1978:47).

From about A.D. 900 on, *hiragana* became the preferred means of writing texts in Japanese. A century later, literary works were appearing in all-*hiragana*, such as *Taketori monogatari* (Tale of the Bamboo Cutter) and

Ise monogatari (Tales of Ise), which are believed to mirror the spoken language of the time. Thus by the Heian period (794–1185) Japanese had two distinct ways of writing. There were *kambun,* or Chinese-style texts, written in characters used primarily for their semantic value, with annotations supplied to make the text read like Japanese. And there were all-*kana* texts of colloquial Japanese, known until the Tokugawa period (1600–1868) as *onnade* (woman's hand) from the fact that *kana* were used primarily by women.

Between these two extremes, various intermediate conventions emerged that led to the mixed character-*kana* script used today. One example is the use of *katakana* symbols in *kambun* texts to designate character readings and grammar particles. Another hybrid style, represented by the *Engishiki* (Institutes of the Engi Period, 927), used Chinese characters of two sizes, the larger for *shōkun* ("regular *kun*") characters and the smaller as *manyōgana* for particles and inflectional suffixes; word order followed Japanese syntax. Meanwhile, the *monogatari* ("tales"), previously written entirely in *kana*, began using characters semantically for the content words. The two styles merged, according to Miller, partly because the thousands of Sinitic loanwords coming into the language lent themselves readily to expression in characters (1967:130). Another cause was the influence of *kambun* on the structure of the language and its effect on the attitude of Japanese in persuading them that proper writing is done with Chinese characters.

The outcome of these processes is known today as *kanji-kana majiribun* ("Chinese characters–*kana* mixed script"), the only style with official sanction and significant popularity. Ideally, the style requires Chinese characters to be used for morphemes that convey meaning and *hiragana* for the syntactic elements. *Katakana,* the other phonetic system, is used for foreign (non-Chinese) words, colloquialisms, and "as a typographical device equivalent to italics" (Sansom 1928:42). It also appears as a substitute for characters that have been proscribed (see below) and as a phonetic gloss appended to the sides of Chinese characters *(furigana).*

It is worth reflecting on the reasons why the *kana* syllabaries did not follow the course taken in the West and evolve into alphabetic symbols. The answer usually given is that the phonetic structure of Japanese, with its restricted inventory of syllable types, lends itself naturally to this form of representation (Suzuki 1975:178). Miller has another explanation, which makes more sense: the Japanese settled on the syllabic *kana* not because of the structure of their language, but because of the effect the Chinese model of one symbol equating to one syllable had on their way of thinking (1967:98). In other words, not only did Chinese characters lead to the importation of thousands of phonetically vague words and morphemes; they also helped prevent the emergence of a segment-based orthography that would have supported the development of more spoken syllable types, relieving in time much of the language's phonetic monotony. Writing Japanese with Chinese characters thus was not simply a case of inventing convoluted mechanisms so that the two would fit each other; the Japanese language itself was bent out of recognition.

Prewar Japanese Writing Reform

If we exclude the reforms that took place in China during the Qin dynasty, then the first to become involved with writing reform in East Asia were individual Japanese. It is clear that the impetus for this involvement was provided by contacts with the West. Japanese had been aware of the alphabetic principle at least since the sixteenth century through Portuguese missionaries. In 1715, Arai Hakuseki (1657–1725), an official of the Tokugawa government, wrote a book praising the alphabet based on information he obtained from an Italian missionary. Although Arai stopped short for political reasons of endorsing the romanization system used by missionaries in Japan, he could appreciate the connection between these foreign phonetic systems and Japan's own *kana* syllabaries. The monk Monno (1700–1763), whose work *Waji daikansho* (Survey of Japanese Writing) appeared in 1754, was another early supporter of an all-*kana* script. The notion that writing could be done without Chinese characters was not especially innovative, since *kana* had been the medium for imaginative literature in Japan since the ninth century. The innovative suggestion was that an all-*kana* script could be used, without stigma, for other types of serious writing, including scholarly discourse.

Another model of a successful phonetic writing system was provided by Dutch traders in southern Japan, whose language and Latinized transcription of Japanese were known to the Rangakusha or "Holland Studies" group of Japanese. In 1783, Otsuki Gentaku (1757–1827) pointed out how easily Dutch writing could be learned by comparison with Japanese. Shiba Kokan (1747–1818), author of *Waran tensetsu* (Holland's Divine Teachings, 1796), was another admirer. Shiba saw no reason why Sinitic vocabulary could not be written phonetically in *kana* instead of in characters as was the practice (Twine 1983:116). In 1798, Honda Toshiaki (1744–1821), another Rangakusha, suggested that the Latin alphabet was the better choice since it is used internationally and can represent more sounds than *kana* with half the number of symbols (Thranhardt 1978:108).

These speculations on the propriety of writing Japanese phonetically did not constitute a movement to replace the character writing system in terms of popular support or as articulated by the various individuals. It was only toward the beginning of the Meiji period (1868–1911), as part of an effort to catch up with the West, that concrete programs to alter the writing system began to appear and attract support. In 1866, Maejima Hisoka (1835–1919) proposed to the Tokugawa Shogun comprehensive reforms that would lead to an all-*kana* script. As founder of Japan's modern postal

system, Maejima was more aware than most of the practical difficulties the
character script entails. He argued that in order to replace Chinese characters, the abbreviated, telegraphlike style of written texts had to be replaced
by something closer to speech *(gembun itchi)*. In addition to eliminating
obsolete grammar forms, this reform also supposed an end to the affected
practice of using unassimilated Sinitic vocabulary in Japanese.

Maejima did not propose replacing all Sinitic *(kango)* compounds in
Japanese, which he saw as the equivalent of Latin loanwords in English,
but he did acknowledge that ambiguity would arise if these words were
written phonetically (Twine 1983:128). The problem, however, was solvable: (1) While Sinitic terms may be ambiguous in isolation, they rarely are
so given enough context; hence the demand for speechlike redundancy. (2)
Compilation of word (not character) based dictionaries would inhibit the
practice of arbitrarily creating new compounds or using those with little
currency. (3) Finally, writers would have to pay more attention to grammar,
to make their texts more predictable. Maejima was aware of transitional
problems and proposed that the changeover occur in several stages through
an eight-year period, during which time dictionaries would be compiled,
orthographic rules established, *kana* textbooks written, and teachers
trained (ibid.: 118–119).

Three years later, in May 1869, Nambu Yoshikazu (1840–1917)
became the first Japanese to argue explicitly for a script based on the Latin
alphabet. Like Maejima, Nambu believed that the major obstacle to eliminating Chinese characters was the language's Sinitic vocabulary, which
could not always be understood when written phonetically or even when
spoken. This problem could be solved in a decade, he argued, by compiling
word-based dictionaries and rewriting texts in the colloquial style.
Nambu's proposals were enthusiastically supported by Japan's new class of
Westernizers. One of them was Nishi Amane (1829–1894), a philosopher
who had coined from Sinitic morphemes many of the new Western-inspired
loan translations then entering the language. His own accomplishments
notwithstanding, Nishi maintained in an 1874 article for the inaugural
issue of *Meiroku zasshi* that it would have been easier to introduce this new
vocabulary directly from the Western languages through a romanized
script. Just as Chinese characters were used at a time when Japan's model
was China, so should romanization be used now that the model had
changed. Neither reducing the number and complexity of the characters
nor using an all-*kana* script would suffice in the long run.

A good example of the extent to which some Japanese were prepared to go in dealing with the complexity of their writing system is provided by Mori Arinori (1847–1889), later head of Japan's Ministry of
Education, who in the same issue of *Meiroku zasshi* proposed that
English supplant the Japanese language entirely, the latter being unsuited
to modern times. Other reformers, disenchanted with the alternatives,

invented their own writing systems based on characters, *kana,* the Roman alphabet, Braille, shorthand, or a combination of these systems, none meeting with any acceptance (Kim Min-su 1973:491). Of greater value was the work of Shimizu Usaburo, a founder of the Kana Society, who backed up his dismissal of the homonym problem with an all-*hiragana* translation of a three-volume German science textbook done entirely in the colloquial style with word division, Western-style punctuation, speechlike grammar, and as many indigenous Japanese words as possible (Thranhardt 1978:134–135).[10]

Other reformers took a different approach to simplification. Fuku-zawa Yukichi (1834–1901), in the foreword to his textbook on Chinese characters *Moji no kyō* (Teaching Writing, 1873), proposed a sharp reduction in the number of characters in use. In his view, one thousand could serve as a basic vocabulary, with two or three thousand the upper limit. Fukuzawa's ideas were taken a step further by his student Yano Fumio (1850–1931), who in 1887 announced that his newspaper would adhere to a three-thousand-character limit. Yano also recommended universal use of *furigana,* which he felt would eliminate the shortcomings of both systems while preserving their respective advantages. According to Twine, Yano "took into consideration the real needs of the Japanese people and the urgency of the problem rather than chasing after attractive but impractical ideas of full-scale change" (1983:130). One might add that he perpetuated the problem and postponed the day of reckoning by making the system marginally serviceable.

From about 1880 on, individual proponents of writing reform began to organize themselves in groups according to their respective viewpoints. One such group was the Kana no kai ("Kana Society"), patched together in 1883 from three smaller clubs formed a year earlier. As the name suggests, members were committed to promoting an all-*kana* script, although they never could agree on what form it would take. One faction advocated continued use of what is now called "historical" *kana* spelling, which by Meiji times was as remote from actual pronunciation as English spelling is from spoken American. A second faction argued for *kana* spelling based on contemporary pronunciation, while a third would tolerate some character usage and was neutral on the spelling issue (Ono 1982:34).

Besides their inability to agree on a common convention, the group was also hurt by its failure to address the problem of style reform. Some of their all-*kana* publications were simply transliterations of original mixed character-*kana* texts and hence were unreadable. They need not have been so, as Otsuki Fumihiko (1847–1928), a prominent member, demonstrated by reworking a text chosen by his critics as particularly bad and making it understandable through punctuation, word division, and consistent use of diacritics that were already part of the *kana* tradition. Another difficulty these reformers encountered was a lack of recognized standards. Though less of a problem here than in China, more stringent norms were needed for pronunciation, syntax, and vocabulary to compensate for the loss of redundancy (predictability) when the characters disappeared. In 1885, the group split over the spelling issue. Although membership in the various *kana* societies continued to grow to a high point in 1888 of more than ten thousand, by 1891 the movement was irreversibly in decline.

The same problems facing the Kana no kai were also encountered by the Romaji-kai, a similar organization founded a few months later in 1883 by advocates of a romanized writing system for Japanese. Its development followed that of the Kana no kai in all essentials. Within two years of its founding, the organization was locked in an internal dispute over which of two romanizations should be adopted. The first option was the so-called Hepburn system devised by an American missionary in 1867, in consultation with native Japanese specialists. The system is largely phonetic. Pronunciation of the consonant letters is based on English, and the vowel letters are based on German and Italian. It can, accordingly, be pronounced reasonably well by foreigners unfamiliar with Japanese phonemic conventions. The other option was a system devised by physicist Tanakadate Aikitsu (1856–1952) and presented to the Romaji-kai in January 1886. Tanakadate's system, which also used the letters of the Roman alphabet, followed a phonemic approach that parallels the *kana* syllabaries, thus earning the title *Nihon-siki* ("Japanese style"). Although arguably easier for a Japanese speaker, particularly one schooled in the *kana* conventions, it is unquestionably less suitable as an international notation. Like the *kana* societies, the Romaji-kai also failed to concern itself seriously with the need for a new writing style. According to Twine, "they merely changed their script to romaji while continuing to use traditional literary styles. Again, this achieved the very reverse of their objectives" (1983:126).

By 1892, the internal dispute had brought the Romaji-kai's activities to a standstill. The dispute and a loss of enthusiasm among Japanese for Western culture in general led to a decline in the society's membership from its 1887 peak of 6,800. Immediately after the Russo-Japanese War (1904–1905), the two factions resurfaced as the Romaji hirome-kai ("Society for the Spread of Romanization"), which supported the Hepburn system, and the Nihon no romaji-sha ("Romanization Society of Japan"), which backed *Nihon-siki*.[11] By this time, however, the locus for change had shifted from private organizations to government. As a direct result of a petition from Maejima's Imperial Education Society, a National Language Research Committee (Kokugo chōsa iinkai) was established within the Ministry of Education in March 1902 to examine phonetic scripts, conduct research on the unification of spoken and written styles, study the language's phonetic system, and choose a standard dialect. Nothing major seems to have issued from the organization until December 1919, when, under the directorship of Hoshina Koichi (1872–1955), it announced a plan to limit the number of characters to 2,616 and consolidate variant character forms (Ono 1982:53–57).[12] Hoshina believed that a limit on Chinese characters was meaningless without measures that applied to Sinitic vocabulary. Among those devices considered were (1) representing the same words with different, easier characters; (2) substituting indigenous Japanese words; and (3) writing the Sinitic words in *kana* while finding other ways to avoid homophony. His concern with vocabulary followed from the premise that characters would eventually be replaced by an all-phonetic script, which meant written words had to be intelligible as if spoken.

In June 1921, the National Language Research Committee was succeeded by the Interim National Language Research Council (Rinji kokugo chōsakai). Unlike its predecessor, the organization included besides scholars representatives from major newspapers eager to reduce the number of characters in regular use. Accordingly, in June 1923 a "List of Commonly Used Chinese Characters" *(Jōyō kanjihyō)* was drawn up consisting of 1,960 characters, 154 of which were simplified replacements of complex forms. A revised version of this list with 2,108 characters was adopted by newspapers in 1925 (Seeley 1984:270). These efforts were ineffective, however, because they did nothing to address the dependency on characters that the language had acquired. Simply rewriting certain characters with *kana*, besides leading to obscurity, confused the reader by splitting the representation of Sinitic compounds, disrupting what few clues the mixed character-*kana* system has (in principle) to offer, namely, a rough division of functions between characters used for content and *kana* for grammar.

In 1934, the National Language Council (Kokugo shingikai) replaced the Interim Council within the Ministry of Education, which in June 1942 issued a "List of Standard Chinese Characters" *(Hyōjun kanjihyō)*. Its 2,528 characters and variants rose to 2,669 in the final document that appeared at the end of the year (Hayashi 1949:70). Originally, only the high-frequency characters numbering 1,134 had to be written; it was considered sufficient for Japanese to acquire just a reading knowledge of the remainder. When the final version was released, the high-low frequency division was abolished (Seely 1984:272). These lists were intended as informal guidelines to be followed at a writer's own discretion. No attempt was made to force them on the publishing industry at large. Nor was there any will to do so amidst the conservative atmosphere that had gripped the country by this time.

Japan's Postwar Writing Reforms

It was not until the end of the Second World War that Japanese once again began to take seriously the idea of reforming their writing system. The explanation usually given by Japanese is that reform was forced on Japan by the occupation authorities as part of an Allied plan to democratize society. There is some truth in this, although it seems more likely that those most responsible for the writing reforms that began in 1946 were the Japanese themselves. American impact in this area, it seems, has been exaggerated by Japanese who were both for and against reform, the former as a shield for their own agenda and the latter as a bogeyman to discredit reform.

The belief that Americans were primarily responsible for the postwar language reforms is based on the alleged activities of a Major Robert K. Hall, staff officer of an educational unit with the occupation army, and on a report issued by an American educational delegation eight months before the first reform was enacted. On November 20, 1945, Hall is said to have informed Arimitsu Jiro, chief of the Ministry of Education's textbook division, that henceforth romanized writing was to be used in Japan's school textbooks. Chinese characters would be gradually phased out of Japanese society, beginning with a 1,500-character limit. The reasons Hall gave for the proposed measures were to increase the time available to students for acquiring substantive knowledge and to facilitate the learning of foreign languages (Sugimori 1982:96–98). Toward the end of the meeting, however, Hall's superior is supposed to have stepped in to announce that these recommendations were not official policy, and that the questions were still under review. Hall, a graduate of Harvard and Columbia with specialties in education and East Asian studies, apparently was expressing his personal views. Unable to win the support of others in his division, he was later transferred out of the section handling textbooks. Hall's views, although not shared by his peers, were consistent with those held by Japanese reformers controlling the National Language Council, with whom Hall had been in contact.

The same interpretation can be given to a report issued by the American Education Delegation to Japan on March 31, 1946, that called for replacing the character script with *rōmaji* (romanization). The reasons given for this recommendation were to facilitate education, simplify mechanization of writing, help spread knowledge, and make research of foreign (i.e., Western) literature easier. It is extremely unlikely that these views could have arisen from any firsthand acquaintance with the problem, since only one of the delegation's twenty-seven members understood Japanese (Maruya 1982:290). The Americans, who had been in Japan only sixteen days before issuing the report, seem to have accepted uncritically the recommendations of a group of Japanese phonetic script advocates who had cooperated with them during their stay.[13] The ability of this group to dominate postwar language policy through control of the National Language Council was insured by the practice of appointing new members to the council on the recommendation of current members only. Together they were responsible for most of the directives listed in Table 1 (Yamada Yoshio 1967:713–714; Neverov 1977:235).

Table 1
Japan's Postwar Writing Reforms

1946	List of 1,850 characters for daily use *(Tōyō kanji)*
	New *kana* spelling rules
1948	Supplementary list of characters for daily use
	Approved "readings" of characters
1949	List of new character forms
1951	Supplementary list of characters for personal names
1952	Principles for composing official documents
1954	Rules for romanized writing
	Rules for writing borrowed foreign words
1956	Rules for homonym substitution
1958	Pronunciation and writing of geographical names
	Guidelines for stroke order of characters
1959	Rules for appending *okurigana*
1973	Amendments to the 1959 *okurigana* rules
	Amendments to the 1948 "readings" list
1981	List of 1,945 frequently used characters *(Jōyō kanji)*

The first of these directives, the *Tōyō kanjihyō* (List of Chinese Characters for the Time Being), which limited the number of characters that could be used in official documents and, by extension, in society generally, was also the most controversial. Intended only as a transitional step on the path to complete romanization, the list was criticized for failing to reflect linguistic realities both in terms of the number of characters and the particular ones chosen. Its acceptance by the Japanese people in the early postwar era has been attributed to its "symbolic character as an instrument of a new political way of thinking and . . . criterion of democratic consciousness" (Muller 1975:65), and to the disposition of a defeated people to accept whatever carries the stamp of official policy. Despite their linguistic shortcomings, which given the magnitude of the task and its inherent contradictions (see Chapter 9) were inevitable, the reforms carried out between 1946 and 1959 unquestionably were effective in eliminating many abuses of the character writing system that derived from elitist social conventions rather than linguistic necessity. They also seemed to have played no small role, directly and symbolically, in the democratization of education. Assuming some linkage between the difficulty of the writing system and Japan's intellectual and material progress, the relative success of these limited reforms makes one wonder what effect a genuine alternative to the character script would have on the country.

As the chronology in Table 1 shows, no new initiatives were taken to reform written Japanese after 1959. The 1973 amendments to *okurigana* rules stipulated that characters would subsume a greater share of a word's representation, meaning that less of the word's phonology would be patently specified. In the same year, 357 more "readings" were added to those available for character representation. The spirit of reform seems to have vanished with time and prosperity. This pattern is typical of the relationship between writing reform and sociopolitical change in East Asia generally. East Asians, for the most part, seem willing to tolerate the inefficiency of character-based writing until a foreign threat causes them to take stock of their social institutions. When the crisis has passed, thanks in part to changes brought about by a more rational orthography, tradition reasserts itself, reform is jettisoned, and retrograde practices creep back in through the writing habits of the conservative elite who were dissatisfied with the reforms to begin with, and, in some cases, through those of the new elite who had engineered the reforms but to whom success gave a new perspective.

This cycle is played out partly because reform of character-based writing is basically a zero-sum game, where changes introduced in one area lead to problems in another, until the whole effort falls apart because of the shortsightedness of reformers who cannot perceive that there is no solution within the context defined. The other reason for the cycle is people's tendency to forget the root causes of problems after they have managed temporarily to squirm out of them, especially when the solution to the problem involves an immediate effort or giving up something one has more or less learned to live with. Most people never get this far, and most of those who do are put off by the fact that the new paradigm, in the early period while adjustments are still being made, almost always leaves people worse off than they were before.

This reform cycle is evidenced independently in all three East Asian countries that are still using Chinese characters. China's early colloquial language *(báihuà)* movement, the emergence of sanctioned phonetic notations, and the People's Republic's first two character limitation and simplification plans (1956, 1964) were enacted when China and Chinese culture were under heavy foreign pressure. By the 1970s, when the regime had consolidated itself, its leaders had aged, and the threat of hostile competition had become less imminent, positive reform of the character writing system was abandoned. In Korea's case, the all-*hangul* legislation enacted during the political reforms of 1894 and in both Koreas immediately after liberation from Japanese rule, was inspired by a perceived need to revitalize society in the face of foreign competition.[14] After some initial successes, the tempo of reform was slowed, sidetracked, and to a limited extent reversed, because of inevitable linguistic problems, but mostly because success had freed these societies and their leadership from the absolute need for more urgent measures. In Japan, organized calls for writing reform began in the Meiji period, when Japanese were obsessed with "catching up" with the West, disappeared with the false confidence that was part of the militarist state, and blossomed again, this time with some success, when Japan lost faith in its institutions through defeat in war.[15]

As Japan recovered from the material and psychological ravages of a lost war, those responsible for the *Tōyō* reforms lost the government's and vocal public's support. In 1962, the National Language Council was downgraded from a "policy recommending" *(kengi)* to a "deliberative" *(shingi)* organization. There was also a change in the membership procedure that opened the council to other, more conservative views (Kondo 1977:117; Gottlieb 1994:1187–1189). In November 1972, the National Language Council reconsidered the *Tōyō kanji* list, and two years later it issued a report stating that (1) such a list is necessary, but should not be "restrictive"; (2) a character list should not try to define usage for science, arts, or individual persons; and (3) the list should apply to modern Japanese only (Seeley 1984:278). In January 1977, the council published a *Shin kanjihyō shian* (New Chinese Character List Draft Plan) containing 1,900 characters and the proposal that the list be considered a "guideline" *(meyasu)* instead of a prescriptive set. The draft dropped thirty-three characters from the *Tōyō* list and added eighty-three. After more deliberation, a final Frequently Used *(Jōyō)* list of 1,945 Chinese characters was issued in 1981, along with a new list for personal names that increased the latter from 120 to 166. More important, the final version included in its Preamble an explicit denial that the list *had* to be followed, and endorsed the use of *furigana,* which had never really gone out of business.

Gottlieb concludes her study of postwar Japanese writing reform by noting that with "the current success of the Foreign Ministry policy in promoting the study of Japanese [language] overseas, the advent of the word processor, which has revolutionized document production in Japan,[16] and the re-establishment of economic security despite the continued use of characters, it is generally believed that many of the earlier arguments for script reform are no longer valid." Writing two and a half decades ago, Miller, typically, was more blunt about it: "Japanese society today appears to have not even an idiot fringe which still seriously proposes 'doing anything' about the writing system" (1967:138).

3. Korean

ON THE CONTINUUM from full use of Chinese characters to no use, Korean occupies an intermediate position. It can optionally be expressed in a mixed character-phonetic script, as is done for some types of writing in the South. Or the language can be written in a phonetic alphabet entirely, which is the practice for most nontechnical works in South Korea and for all writing in the North. Unlike the Japanese, who also use a mixed character-phonetic script, Koreans, when they want to at all, use Chinese characters only to represent Sinitic vocabulary; indigenous words must be written in the *hangul* alphabet. Korean thus has moved further away from characters and closer to full phonetic writing than Japanese, which uses characters for both borrowed and native vocabulary, and when the convention calls for it, does so obligatorily. Although Koreans in the South and the North still rely to some degree on a latent knowledge of Chinese characters to distinguish the language's many Sinitic terms, most Koreans feel no attachment to the characters and would just as soon be rid of them entirely.

I begin the present chapter by describing the linguistic factors that enabled Korean to break the association with characters more completely than Japanese, despite the fact that the two languages historically had similar conventions for character use. I will then explain the cultural dynamics that shaped Koreans' attitudes toward writing reform and gave the movement its unique focus. Finally, I will delineate and compare the steps taken in the two Koreas to eliminate Chinese characters in favor of all-phonetic writing. Thanks to the efforts of linguists in both parts of the country, Korean is well on its way to becoming East Asia's second major language, after Vietnamese, to free itself from the Sinitic paradigm.

Relationship of Chinese Characters to Korean

Korean language and writing are finally getting the attention they deserve. I recall in 1979 looking at a world map at an institute for Korean studies outside Seoul. The institute, which was tasked with promoting worldwide interest in Korean culture, had put pins on the map to mark places outside Korea where the Korean language was being taught. I did not embarrass my hosts by counting them, but it wouldn't have taken long. Our interpretations, in any case, were quite different: the Koreans running the institute were clearly proud that non-Koreans were learning the language, while I was mildly appalled that the numbers were so few. This gap between the number of people who were studying Korean and the number who, by every statistical measure, should have been studying it presented a unique career opportunity for me and real incentive to work at learning the language.

My expectations have not been disappointed. Korean language programs have proliferated in the United States in the past few years, encouraged by Republic of Korea government funding, community support, the availability of first-rate teaching materials and, most important, South Korea's own economic success. Korean ranks among the world's ten most common languages, and is worth learning for that reason alone. Other people are attracted to the language for its value in linguistic studies. Like Japanese, Korean borrowed most of its so-called learned vocabulary from Chinese, giving it a superficial similarity to Chinese that is reinforced—in the South—by the use of Chinese characters in technical works, university textbooks, and other types of nonfiction writing. But Korean has no genetic affiliation with Chinese. It is, like Japanese and Mongolian, an "Altaic" language, with typological features characteristic of that hypothetical family, including subject-object-verb word order, agglutinative morphological affixes, postpositions, and a core vocabulary of indigenous morphemes of varying syllable length. Although its genetic relationship to Japanese remains uncertain, the two languages are so similar structurally that a sentence translated from one of the languages to the other often can be superimposed on the original without disrupting the morpheme sequence.

Phonologically, however, the similarities between Korean and Japanese disappear almost entirely. The latter has a restricted inventory of about one hundred different syllables of the vowel (V) or consonant-vowel (CV) type,[1] enriched by a few morphophonemic sound changes that operate between some syllables within a word. Korean has many times that number of syllables, with V, VC, VCC, CV, CVC, and CVCC configurations, and a complex system of cross-syllable sound change rules. Although only a part of the Korean syllable inventory is available to represent borrowed Sinitic vocabulary, the fact that the language has a much larger total number of syllables than Japanese means that potentially ambiguous Sinitic words are less confusing phonologically. Koreans are better able to identify to what part of their lexicon a word belongs, whereas in Japanese the distinction between Sinitic and indigenous sounds is less apparent.[2] These innate differences are magnified in Korean by spelling conventions that preserve distinctions lost in speech.

Korean's larger number of syllables, besides helping to make phonetic ambiguity less of an issue than in Japanese, also had a crucial effect on the development of writing in Korea. As we saw in the preceding chapter, the limited number of syllables in Japanese meant that a few dozen Chinese characters could represent the entire inventory of Japanese sounds.[3] Characters used for their sound lost their original semantic connotations while their shapes became increasingly stylized, until they evolved in both form and function into a qualitatively different type of symbol. The result was an indigenous writing system that imposed its own requirements on the phonology of Japanese speakers, reinforcing even more than the characters a psychological fixation on syllables of the simplest types, thus both preempting and precluding the emergence of a segment-based orthography.[4] It was not for lack of trying that Koreans failed to follow the same path. Like the Japanese, Koreans developed the same kind of mixed writing systems, with *on*- and *kun*-style readings for Chinese characters and the same convention of using characters phonetically to represent Korean sounds. The "problem" was that there were so many more syllables in Korean that its users were unable to work the hybrid script into an efficient system. Not only was there more incentive for Koreans to develop a segmental orthography, there was nothing, practically speaking, standing in its way.

This brings us to *hangul,* Korea's acclaimed phonetic alphabet. *Hangul,* literally "Korean writing," from the Sinitic morpheme *han* and the indigenous Korean word *kul > gul,* is the modern term for what was originally called *hunmin chŏngŭm* ("correct sounds for instructing the people") from the name of the 1446 imperial rescript that promulgated the system.[5] The term *hangul,* however, which is half Chinese and half Korean, is particularly apt because etymologically it portrays the system's essence quite accurately, although in a way most Koreans would prefer not to dwell on. It is customary at the beginning of one's account of *hangul* to praise Korea as a nation and King Sejong (1397–1450) personally for independently inventing an alphabetic system that put literacy within reach of the common folk and has made it possible—linguistically and culturally—to break the cycle of dependence on Chinese characters. All of this is true, and it is certainly laudable, but after hearing it a hundred or a thousand times, the ritual gets tiring. I am also put off by the *hangul* cult's incessant harping on the magnificence of their ancestors' accomplishment, because the more they tout it, the more it draws attention to all the things Korea *didn't* do. So let's leave it at that. Korea, the South at least, has a lot going for it these days, and it can do without this worn out form of condescension. Genuine Korean patriots will know what I mean and thank me for it.

Hangul, in fact, is less than it could be, owing to a quirk of fate that can be traced back to China and Chinese characters. Typologically, *hangul* is an alphabet of twenty-four basic (twenty-eight historically) and sixteen compound letters representing nineteen consonants and twenty-one vocalic elements. The system looks more complex than this, because instead of combining the letters serially, Koreans group them into syllables shaped like blocks, by modifying the size, shape, and position of the letters depending on where they appear in the spoken syllable. As a result, *hangul* bears a superficial resemblance to Chinese characters, which is not coincidental.[6] My immediate point, however, is that *hangul,* while alphabetic, was like every other writing system in East Asia unable to escape the Sinitic paradigm that accords prominence to syllables and not words. Although modern Koreans are addressing the issue with rules for word division, this connection with Chinese characters, exemplified by the use of a Sinitic term in the word for "*Korean* writing," is still evident and has had important effects on the language's development.

Hangul's connection with Chinese characters goes further than just appearance. In order to sell the idea of a non-Chinese invention to a China-oriented court, those backing *hangul* not only had to make it look like Chinese characters, they also had to promote it as an auxiliary system for helping people pronounce Chinese characters correctly. Although its use expanded beyond this, *hangul* for most of its history was regarded as a poor person's substitute for *real* writing, which was either classical Chinese (*hanmun*) written in characters or stilted Korean written in Chinese characters used—as in Japanese—to represent Korean sounds or as symbols for Korean synonyms. Of course, characters were also used for the large number of Sinitic loanwords coming into Korean. The result was the same as what we have noted for Japanese: an enormous collection of foreign, syllable-sized morphemes, which make perfectly good sense written in characters, but which contain too few phonetic distinctions even when combined into words to be understood easily when spoken or written phonetically.

This is the linguistic rationale, as it were, for the use of Chinese characters with *hangul* in technical and scholarly publications in the South: Since many Sinitic words are ambiguous, the argument goes, they must be presented in the medium through which they were borrowed, while indigenous and fully indigenized Sinitic terms, which are phonetically more diverse, can be written in *hangul*. Needless to say, this "solution" perpetuates the problem by sanctioning the very conditions that brought it about. Not only are users of the *hangul*-character mixed script deprived of any incentive to rectify the cause of the ambiguity, the availability of characters with their own unique rules of redundancy allows character-literate Koreans to go on borrowing and inventing new Sinitic terms, digging the hole even deeper. This practice applies almost exclusively to the more formal genres, where Sinitic vocabulary is used in greater proportions. Unfortunately, the readers and creators of mixed script materials are the ones most likely to have learned a large number of Chinese characters in high school and college, and hence those with the least incentive to do anything about it.

South Korean literature, popular writing, and newspapers for the most part make little or no use of Chinese characters, being written instead in all-*hangul*. For a while, all-*hangul* novels would occasionally add characters in parentheses after ambiguous Sinitic words, but even this practice seems to be dying out. Korean newspapers that still use the characters have developed an interesting variation on this, whereby the first appearance of a potentially confusing Sinitic term is in characters and subsequent appearances are in *hangul,* or (less commonly) vice-versa. Both practices evidently are designed to specify the word in a way all readers can relate to, but they can also be viewed as a device to indigenize poorly assimilated terms. To many South Koreans, all-*hangul* writing is an ideal that is gradually being realized across all genres. In the North, however, it has been a reality for nearly five decades, although it has not been without problems. The chief difference between the two Koreas' respective efforts to replace Chinese characters entirely with *hangul* is in the nature of the transition. In the South, it has been by fits and starts, accompanied by the gradual evolution of mechanisms that have led to the suppletion of the mixed character script in some areas and a reduction in the number of Chinese characters where the mixed script is still used. North Korea, by contrast, jumped into all-*hangul* with both feet; their problem has been how to engineer mechanisms to make it work.[7]

It is easy to dismiss the relationship of Korean to Chinese and Chinese characters as the equivalent of a Japanese-style character-*kana* mixed script, and indeed there are many similarities. To begin with, both systems had comparable historical antecedents: equipped with the same basic tool and facing roughly the same set of problems, the two languages with their remarkably similar structures developed the same types of semantic and phonetic conventions for using Chinese characters. Moreover, the two countries were probably aware of each other's systems, as suggested by their shared use of certain abbreviated characters as phonetic symbols (Lee Ki-mun 1977:71). And in their modern forms, both the Japanese and (South) Korean systems mix Chinese characters with indigenous phonetic systems, partly from habit and partly to reduce the ambiguity of the Sinitic vocabulary.

Nevertheless, there are important differences. Although Chinese characters can, exceptionally, have more than one sound in Korean, these multiple values (usually two at most) parallel those in standard Chinese, from which the sounds derive. Whereas a second or third reading may exist in principle and may still appear in dictionaries, in practice Koreans have narrowed the choice to one reading for all but a handful of cases. A character-literate Korean therefore can look at a Chinese character and read off one sound, without bothering to contemplate the character's role in context. There is none of the guesswork that attends decisions in Japanese on what *(on)* reading is meant. In addition, modern Korean uses Chinese characters for Sinitic morphemes only, not for indigenous (let alone English!) vocabulary. The mapping relationship between language and script is, unlike in

Japanese, entirely straightforward. This relationship makes the South Korean system much easier to learn and operate, so that one would think there would be less pressure to get rid of Chinese characters in Korea than in Japan. Paradoxically, exactly the opposite is true.

While editorial styles vary, South Koreans writing in the mixed script are pretty much free to decide whether a Sinitic word should appear in characters or be rendered phonetically in *hangul*. By and large, the expectation is that if the term can be understood in *hangul,* then it should be written in the country's indigenous script. In Japanese, the rule seems to be that if a noun or verb, Sinitic *or* indigenous, has a Chinese character and the character is among those on the sanctioned list, then it should be written in characters. These differing practices, besides their long-term linguistic effect in making the languages more or less amenable to phonetic representation, have the net social effect of convincing their users that the characters are or are not intrinsically part of their linguistic systems. Nothing drives this point home more than the use in Japanese and nonuse in Korean of Chinese characters for indigenous vocabulary. As we have seen, in Japanese the characters were grafted onto native words, acquiring in the process a kind of proprietary relationship with the language and a sense among its users that the characters belong. Koreans feel no such attachment, because Chinese characters can represent only borrowed Chinese terms.[8] In fact, Koreans have to be persuaded by linguists that Chinese characters—whatever their linguistic failings—are historically as much a part of Korean writing as *hangul*. Koreans just do not accept this on a gut level.

These different psychological dispositions toward the characters are matched by performance differences, which further the users' attachment or alienation. The true test here is not in the ability of Japanese and Koreans to read characters (although the differences are apparent here as well), but in their ability and inclination to write them. A Japanese person, like a Chinese, will draw a character (not the *kana*) when asked to write a word, if he or she can remember it, or be embarrassed if he or she cannot. By contrast, although I have been in contact with educated Koreans almost daily for twenty years, I have only rarely seen a Korean who had not undergone special training in Chinese or Japanese volunteer to write a character. If asked specifically to do so, Koreans usually find some way to parry the request or end up writing it mechanically, without the grace and style of long habit. Nationalism also plays a role in the equation. *Kana,* after all, were derived from Chinese characters, and while Japanese can take credit for that process, they can hardly claim that the symbols are entirely indigenous. *Hangul,* in contrast, was built from the ground up by Koreans, giving them nationalistic grounds to replace the Chinese characters.

Finally, there are linguistic reasons why Koreans are apt to abandon the characters before the Japanese. First, Japanese is phonetically less distinctive than Korean, at least within the syllable boundary, which with Chinese characters is all that counts. Second, because characters in Japanese can represent polysyllabic indigenous words, *kanji* from the publisher's viewpoint are more economical than single-syllable *kana,* which like a character is made with a single impression and takes up the same amount of space. Third, since romanization is not yet an option, the alternatives are the mixed script orthographies as they now stand or writing in all-*kana* and all-*hangul.* All-*hangul* not only has a sanctioned and viable tradition that *kana* at present lacks, *hangul's* perceptual unit—syllable blocks—carry more graphic distinctions than are provided by a *kana* symbol occupying the same physical space, making it easier for the eye to distinguish one cue from the next. Chinese characters designate morphemes, and these patterns can be stored in the mind as such. *Hangul* identifies discrete phonological segments, which in phonetic writing provide early cues that are indispensable to practical reading strategies. *Kana,* a true syllabary, falls somewhere between the two, offering neither a clear picture of the morpheme nor a discrete look at its phonology.

For all of these reasons—linguistic, cultural, and psychological—Korean writing has moved much faster than Japanese toward complete phoneticization. The remaining linguistic problems are being solved or are solvable, while the conventions for use seem designed to make the transition as painless as possible. The North is already using all-*hangul,* and the lessons learned there can be applied to problems that develop in the full phoneticization of writing in the South. South Koreans, for their part, practice what can be considered two forms of digraphia: a mixed script for formal applications and all-*hangul* for an expanding variety of other genres constitute one form. Freedom of movement within the mixed script to use as few or as many Chinese characters as society wants is another.

Development of Writing in Korea

The availability of two or more forms of writing has characterized Korean orthography throughout most of its history. According to legend, Chinese characters reached "Korea" in 1122 B.C. through Jizi (Kor. Kija), a member of the Shang dynasty nobility who fled China when the Zhou dynasty was established (Liu Shih-hong 1969:70). Actual records place the first known use of Chinese characters on the peninsula sometime before 108 B.C., when China's Lo Lang (Kor. Lak Lang) colony was established in northern Korea. There is no evidence of writing in Korea before this, nor any reason to believe that the characters were first used there for anything other than to write unadorned classical Chinese.

By the fifth century A.D., however, Chinese characters were being used in Korea's Silla kingdom both semantically and phonetically to record elements of the Korean language. Known subsequently as *idu* (lit. "official readings") after its main body of users,[9] the practice gradually evolved into a regular system that rearranged Chinese morphemes to fit Korean grammar and alternated between the two usages of Chinese characters according to the nature of the text. Although it shared (and predated) the Japanese practice of using characters to represent indigenous morphemes on the basis of meaning or sound, there was nothing remotely comparable to *idu* in Japan until about the twelfth century, when Japanese *kambun* texts began to follow Japanese word order. A third form of early Korean writing has been identified by Lee Ki-mun as the "oath record style" from its use on a stone inscription dated 552 or 612 (1977:52–53). Texts were written entirely in Chinese characters used for their semantic value, with no provision made for Korean grammar particles. It differed from pure Chinese only by some variations in word order and should probably be considered a transitional form between classical Chinese, which remained the written language of the Korean scholar elite up to the early part of the twentieth century, and the emerging *idu* convention.

In its early form *idu* used characters semantically to represent even Korean grammar particles, for example, 者 (Chin. "that which, one who") for the Korean topic particle, 以 (Chin. "by means of") for the instrument particle, and 中 (Chin. "among, within") for the Korean possessive particle (not 之, which was used for its sound to indicate a verb-final form). This practice later gave way to use for grammatical morphemes of a restricted set of characters whose association with Korean was phonetic. In reading *idu,* one supplies semantically equivalent native readings for characters representing "content" words, in the manner described above for Japanese *kun*. Or if the word was borrowed from Chinese, one reads it directly in its Sino-Korean pronunciation. The meaning in either case is that of the characters. Since the system was used primarily for prose, Chinese vocabulary dominated, so that the system, though awkward, was still manageable.

Closely related to *idu* was another technique used in the ninth and tenth centuries known as *hyangchal* ("local writing"). In this system, the distinction between characters used with *kun*-type readings for "content" words and phonetic use of the characters for grammatical affixes was more strictly maintained. Nevertheless, the reader still needed to grasp the meaning of the text to know whether a Chinese character was to be interpreted semantically as a substitute for an indigenous Korean context word or read in its Sino-Korean pronunciation and linked with a (nearly) homophonous Korean grammatical particle. Not all scholars treat *hyangchal* as a separate system. Lee Ki-mun views it as a further development of *idu* (1977:59), while Blank believes "the difference is in the degree of semantic or phonetic use" of the characters (1981:39). In fact, the difference may be not one of design, but a reflection of the type of text being represented. *Hyangchal* was used mainly for lyric transcription, where native Korean vocabulary dominates; with fewer Sinitic words to represent, the alternation between *on*- and *kun*-type readings for content words as practiced in *idu* would disappear of its own accord. *Hyangchal,* whether it was a deliberate or a de facto convention, in any case fell out of use entirely by the fifteenth century, when *hangul* superseded its function.

Idu was fully systematized by the seventh century and continued to be used until the end of the nineteenth. No significant abbreviations, comparable to those used in Japanese, were made to the forms of characters used for their phonetic values until much later, when some of the signs used to indicate grammatical particles began appearing in reduced forms developed to gloss classical Chinese texts. Moreover, although the system could be regularized in the sense of using the same Chinese character for the same Korean sound, the inventory of characters used in this manner could not be significantly reduced, even if the Korean bureaucrats using the system had wanted to "spell" out indigenous content words, because of the large number of syllables in Korean. The use of this difficult system over such a long period of time, even after *hangul* became available, can be explained by its status as the official script of government and by its external resemblance to Chinese, which continued to enjoy the highest prestige.

Between these two systems—*idu* and pure Chinese—was a technique developed in the fourteenth century, similar to Japanese *kambun,* known as *kugyŏl* ("the knack of [reading] orally") or *to* ("to utter"), in which Chinese texts were read with Sino-Korean sounds. The use of *kun*-type readings in this genre was extremely limited (Hayashi et al. 1983:8). As was the case with *kambun* in Japan, *kugyŏl* in Korea helped establish a false identity between Chinese and the indigenous language, leading to the introduction of countless Chinese loanwords with important consequences for the language. It would seem, moreover, that in eschewing *kun*-type readings, the genre also helped to establish the subsequent practice of writing only Chinese-derived words in characters. *Kugyŏl* is further distinguished by its use of abbreviated characters for symbols that designated grammatical inflections and particles. Examples are 伊 > イ *(-i),* 尼 > ヒ *(-ni),* and 隱 > ß *(-un).* The relationship both in function and form to the *katakana* used in Japanese *kambun* is obvious. Some sixteen symbols seem to have been shared by the two languages, although the direction of diffusion is uncertain. Another method was to combine two *kugyŏl* forms to accommodate polysyllabic words, for example, 爲 > ＼／ (Kor. *ha,* the root of *hada* "to do"; the original connection with the character was semantic) plus 口 (Kor. *ku,* a phonetic use of the character) formed 匃, read *hagu (hago),* meaning "with, and."

Despite these conventions for writing Korean with Chinese characters, their evolution into a systematic phonetic script (a syllabary) as had happened in Japan and the Middle East was frustrated by the phonetic characteristics of the language. With only 102 syllables, Japanese can be practically represented by a small number of syllabic signs. Korean, for its part, has some 1,096 currently used spoken and 1,724 written syllable forms. Even with generic, subsyllabic indicators equivalent to the *kana* diacritics, the richer phonology of Korean would have required an inventory of as many signs as there were spoken syllables if each were to be represented uniquely. That is, a fully "modernized" writing system for Korean based on indivisible syllable units would entail a degree of complexity approaching that of the character script itself.

Having reached this impasse, further refinement meant rethinking the problem from the ground up. If there are too many syllables for a practical syllabary, are there smaller units in the language's phonology on which a writing system can be based? This solution seems obvious to us today, but it bears pointing out that the transition from syllable to phoneme is a enormous feat of abstraction, which may have been accomplished only once in history (Gleitman and Rozin, 1973a:464). Accordingly, it was first believed that the *hangul* alphabet, completed in 1443 and disseminated three years later, was an adaptation of some other phonetic script instead of a deliberate creation as claimed traditionally, and a number of different theories emerged to explain its origin (Blank 1981:59).

Scholarship over the past few decades, while recognizing a foreign contribution to the idea of alphabetizing Korean, now regards the units of the script and the specific theories for their composition as purely indigenous. Koreans had known of Sanskrit and the phonetic writing system of Tibet through Buddhism. During China's Yuan dynasty (1279–1368), the Mongols had sent printed material to Korea in the *hP'ags-pa* alphabet. Correspondence was also carried out in the phonetic Uighur script. The Mongol alphabet itself, adapted from Uighur writing, was also known in Korea by the fifteenth century (Kontsevicha 1979:24–25). Koreans, moreover, had extensive experience with the phonetic recording of language through their own adaptations of Chinese characters for *idu, hyangchal,* and *kugyŏl*. As they were versed in the phonetic principle and aware of its application to subsyllabic segments of phonology, it seems probable that the conceptual jump made by the inventors of *hangul* from syllable to segment was eased by foreign precedent.

Regarding its concrete design, however, *hangul* was all invention. This proposition is supported by the failure of competing theories to demonstrate a systematic connection between the shapes of *hangul* letters and those of any other alphabetic script, and was confirmed by the discovery in 1941 of an authentic example of the original *Hunmin chŏngŭm* text of 1446, in which the principles of its creation are described.[10] In the section on "Notes and Usage," *hangul* shapes are explained as being patterned after the speech organs used to make the corresponding sounds. The symbol ㄱ is the basic velar consonant, showing "the back of the tongue on the soft palate of the open mouth." ㄴ is the alveolar consonant, "with the tip of the tongue touching the upper alveoli." The bilabial consonant is represented by ㅁ, showing "the form of the mouth using both lips." ㅅ is the dental and ㅇ the glottal consonant (Lee Ki-mun 1983:82). These five basic forms are modified according to fixed principles to accommodate the remaining homorganic consonants, for example, aspirate consonants add a stroke to the basic symbol, tense consonants double the sign used for their nontense counterparts, and so forth. The shapes of basic vowels and rules for representing their combinations followed different but systematic linguistic principles.

Hangul follows a phonological theory that, unlike the Chinese theory, analyzes the syllable into three (versus two) parts including initial, middle, and final sounds. These parts are combined into syllable-size graphic units containing from one to four *hangul* letters, for example, 이 = *i* (the small circle, in this position, is a dummy symbol that means "vowel follows") or 몫 (*moks* "portion, share"), where ㅁ = *m*, ㅗ = *o*, ㄱ = *k*, and ㅅ = *s*. The scholars who systematized *hangul* spelling in the first half of the twentieth century chose to depict the etymology of morphemes by preserving in the script their basic phonology, despite the operation of morphophonemic sound change rules; the reader makes the necessary adjustments, for example, 압력 *ap + ryŏk* ("pressure") is read *amnyŏk*. The result of all this, according to Samuel Martin, is an orthography that "incorporates representation of phoneme components, phonemes, morphophonemes, syllables and—to the extent that certain morphophonemic shapes (such as *kkoch* 꽃 'flower') are unique shapes—morphemes" (1972:83).

Hangul goes to great lengths to preserve the syllable as a unit of orthography by squeezing, bending, and reordering the sequence of letters so that they fit into an imaginary block. Often this process results in configurations that are less distinctive than they might have been if the letters were strung out serially. For example, 꾹 *kok*, 꾹 *kuk*, and 끅 *kŭk* can be hard to distinguish in substandard print. CVC syllables with compound vocalic elements can get pretty crowded. The focus on syllables is also evident in *hangul*'s treatment of vowels, which, as we have seen, are preceded with a small circle when there is no initial consonant (in the morphology). Although it is possible that the circle actually represents a voiced laryngeal consonant present in speech (Sampson 1985:128), this interpretation would not apply to V or VC syllables *within* words, particularly those preceded by syllables with final consonants that transfer in speech to the next syllable, where the circle-plus-vowel orthographic convention is still maintained. It seems far more likely that the circle before vowels was designed (or was generalized throughout the system) to maintain the visual syllable format, which some psycholinguists regard as "a natural unit for representation in an orthography" (Gleitman and Rozin 1973:464).

In view of the ingenuity demonstrated in creating individual *hangul* letters, it is tempting to attribute the retention of a syllable format to this same perception. Coulmas, for example, writes that "it is possible to write *Han'gul* in linear order, but the system's designers must have been aware

지루하던 비가 정오(正午)가 지나서야 개었다. 준은 자리를 거두고 가까운 음식집에서 아침 겸 점심을 하고 들어왔다. 그는 오늘 아무 예정도 없었다. 식사를 하고 난 다음에는 으레 담배가 당긴다. 보통 때는 기계적으로 담배를 꺼내서 물게 되지만 문득 이상해질 때가 있다. 그가 첫 담배를 피우기는 군에 들어가서의 일이니까, 벌써 삼사년 경력이 붙은 셈이다. 복학(復學)한 다음에도 그럭저럭 피우고 있다. 사실 군대 생활을 하는 동안 담배는 요긴한 몫을 했다. 하필 배속된다는 게 엠 비 피 사단의 수색 중대였다. OP라는 곳은 독고준과 같은 남자에게 안성마춤으로 잔인한 자리였다. 이북 출신은 되도록 OP 근무를 시키지 않는다는 것으로 되어 있었으나 그는 거기서 근무하게 되었다. 지호지간(指呼之間)이란 이런 것을 말하는 것일 게다. 바로 눈앞이었다. 녀석들이 호(壕) 밖으로 나와서 평행봉하는 것이 보인다. 자식들은 저것도 체육 사업이라고 부를 테지. 두 개의 막대기 사이에서 흔들리는 몸뚱아리를 바라보면서 그는 쓴웃음을 지었다. 포대경(砲臺鏡) 속에서 바라보이는 그들의 옷차림은 예나 지금이나 초라했다. 이런 산굽이를 돌아 나와 이쪽의 관측에 백 미터 가량 노출된 보급로를 소달구지가 지나간다. 이런

Hangul text used in a South Korean novel. (*Hoe Saek In*, by Choe In-hun. Minjung sogwan, Seoul, p. 60)

that breaking down the continuum of linguistic sounds into phonetic features . . . is inconvenient for reading. They also recognized the syllable as an
important unit of speech" (1989:120). Evidence that the syllable format
was a carryover from the use of Chinese characters, however, is persuasive.
In his preface to the *Hunmin chŏngŭm*, Sejong wrote: "Those signs are
modeled on the old Chinese seal characters. . . . When put together they
form the written character." Lee Ki-mun believes the design of *hangul* was
attributed to the characters to forestall the objections of Korea's Confucian
scholars (1977:60). Kontsevicha concurs, adding that there was a demonstrable need to disguise the idea of a "Buddhist-Indian alphabetic script"
from a court dominated by Chinese Confucian ideology (1979:28).

In terms of *hangul*'s intended use, the original 1446 edict did
acknowledge that existing character-based systems are "too complicated,
imperfect, and inconvenient a system for Koreans to use freely in expressing their own ideas and thinking, because too many Chinese characters are
involved in it" (cited by Lee Sang-baek 1957:2). Nowhere, however, was
mention made by those promoting the new script or by their immediate
successors of using *hangul* to replace Chinese or Chinese characters; in fact,
they took pains to avoid the inference. The literate upper stratum continued using classical Chinese after the invention of *hangul* just as they had
before. Lesser officials did begin using *hangul* instead of *idu*, while an
emerging middle class was identified by its use of both *idu* and a mixed
hangul–Chinese character script (Kim Min-su 1973:342). All-*hangul* meanwhile became the common person's tool for writing personal letters, bills,
in short "all areas of 'everyday' life matters" (Blank 1981:86).

Thus by 1894, some four and a half centuries after *hangul*'s appearance, there were four different writing systems in use in Korea. *Idu* gave
way that year to a new official style called "national Chinese writing"
(kukhanmun), which transposed elements of what was essentially classical
Chinese to match Korean word order and added enough grammatical
affixes, written in *hangul,* to make the text readable as Korean. While an
improvement on *idu,* the system could not compete with the popularly used
character-*hangul* mixed script and the all-*hangul* script, which were both
based solidly on the Korean language. By 1919, it went out of use entirely.
Classical Chinese *(hanmun),* for its part, continues to be taught in South
Korea as a foreign language much as Latin used to be taught in American
high schools. As a practical tool for writing, it, too, dropped out of use in
Korea some eight decades ago.

Hangul's fortunes have shifted throughout history with changes in
political climate. It was banned outright in 1504 after the Kapja revolt. For
a brief period at the turn of the nineteenth century, it was accorded official
status by the reformist government. Suppressed during the Japanese occupation, it emerged afterward as the only script recognized in North Korea
and one of two scripts used in the South. These latter developments were as

much the result of conscious reform, however, as they were a product of evolutionary change.

Dynamics of Korean Writing Reform

To understand writing reform in Korea it helps to keep several factors in mind. The first is that the issue, as understood by Koreans, has nothing to do with romanized scripts. This may disappoint internationally minded partisans from other countries, whose own involvement with writing reform has predisposed them to view the conflict essentially as one between Chinese characters and the letters of the Roman alphabet. For most Koreans, so far, this dichotomy is not relevant. One can write either in all-*hangul* or by using Chinese characters for some or all of the Sinitic vocabulary. Other possibilities are imaginable. Romanized notations for Korean have been available in their limited applications for decades, and there is no reason why one of them could not be pressed into service as a regular orthography. If all-*hangul* writing is practicable, ipso facto, so is any other consistent (morpho-) phonemic representation.

Replacing *hangul* with a romanized script would, moreover, solve certain problems associated with the former, such as its nonuse internationally; its incompatibility with much foreign, alphabet-based computer software; the relative inefficiency of *hangul* computer input and output; and, most important, the syllabic mentality that frustrates genuine writing reform and leaves the Korean language hostage to the Sinitic paradigm. There have been signs recently that at least some of these considerations are forcing Koreans to take more seriously the prospect of a romanized script for at least some applications.[11]

Korean romanization has also been set back by the division of the country. As we shall see, the separate paths taken by the two Koreas in this arena are a microcosm of what has happened with the problem of Korean writing reform in general. North Korea's romanization system was specified, for once and for all, in a document titled *General Rules on Writing Reform with the Roman Alphabet* issued in January 1956. The protocols differ from the 1939 McCune-Reischauer system minimally by using [*h*] instead of an apostrophe for aspirated consonants, a different set of letters for the palatal affricates, and [*i*] instead of [*e*] as the second element used to indicate certain vowels. The system was intended for use by non-Koreans reading Korean, as evidenced by a rule prohibiting readings for letters that differ from those commonly used internationally.

In South Korea, McCune-Reischauer, which was also devised with the foreigner in mind, was the de facto romanization until 1959. The system is phonetic, not phonemic, and assumes no knowledge of Korean phonology on the part of the reader. In February of 1959, in an act similar to an event that took place in Japan some two decades earlier,[12] the Republic of Korea's

Ministry of Education adopted a new *Method for Writing Hangul in Roman Letters,* which is almost entirely phonemic and was clearly intended for Koreans reading Korean. Although its internal logic is impeccable, the system leads the foreigner to strange pronunciations and to what an English speaker might regard as some rather awful spellings, like "dog lib" for "independence" and worse. It was never able to displace the better established McCune-Reischauer and has had to compete with a variety of different contrivances used in pedagogy. Then in January 1984, with an eye on the upcoming Olympic Games, the South Korean government shifted to a foreign-oriented system for street signs not much different from McCune-Reischauer (Yi Sang-ok 1989:118). By 1988, the Ministry of Education was back to McCune-Reischauer entirely (Yi Un-jong 1989:336–339). Finally,

【 펑양 7월 3일발 조선중앙롱 신 】

경애하는 수령님의 서거 2돐에 즈음하여 《위대한 수령 김일성동지는 영원히 우리와 함께 계신다》 중앙미술전시회가 개막 되였다.

전시회장에는 일찌기 혁명의 길 에 나서신 첫날부터 생애의 마지 막순간까지 조국의 부강번영과 인민의 자유와 행복을 위하여, 온 세계의 자주화위업 실현을 위하여 모든것을 다 바치신 경애하는 수령 김일성동지의 혁명활동과 불 멸의 업적을 형상한 작품들을 비 롯하여 70여상의 미술작품이 전 시되여있다.

All-*hangul* newspaper text, North Korea.
(*Minju Chosŏn,* 4 July 1996, p. 1)

at the 1992 Paris convention on North-South romanization, the South proposed rules based largely on the original phonemic system adopted in 1959! The lesson to be drawn here, besides the one on comparative politics, is that romanized writing in Korea will not replace *hangul* any time soon.

A second point to remember in trying to understand Korean writing reform is the conditions that brought about this exclusive attachment to *hangul*. Leaving aside the practical features of the script, the fact that it was invented and could persist at all in the face of hostility from China, Japan, and through most of its history from Korea's own Confucian upper class is a monument to Korean national spirit. This feeling is so strong that Koreans have designated a national holiday (October 9) to commemorate *hangul*—the only country in the world to so honor a writing system. Being entirely Korean, highly visible, and a first-rate achievement, *hangul* has in addition to its linguistic function also taken on an independent role as a symbol of Korean identity, which flourishes whenever political conditions allow. One such period was during and immediately after the Kapo Rebellion of 1894, a farmers' revolt against the China-oriented court that instituted a number of egalitarian reforms. In 1895, *hangul* was decreed the primary writing system of government. That same year, Yu Kil-jun, the first Korean to study in the West, wrote his *Sŏyu kyŏnmun* (Observations from My Journey to the West) in the mixed *hangul*-character script, the first serious work to so appear (Blank 1981:87–89). In April 1896, the newspaper *Tongnip sinmun* began publishing in *hangul* exclusively. All-*hangul* novels had appeared even earlier. It was during this period that the term *hangul* itself first came into use as a replacement for the earlier term *ŏnmun*. Promotion of the script was aided by the appearance of all-*hangul* translations of the Bible and other Western religious publications.

By the 1920s, however, an equilibrium had been reached between attempts to oust Chinese characters completely and the preference of the character-literate public for their retention in limited number (Nam 1970:13). The effect of the Japanese occupation (1910–1945) on the all-*hangul* movement worked two ways. Instead of moving ahead openly with the tedious work that popularization of a practical *hangul* orthography entailed—defining word boundaries, establishing spelling conventions, laying down rules of grammar, ridding the language of obscure Chinese compounds, and encouraging development of a new, colloquial style—supporters of the movement were forced to conceal these activities or face imprisonment. Without meaning to belittle their accomplishments, I suspect that if the same zeal and determination could have been applied in a milieu where such efforts were rewarded, the stage would have been set for the emergence of a truly competitive all-*hangul* script before the language had absorbed through Japanese the thousands of new Sinitic compounds introduced by bilingual Koreans. At minimum, the language would have been free to develop corresponding terms on the basis of its own morphology or to assess new Sinitic vocabulary as it emerged, instead of lying dormant for thirty-five years. As it was, the Japanese authorities forbade both the use of *hangul* (1933) and the Korean spoken language (1938). *Hangul* publications simply disappeared (Kim Jin-p'yong 1983:97).

The other way the occupation took its effect was on the attitude of Koreans toward writing reform after these sanctions were lifted. Whatever the linguistic merits of all-*hangul* may be, debate on the question was drowned out by a groundswell of nationalism that sought to establish in one leap what Japanese colonialism had suppressed for over three decades. The result was hasty reforms in both the North and the South, which might have succeeded with less turmoil and disruption if given better planning and preparation. However, if Korean linguists had not taken advantage of popular sentiment to enact their reforms, who knows how long the process might have been delayed.

A third factor in understanding Korean attitudes toward writing reform is the manner in which Chinese characters are used. I have discussed *idu* and other techniques used previously by Koreans to make a character text represent indigenous vocabulary. The movement to unify written and spoken language styles at the beginning of the twentieth century caused these practices to fall into disuse, which meant that the sole representata of Chinese characters became the borrowed Sinitic vocabulary. There was no attempt to preserve the tradition of reading indigenous words from semantically equivalent characters, as the Japanese do with their *kun* readings of characters. Native Korean words are simply spelled out in *hangul,* while writers, depending on their subject and editor, represent the borrowed Chinese words in either characters or *hangul.* The effect of this practice on Koreans' attitudes has been twofold: on the one hand, characters are still seen, even among those comfortable with them, as something alien. They may revere the characters, use them at every opportunity, sign petitions demanding their use in the school curricula, and regard them as an inseparable part of national culture; but the characters just are not Korean, not in the same sense the Japanese view these symbols as something truly Japanese.

The other effect has been on Koreans' attitudes toward vocabulary itself. It is commonly accepted in countries whose languages include a large number of Sinitic morphemes that in order to write intelligibly without characters, one must address the problem of how concepts represented by phonetically vague Sinitic words can be expressed. One method is to replace the words with equivalent indigenous vocabulary, an approach that has won adherents in Japan and Vietnam. In Korea, however, this practice has been carried to extreme lengths. Not only have reformers sought to replace what they call "Chinese character words" *(hanja'ŏ)* that are ambiguous.[13] The general feeling in the purification campaigns that surfaced in both the North and the South was that the entire corpus of borrowed vocabulary is fair game.

For example, between February 1962 and July 1963, a special committee established in South Korea to promote all-*hangul* worked up a list of indigenous replacements for Chinese loanwords that when published filled five volumes (Kim Min-su 1973:348). Most of these replacements do not have and never had any real currency. They were built ad hoc from indigenous morphemes, many of which themselves had long ago fallen out of use. This process can be explained partly on linguistic grounds: In Japanese, native words were grafted onto characters *(kun)* and, accordingly, were able to coexist with their Sino-Japanese *(on)* counterparts. In Korea, borrowed Chinese vocabulary simply drove the indigenous words out, impoverishing the language's native component and necessitating recourse to artificial constructs. Still, it is hard to escape feeling that the drive to resurrect the language's indigenous elements (and purge established borrowings) owes more to Korean nationalism than to the requirements of a phonetic orthography.

Writing Reform in the Koreas

Efforts to replace Chinese characters with all-*hangul* writing followed different paths in North and South Korea and have met with different levels of success. Just as in their respective programs for romanization, both countries acted in this larger arena in a way that betrays the nature of the societies themselves. In the North, all-*hangul* writing was put on a philosophical basis that tied its fate to the sanctity of Marxism-Leninism and to the Democratic People's Republic of Korea's own *chuche* ("self-reliance") ideology. Once all-*hangul* writing was embraced, the North was committed to seeing the reform through no matter what difficulties were later encountered. In South Korea, all-*hangul* was greeted initially with the same enthusiasm that launched writing reform in the North. When the inevitable problems developed, however, opponents of the reform were able to dilute it and prolong the transition to all-*hangul*, but only after the pendulum had swung back and forth so many times that the embarrassment became worse than the nuisance of writing in the mixed script. Reform in the South, in other words, was encumbered by a kind of pseudopluralism that let the faction in power impose its program on public education, only to have the entire policy reversed when the other faction gained control over government policy. Ideology's role was negative, since the reform's opponents could and did attack its advocates as Communist sympathizers.

Despite the North's and the South's different approaches to reform, there are commonalties in the way these reforms played out in practice, which derived from the fact that the linguistic problems facing both countries were the same. Differences in policy should not obscure our perception of what actually happened. In the South, the situation was less chaotic than the shifting government regulations make it appear, simply because people's linguistic habits do not change overnight. Changes effected from the top down were limited to what South Koreans could learn in six years of schooling. There were many other opportunities for individuals interacting with society to acquire some proficiency with the characters (recognition, most significantly) or to become gradually acclimated to depending on fewer of them. The absence of a consistent legal norm is not the same as the absence of standards generally, as every linguist knows. It is naive to imagine that South Korean society was thrown into chaos as a result of these changes or to assume that the government had any more effect here than it has had elsewhere. The South Korean government, or that part of it that supported reform, was unable to effect all-*hangul* by decree because the society and the language were not ready for such a sweeping change. Conversely, efforts to teach South Korean high school students characters have been less successful than the procharacter camp had hoped, because they contradict society's heartfelt wish to get by with as few Chinese characters as possible.

The North had its problems with writing reform, too, but the government did a better job keeping them bottled up. In 1946, two years before the Democratic People's Republic of Korea (DPRK) had been established, the Korea Language Research Society (Chosŏn ŏmun yŏnguhoe) was created as a civilian advisory group supported by the People's Committee. A year later, its headquarters was moved to Kim Il-song University, and in 1948 it became part of the new government's Ministry of Education. From its inception, the organization busied itself forming conventions that would facilitate the elimination of Chinese characters and help institute an all-*hangul* script, such as revised *hangul* spelling rules and horizontal writing, which the reformers regarded as part of the package. By the end of 1946 and the beginning of 1947, the major newspaper *Nodong sinmun*, mass circulation magazine *Kulloja,* and similar publications began appearing in all-*hangul*. School textbooks and literary materials converted to all-*hangul* at the same time or possibly earlier (So 1989:31). At first, Chinese characters were appended in parentheses to ambiguous Sinitic terms. By 1948, even this crutch was being phased out. Finally in 1949, three years after the reform had started, scientific publications and even Korean classic works were being written without the aid of Chinese characters (Ko 1989:26). This is how writing has remained in the North for all but a few specialized works and certain textbooks, which I will discuss presently. On this level, there can be no doubt that the reform succeeded.

North Korea's campaign to eliminate Chinese characters was motivated by three factors, according to an official account: "to popularize writing, of course, to eliminate flunkeyist and bourgeoisie elements from the sphere of language, and to satisfy the demands of the new times."[14] Stamping out illiteracy through the introduction of all-*hangul* was a priority goal, in consideration of the position Marxism-Leninism accorded language as a "weapon" in the socialist struggle. The DPRK in this respect was following the same utilitarian logic that motivated writing reform in the Soviet Union and in the communist "base areas" in China when *pinyin* was still being treated as a replacement for the character script. There was also a strong nationalist element in the program. Chinese characters were seen as leftovers from the "feudal" era when Koreans worshiped all things foreign. Besides weakening the role of *hangul,* the characters were seen as causing the language to be tainted with Sinitic sounds, "Chinese character-style foreign borrowings" (i.e., nonwords, or words that cannot stand alone phonetically), and classical Chinese morphology (Ko 1989:24).

Although Kim Il-song is officially credited with spearheading the DPRK's crusade against Chinese characters, there is evidence that he was not the movement's most enthusiastic supporter. According to Ko Yong-kun, Kim went on record as early as February 1949, when Chinese characters had already been removed from most DPRK publications, as advocating their *gradual* abandonment (1989:25). The Great Leader reportedly was concerned about the adverse effects a hasty reform would have on education. His reservations were further confirmed by the appearance in August 1959 of a "Chinese Writing Textbook" *(Hanmun kyokwasŏ),* which despite its misleading title was used to teach eighth to tenth grade students Chinese characters and Sinitic terms in the mixed script. More evidence of backsliding appeared in 1964, when Kim issued an instruction to DPRK linguists on the use of Chinese characters in education. Although couched as a measure to prepare the North Korean people for "unification" with the South, where Chinese characters were still used, Kim complained about the overly zealous attitude of reformers who were trying to remove indigenized Sinitic words from circulation and hinted that the all-*hangul* policy, as it was then being implemented, was in trouble: "Even students coming out of college make mistakes in Korean" (Kim Il-song 1964:7).

Kim Il-song spoke out even more forcefully about the need to reintroduce characters in the educational curriculum in another pronouncement on May 14, 1966: "While we should use as few Sinitic terms as possible, students must be exposed to the necessary Chinese characters and be taught how to write them" (1966:7). Kim explained the turnabout in terms of a need to train specialists to translate classic Korean works into the vernacular. This reasoning is questionable, since the translations he spoke of had started appearing in 1955 and were nearly completed by the time of the speech. Between 1968 and 1969, a four-volume textbook appeared for use in grades 5 through 9 designed to teach 1,500 characters, confirming the applicability of the new policy to the general student population. Another five hundred were added for grades 10 through 12 (Yi Yun-p'yo 1989:372). Although Chinese characters did not reappear in newspapers, technical works, or any other nonpedagogical publications, their reinstatement in the schools on this scale suggests that North Korean linguists had accepted the need for an underlying knowledge of the characters to make all-*hangul,* in its present state, work more effectively.

In 1971, a new *"hanmun"* textbook written entirely in the mixed script was published for use in university history departments. It contains 3,323 different Chinese characters, and draws heavily from Kim Il-song's *Selected Works* and other communist tracts. In March 1972, a "Mixed Script Reader" *(Kuk-Hanmun tokbon)*[15] appeared for college students in general with three thousand different Chinese characters, including the two thousand taught from grades 5 through 12 plus one thousand entirely new forms taught in thirty lessons. Examples are thoroughly modern, and there is no interest shown in *hanmun* (classical Chinese used in Korea) per se (Sim 1989:200). Yi Yun-p'yo believes the characters were picked for their applicability to high-level terminology in modern Korean (1989:372). The textbook includes a preface by Kim Il-song endorsing its goals as a prelude to "national unification." Although North Korea has removed Chinese characters from its written materials, it has, paradoxically, ended up with an educational program that teaches more characters than either South Korea or Japan, as Table 2 shows.

The importance Chinese characters have in the DPRK's educational system is apparent in the time formally allotted for their study. Characters are taught for two of the school week's thirty-one and thirty-two hours in the fifth and sixth grades, and for one hour per week thereafter (Sim 1989:200). According to Yi Yun-p'yo, Chinese characters were reintro-

Table 2
Number of Chinese Characters Taught in the Koreas and Japan

Grade	North Korea	South Korea	Japan
1		·	80
2			160
3			200
4			200
5			185
6	500		181
7–9	1,000	900	939
10–12	500	900	
Total	2,000	1,800	1,945

Source: Adapted from the Seoul Choson ilbo, February 7, 1994, p. 1.

duced into education to compensate for a "hasty" reform that was conducted without adequate preparation. Although other devices, such as revised *hangul* spelling, word division, "adjustments" to Sinitic vocabulary, ridding the language of Japanese borrowings, rehabilitating traditional morphology, and regularizing Korean grammar, were instituted in support of the reform, these "after the fact" measures in themselves could not, in Yi's view, "prevent a decline in the mental abilities of the students and people, and a decline in their ability to understand Sinitic vocabulary" (1989:367). However, far from being an indictment of the all-*hangul* reform, teaching Chinese characters in DPRK schools probably serves multiple purposes, much as Latin did for generations of high school students in the United States, namely, historical and cultural continuity, helping Koreans understand their language's etymological roots, and, I would suppose, even in this communist state, keeping obscurantist pedagogues employed and happy.

Writing reform in the South began in much the same way. In November 1945, a Korea Education Council (Chosŏn kyoyuk shimuihoe) was established that was composed largely of members of a committee that had been set up two months earlier to promote all-*hangul*. By December the council had achieved legal status within Korea's Ministry of Education, and on December 8, 1945, it voted to eliminate Chinese characters from elementary and middle school textbooks (An 1984:331). Textbooks were published in all-*hangul* and included characters in parentheses only after ambiguous terms. Then on October 1, 1948, shortly after the South Korean government was formally inaugurated, the State Council under the advice of the reformist group passed Law Number 6 titled "Law Regarding the Complete Use of *Hangul*," which extended the ban on characters to public documents. Both Korean scholars who favor reform (Blank 1981:146) and those who oppose it (Nam 1970:5; Oh 1971:89) agree that the law was enacted on the strength of the patriotic movement that followed liberation from Japan. No genuine debate preceded the act, and it is doubtful whether the public had prior knowledge.

The reformers' decision to push these measures through without a public airing was rewarded with widespread apathy toward their goals. Of the major South Korean newspapers, only the government paper *Seoul sinmun* adopted an all-*hangul* policy (it has since been rescinded). All other newspapers, magazines, and publishers in general continued to use Chinese characters in unlimited number (Nam 1970:6). Even within the Republic of Korea government itself, only the Education Ministry was able to enforce compliance (Blank 1981:151; An 1984:332). Lacking public support and faced with a growing professional countermovement, the ministry in 1950 restored one thousand characters to school textbooks, to be used only in parentheses. The chief difference between this and the former practice was that now the characters were to be used whenever a new Sinitic word appeared, not just when it was judged to be ambiguous. Moreover, there now existed a government-approved list of characters, whereas before there had been none.

The rest followed logically. In November 1957, the list was expanded to 1,300 with formal training in characters reinstituted for grades 7 through 12. According to An, the list was meant to cap newspapers' use of characters (1984:332), although in retrospect it is apparent that the measure only sanctioned their usage. In February 1963, the countermovement was able to force the ministry to eliminate parentheses around characters beginning with textbooks published in 1964. Characters were used directly in the text in the traditional mixed script manner, without the aid of *hangul* glosses. Moreover, they were actually taught, in three stages: six hundred in elementary school (two hundred per year from grade 4), four hundred in middle school beginning in 1966, and all 1,300 characters in high school by 1968. The purpose of these new measures, according to Kim Min-su (1973:328), was to reduce the gap between students schooled in all-*hangul* and society at large, although it seems obvious enough that this "gap" is precisely what the planners of the original legislation had intended.

While the characters were making a comeback in the schools, reformers in the Education Ministry were trying to make inroads in other places. In December 1957, they persuaded the government to adopt a *Revised Hangul Plan,* which required public notices, commercial signs, and government announcements to be in all-*hangul.* The ban extended even to scrolls in government offices. In August of the following year, police supervised the removal of Chinese character store signs. Private publishers were also encouraged to comply (Kim Min-su 1973:347; An 1984:333). The program was defeated by members of the opposing camp, who claimed the proscription on characters violated their civil rights. In November 1965, the Ministry of Government Administration tried again to enact a *Revised Bill for All-Hangul,* which also failed for lack of support.

Things finally came to a head. In December 1967, the National Language Committee (Kuk'ŏ shimui wiwŏnhoe) recommended 198 simplified replacements for characters on the basic list of 1,300, a move that would further shore up their status. Seeing which way things were going, the Hangul Society appealed successfully to President Pak Chong-hui on January 6, 1968, to implement a thorough all-*hangul* program that would apply to both public and private sectors.[16] Pak, who sympathized with the movement, had his cabinet in May of that year draft legislation for yet another reform program, which was to be carried out over a five-year period. Issued as "Prime Minister's Instruction No. 68" on October 25, 1968, it required government institutions and private publishers to limit the number of characters they used to two thousand by the end of 1968, to 1,300 by the end of 1969, and to zero by 1973. The deadline for total elimination of the characters was then advanced to January 1, 1970, probably to preempt

실내의 라돈濃度는 1일중에도 氣象條件
環境條件의 변화에 따라 요동이 심하므로[4,5]
度의 변화요인에 관계없는 장기간동안의 평
濃度를 측정할 수 있는 受動的 라돈濃度測定
式[9]은 라돈 및 子核種의 연속호흡으로 인한
체의 被曝線量 평가에 유용하다. 본 연구에
는 1989년에 확립된 'CR-39 라돈컵에 의한
動的 라돈濃度測定方法'[8]을 이용하여 실내
라돈濃度를 측정하였다.

Mixed *hangul*-character script in South Korean technical journal.
(*KAERI Journal* 11.1, June 1991, p. 76)

countermoves. Once again school textbooks were rewritten in all-*hangul* (Kim Min-su 1973:349–350).

No sooner had *these* reforms been mapped out than the pendulum swung back again. In December 1971, less than a year after the policy had been put into effect, the decision was taken to resume teaching Chinese characters in public schools. This became policy in August 1972 under a new arrangement that called for 1,800 characters (five hundred more than before) to be taught, half in middle school and half in high school. In July 1974, the Ministry of Education agreed to put the 1,800 characters in parentheses into textbooks of all types, beginning with history and Korean language (Yu Pong-yong 1974:154). The impetus for this reversal was an open petition signed by 140 prominent South Koreans, opposed to all-*hangul* for linguistic and cultural reasons, which outlined a multipoint program that would, in essence, have re-Sinified South Korean education from primary school up.

A balance was struck in August 1976, when the Ministry of Education agreed to keep Chinese characters out of the elementary schools and teach the 1,800 characters in special courses, not as part of Korean language or any other substantive curricula. This is where things stand at present. In a letter to the Education Ministry in August 1977, President Pak stated that "the extreme view that advocates eliminating commonly used Chinese characters is, practically speaking, incorrect." The reasons given by the ministry for reinstating Chinese characters are (1) all-*hangul* education was not preparing students for life in a society that continues to use the characters; (2) all-*hangul* created ambiguity, especially in high-level vocabulary; and (3) publishers were being forced to append English glosses to ambiguous *hangul* words (Han 1975:464). Unquestionably, the reluctance of character-literate intellectuals to abandon Chinese characters for reasons of culture, emotional attachment, and personal convenience has also been a strong force for their retention.

4. Vietnamese

OF THE FOUR MAJOR languages that have used Chinese characters, Vietnamese is the only one to have abandoned them completely for all-phonetic writing. Nevertheless, Vietnamese has been largely ignored in this regard. One reason for this neglect is the language's exotic flair, it being the least commonly taught of East Asia's less commonly taught languages. Paradoxically, another reason may be because Vietnamese writing reform has already succeeded, which to many scholars puts the language and the country outside the Chinese character cultural sphere and beyond linguists' related concerns. A more subtle factor behind the neglect may also be the most telling: in Vietnam, writing "reform" was accomplished over the long term and from the bottom up. For planners eager to engineer social change, the Vietnamese model has nothing dramatic to offer. It did, however, work.

This chapter begins with an overview of the language that the writing is tasked to represent. Some "naive" first impressions of the present writing system may offer a clue about a problem affecting writing reform throughout East Asia. I then take up Vietnam's *chữ nôm* character writing system, its structure and history, and factors leading to its replacement with a romanized script. The genesis of the latter, known as *quốc ngữ*, is traced through time and analyzed in terms of how it was able to displace Chinese characters. In the final section I will suggest that although the characters disappeared from Vietnam, their legacy continues to operate in such a way as to make Vietnamese orthography less efficient than it might have been. There is still work to be done.

Vietnamese Language and Sino-Vietnamese

First impressions are important, because they impinge on us directly, unfiltered by the tolerance one acquires through understanding. People who live with or are part of a system often are the poorest judges of its utility, because, immersed in the system, they have no objective reference from which to evaluate it. Scholars fare no better. Attracted by the challenges of a problem, as their understanding of it deepens, they often lose sight of the fact that it is a problem. Contradictions understood on their own terms begin to seem reasonable. Add to this the comfort one realizes from having mastered the problem's complexities, and the scholar is soon the system's most outspoken defender.

It is unusual to find an informed critic of East Asia's character writing system, not because the system is not badly in need of criticism, but because those able to provide it have lost the incentive. The problem begins with East Asians themselves. Just as it is marginally easier for me to pay 42 percent of my income in taxes than to try doing something about it, people born into the "Chinese character cultural sphere" who have to deal with the characters' foibles and disutility on a daily basis acquiesce in their fate because they have no real choice. The brighter members of society, whom you would expect to be in the vanguard of reform, revel in their mastery of the character writing system, their achievement made sweeter by the failure of many of their contemporaries to rise to the task. East Asian linguists and scholars have their own complex web of loyalties and intuitions, which on balance tend to flatten out expressions of discontent. While many do see the problem for what it is and are willing to say so privately, they see no present alternative viable enough to risk their reputations and careers pointing out the way. Other Asian intellectuals are so consumed by their distaste for Western artifacts and the Western arrogance that has accompanied them that they are willing to hold on to their Chinese characters at any cost.

When Westerners view Chinese characters, it is from the perspective of someone who already has command over a much simpler writing system that for all intents accomplishes the same functions with far less hassle. Their first reaction typically is a mixture of awe and confusion, followed by the question, asked in innocence, "Why don't they just write with letters?" Some go on to study the characters and end up dabbling in them just enough to persuade themselves that the system, potentially, can be mastered and that it really is a genuine alternative to the alphabet. They then retreat to their own alphabetic world with the same smugness and righteousness that a Western student gets from a two-week tour "laboring" in a Chinese peasant commune. Others actually do hang on long enough to learn the characters well, and in the process acquire a stake in preserving the value of their investment. Still others make the effort to study the structure of the system and its workings and conclude, under the influence of the enlightened relativist paradigm, that the writing system really does match up quite well with the languages it is used for—without ever asking themselves how the languages got that way in the first place.

If these patterns ring familiar, it is because many of us have been there. It just takes some a little longer to wise up. With our later experience in mind, it might pay for us to go back and reconstruct our first impressions of Vietnamese orthography, those that struck us before the morass of dots, squiggles, and other marks began to make sense and take their place along with taxes and Chinese characters as part of the rational universe. Written Vietnamese appears to most Westerners as a strange blend of familiar alphabetic letters and unfamiliar diacritics—lots of them. There are good reasons for these diacritics—"good" in the sense that the syllable-based orthography, for reasons that we will get into, would not work without them—but we are dealing with first impressions, and in my case it was one of severe clutter. Colleagues knowledgeable in linguistics who have not studied Vietnamese have commented similarly. One complained that the system "piles up" so many diacritics that the syllabic units on which they are based seem almost as complicated as Chinese characters. Another linguist, with an active command of several alphabetically written languages and familiarity with many more, responded to my suggestion that Vietnamese is an example of a language that successfully rid itself of Chinese characters with the comment, "You call that a 'success'? I've never seen an alphabetic system more in need of reform."

Compared to Chinese characters, there is no question that Vietnamese writing is a stunning success. Written Vietnamese seems busy because it is close enough to what alphabetic users expect to be judged by the same standards of efficiency and simplicity that users apply to alphabets in general. In other words, it is within the pale, whereas Chinese characters are outside the pale altogether and hence not held accountable to the same rational standards that are applied to other systems—a neat psychological trick that has served China in more than one respect. But this brings up another question that we should register before getting lost in descriptive and analytical details. That is, given what we have seen so far about the connection between complexity and Chinese characters, on the one hand, and the simplicity we have come to expect of alphabetic systems on the other, is there any possibility the characters in some way are responsible for Vietnamese writing's aberration from the alphabetic norm?

I shall return to these questions at the end of the chapter. Meanwhile, let's look at the Vietnamese language, its writing system, and how the latter got to be what it is today. Vietnamese, like Chinese but unlike either Japanese or Korean, is an isolating language whose forms are not inflected and whose grammar is based largely on the order in which morphemes appear in sentences. Vietnamese, however, has no genetic relationship to Chinese. Linguists believe Vietnamese either developed from a Mon-Khmer language and acquired a tonal system from Thai, or was a Thai language that borrowed a large part of its early lexicon from Mon-Khmer languages. A third possibility is that it developed from the same protolanguage as Malaysian. Although unrelated to Chinese, three other features of the language besides its typology tend to give people the impression that it is.

The first of these is phonemic tone. Chinese syllables are distinguished by three to nine or more different pitch contours, depending on the particular Chinese language and dialect (and according to how "tone" is defined). Southern Chinese languages tend to have more tones, and Vietnamese with its six phonemic tones (in the Hanoi dialect; Saigon speakers do not distinguish the *ngã* and *hỏi* tones) is in good geographic company. This shared characteristic, however, can be accounted for by what linguists refer to as "areal tendencies" that are spread between languages in contact for long periods of time, and has nothing to do with genealogy. In the case of Vietnamese, the connection with Chinese was in the way the former, with its system of tonal contrasts, was able to accommodate Chinese tones (or phonetic features that led to the development of tones) present in the thousands of Sinitic terms borrowed into Vietnamese—distinctions that were simply leveled out in the Sinitic vocabularies of Korean and Japanese.

The second way in which the two languages emulate each other is in their emphasis on the syllable as a basic phonological and morphological unit. Part of the reason are the tones themselves, which in Vietnamese and Cantonese—the Chinese language geographically closest to Vietnam—are fairly consistent within syllable boundaries and little affected by the tones of neighboring syllables. Syllable shapes are also of the same basic variety: a nuclear vowel optionally preceded by a single consonant and a medial glide, and followed by nothing, a consonant or semivowel, or "a cluster of two vowels or a diphthong followed by a final consonant or semivowel" (Thompson 1987:47). The orthography notwithstanding, Vietnamese syllables have no consonant clusters leftover from defunct morphological processes or any form of cross-syllable morphophonemic changes, such as occur in Korean and to a limited extent in Japanese, to detract from the syllable's autonomy. Also, just as Chinese characters tend to focus users' thoughts and pronunciation habits on the single syllables that they represent, so does Vietnamese orthography, which puts blank spaces (or a hyphen) between every written syllable.

Not surprisingly, these features and practices have led people to the same false assumption applied to Chinese that Vietnamese is a "monosyllabic" language, whose "words" are each one syllable long. Fortunately, Vietnamese has not been maligned by the same corollaries to its alleged "monosyllabism" that have distorted our understanding of Chinese, namely, the supposed inability of its speakers to move beyond primitive levels of discourse because of a severely restricted inventory of "words," and the absolute "need" for a character script to distinguish between words that all sound the same. Vietnamese has been spared the former allegation because its syllables outnumber those of standard Chinese Mandarin by a factor of five, or perhaps simply because no one has gotten around yet to making the assertion. The second claim has not surfaced because the Vietnamese stopped using characters long ago! Discomforting as this fact may be to Sinophiles and supporters of character writing systems, Vietnamese have "managed" without Chinese characters in their writing, educational system, and other functional areas of society for nearly a century, despite the high proportion of Sinitic terms in the language and its alleged monosyllabism. Today, the only Vietnamese who know Chinese characters are those who have learned them through Chinese and a handful of scholars who study old Vietnamese texts.

As a matter of fact, Vietnamese is no more monosyllabic than Chinese or other languages. Lexical items, indigenous or borrowed, consist of single- and multiple-syllable words, the latter predominating both in absolute number and in the percentage of words they account for on higher levels of discourse. What Vietnamese does share with Chinese is a monosyllabic morphology that, in my view, evolved in both languages under the influence of Chinese characters, which encouraged a semantic interpretation for every syllable even where there was none and preserved the semantic values of other syllables long after these associations functionally disappeared. Although the characters have gone out of Vietnamese, their legacy remains in an orthography that divides syllables instead of words; in dictionaries that index their polysyllabic entries by syllable type;[1] and through the influence of Sinitic vocabulary, coined in Vietnam or other East Asian countries, whose monosyllabic morphemes remain morphemes by virtue of their Chinese character base.

A third reason Vietnamese seems related to Chinese is because, as I have just intimated, a large part of the Vietnamese lexicon *is* Sinitic in origin. Estimates range from 30 to over 60 percent (DeFrancis 1977:8). Calculating the exact size of the Sino-Vietnamese inventory, however, is not a straightforward process. Is the count based on the percentage of Sinitic words in connected discourse, in which case the Sino-Vietnamese vocabulary runs from under 30 percent for everyday speech to a figure near 90 percent for patches of text in a Marxist editorial? Or do we base the count on the lexicon itself, where other problems come into play, including trying to sort out nonindigenized Sino-Vietnamese terms, used by a minority of educated Vietnamese who learned the terms through international Sinitic,[2] from terms that have become part of the common repertoire? More fundamentally, can we include among the Sinitic part of the Vietnamese lexicon words so thoroughly indigenized that their Chinese origin is obscure to all but a few etymologists?

Sifting out Sinitic from native vocabulary is more of a problem in Vietnamese than in Japanese or even in Korean because of the longer history of contact between Chinese and Vietnamese, and because of the intimacy (most Vietnamese would use a different word to describe it) of this contact. Vietnam was under Chinese "suzerainty" for nearly a millennium: from 111 B.C. to A.D. 39, from 45 to 544, and from 602 to 939. During this long period, the Vietnamese language itself was overshadowed and to some extent replaced by Chinese, opening the door to thousands of Chinese terms and, I would conjecture, to the monosyllabic Sinitic morphology enforced by written Chinese, which was the only writing known in Vietnam at the time. Instances of multiple borrowing of the same Sinitic morpheme were fairly common, as the term entered the language from different parts of China with different pronunciations. Or the Sinitic morpheme was reintroduced centuries later with a changed pronunciation, the original borrowing having become so well indigenized that users were unaware the morpheme was already part of Vietnamese. Typically, Chinese terms introduced through characters retained their Sino-Vietnamese pronunciations, while those whose primary realization depended more on speech were assimilated to native pronunciation habits (Hai 1974:2).[3]

Even after the Chinese occupation ended in the tenth century, the influence of Chinese language and writing continued to be felt through Vietnam's bureaucrats and scholar elite, for whom classical Chinese remained the preferred medium of expression. What had until then been haphazard, continuous borrowing of Chinese vocabulary gave way to systematic, deliberate adjustments to the Sino-Vietnamese lexicon. Pronunciations of Sinitic terms, based as they were on a written medium that had become severed from colloquial Chinese language, were read in a fixed (albeit Vietnamese-like) fashion. These latter practices, while relevant only to the 3 to 5 percent of the population who were literate (DeFrancis 1977:19), succeeded in establishing character-based, phonetically marginal Sinitic as the vehicle through which new upper-level vocabulary was formed.

At the end of the nineteenth and the beginning of the twentieth centuries, the number of new Sino-Vietnamese words coming into Vietnamese directly or indirectly from Chinese increased under the pressure to create new terms for new Western concepts. Whereas before, poorly assimilated Sino-Vietnamese terms were confined chiefly to diplomacy and Buddhism, these newer terms were scientific and intellectual, and hence found their way into the common language through newspapers and school textbooks (Hai 1974:41). The result was the same sort of transformation that simultaneously characterized the other major languages of East Asia: an expansion of the identifiably Sinitic part of the lexicon and a growth in the number of people who had to deal with it.

Vietnam's Character Writing System

According to Hai, Chinese writing acquired official status in Vietnam in 1010 and retained it until the twentieth century (1974:1).[4] Although the earliest extant Chinese texts written by Vietnamese date from the end of the tenth century,[5] it is likely that Vietnamese were using Chinese characters to record elements of their own language as early as the eighth century (DeFrancis 1977:23; Thompson 1987:57). Even this time frame may be conservative, since it postdates the use of Chinese characters to record indigenous Korean and Japanese by a century or more, although the Chinese influence in these latter countries had a later start and was less intense. Nevertheless, the earliest examples of the practice do not appear in Vietnam until the end of the thirteenth century, in poetry written by Nguyen Thuyen, and on a stele in Ninh Binh province dated 1343 listing some twenty names of Vietnamese villages (Nguyen 1959:271).

Using Chinese characters to record non-Chinese languages was, as we have seen, normal practice in East Asia. There were three ways this could be done, and each language made use of all three methods. Chinese characters could be used semantically to represent indigenous words with the same or nearly the same meaning, in which case one would look at a character and read off a native sound corresponding to the word in one's own language. Conversely, the characters could be used for their phonetic value, regardless of what they meant in Chinese. People would simply pick a character that sounded in Chinese like the pronunciation of the target word, and read it as such with the meaning of the indigenous homonym as the one intended. Finally, characters were used to represent Sinitic vocabulary borrowed into the indigenous language, in which case the assignment was both semantic and phonetic. As we saw in the examples for Korean and especially for Japanese, as these practices became established, users reduced the complexity of the forms, particularly when the characters were being employed solely as phonetic indicators. In Vietnam, however, the opposite mostly happened: the system (or many of its forms at least) actually gained in complexity.

The application of Chinese writing to Vietnamese, called *chữ nôm* ("southern writing," *nôm* < *nam*) as distinct from *chữ nho* ("writing of the scholars," i.e., classical Chinese), differed from its application to Korean and Japanese in three other respects. Lacking inflected forms, Vietnamese put less pressure on the system to evolve a restricted set of phonetic indicators, which in Japan led to a full-fledged syllabary. With some 4,800 spoken syllables in today's Hanoi dialect (2,370 discounting tone), Vietnamese would have been a worse candidate than even Korean to be represented by a syllabary. Second, unlike Japanese and Korean, Vietnamese syllables are almost always morphemes, hence more logical candidates for depiction by characters—although one cannot help wondering how much the character-based Chinese morphology forced or reinforced this tendency in Vietnamese. In any case, the fit between Chinese characters and Vietnamese morphology was (or became) closer.

Finally, although the Japanese and Koreans did coin some two to three hundred Chinese characters of their own, mostly they were content to use the Chinese system as it was. The Vietnamese, however, not only adopted the Chinese forms, but went on to create thousands of new forms for their own language. Although these symbols appear extraordinary to people familiar with the Chinese system, one should keep in mind that the conceptual leap between Chinese writing and *chữ nôm* is far less than the gap between characters and *kana,* not to mention *hangul* or the Vietnamese alphabet. *Chữ nôm* just *seems* more exotic because of our fascination with the complex, which may make an interesting pastime for some people, but is a poor foundation indeed for a practical writing system.

There appear to be as many classification schemes for *chữ nôm* characters as there are people who have analyzed it (Huang 1954:126; Nguyen 1959:274; Jensen 1970:184; Hai 1974:5–7; DeFrancis 1977:24; Li 1980: 243). The following breakdown of borrowed and newly created forms gives some idea of the system's composition.

In the first set of cases, Chinese characters are borrowed intact and

1. used phonetically to represent Vietnamese words.

没	một	one
固	có	have
埃	ai	who

The Sino-Vietnamese pronunciation of a character is homophonous, or nearly so, with an indigenous word, allowing that character to represent the Vietnamese word. There is no semantic relationship.

2. used semantically to represent "Vietnamese" words.

(a)	味	mùi	smell, odor
	役	việc	work, event
	本	vốn	capital, funds

A character is assigned to a Vietnamese word, typically an early Sinitic borrowing that has been fully assimilated, on the basis of that character's meaning in Chinese. However, the same character can also be read in what was recognized as its Sino-Vietnamese pronunciation to designate more recently borrowed Chinese vocabulary, as in the following:

(b)	味	vị	flavor, taste
	役	dịch	service, corvee
	本	bản	root, foundation

The two usages (2a and 2b) parallel the *on-kun* dichotomy in Japanese, wherein Chinese characters are read with their Sinitic pronunciations when the meaning is that of the borrowed Chinese morpheme or with native Japanese pronunciations when the character is used to represent an indigenous word with nearly the same meaning. The chief difference is that here the "indigenous" Vietnamese words all seem to be early Chinese borrowings.

None of the *chữ nôm* examples cited in any of the above sources shows an entirely indigenous Vietnamese word being depicted by a Chinese character on the basis of shared meaning. Nor did my check of a large *chữ nôm* dictionary turn up any such cases.[6] Although many borrowed Chinese characters are glossed with multiple pronunciations, all of them seem to be earlier, later, or geographically diverse renderings of a common Sinitic etymon.

Vietnamese did distinguish between fully assimilated Sino-Vietnamese terms and more recent Chinese borrowings expressed by the same characters through use of special diacritics with the former (Hai 1974:4). For example, 本 (SV *bản*) above could be written 本ᒼ when meant to be read as the indigenized expression *(vốn)*. These diacritics were also used with forms in category 1 above to identify characters that represented genuine native words phonetically in cases where the same character happened also to be used with a wholly borrowed Sinitic word, as in 木 for Sino-Vietnamese *mộc* (wood, tree), but 木ᒼ for pure-Vietnamese *mọc* (to grow, rise). Given this use of the diacritics with category 1 forms, where the congruence between character and word was based solely on phonetics, it is apparent that these diacritics meant something on the order of "read as Vietnamese word."

3. used to represent Sinitic words.

頭	đầu	head, beginning
少	thiếu	lack
册	sách	book

In this case, the character represented the borrowed Chinese word in the same, straightforward manner used throughout all of East Asia. The Vietnamese, however, did not stop at borrowing Chinese characters and stretching their applications, but created entirely new character forms as well.

In the second set of cases, characters were made specifically for Vietnamese, including

1. forms created on the "compound ideographic" principle.

丕	giời	sky, heaven
𡗋	mất	lose
𦝄	tuổi	year of age

The first form is a combination of the Chinese characters 天 (Mand. *tiān*) meaning "sky, day, heaven" and 上 *(shàng)* meaning "up." The Vietnamese character's components thus are both semantically motivated. The same is true of the second form's, 亡 (Mand. *wáng*) and 失 *(shī)*, both of which have "lose" among their meanings. The third example, consisting of the Chinese characters 年 (Mand. *nián*) "year" and 歲 *(suì)* "year of age," is interesting because the word *tuổi* is probably an early borrowing of the Chinese word *suì*, which, if it had not been regarded as a fully indigenized word, could have been written simply with the original character 歲.

2. new Vietnamese "semantic-phonetic" compounds.

羙毋	mẹ	mother
巴三	ba	three
庶	mà	but, however

The character for *mẹ* is made up of the Chinese forms 美 (Mand. *měi*), functioning as a phonetic indicator, and 毋 (Mand. *mǔ*) "mother," serving as a semantic component. The second and third characters are built up similarly: 巴 and 麻 have Mandarin sounds *bā* and *má,* while 三 and 而 carry the Chinese meanings "three" and "but." Some hybrid examples also occur of Chinese characters used as semantic components with Vietnamese *nôm* characters used for their phonetic value, the whole representing a (nearly) homophonous indigenous word, such as 口丕 *lời* "spoken word," made up of the Chinese character for "mouth" 口 and the Vietnamese form 丕 pronounced *giời*.

3. forms created by removing features from the Chinese.

爲	>	𬈂	làm	do, make
衣	>	𬈂	ấy	that, those
羅	>	罗	lạ	strange

The first example appears to be a real case of a Chinese character, reduced in form, used to represent an entirely indigenous Vietnamese word on the basis of semantic agreement. The last two forms were both phonetically motivated (衣 Mand. *yī* was pronounced **ei* in ancient Chinese).

For both linguistic and social reasons, *chữ nôm* was never able to supplant Chinese (i.e., classical Chinese, written in Chinese characters) in Vietnam or to develop into an efficient writing system on its own terms. The linguistic defects are the same as those noted throughout this book for Chinese characters generally, caused by the large number of tokens (some twenty thousand in *chữ nôm*), the arbitrariness of their composition, and the inconsistent way the units and their components connect with the sounds of the language. We have already noted that many of the *chữ nôm* characters had multiple readings depending on whether they were used for indigenous words, indigenized words, or Sinitic terms not fully assimilated, and also according to when and from what part of China the terms entered the language. None of these pronunciations was tied to the structure of the character in a way that would allow the user to derive or reconstruct the sound in any clear fashion. The most the characters offered were hints, made by analogy, of the sound, which could be misleading if the roles of their components were misconstrued.

For example, the components 女 and 多 are used semantically in 妚 *gái* "girl" and 嚤 *nhiêu* "much, many," but reappear as phonetics in 奼 *nửa* "half" and 䂮 *đá* "stone." Besides characters with multiple words, some words had multiple character representations, such as 𦥃 or 𦥯 for *đến* "arrive," and 朕 or 腷 for *béo* "fat, greasy." Although it is likely that some of these inconsistencies would have been ironed out if *chu nôm* had been in wider use, with nearly five thousand distinct syllables in Vietnamese the system was hard pressed to come up with enough structures of any type to cover the inventory of sounds, not to mention doing so consistently and unambiguously. If, as DeFrancis has observed, the Chinese "syllabary" is large and inefficient, the prospect *chữ nôm* had for evolving, like Japanese *kana*, into an efficient form of phonetic representation was zero.

Socially the system did not have much going for it, either. As Hai noted, the only reason Vietnam got away with having an indigenous script under Chinese suzerainty was that *chữ nôm* borrowed heavily from Chinese and resembled it (1974:8).[7] Otherwise it would have been suppressed, just as the French tried to suppress the script in the latter part of the nineteenth century because of the nationalist associations it had acquired (DeFrancis 1977:99). *Chữ nôm* was known only by the 5 percent or less of Vietnam's educated population, who used it not as a primary medium but rather as an aid to learning Chinese and for recording folk literature. It was not viewed as worthy of serious composition, and in this respect its status paralleled that of every other indigenous writing system in East Asia. An exception was during the brief Ho dynasty (1400–1407), when Chinese was abolished and *chữ nôm* became the official script, but the subsequent Chinese invasion and twenty-year occupation put an end to that (Helmut Martin 1982:34).

Chữ nôm was used more widely—in its limited role—as time passed and accumulated a considerable volume of literature in the nineteenth century particularly (Hai 1974:9). However, the script had a home-grown air that marginalized its applicability in the eyes of the educated, bureaucratic elite to areas of local (native Vietnamese) culture. For the elite group, classical Chinese, the lingua franca of East Asia, was the language of state and scholarship, and their symbol of group identity. Partly for this reason, *chữ nôm* became the preferred vehicle for social protest during the Le dynasty (1428–1786), which led to its being banned in 1663, 1718, and 1760. There was a final attempt during the Tai Son "rebellion" (1788–1802) to give the script official status, but this attempt was reversed by the rulers of the subsequent Nguyen dynasty (1802–1945). Gia Long, founder of the

Nguyen, seems to have supported *chữ nôm* for as long as it took him to climb into power, then reverted to Chinese almost immediately after establishing his dynasty; his successors strengthened this tendency (DeFrancis 1977:35). Chinese was not to be replaced in Vietnam by a writing system derived from it.

Writing Reform and the Vietnamese Alphabet

Evolution of Vietnam's character-based script had reached the same dead end as *idu* had in Korea, and for the same reasons. While both systems could render the indigenous languages, given their large number of syllables, the use of characters as the basic units of writing guaranteed that the orthography would be as complex as the Chinese with which it was competing, with none of the latter's status. Further development meant cracking through the syllable barrier so that subsyllabic segments could be identified and their abstract role in forming concrete syllables applied. In Korea, this process was manifested through the invention of a wholly indigenous phonetic writing system, backed by the country's monarch, whose efforts to popularize the system from the top down are legendary. Although *hangul*'s creation was a stroke of genius, Koreans some five hundred years later are still using or at least learning Chinese characters. Despite massive, state-sponsored efforts to eradicate Chinese characters, the latter still constitute an important adjunct to the phonetic *hangul* orthography in the South and are taught in the North in even greater numbers, in part to facilitate recognition of Sinitic terms.

In Vietnam, the development of a phonetic writing system was less dramatic, but in the end proved to be even more effective in its ability to displace the patent vestiges of the Chinese system. There are several reasons for Vietnam's success, which I will take up in detail in the next section, but the most compelling factor behind this success is that Vietnam never had a top-down, coordinated, state-backed movement to effect the reform. Rather, the impetus for change began innocuously and trickled around slowly until the characters were removed not by fiat but by their inability to compete with a viable, tested, popularly based system, grounded on solid phonetic principles and more the product of growth than invention. Although the Vietnamese system still leaves something to be desired in terms of simplicity, adaptability to mechanization, and some other linguistic areas that I will discuss later, these are minor issues in view of the distinction the script earned in being the only writing system fully to displace Chinese characters in East Asia. The incredible part is that the process was carried out without any central planning whatsoever.

Vietnam was first introduced to alphabetic writing by European missionaries in the early seventeenth century, when similar activities were happening in China and Japan. According to Thompson, by the 1620s there were several alphabetic systems being used in Vietnam to record words for scholarly purposes and for use by missionaries studying the language (1987:54). These systems were collected by the Catholic missionary Fr. Alexandre de Rhodes, who had been in Indochina since 1642, and "codified" into a writing system for use in his own materials. The latter included the first known work to be published in romanized Vietnamese, Rhodes' *Annamese-Portuguese-Latin Dictionary*, which appeared in Rome in 1651. The work was also noteworthy for its use of what DeFrancis believes to be the first "systematic scheme for the romanization of Vietnamese" (1977:54).

These early systems were intended to serve not as full-fledged orthographies, but as working notations meant to fulfill limited, real-world functions. Although they were based on good phonological theory, no immediate attempt was made to expand their sphere of application. DeFrancis, who has written the standard work on this subject, finds "no evidence that [Rhodes] intended any extensive use even within the Vietnamese Catholic community, much less among the Vietnamese as a whole" (1977:59). Although some writing on clerical matters was done in romanized Vietnamese, it appears not to have been used even in proselytizing. The system, as it were, lay in a state of incubation for nearly two centuries until 1838, when Fr. Jean-Louis Taberd published a second dictionary in romanized Vietnamese based on corrections made by Monsignor Pigneau de Behaine to Rhodes' system (ibid.: 64).

Romanization was given a major boost by French colonialists shortly after they annexed Vietnam's three southern provinces in 1862. It served both as an aid to their own study of the language and as a counter to Chinese writing and *chữ nôm*, both of which entailed unwanted associations with another semicolonial power. In 1864, a decree was issued providing for elementary schools that used romanized Vietnamese. A year later, the romanized Vietnamese magazine *Gia Dinh Bao* began publication under French auspices. French support for the script, which by the turn of the century had acquired the improbable name *quốc ngữ* (lit. "national language"),[8] had put the colonialists in somewhat of a bind. On the one hand, they were eager to stem the growing popularity of *chữ nôm*, the indigenous Vietnamese character script, as a vehicle of anticolonial protest by offering a Western-style alternative. Some saw the romanized script as an indirect path to teaching the Vietnamese people French (DeFrancis 1977:136). Others feared that promoting *quốc ngữ* would lead to a movement away from French, as the notation took on the function and trappings of a regular orthography and as it acquired the nationalist image that its name implied.

While romanized Vietnamese was being transformed, through actual usage, into a script able to represent the Vietnamese language, the language itself was being transformed by an influx of new words coined to represent Western scientific, technological, and cultural concepts. Some of these terms, which were mostly based on Sinitic morphemes, came into the language through Vietnamese students studying in Japan. Most entered through translations of Chinese and Japanese texts, which themselves were translations of or heavily inspired by Western-language works. These romanized translations enjoyed a wide readership, particularly among younger Vietnamese who saw mastery of the new Western knowledge as the key to liberation from colonial domination. As *quốc ngữ* spread, its forms became increasingly standardized, not by government fiat but through adaptation, imitation, and decentralized decision making, the same "patchwork of parallel operations" (Kelly 1995:21) that creates order in any complex system, including (or especially) language. Meanwhile, the importance of Chinese in Vietnam, particularly in the post–World War I era, continued to drop through natural attrition of scholars, deliberate deemphasis in the schools, and the disutility of using Chinese language and writing in French colonial society (DeFrancis 1977:205). *Chữ nôm* suffered for the same reasons.

The period between the two world wars saw a substantial increase in the number of *quốc ngữ* publications. In 1925, the first Vietnamese novel was published in the romanized script. Dictionaries began to appear. By 1930, there were seventy-five *quốc ngữ* newspapers in Vietnam. Helmut Martin, the author of a book on Chinese language planning, opines that this series of publications was more effective in promoting the spread and acceptance of the script than any long-range planning or discussion could ever have been (1982:37). DeFrancis' view is similar: "What is of decisive importance in the establishment of a system of writing is not the existence or availability of such a system but the extent of its actual use in publication" (1977:193).

Quốc ngữ as it appears today uses the twenty-six letters of the English alphabet, minus *f, j, w*, and *z*. Special letters *đ* and *ă, â, ê, ô, ơ*, and *ư* have been added, for a total of twenty-nine letters. Consonant phonemes are represented by single letters, by a cluster of two letters corresponding to a single phoneme (e.g., *th-, nh-*), or by different letters in complementary distribution before different vowels, for example, *c-, k-*, and *q-* for the phoneme [k]. Phonemic tone is depicted by marks added above or below the vocalic nucleus of each syllable, except level tone which is unmarked. Spacing occurs between all syllables, although there is a tendency in some types of writing to use a hyphen between the syllables of polysyllabic words, especially Sinitic compounds. The script functions entirely without the aid of Chinese characters. According to Thompson and Thomas, Vietnamese orthography "shows more distinctions than are actually found in any modern dialect, but . . . is otherwise nearly wholly consistent and comes very close to being phonemic. Once the system is understood, any written syllable can be correctly pronounced by a native speaker and there are relatively few special spellings to learn. As the world's writing systems go, this is a rather good score" (1967:817).

With the French departure in 1954, the Vietnamese language and alphabet became national standards, promoted by the government as the sanctioned media in education and all forms of communication. Chinese characters have been displaced entirely and are of as little importance to Vietnamese in Vietnam as they are to Americans in the United States. Interestingly, both the Koreans and the Vietnamese addressed similar concerns about a potential loss of cultural heritage through crash translation programs of character-based classic works into *hangul* and *quốc ngữ,* with the result that the national literary record was made available to wider groups of the population than had ever been possible through the character scripts. As for the loss of the "special" relationship Vietnam had with China through the shared character script, this seems to bother the Vietnamese even less than it bothers Koreans.

Why Romanization Succeeded in Vietnam

A few linguists interested in writing systems and their reform have pointed, correctly, to Vietnamese as an example of a language that was able to switch from a character-based to an alphabetic orthography.[9] Most people concerned with the general problem, however, act as though the Vietnamese evidence does not exist. I have always been perplexed at how scholars can debate whether Chinese, Japanese, or Korean, with their character writing systems and heavy overlay of character-dependent Sinitic morphemes, are capable of being represented by a phonetic system of writing, when a living proof-of-concept lies right under their noses. But this proof itself may be part of the problem.

   In their search for language universals, linguists seem to have overlooked a basic commonality, as well established in sociolinguistics as Murphy's Law is in metaphysics, namely, the "Principle of Substandard Southern Speech." This principle holds that the farther south one descends in a speech community, the more barbaric the speech becomes and the less worthy these patterns are of emulation. The truism applies worldwide but is honored especially in East Asia. "Standard" Chinese Mandarin speakers in the north have little regard for the quaint "dialects" spoken in the south (and southeast and southwest) of China; they are tolerated as faits accomplis, in a gesture of Great Han magnanimity, but have no part in the central government's plans for the future (never mind that some users of these lesser speech forms have their own vision of how things will turn out). In Korea, Kyongnam speech is stigmatized in the educated estimate of standard Seoul speakers, just as Kyoto-ben is a Tokyo speaker's laughingstock. At the very bottom of the East Asian linguistic hierarchy, as the name Vietnam (lit. "south of Yue," Yue being a southern Chinese region) implies, is Vietnamese, and within that country, the southern speech centered on what used to be called Saigon is barely fit to be heard, as any Hanoi speaker will tell you. Linguists study these southern forms and even make a superficial show of professing their "equality," but in their hearts they—like everyone else—know better. Psychology can easily account for the abnormal circumstance that the best academic linguists (e.g., Charles Hockett, Y. R. Chao) were nonstandard speakers of their own languages.

Now, before I get into the same trouble that Mencken did with his bathtub hoax or John DeFrancis ran into with his "Singlish Affair" (1984a:19), let me state clearly that most linguists do in fact believe in the truth of their maxim that all languages are equal with respect to the utility they provide to their speakers and that they would attack my "principle" with the scorn it deserves. I will concede that not all linguists or scholars of Chinese writing have had the leisure or opportunity to get close enough to this "peripheral" language to accept it viscerally as a genuine East Asian language and member-in-good-standing of the Sinitic cultural sphere. This lack of exposure may be why Vietnamese is not taken as seriously as it ought to be by language planners looking for a way out of the Chinese character trap. But isn't the fact that Vietnamese did shake off the characters one of the main reasons why the language is considered, by North Asians especially, to be outside the pale of meaningful comparisons? Having made itself different, the language and hence the experience of becoming different are made irrelevant. Vietnamese no longer "belongs," so what can we learn by studying it?

I will not pretend that all or even most of the twelve factors listed below to explain how Vietnamese was able to convert to phonetic writing can apply to other East Asian languages, which have not yet made the transition or have done so less fully. Some of the lessons, however, are relevant.

1. Vietnamese makes more phonetic distinctions than other East Asian Languages. One of the major facts that must be taken into account in writing East Asian languages phonetically is that the Sinitic terms that make up such a large part of their vocabularies are syllable-based. Since these single-syllable morphemes are distinguished by Chinese characters that contain a high degree of graphic redundancy, they did not have to be distinguishable by sound in Chinese. Nor did the languages adopting them have much incentive to preserve the morphemes' phonetic intelligibility, since the terms could be understood through characters. Nevertheless, not all languages lost or reduced phonetic distinctions at the same rate, and some had more to begin with. Compared to Mandarin's 1,280 syllables (with tone), Korean's 1,100 spoken syllables, and the 100 to 319 syllables in modern Japanese (according to how the inventory is counted), Vietnamese stands alone with 4,500 to 4,800 spoken syllables, depending on the dialect. The figure rises to over 6,200 for written syllables, since Vietnamese orthography was designed to accommodate more phonetic distinctions than a speaker of any one dialect makes. Although only some fraction of

these syllables actually apply to Sinitic, the total figures are still relevant because a greater number of syllables overall means that indigenous terms are spread over a wider phonetic base and are less likely to clash with borrowed Chinese terms as homonyms and near homonyms.

2. Sinitic sounds are more fully assimilated in Vietnamese than in Japanese and Korean. It is difficult to give an exact accounting, as I did in the preceding chapters for Japanese and Korean, of what portion of Vietnamese syllables are Sinitic, because many sounds that may have originated as Chinese borrowings are so thoroughly indigenized that they are no longer considered as such. Moreover, the process of adaptation had been going on for so long that for any given Chinese character, Vietnamese had several different "Sinitic" pronunciations available to represent it, whereas Chinese and Korean, for the most part, had only one. In Vietnamese, not only is the overall inventory of syllables much higher than in the other languages, the "Sinitic" vocabulary—which is where most of the ambiguity problems arise in East Asian languages—is diffused throughout a larger part of the inventory.

3. Vietnamese grammar adds redundancy to Sinitic terms that is not available in other East Asian languages. In Vietnamese, attributes follow nouns instead of preceding them in the normal Sinitic word order. This fact would not add any distinctions in itself, were it not that Vietnamese sometimes borrowed Sinitic terms as units and other times analyzed the borrowings and rearranged the morphemes to fit Vietnamese word order, which cuts down on repetitive patterns. Vietnamese grammar also specifies the use of semantic classifiers before many types of nouns (e.g., **con heo,** "a pig"; **chiếc xe hơi,** "an automobile"), which helps show their grammatical function at the same time it cuts down on homonyms. These classifiers are not limited to use with numbers and demonstratives as in Chinese Mandarin, but are considered to be part of the word itself. An extension of the use of classifiers is the more recent practice of prefixing terms with indigenous (or indigenized) morphemes that give a clue to the term's semantic category, for example, *nha* before buildings, *quả* before round objects, and *máy* before machines (Aleshina 1977:204). Entire noun phrases can be flagged by prefixing them with the words *sự* or *việc* ("thing, matter, affair"). These devices help the reader zero in on the meanings of phonetically ambiguous words by constraining the range of possible interpretations.

4. *Quốc ngữ,* a national symbol, won popular support over its stigmatized competitors. Although introduced by Westerners, romanized Vietnamese had been around long enough to lose its foreign association. Tied to the sounds of the national language, it easily acquired the latter's status and prestige. *Chữ nôm* by contrast represented the sounds of the language poorly (i.e., in a less motivated fashion), and its symbols were too closely connected etymologically and psychologically to those used in China, which had stifled Vietnamese national culture not for two hundred years but for two thousand.

5. Romanized Vietnamese had the active support of the government. While wary of the nationalism *quốc ngữ* could inspire, the French essentially had no choice but to support it as an alternative to the systems associated with France's colonial rival. They also hoped that their Vietnamese subjects, having become literate in one type of romanized system, could use that knowledge to become proficient in French. Consequently, the colonialists not only backed *quốc ngữ* with schools, publications, and official sanction at a time that was critical in the new script's development, they also did what they could to discourage use of Chinese characters.

6. From a linguistic angle, there was little that romanized Vietnamese had to compete against. Chinese writing did not represent Vietnamese; it was used to write classical Chinese and hence was completely out of tune with the needs of the times. *Chữ nôm,* for its part, was "too unsystematized, not widespread, and even more complicated than the Chinese characters" (Martin 1982:39). Whereas Japanese and Korean had been able to work out a modus vivendi with the characters and take some pressure off the user by mixing the characters with elements of their own phonetic writing, *chữ nôm*'s incorporation of an indigenous element led, conversely, to even more complexity.

7. The transition to alphabetic writing in Vietnam happened early, before literacy was widespread and before the language had acquired many of the modern Sinitic terms that contributed to ambiguity in the other East Asian languages. In Vietnam, there was less to unlearn and fewer people who had to unlearn it. According to DeFrancis, even by the end of the 1930s only 5 to 20 percent of Vietnam's population was literate (1977:218). DeFrancis also quotes the editor of a major *quốc ngữ* journal, who wrote in 1923 that Vietnamese still lacked the "abstract and technical vocabulary of modern knowledge" (p. 208). The absence of these terms, which in other East Asian languages are almost entirely Chinese-based, gave Vietnamese the option of acquiring alternate terminology that fit the language and alphabetic writing, instead of adopting a batch of imports coined with the requirements of a different writing system in mind.

8. The writing system was grown, not manufactured. As I described earlier, Rhodes' alphabet was a synthesis of other individual creations and, in turn, was improved on by others whose interests lay in developing a practical phonetic notation that could meet real-world needs. All of this synthesis occurred, moreover, before the system had moved to the center of the stage as a national and then *the* national orthography. The same was true of the acquisition of vocabulary. As DeFrancis observed, new words were added to Vietnamese "largely through the uncoordinated efforts of individual writers. . . . These originated from various sources and were created in various ways" (1977:211). No one person or committee had responsibility for declaring how the language's vocabulary would be constituted and how these words would be represented in the writing system. Dif-

fuse input led to sound "choices" whose sanction was implied in the process itself.

9. *Quốc ngữ* was not thrust on the people to sink or swim, but had the luxury of sharing orthographic responsibilities with two other systems in a trigraphic relationship. Whatever their linguistic and social shortcomings, Chinese writing (of Chinese) and *chữ nôm* were established writing systems in Vietnam used by the literate population in a number of tasks for which *quốc ngữ* at the time was not well-suited. As the demands of the times changed and as romanized Vietnamese established its conventions and popularity, it gradually assumed (or displaced) the earlier practices. The upshot of the process was that Vietnamese people were weaned away from Chinese characters to a phonetic script over a span of half a century, a lesson that has not been lost on some Chinese supporters of writing reform (e.g., Cheng Fang 1981:198), who see *pinyin* and characters functioning side by side in different applications for years to come.

10. Similarly, the Vietnamese language itself was and to some extent continues to be supported by two other well-developed languages, French and English, which were and are known by a significant part of the educated populace. This phenomenon has had two effects. Just as *quốc ngữ* shared with two other systems the functions of writing, giving the former enough breathing space to establish itself gradually and on its own terms, so have French and English provided Vietnamese—and the phonetic orthography with which it is intimately associated—a needed respite from the pressure of having to deal at once with all of the demands modern society puts on language. Vietnamese and Vietnamese writing have had time to assimilate (not choke on) new forms or develop forms of their own, while these other languages take up the slack. The second effect is the benefit the indigenous language receives from exposure, through the minds of bilingual Vietnamese, to non-Sinitic models.

11. Since overt, centralized planning did not enter into the equation, there was no need for the system to be pre-engineered to "perfection" before being implemented. While experts debate the feasibility of an all-*hangul* policy or spend their time working out the fine details of word division for *pinyin*, Vietnamese people in the course of their day-to-day activities are improving the language and writing system as they go along. Language, an open-ended system if there ever was one, can never be "optimized" or perfected because it is constantly changing, as its users adapt it to a changing universe. The language and its universe coevolve. Waiting until every last flaw in the scheme is worked out abstractly before using it means waiting forever.

12. Finally, *quốc ngữ* triumphed because of its own intrinsic qualities. These include its close ties to the spoken language, its ability to span dialectal differences without sacrificing motivation or accuracy, and its international character, which, among other things, puts conventional word

processing equipment and programs within easy reach. This last quality has benefits that extend to the language itself. Early borrowings from European languages into Vietnamese were reduced both phonologically and in length to correspond with native phonology and the isolating morphology. For example, French *gas, gare,* and *garage* all became Vietnamese *ga,* French *gramme* became *gam,* and so on. Later European borrowings began to show a greater tendency to preserve the words' original form, including alien phonology that has begun to influence the indigenous phonological system (Aleshina 1977:203). If, as I maintain elsewhere in this book, a writing system influences the language that it is used to write, Vietnamese may experience through the importation and wholesale representation of polysyllabic European words a return from the syllable-oriented structure that Chinese characters helped to create in the past.

China's Legacy and the Unfinished Reform

The direct adaptation of Western vocabulary into Vietnamese, though facilitated by the romanized writing system, runs into an obstacle created by that same system, namely, its practice of putting spaces between every written syllable. As described above, *quốc ngữ* orthography, while alphabetic, divides the discourse at the syllable level, so that blank spaces appear every one to seven letters, depending on the number of letters in the syllable. There is no word division per se, since there is no way of knowing from the orthography whether a space after a syllable coincides with a word boundary. Exceptions are proper nouns—which lie at the fringes of the lexicon and for that reason can or must be supplied with some kind of identifying feature that signals them as units. For indigenous and Sinitic names, this function is provided by use of the uppercase for the first letter of a word, as in *Bộ trưởng Ngoại giao* ("Foreign Minister"), and *Phó Bí thư Thành ủy* ("Vice-Secretary of the Municipal [Party] Committee"). Western proper nouns are simply written as is, without spacing between syllables, unless the term is common enough to be indigenized, in which case hyphens may be inserted between a word's syllables.

This absence of word division in Vietnamese orthography has been excused by the alleged circumstance that if written syllables were run together, users would have no overt way to know if a consonant between vowels in the middle of the word ends the first syllable or begins the next. This claim seems superficial to me, because it assumes that with a word-based orthography users would still care about how a word's syllables were constituted or that users could not figure this out anyway from their knowledge of the word, its meaning, and the language's morphology. English lexicography acknowledges considerable disagreement on how dictionary entries should be syllabified, but this does not prevent people from reading the language and identifying morphological components

(SGGP). - Tới 21-6-1996, nói chuyện tại Câu lạc bộ giao lưu văn hóa (LAAP) về thành tựu của ngành tư pháp, Bộ trưởng Bộ Tư pháp Nguyễn Đình Lộc cho biết: Sẽ có nhiều đạo luật được trình ra Quốc hội trong thời gian cuối năm 1996 và đầu năm 1997, trong đó có 3 đạo luật quan trọng là: Luật Hình sự, Luật Hôn nhân và Gia đình, Luật Đầu tư.

Vietnamese newspaper text.
(*Sàigòn giải phóng,*
22 June 1996, p. 1)

Vietnamese alphabet written in Chinese character style for ancestral altar.
(Courtesy of Tinh P. Ha and Mai T. Ha)

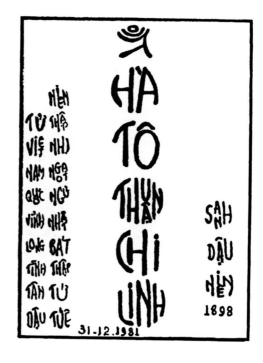

where the latter are worth identifying. As we shall see in a later chapter, the Sinitic compulsion to supply every syllable with its own semantic interpretation often leads to artificial associations that stand in the way of understanding.

A more plausible explanation for Vietnamese syllable spacing relates back to the origins of writing in Vietnam. Neither Chinese writing nor its *chữ nôm* derivative bothers with word division, because the individual units are already supplying a semantic gloss of sorts to the reader that together with context enables users to get by (although not without penalties). As a result, the concept of the word—a decidedly written-language concept—never caught on in Vietnam any better than it did in other East Asian countries. Nguyen Dinh Hoa's *Vietnamese-English Dictionary* (1966) gives the following meanings for *chữ*, the term bilingual Vietnamese usually associate with English "word": "letter [of the alphabet], (written) character, word, type, script, written language, handwriting." A Vietnamese-Chinese dictionary begins a like string of equivalents with "1. 字" (*zi*, "Chinese character"). Thompson observes that *chữ* "most often refers to a written or printed syllable—the unit appearing with a space preceding and following—although it sometimes refers to a longer sequence, the syllables of which are connected by hyphens." The notion of "word," Thompson writes, is outside the Vietnamese tradition. Rather, *chữ* (and its Sino-Vietnamese equivalent *tự*) "refer fairly regularly to monosyllabic elements identified here as morphemes" (1987:121–122).

Vietnamese lacks word division because it lacks well-defined words and, until recently, even the concept of "word." This lack is evidenced in the composition of dictionaries and in the frustration users experience in trying to look up sequences of text that are obviously words. To continue from Thompson: "The student cannot expect to find a single reference work which will list all or even a large proportion of the forms he will meet in reading texts in the language. In fact, wholesale coinage of new terms during the last decade makes recent texts quite difficult for foreign readers until they have acquired a deep sense of the word building habits of the language and the intimate knowledge of a large number of basic meaningful forms" (1987:67).

Now if this description sounds a lot like what readers of Chinese texts encounter routinely in their efforts to make sense of two- and three-character combinations that are forever cropping up in texts but cannot be found in any dictionary, there is good reason. Absent word division in their orthographies, neither language has any clear device for indicating what is a word or what can be a word, leaving the field wide open for users to create pseudowords willfully. It is not, as Thompson suggests, that dictionaries cannot keep up with new coinages so much as it is a case of these "coinages" being done arbitrarily and without restraint.[10] In written languages with word division, coining new terms is risky, because even with the hyphen as a hedge, the innovator must come forward openly with the creation for ratification before his or her peers. East Asians are not so encumbered. Morpheme sequences can be created as the writer writes that correspond as units to nothing in anyone else's lexicon, but the writer may assume, with only partial justification, that the reader will be able to assemble to arrive more or less at the meaning the writer was aiming at.

Thompson may also have been too generous in stating that the problem of piecing together whole meanings from newly arranged fragments is endemic to foreign students of Vietnamese alone. On many occasions I have sought the counsel of well-educated native speakers on the meanings of Vietnamese morpheme sequences used as words but not listed in any dictionary, with the result that we both went away perplexed. Sometimes when the sequence is meant to translate a foreign word, it is possible to identify the word that is meant from context, what clues the morphemes provide, and one's knowledge of the foreign language and subject matter—and in these cases native speakers actually tend to fare worse than the foreigner who has active reference to the base language. When the sequence is entirely original, its meaning is anyone's guess. Professional translators know what I am talking about and are nodding their heads as they read this.

Words are poorly distinguished in Vietnamese because the traditional writing systems did not require it. *Quốc ngữ* simply bypassed the problem by taking the same syllable units as the basis for its orthography, although there is evidence that this convention is not entirely satisfactory. Hyphens are occasionally used in some types of publications to link separate morphemes together. Thompson stops short of calling these sequences words, noting that "they signal combinations of syllables which form units from the point of view of their use in sentences. To some extent their use relates to the problem of just what a word is in Vietnamese" (1987:73). Although some guidelines for use of the hyphen can be elucidated (ibid.: 74–75), in practice usage is erratic, even within the same publication. Their presence suggests that Vietnam's syllable-based orthography, while obviously serviceable, is in the world context still a transitional artifact. Put a little more bluntly, Vietnamese writing still carries part of the Chinese character legacy and many of the problems that go with it.

Let's go back now to our first impressions of the writing system to see how they tie in with this thesis. I noted earlier that the script conveys to the novice a feeling of clutter, owing to the use of diacritics for special letters and another set of diacritics to indicate tone. The result is a script that is largely phonemic. But is it really necessary to specify all of these details, especially when doing so makes typing on standard keyboards difficult and since, given the quality of some contemporary Vietnamese printing, they are often superfluous anyway because the individual marks cannot be distinguished? This problem is serious enough to have warranted calls for script reform by Ho Chi Minh, who in 1943 and again in his last testament

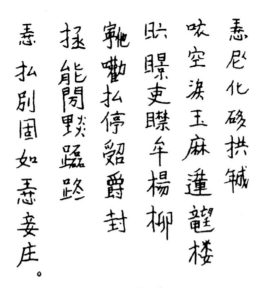

Vietnamese *chữ nôm* character text.
(Courtesy of Pham Van Hai)

in 1969 urged simplification of the orthography, especially the diacritics (Martin 1982:39).

Hangul gets by without marking long vowels just as English gets away without indicating stress and some phonemic features. Though hardly a model for emulation, it is noteworthy that English is able to use only twenty-six letters (and no diacritics) to accommodate the language's forty phonemes, while Vietnamese needs twenty-nine letters to write just thirty segmental phonemes (eleven vowels and nineteen consonants, including a coarticulated stop final). English writing and other alphabetic systems are able to function without specifying every phonetic or phonemic detail, because they incorporate another feature that allows the phonology to be depicted, as it were, from the outside in, namely, word division. Grasping the whole, users are able to retrieve from the information stored in their heads whatever additional phonological data they need to process or communicate the word, even though much of this information is missing from the orthographic record. Vietnamese forms lack this added level of redundancy; hence they require other, more overt cues to compensate. Tones, segmental phonemes, and written distinctions no one speaker makes must all be there to insure that the syllable itself, in context, can be identified with a particular morpheme. In this sense, Vietnamese orthography is still behaving like a Chinese character–based script, albeit one in which the sounds are rationally specified.

The likelihood that many of the tonal diacritics can be removed in a word-based Vietnamese script is suggested by China's experience with its *pinyin* alphabet, which does use word division. Computer experts have discovered that *pinyin* Chinese text entered as words gains little in clarity when the four tones are specified. For both languages, a practical word-based orthography will most likely require partial marking of tones, although it is hard to know beforehand how much and where. The correct balance can be established only through practice, as users themselves decide what makes up the languages' words and how these words are to be identified in writing.

Part 2 CRITIQUE OF CHINESE CHARACTER–BASED WRITING

5. Representation

ONE OF THE THORNIEST of the many problems pertaining to Chinese characters is determining what these symbols represent. Although a consensus seems to be emerging among specialists that the characters map onto morphemes—normally defined as "minimal units of meaningful sound"—uncertainty about how this mapping relationship takes place has led them to widely divergent views. At one end of the scale, scholars cite an alleged direct connection between "meaning" and symbol as prima facie evidence that Chinese characters are "ideographic," that is, they represent ideas. Although the characters are used with languages, their primary connection with meaning as such implies that they need not be restricted to any one language, as the facts *seem* to show, or for that matter to language at all. In this view, they are language-independent.

Other researchers grounded in mainstream, speech-oriented linguistics properly reject this "aphonic" interpretation of Chinese characters. But in doing so, they go too far in the other direction and end up making claims about the phonetic properties of characters, which, while true on one level and for some languages, do not sufficiently take into account other facts that point to a primary identification with meaning-based linguistic elements in all of the languages. I will try in this chapter to reconcile these opposing views by presenting a broader and, I hope, more accurate description of the morpheme—which many seem to forget is as tied to sound as it is to meaning—and its relationship to Chinese characters. Along the way, I will consider other common or possible interpretations of what these symbols are or represent.

Chinese Characters as Pictograms

Chinese characters are sometimes called pictographic. This view is held widely by nonlinguists and by many people who read and write languages that use characters. One source for their belief is a tendency language and area studies teachers have to use the system's novel aspects to attract the interest of their pupils. Every year beginning Chinese students are made to marvel at the similarity between 馬 and a horse, 門 and a door, 火 and fire, and so on, the similarities usually being apparent only after they are explained. This pedagogical trick loses its appeal later, when students face up to the task of memorizing hundreds, then thousands of symbols whose origins have no relevance to their present task.

With mastery and age, however, comes for many a renewed ability to discern in some characters vestiges or whole images of what is depicted. One of my first Chinese teachers, a native speaker, claimed she could "see" water pouring from a page that had several characters with the *shǔi* or "water" radical. Her sentiments are echoed by poets and literary critics, who wax on about how the pictographic quality of the characters adds another dimension to their art. One eminent sinologist, who should have known better, was moved to write, "The Chinese have specialized on making their writing so suggestive to the eye that it immediately calls up ideas and vivid pictures" (Creel 1937:159). Although few specialists entertain that position today, their contribution to this belief took the form of an early fascination with so-called etymological dictionaries that reproduced ancient forms of some characters that did, in their own way, bear a resemblance to the objects they represented. Since these were by far the most charming examples of an otherwise dry and incomprehensible set, the identification of Chinese characters with pictograms became common.

There are several problems with this view, however, particularly when applied to the system as a whole. As noted in Chapter 1, Chinese very early on abandoned the practice of trying to represent the objects of nature with pictures that resembled them. The process was self-defeating, not only because of the difficulty of creating enough distinctions to differentiate in a relatively small space one icon from thousands of others, but also because many things worth depicting are not amenable to this approach, such as names, relations between objects, and abstract concepts. Although some of these problems were overcome by using graphs that mirrored the abstraction, for example, 上 for "above" and the character 一 for "one," or that combined the senses of two or more existing graphs into one, such as a single 木 "tree" becoming a 林 "forest," Chinese eventually discovered a better way. Instead of creating an entirely new semiotic system, they simply tapped into natural language, which had already evolved principled techniques for expressing the things people wished to express.

At first this took the form of borrowing a character used for one word to write another word that had no character but had the same or a similar sound—a step that seems to have been taken by all the world's major writing systems (Jensen 1970:51–52). By extending the use of characters to unrelated concepts identified in speech with the same pronunciation, Chinese writing moved decisively and irrevocably away from iconicity and toward phonetics as the dominant principle governing the creation of new character forms. Had the process continued, Chinese today would be using a fully developed syllabary with one unique graph for each syllable in the language. It is more likely, however, that the practice would have led to a rejection of the characters outright, as Chinese found it increasingly harder to justify using thousands of symbols to accomplish what a few dozen alphabetic symbols could do in combination.

What prevented Chinese characters from becoming identified entirely with sound was the practice that Chinese evolved of attaching to these sound-bearing or "phonetic" elements other characters (or their abbreviated substitutes) chosen for their semantic value, eventually forcing the two into the same squarish frame.[1] The result was an entirely new character, distinct from all other characters having the same phonetic element and read in the same or a similar way. These semantic-phonetic compounds grew rapidly in number and now account for some 85 percent of the forms in use. What this type of character means for the classification of the system as a whole will be discussed below, although it is evident that they and most other types of characters discussed have nothing in common with pictograms.

Even those characters that began as pictures lost the resemblance they had to their referents as the forms became increasingly stylized. Even in cases where some identity was preserved, the association must be regarded from a synchronic point of view as strictly arbitrary. 日 looks more like a window than like the sun. 月 resembles a stepladder more closely than the moon. The absence today of any motivated connection between Chinese character forms and their meanings was demonstrated by Koriat and Levy in an experiment that measured the ability of subjects with no background in written or spoken Chinese to guess the semantic domains of concepts represented by characters (1979: 353–365). They concluded, "The inability of subjects to guess the dimension conveyed by each pair of Chinese characters suggests that the Chinese ideographs [*sic*] employed in the present study have retained few traces of literal representation."

There is not and, in most cases, never was anything in the shape of the characters that would enable an uncoached reader to see the form of the object represented. The connection becomes evident, in those relatively few cases where the pictographic principle did apply, only after it is pointed out. For example, we know 門 "door" was an icon of the concept it represents. Likewise, the character 馬 is a stylized representation of a horse. Without being told, however, few would make these connections. And virtually no one would choose for 闖 the correct meaning "rush in suddenly" if given a choice between that and a more logical interpretation such as "horse in a stable"—let alone make the proper connection without any hints at all! None of these symbols has the universality of a true pictogram such as →, the general meaning of which is apparent to most people at a glance (Shibata 1987:9–10).

These arguments all apply to the extralinguistic relationship of characters with the nonlinguistic world. But in classifying a writing system, one cannot focus exclusively on the nature of the system's units while neglecting their "interlingual" relationship to each other in connected discourse (Haas 1976:133). Even if we were to allow the argument that some characters are pictographic, it does not follow that the sense of these symbols, strung together one after another, can be derived without recourse to an extrinsic grammar. If there is no motivated connection between meaning and the forms of individual characters, there is even less between the collective pictorial sense of characters in combination and what is actually meant by a page of idiomatic Chinese.

Chinese characters—or at most a small percentage of them—can be called "pictographic" only by dropping the requirement of necessary association and by admitting conventional association as the criterion, which invalidates any claim that the forms or the system are universal. This is not to say Chinese characters do not evoke in different people different extra-linguistic associations, based on their understanding of the connection between meaning and form (which may or may not be correct) and a host of other subjective factors peculiar to the individual. What utility such associations could have for present day users, however, escapes me. Some people even complain that these peripheral associations, when they occur at all, only get in the way of understanding.

Chinese Characters as Ideograms

The degree to which someone, armed with an etymological dictionary or an active imagination, can identify a handful of characters with original pictographic elements is, in any case, a diachronic exercise, irrelevant to an inquiry aimed at elucidating the formal synchronic relations between these symbols and other units. Only a few specialists are even remotely concerned with their origins. What users of Chinese characters look for when they read or intend when they write goes beyond the form of the symbol itself and into the realm of what the symbol currently represents, in other words, what it means. The interesting question, therefore, is not where the symbols came from but how they mediate meaning.

There are two approaches to this problem. One can study the mental processes of users as they interact with Chinese characters and draw inferences about how the mind relates the characters to meaning. This *functional* approach will be treated in Chapter 7, which deals with psycholinguistic aspects of Chinese characters, although its findings have some bearing on conclusions we shall reach presently. The task for the remainder of this chapter will be to establish how the characters represent meaning in a formal, *structural* sense.

One of the earliest and most persistent formulations equates Chinese characters directly to meaning, without the intervention of language. This is the so-called ideographic principle, long held by intellectuals who believed they saw in the characters a neutral medium available to all human beings for expressing "pure thought," unfettered by the cultural baggage attached to language.[2] Chinese characters, in this interpretation, act much the same way as numbers and mathematical formulae in directing users to concepts that can be identified without reference to the names different people give them, or even if no name is given (Sokolov 1959:185). Two types of evidence are used to support this view: (1) the alleged ability of Chinese characters to signify meaning within a community of people who use the same language, but without recourse to the sounds of that language, and (2) use of the same characters with the same meanings in different languages. Neither of these proofs will stand up to logical analysis.

In the first case, even if one were to accept the (untenable) argument that the characters have no necessary relationship to sound, it by no means follows that the absence of such a relationship implies no connection with language. Quite the contrary. If linguistics has taught us anything over the past four decades, it is that language is more than sound. It encompasses the entire set of structures and relationships linking an observable physical phenomenon (speech or writing) with thought processes that precede language and are largely independent of it. To call Chinese characters ideographic, one would have to show that the graphic forms bypass all intermediate linguistic structures, not just sound, and equate directly to the ideas that lie beyond language, ideas that, owing nothing to language, are directly accessible by different people of the same or different cultures.

The flaw here lies in lumping together under the single category of meaning two different types of mental phenomena. There is thought, on the one hand, which is meaningful to the individual thinking it, but cannot without language be delineated, identified, maintained, and manipulated, or communicated with any precision. It is hard to see how Chinese characters can refer to meaning at this level, since there is nothing constant for the symbols to map onto. For symbols to have utility to the individual, they must refer to persistent facts of consciousness, and for the symbols to be effective between individuals presupposes what Olson has called an "agreed upon or presupposed possible world" (1982:155). These conventions are precisely what constitute the semantic content of language. It is not meaning per se, but linguistic meaning that makes up the representata of Chinese characters. This changes the score completely. The characters do not deal with "naked ideas," but identify concepts peculiar to particular languages, and in this sense function no differently than the symbols of any other writing system whose relationship to sound is more directly motivated.[3] One can argue (as I shall later) over where in the chain of linguistic phenomena the tie-in with Chinese characters occurs, but one cannot argue their connection with language itself.

Moreover, one need not claim that Chinese characters map directly onto sound to appreciate that some connection with sound is inescapable. The connection manifests itself on three levels and in each case is so pervasive that one can only call the characters ideographic by closing one's eyes to the greater part of reality. Etymologically, we have seen in Chapter 1 that most characters owe their shapes to the sounds of the language they represented. This is a panlinguistic phenomenon that applies to Chinese no less than to any other developed writing system. Functionally, psycholinguistic studies have shown beyond doubt that sound plays a role in the way human minds process these symbols. Although the precise nature of this connection can be argued, its presence cannot. However, my main concern here is to demonstrate a formal connection to sound, and to do that I need only point out that every character without exception has a pronunciation. Being able to understand a character's meaning without knowing the correct pronunciation is irrelevant: the same happens to users of alphabetic writing systems. Understanding the meaning of a character with *no* knowledge of its sound (the pronunciation was forgotten or never learned) does not demonstrate its ideographic nature either; formally a reading does exist. The phenomenon is pathological by definition and as witnessed by the inability of the reader to focus on the concept represented.

Nor can characters in Chinese and Korean with two or more pronunciations, each with different meanings, be cited as evidence of ideography. First of all, the meanings represented are *linguistic* meanings, not vague, indeterminate ideas. Second, if the meanings are unrelated, for example, Chinese 率 which is read *shuài* ("to lead") or *lǜ* ("rate, ratio"), it is simply a case of one symbol being used for two different words or morphemes, just as *desert* in English has two unrelated meanings and pronunciations determined by context. Having nothing in common semantically, the form representing the two meanings can hardly be construed as a symbol for a more basic or primary concept.

The phenomenon in any case is rare. It is far more common in Chinese to find among the exceptions to the one-character-one-sound-one-meaning paradigm characters with (1) related meanings and different pronunciations, (2) related meanings and the same pronunciation, and (3) different meanings and the same pronunciation. The last two phenomena need not concern us at all, unless we are prepared to call the alphabetic writing used in Western languages ideographic as well. Nor need we dwell long in this context on the first category, since the only thing that distinguishes it from category (2) is a difference in sound, that is, a linguistic factor. Specifically, it is worth noting that in Chinese and Korean, differences in a character's pronunciation that correspond to different though related meanings are usually minor: a changed tone, the presence or absence of aspiration, or a syllable-final consonant. There is reason to believe that many of these pronunciation differences are the residue of morphological processes that operated historically, in which case the phenomenon parallels what we find in English spelling, where a single graphic form can be pronounced differently (as in Chinese) depending on what syntactic and semantic characteristics are intended.

This brings us to Japanese. Unlike in Chinese and Korean, it is usual for characters to be read in Japanese with two or more pronunciations, tied to concepts that share a common semantic core. Moreover, the readings vary grossly, the typical case being an *on,* or Sinitic, pronunciation joined by a *kun* reading drawn from the indigenous lexicon. This unusual convention, found today only in Japanese, is used to support two arguments aimed at demonstrating the ideographic function of *kanji.* One argument alleges a "dual phonetic realization" of the same concept: the concept itself, being realized in two (or more) linguistic forms, must therefore lie beyond language, that is, be prior to it. The flaw in this reasoning is simply that we are dealing here not with one concept but with as many concepts as there are readings for the character. Associated with the different readings are different syntactic constraints, sociolinguistic variables, and even emotional links with the pronunciation itself, all serving to distinguish the meanings overall. Even if one were to rule out these considerations, there are too many cases where the *on* and *kun* readings are accompanied by large semantic differences, the former usually designating an ill-defined semantic area and the latter one or more specific aspects of it.

Another argument looks at this same fact of one character representing two or more concepts, one general and the other(s) more specific, and concludes that the graph must be representing a kind of supraconcept, more comprehensive than any one concept realized in the language. For example, 人 in Japanese has the narrow meaning of "person" at the same time it carries a broader meaning relating to humanity in general. It is interesting to note, however, that this distinction between general and specific does not parallel the *on* and *kun* distinction exclusively and can be more striking within the range of meanings covered by the *kun* reading alone. Nelson's *Japanese-English Character Dictionary* lists for *hito,* the *kun* of 人, these English translations: "man, human being, mankind, person, people; character, personality; a true man; man of talent; adult; other people; messenger; visitor." These associations together seem to carry as broad a meaning overall as the less specific *on* readings *jin/nin* or the combinations in which the latter appear. The character 口 is assigned by Nelson one general meaning "mouth" for its *on* readings and twelve separate groups of meanings for its *kun* reading *kuchi.* 筋 is realized in Japanese as "muscle, sinew, tendon" in its *on* reading *kin* and as "muscle, sinew, tendon; vein; fiber; string; line; stripe, streak; plot, plan; reason, logic; circumstances; thread, sequence; quarters, sources, authorities; lineage, strain, stock, descent; grain, texture" when read with its *kun* reading of *suji* (Nelson 1962:684).

These observations in themselves go far to dilute the significance attached to the "multivalent" semantic qualities of *kanji* by proponents of the ideographic theory, since the spread in meaning in many cases owes more to the indigenous word represented than to any bridge the character effects between the indigenous word and its Sinitic counterpart. Moreover, if we ignore pronunciation and consider only the character itself and its meanings, it is clear that the character 人 functions semantically in precisely the same way as the graphic complex "person" does in English, both as a word in itself (with several distinct meanings) and as a basis for other words that incorporate this semantic attribute into their overall meanings, for example, the written forms "personal," "personnel," "personality," "personable," "impersonate," "personage," "persona," "personification," and "impersonal." If Japanese writing is ideographic, then so is English.

So far our discussion has focused on the functioning of Chinese characters within languages. Another argument looks at their use *between* languages and concludes that the representation must be ideographic—otherwise how could monolingual speakers of one language understand the symbols when used in another? That Chinese characters have meanings (which have sounds) on the strength of their forms alone and not because the forms represent sounds that have meanings is, I believe, indisputable. But it does not follow that they function ideographically, without regard to language or even without regard to a specific language. Users of Chinese characters, if they understand a character in a different language, are reading it or thinking of it in their own pronunciation. The sound may not be needed to access the meaning or even to support the fact that it formally does have meaning, but it will inevitably be recalled at some stage in the process of using it.

More important, the ability of users of one language to understand Chinese characters in another does not hold up for the entire inventory. Many characters are used in one or two of the languages that use Chinese characters, but not all three. Others have different meanings in different languages, alone and even in combination. All have different meanings if extended (linguistic) meaning is taken into account. Finally, the same claim can be made for shared or borrowed words, which number in the thousands, in alphabetic languages. The spellings (shapes) of these cognate forms need not even correspond exactly; all they need do is resemble each other visually and share the same basic sense to equal or exceed the transitivity claimed for Chinese characters in East Asia, where independent reforms have changed the shapes of many characters between countries and languages, often beyond recognition. One can argue that the changed character forms really stand for the same thing, but then so do the written forms of cognate terms in Western languages spelled with the Roman alphabet. If the claim to ideography is based on the relationship across languages between visible form and meaning, then it can be said of other writing systems too, even those based more directly on phonetic principles.

It is high time to reject the notion that Chinese characters represent "ideas" divorced from language. There is no evidence supporting the claim, and every argument allegedly in favor of it either overlooks a fundamental linguistic connection or trivializes the concept by extending ideography to all writing generally.

Chinese Characters as Logograms

Astute Western observers since DuPonceau (1838) have suggested that Chinese characters correspond to words, that is, familiar linguistic elements known to all languages, and not to "ideas" independently of language. While this formulation is not strictly correct either, it is a step closer to the truth. It also provides an opportunity to introduce the types of writing systems to which Chinese characters might conceivably belong, since neither of our earlier formulations—pictograms and ideograms—qualifies as "writing" as the term is normally understood. People can and do create symbolic systems with limited applications that are not formally based on language (although their articulation would depend on it), mathematics and scientific notation being well-known examples. However, such systems symbolize only a small fraction of the phenomena expressed by natural language. Pictograms in principle are less restrictive, but their interpretation rests loosely on the "reader." Neither expresses language; and since Chinese characters clearly do, our search can be limited to systems that connect with language on one level or another.

There is broad but not total agreement among linguists on how writing systems should be classified. Pulgram, for example, identifies seven types of writing, which he labels pictorial, logographic, syllabic, alphabetic, phonemic, phonetic, and spectrographic (1976:4). Pictorial "writing," however, is dismissed by Pulgram as "comparable to a cartoon without a caption." Lacking a formal connection with language, the "translation of the picture into words is necessarily free" (p. 6). "Spectrographic," on the other end of the scale, refers to machine-made representations of the physical properties of one person's speech. While of great value to linguists and engineers, it cannot properly be called a "system" since, like pictograms, there is no discrete set of units governing the representation and hence no reliable means of insuring that the representation will be generally understood.

Sampson's (1985) analysis distinguishes two fundamental types of "writing" according to whether a direct connection with natural language exists. One group, called "semasiographic," is used in lieu of the ambiguous term "ideographic" to mean systems that "indicate ideas directly," including mathematics, road signs, pictograms, and other types of symbolic

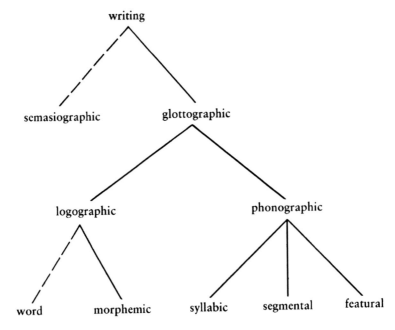

Figure 1. Possible types of writing (adapted from Sampson 1985:32)

systems. "Glottographic," by contrast, includes only those systems with formal relationships to a spoken language, as shown in Figure 1.

The dotted lines in Figure 1, according to Sampson, show that although these categories are conceivable (in his view), no fully elaborated specimens have been developed. He further contends that people have not invested semasiography with the same range of expression available in natural language because we have the latter at our disposal, although the notion that a comparable system not based on language could exist is implausible as it stands. Lacking concrete and full examples of such systems and even the likelihood that such will appear, it is hard to argue with DeFrancis' suggestion that the term "writing" be reserved solely for systems that represent language directly (1989:5). DeFrancis' proposal would eliminate much of the confusion surrounding these matters, and our understanding of Chinese characters in particular, since there is nothing in the latter that supports the existence of a non-language-based "writing," either.

Having confined our search to language-based systems, two major possibilities remain, identified in Sampson's scheme as "logographic" for systems based on units of meaning and "phonographic" for writing based on phonologic (sound) units (1985:33). By "meaningful units" Sampson is referring to units of thought "that the language isolates," and not language-independent abstractions. French also sees the main distinction in writing systems as between "scripts the graphemes of which typically represent meaningful linguistic items and, on the other hand, scripts the graphemes of which typically represent meaningless linguistic items" (1976:117). The former, meaning-based scripts he calls "pleremic," in contrast to "cenemic" scripts based on meaningless sound. Coulmas adopts the same distinctions and terminology, using "pleremic" to denote scripts with "elements that carry meaning" and "cenemic" for scripts with elements that *distinguish* meaning (1989:49). Within each category, Coulmas goes on to distinguish two subtypes (four "levels of analysis"), including "lexemic" and "morphemic" under the meaning-based systems, and "syllabic" and "phonemic/phonetic" under the sound-based systems. The four subtypes correspond exactly to Sampson's "word," "morphemic," "syllabic," and "segmental" taxonomy. DeFrancis points out that Sampson is alone in treating Korean *hangul* as a fifth or "featural" subtype (1989:62), and I see no justification for doing so either, since the feature-based origins of some *hangul* letters (segments) have no more relevance to the system's classification than do the pictorial origins of some Chinese characters.

In Sampson's depiction of "logographic," or meaning-based systems, in Figure 1, note the dotted line to "word," showing it as a hypothetical subtype with no actual examples. Nor will any appear soon, according to French, in view of the fact that such a system requires a separate symbol for each of the "many tens of thousands of words" in a modern language (1976:105). Russian linguists have come to the same conclusion about the impracticality of any writing system whose indivisible elements run into tens or hundreds of thousands (Sokolov 1959:195; Solntsev 1985:7). Chinese characters in practice number today from roughly two to seven thousand, depending on the language, and clearly cannot be representing words primarily, since the words in any of these languages easily number more than ten times the highest figure.

If meaning-based writing systems are limited to the single subtype "morphemic," why bother with the word "logographic" at all? The term is just familiar enough to those professionally concerned with language to be recognized as "meaning-based," but not well enough understood for many to be aware that the class includes words and morphemes, and that the latter is all the system really represents. This misunderstanding is abetted by imprecise use of the term by linguists themselves and use by different linguists in different ways.[4] The confusion can have serious consequences when, for example, two well-known reading researchers comment that Chinese are handicapped by a shortage of words because their "logographic" system contains only a few thousand symbols compared to the tens of thousands known by adult readers of English. (Gleitman and Rozin 1973b:497). The real distinction to be made comes down quite simply to writing systems whose units in principle represent morphemes and systems whose primary units represent sounds.

Chinese Characters Representing Morphemes

As mentioned at the beginning of this chapter, the view that Chinese characters primarily represent morphemes is shared today by most specialists.[5] "Morphemes" have been defined in general terms as "the smallest individually meaningful elements in the utterances of a language" (Hockett 1958:123). This characterization is not entirely satisfactory, since it defines what is essentially a fusion of meaning and (by most accounts) sound in terms of the latter, but as a working description it will suffice for the moment. Examples of morphemes from English are "old" and "-er" in the word "older," but not the "-er" in "sister" (ibid.: 124–125). The "-er" of teacher is also a morpheme but distinct from its homophone in the first example because of its different meaning. It is evident that a morpheme can be a word, that is, it can stand alone, although it can also be used as part of a word, depending on its ability to function in other words while maintaining the same sound and overall meaning.

The distinction between morphemes as words and morphemes as parts of words corresponds in Chinese to what are usually identified as "free" and "bound" morphemes. The former are able to stand alone as an utterance, and the latter are dependent on other morphemes for their realization. Examples are *lǎo* and *shī* in the Chinese word *lǎoshī*, meaning "teacher." Both syllables are "representing" morphemes, *lǎo* meaning "old" and *shī* a "master" or "specialist," but only *lǎo* can stand alone as a minimum free form. *Shī* (the morpheme) only appears in modern Chinese in combination with other morphemes. Free or bound, these morphemes are nearly always identified by users of Chinese, Japanese, and Korean—and by lexicographers who describe that usage—with unique Chinese characters. The *lǎo* used to mean "old" is written with the character 老 and not with any of a half dozen other modern forms that have the same sound but different meaning. The morpheme used to mean "master" or "specialist" and pronounced *shī* corresponds to the character 師 and not with other characters used to convey a similar sense but pronounced differently.

By and large, Chinese characters correspond to the morphemes of the languages in which they are used. In Chinese and in the Sinitic lexicon of Korean, the relationship usually takes the form of one-character-one-syllable. As described by Coulmas, "Chinese characters refer at the same time and in parallel both to the sound and to the meaning of the words/morphemes which they represent" (1983:186). This relationship also holds true for the indigenous part of Japanese to which characters have been assigned (the *kun* readings of characters), where the phonetic part of the equation is not limited to one syllable but can run to as many as five, for example, in 詔 *mikotonori* "imperial decree." Japanese normally distinguish the written forms of conjugated words by using a character for the essential element (i.e., the base morpheme) and phonetic *kana* for the remainder.[6]

Moreover, they make a determined effort to slice what is clearly one and the same indigenous morpheme (in terms of the sound system of their own language) into as many separate morphemes as they can assign to appropriate Chinese characters. These latter two practices are significant because they demonstrate a primary connection between characters and morphemes that is not self-evident in the Sinitic lexicon, where the characters also represent a syllable.

While there can be no question that Chinese characters map onto morphemes, there are some apparent and real problems with this formulation that need to be addressed. Among the apparent inconsistencies are cases of two or more characters being used to represent one morpheme, which will be dealt with toward the end of this section, and nonmorphemic phonetic use of Chinese characters, which will be treated in the following section on Chinese characters used as a "syllabary." Less easily dismissed are examples of Chinese characters being used for more than one morpheme, with or without the same pronunciation.

I was earlier inclined to attribute this last group of "exceptions" to historical change. No doubt this is a factor, and a strong one. Languages constantly change and do so on all levels with little regard for how innovations affect symmetry. Conversely, the tendency to restore iconicity between units on different linguistic levels is itself a powerful mechanism of change. One finds at any given moment a system in flux, where rules work against exceptions, and new exceptions are constantly created. Add to this the innate conservatism of orthography, which derives much of its utility from ignoring linguistic change, and one can only marvel at how well the "correct" alignment of one character = one morpheme = one syllable holds up.

However, even allowing for historical change, I now feel there are too many persistent cases of Chinese characters identified with more than one morpheme to assume this is the only stable relationship possible. In the People's Republic of China, two sets of reforms have obliterated the one-character-one-morpheme paradigm in principle: today, many characters are used both with their traditional meanings and as substitutes for other, more complex forms with entirely different meanings. For Taiwan and other Chinese areas where the reforms have not taken root, the list of characters having two or more readings that correspond to differences in meaning runs into the hundreds. In Japanese, the association of different *on* and *kun* readings with a character is more the rule than the exception. We must either admit "one character equals more than one morpheme" as a regular feature of the representation or take a fresh look at how we define the morpheme itself. By the same token, it is difficult to explain how a Chinese character can be merely "representing" a morpheme, defined as the fusion of meaning and sound, when the character almost always does a better job identifying the meaning than does the sound to which the meaning is joined.

But let us deal with apparent problems first, beginning with the notorious "butterfly" example and similar cases usually connected with borrowings into Chinese. Specialists from Kennedy (1964:274–322) to DeFrancis (1984a:180–181) have observed that a number of polysyllabic words exist in the Sinitic lexicon that, although represented by more than one Chinese character, cannot easily be construed as being made up of more than one morpheme. The Chinese word for "butterfly," *húdié,* is written with two characters 蝴 and 蝶 sequentially, in keeping with the one-character-one-syllable convention. Since 蝴 appears only with 蝶 in the language and never alone, the character can hardly be considered, by itself, a sign for the morpheme "butterfly." Rather, the word is usually regarded as an unanalyzable morpheme written with two characters. Other examples from the "insect" group are 蜘蛛 *zhīzhū* "spider," 蜈蚣 *wúgōng* "centipede," and 蝌蚪 *kēdǒu* "tadpole," all originally single-morpheme words that were given as many characters as the words had syllables, and a foreign borrowing for "glass," 玻璃 *bōli,* which like the others cannot be split into its constituent characters/syllables and still be used to signify the word in writing or speech.

Kennedy's and DeFrancis' claim that these words are "polysyllabic" is indisputable. One need only open any modern Chinese word dictionary to find tens of thousands of other polysyllabic words, some foreign but most of Sinitic origin. In terms of the words' morphemic status, however, it turns out that the second elements of these compounds are used productively as morphemes in other polysyllabic Sinitic expressions, such as 蝶衣 *diéyī* "butterfly wings," 蝶骨 *diégǔ* "sphenoid bone," and 蛛網 *zhūwǎng* "cobweb." The underlying structure of the *húdié*-type terms thus seems to be (1) a core morpheme, one syllable long in word-final position, which designates the concept generally, and (2) prefixed to the core, in regular attributive-noun configuration, a second element that carries the linguistic meaning of "general > specific." Only the core morpheme is productive or, at any rate, is subsequently analyzed as such. It is hard to escape concluding that Chinese writing favors the morphemic principle of representation even at the cost of redefining what began as phonetic usage of the characters.

In Japanese, there are two other constructions in which a Chinese character seems to be designating less than one morpheme. One is the *ateji* ("characters applied" to a word) or so-called false substitution characters, in which Chinese characters are chosen for their phonetic (*on* or *kun*) values and applied to a word with no regard for the characters' individual meanings. Examples are 矢張 *yahari* "also" and 大方 *ōkata* "almost" (in its *on* reading of *taihō* it means "broadminded"), which owe their associations with these morphemes to a coincidence of sound. Unlike Chinese, no attempt is made to reanalyze the meanings of the constituent characters in terms of the meaning of the word to which they were assigned. The second type of submorphemic use of Chinese characters in Japanese involves using

two or more characters on the basis of their meanings to represent a word
that, in terms of its phonetic representation, is made up of only one morpheme. Sokolov identified three subtypes, including (1) use of characters
for indigenous words that have no equivalent in Chinese, for example,
足袋 "foot bag" for *tabi* "Japanese-style socks"; (2) use of Chinese characters for words borrowed from Indo-European languages that have no
equivalent either in Chinese or in Japanese, for example, 烟草 "a grass for
smoking" for *tabako* "cigarette"; and (3) using a legitimate Chinese combination for the semantically equivalent indigenous Japanese word, for example, 今日 "present day" for *kyō* "today" (1963:126).

Both the phonetic and the semantic assignment of Chinese characters
to indigenous Japanese words date back to the seventh century and earlier,
when Chinese characters were pressed into service to write a language that
is even less well-suited to this form of representation than English. The *ateji*
today are more an artifact of history than an ongoing morphological process. Officially proscribed by the postwar reforms, they have been largely
superseded by phonetic *kana*. Submorphemic semantic use of Chinese characters in Japanese, in contrast, seems to be enjoying a rebirth as the language, flooded with new English borrowings, seeks to compensate for the
overly long or ambiguous representation these terms acquire when transliterated in *kana* by assigning, in addition to the *kana* phonetic symbols, two
or more Chinese characters whose sense mirrors the morphemic structure
of the borrowing, that is, a semantic gloss. The characters are read, however, not with their Sinitic *on* values or even with *kun,* but collectively with
the sound of the transliterated borrowing.

What these apparent counterexamples to the one-character-one-
morpheme paradigm share with the *húdié*-type words in Chinese is that
they usually involve words whose origins lie outside the Sinitic lexicon,
where the paradigm operates most visibly. Indigenous Japanese words in
need of character representation are forced to use two or more in succession when no appropriate single character exists to represent the concept.
But does this mean the characters are individually representing less than a
morpheme? If so, then what *are* they representing? Certainly not sound,
where the connection is even further skewed. The problem can be
resolved only by allowing that, formally, the characters are standing for
an equal number of morphemes, which in turn make up a word that is
analyzed as *one* morpheme in the language's phonetic representation. The
equation becomes enigmatic only if one assumes that the phonetic representation is primary or that the two representations can be discretely
defined in terms of each other. For *ateji* or phonetic usage of characters in
Japanese, however, and for a large number of recent Western loanwords
in Chinese, characters are used for their phonetic values alone, adding
weight to yet another hypothesis that Chinese characters are, at heart, elements of a syllabary.

Chinese Characters as a Syllabary

Although the relationship between Chinese characters and morphemes seems well established, other evidence relating to their internal structures and the way characters are used suggests they may also be representing sound. In modern Chinese, one need not search far for examples where sound is the only thing being represented. It is nearly impossible nowadays to read through a page of Chinese that does not include, at minimum, foreign place and personal names written with a string of characters whose individual meanings play no role at all and that were chosen solely on the basis of how they sound when pronounced. Page one of a September 1993 issue of *People's Daily*, for example, printed the name of the former British prime minister Margaret Thatcher with three characters 撒切爾 pronounced in modern standard Mandarin *Sāqiēěr*. England itself was represented with the usual hybrid combination read 英國 *Yīngguó*, in which the second syllable means "country" and the first is used for its sound alone. On the same day, my intermediate Chinese students were alternately amused and embarrassed by their failure to grasp such textbook forms as 加拿大 *Jiānádà* for "Canada" and 意大利 *Yìdàlì* for "Italy."

The technique of using Chinese characters for their sound value alone extends beyond foreign proper names to foreign terms generally. This is witnessed historically in the *bōli* "glass" example cited above, which began as a phonetic borrowing, and in such neologisms as 雷達 *léidá* for "radar," 修 *xiū* for "show," and a host of other Western terms that have become common enough in speech to force some kind of written representation. Moreover, the practice has been and remains extremely common *within* the Sinitic family of languages, where Cantonese, Taiwanese, and Shanghainese speakers freely borrow characters to represent the sounds of indigenous morphemes. Taken together, these practices constitute a continuation of the same historical process described in Chapter 1: existing characters are pressed into service to represent homophonous or nearly homophonous words that lack a written form. After the extension has taken root, a "radical" may or may not be added to the form to distinguish a particular meaning from others with the same "phonetic." Still later, the whole complex is simplified by calligraphers, users, and reformers; the sound associated with it undergoes natural change, and the form is available once again to represent a new term or borrowing based on sound correspondence. As I have already pointed out, some 85 percent of the character inventory was formed in this manner.

Within this evolutionary process, the only factor that remains constant is the identification of the character in Chinese with a sound one syllable long. The importance of this link in the overall scheme can be gauged from the fact that whereas characters usually represent one or several morphemes, they can be and are sometimes used for no other purpose than to depict sounds. Conversely, there are no cases in Chinese of characters without one or more syllable sounds. Could this system, in essence, be one big syllabary masquerading as morphemic writing?

The thought is tantalizing, inasmuch as it fits perfectly the structuralists' contention that writing is a device for recording sounds. Other types of evidence, elucidated by John DeFrancis, lend credence to the hypothesis that the "Chinese writing system should be considered to be basically a phonetic system of writing of the syllable type" (1984a:125). For example, not only do the majority of characters contain components selected originally for their phonetic value; these components generally constitute the largest or, at any rate, the densest and most conspicuous part of the character. More important, their distribution is uneven throughout the corpus; several such phonetic components appear in a dozen or more characters with the same (or nearly the same) sound. Although their usefulness varies, DeFrancis calculates that these phonetic structures—some nine hundred of them—give a useful idea how a character might be pronounced two-thirds of the time. While this figure can be questioned depending on how one defines "useful," the phenomenon is pervasive enough to allow those versed in the system to hazard reasonably accurate guesses as to the pronunciation of unfamiliar characters or to jog the memory on forms that were nearly forgotten. By contrast, the amount of useful semantic information provided by a character's radical, if you can find it, is minimal.

Weighing against these considerations are other, in my view, more persuasive factors that point to a primary identification of Chinese characters[7] with morphemes (keeping in mind earlier comments about morphemes not being "units of meaning" but units that join meaning and sound). For starters, the syllabary argument cannot be applied to Japanese. Sinitic *on* readings in Japanese are pronounced with one or two syllables, depending on whether the Chinese sound had a syllable-final stop consonant when assimilated into Japanese. *Kun* readings can be several syllables long. Although the Japanese readings are not directly related to what characters represent in Chinese, the fact that the characters do represent morphemes in another language establishes this in principle as a possibility. Moreover, as Kratochvil (1968:155), French (1976:105), Coulmas (1989:50), and others have pointed out, most modern Mandarin syllables can be written by more than one and in some cases dozens of characters. This fact in itself does not rule out the possibility of the system being a syllabary. One need only cite premodern Japanese *kana* usage for examples of single syllables represented by multiple characters used for nothing but their sounds. What clinches the argument for a primary identification with morphemes is the fact that their relationship with characters is almost always one-to-one. 再 *zài* ("again") cannot substitute for 在 *zài* ("in, at,") nor can 事 *shì* ("matter, event") stand in for 是 *shì* ("be"), despite the congruence in sound. As French states, "It is the meaning associated with a syllable in a given environment that determines which character is chosen to represent it" (1976:105).

Granted that characters are used in Chinese for their sound values to represent foreign terms and onomatopoeia, there is nevertheless a tendency to restrict these tokens to a particular subset of the inventory. Often they are identified by affixing the "mouth" radical 口 to the left of the character, especially in the non-Mandarin Sinitic languages, such as Cantonese. Moreover, as I have already discussed, there is overwhelming pressure to reinterpret characters that began their lives as phonetic symbols in terms of the morpheme represented. While there is no disputing that the individual characters' forms consist largely of components tied in some way with sound, the identification of the units as a whole with morphemes is, I believe, beyond dispute. Since morphemes themselves are a fusion of meaning and sound, identifying the characters with morphemes does no harm to the precept that writing offer some principled connection to the sounds of the language it represents.

But there may be more to the story. Although the characters are not serving primarily as a syllabary, there is no reason to disallow the possibility that for Chinese they constitute at the same time a syllabary, albeit in DeFrancis' words, irregular and "appallingly large" (1984a:111).[8] Consider the following. Chinese characters represent morphemes, which in Chinese are one syllable long. A coincidence? I do not think so. It is more likely that under the influence of the character script, a monosyllabic morphology was imposed on the language. This outcome is just one aspect of the enormous impact of Chinese characters on the structure of the languages that have used them. But this hypothesis leads quickly to another question. If the only thing characters usually represented in Chinese were morphemes, why must the morphemes be squeezed down (reanalyzed) into single syllables? Why not have them map onto polysyllabic morphemes in Chinese as they do in Japanese? Clearly, it is because the characters, as the only system available to represent Chinese, have been forced by the canons of what DeFrancis has called "true" writing to map onto sound in a consistent fashion as well, that is, they really are working like a syllabary. A full characterization of the writing system, at least as it applies to Chinese, must take these facts into account.

Chinese Characters as Part of the Morpheme

The problem of trying to determine what Chinese characters "represent" is made worse by a lack of consensus on what the terms proposed as the objects of representation actually mean. John DeFrancis, who has spent more time studying this topic than anyone, offers several pages of examples of how prominent writers have used the terms "pictographic," "ideographic," "logographic," and "morphemic" in different ways (1989:223–226). He concludes, "Again the impression is conveyed that logographic or morphemic writing is characterized by a complete absence of any phonetic component." As we have seen, the hypothesis that Chinese characters operate even in a formal sense without sound is untenable. Yet most evidence does seem to point to morphemes as the units to which characters correspond. Could the problem be the definition of morpheme?

Much of the confusion, it seems, could be eliminated simply by using the term "morpheme" in the full sense that it is intended to convey and not as a synonym for "unit of meaning." I have argued that the notion of "units" implies that these slices of reality have been ordered by reference to an extrinsic marker, that is, the sounds of a given language. Unless a set of semantic features can be identified through something external and concrete, it floats aimlessly, cannot be manipulated in any useful manner, and is quite incapable of maintaining even its own integrity. In other words, the set must be named, which brings the construct firmly and irrevocably out of the realm of pure, unfettered thought and into one's linguistic repertoire. In acquiring a name, the construct takes on a host of other characteristics. These include, at minimum, rules governing its use within a dynamic system;[9] emotional and social values absent from the prelinguistic construct itself; and information relating to the constitution of the vocal and visual elements that cannot be specified until identification with a particular semantic set is made, such as the range of permissible variation in sound and the exact relationship between the vocal and visual signs.

Morphemes thus are neither aphonic semantic sets nor, as Hockett put it, "the smallest individually meaningful elements in the utterances of a language" (1958:123). They are the conventional interface between meaning, on the one hand, and a physical marker on the other. As such, it makes no more sense to call one or the other aspect primary than it would to so identify either side of a coin. David Reed, writing more that two decades ago, reached a similar conclusion: "Some linguists have preferred to think of linguistic forms as physical units that signify meanings that are themselves non-linguistic, and others have thought of linguistic forms as semantic units that are identified by non-linguistic physical configurations." Reed, however, regards "linguistic forms as simultaneously having semantic and physical features, neither of which is paramount" (1970:292). To him, "linguistic forms" are "links between meaning and the symbol systems of writing and speaking but not to be exclusively identified with either meaning or symbol" (1970:286).

If morphemes (Reed's "linguistic forms") are a fusion of meaning and a phonological form, there can be no question of the written symbol mapping onto anything but a linguistic unit. Identifying Chinese characters with the morphemes of a language therefore puts these symbols squarely in the mainstream of linguistic phenomena. The characters do not identify sound irrespective of meaning or aphonic mental constructs. Rather, they meet the two at their junction. The only real question is how the identification is accomplished. Do the characters represent the morphemes, or are they in some way part of them?

I have stated that a set of semantic features cannot exist as part of a language without an extrinsic marker. Humans, according to Hockett, need "some mnemonically satisfactory device for keeping morphemes apart" (1947:229). Although persuaded that this device was "probably" sound, Hockett was less committed to the proposition that it *had* to be sound. Other researchers have claimed that either sound or writing would serve in this regard, since both are physical "functions" of the same unit of content (Uldall 1944:11). Dwight Bolinger argued for the existence of "visual morphemes" which exist "independent of or interacting with the more fundamental (or at least more primitive) vocal-auditory morphemes" (1946:333). More recently, Fowler proposed that in addition to "a grammatical class, a meaning, and a phonological form," that is, the basic elements of a linguistic form, a "fourth property, the graphic form of the word" be added directly to that unit's makeup (1981:182). Goodman proposed a "complementary" relationship between "a written code and an oral code," neither being in any formal sense "primary" or representing the other (1982:53).

The formal parity of a morpheme's phonological and graphic forms is evidenced in Chinese by such facts, adduced above, as multiple readings for characters, on the one hand, and homonyms in speech, on the other. It is impossible to claim, in a formal sense, that Chinese characters are attached to meaning primarily and sound secondarily, because there are too many cases of characters with two or more readings each connected with a different meaning. The opposite claim—that sounds are the primary referent—is also untenable owing to the large number of homonyms whose meanings are distinguished in writing. Maevskiy, a Russian linguist working with Japanese, came to the same conclusion that the graphic forms *are* morphemes "and do not simply designate morphemes which exist somewhere separate from them. From [Maevskiy's] point of view, the character 雨 is a linguistic sign just as the phonetic word *ame* is; both signs, the spoken and the written, carry one and the same meaning, and both signs can be regarded as variants of one morpheme, as functionally identical elements" (1973:70).

In other words, neither the sound nor the graphic symbol represents the morpheme; instead both are part of it. The two physical markers are alternate means of identifying a semantic set, which becomes a morpheme only by adding one marker (sound) or both (sound and a graphic form). Moreover, for Chinese, Japanese, English, and all or nearly all languages that have written forms, the relationship between the written and spoken signs is established only in terms of a given morpheme. Unless one knows the meaning of a sound, one cannot write it according to the language's orthographic conventions. By the same token, removed from context, one cannot read a character correctly in Japanese or all the time in Chinese, unless the particular meaning is understood. This relationship also seems to hold for many alphabetically written languages. The reason users tolerate what would appear to be a patent disutility, that is, the impossibility of converting sound directly to writing and vice-versa, I suggest, is because of the greater clarity one realizes from providing a morpheme with an overall address that is more specific than either of its physical constituents. If only one of a form's concrete markers were available or if the one could be derived entirely from the other, too much would depend on context in distinguishing the tens of thousands of meaningful constructs in a well-developed language.

Depicting the two addresses entirely in terms of each other, in any case, is neither desirable nor possible, unless one is dealing with a very small community of speakers whose pronunciation did not vary much from person to person. One reason so-called phonetic scripts are (or become) phonemic is because by mapping onto sound at an abstract level, individual users with widely different pronunciations are all able nonetheless to identify their own concrete speech habits with a common standard. Writing, moreover, must stand alone and be comprehensible in its own terms without the paralinguistic and extralinguistic devices available to speakers. Redundancy must be added in other ways, for example, by using morphophonemic spellings, which normal sound change itself would produce. The conflicting requirements of speech and writing serve to separate the spoken and written addresses of morphemes, making their primary link the conventional one that obtains through their identification with the same unit of linguistic meaning, although the benefits of maintaining some type of causal connection between the two are obvious.

If a morpheme is invested with either a sound or a written symbol, or both, neither need be unique to the morpheme. However, their combination should be. This formulation enables us to eliminate the problem that arose earlier in this chapter of characters mapping onto more than one morpheme. If a character is viewed as *part* of the morpheme along with the sound that constitutes its phonological marker, there is no more need for that character to be restricted to one morpheme than there is for the corresponding sound to be restricted to one morpheme. 書 and *kak-* in Japanese are coequally part of one morpheme, which has the basic meaning of "write" and certain rules of grammatical association; similarly, 書 and *sho* are the extrinsic parts of another morpheme meaning "write" with different rules of grammatical association. Chinese 率 / *lù* is the physical part of a morpheme that means "rate, ratio," while 率 / *shuài* is part of a morpheme that means "to lead."

Functional support for this proposal is found in clinical and psycholinguistic studies, particularly those involving patients whose ability to access vocabulary has been impaired. Although I will treat this subject in greater detail in a later chapter, some of its findings support my line of reasoning here. Paradis et al., in their summary of the neurolinguistic aspects of Japanese writing, provide evidence for the psychological reality of the character qua morpheme and for regarding graphic forms as part of the overall linguistic construct. They reject a model for the configuration of Chinese characters in the mental lexicon in which "graphemic representations are added on to lexical entries that are already in existence at the time a child learns to read." Although such a model would allow compounds to be accessed directly, it fails to account for "the explicit knowledge that Japanese seem to have of the inherent meaning and all possible readings of most single *kanji*." It is more likely that for "the fluent reader, graphemic representations are part of general word entries, and so familiar words are accessed directly, as above" (1985:26). Paradis et al. cite pathological cases of patients suffering physical lesions who can pronounce *kanji* correctly without understanding them and others who can understand the characters' meanings without being able to offer any pronunciation. In their view, both types "demonstrate the existence of a functionally independent connection between grapheme (character shape) and sound, grapheme and meaning, and meaning and sound, each capable of being selectively impaired" (p. 166).

Deciding which of the two aspects of a morpheme's physical sign to call primary is irrelevant and probably a futile exercise, since both formally enjoy equal status with respect to the unit's meaning and to each other. Functionally, of course, there are differences. On the one hand, the written aspect typically is more specific, providing more distinctions than can be discerned in most speech environments. Its identification with meaning is more discreet, which is one argument for regarding this aspect of the sign as primary. On the other hand, the written sign—or its mental image—plays a decidedly lesser role than the sound trace in internal processing. No one thinks habitually in terms of visible signs, nor can the question be separated from the bigger issue involving the primacy of speech in language, where phonology accounts for a large part of a language's structure and necessary processes.

History does not help much here either. Although few would dispute the evolutionary precedence of speech over the written form, much of the formal part of language, including the identity of words, has depended more on writing than on speech. The same pattern is also true of acquisition by individuals: one's native language is introduced through speech and subsequently refined and expanded through visual media. The two aspects complement each other, and it makes little sense to worry about which of the two should be called primary, particularly in a formal context. One might object that any system of writing can be used to identify a morpheme—for example, Chinese characters, *pinyin, kana,* or *hangul*—

whereas the morpheme has just one sound, which should therefore be regarded as primary. But this argument also fails, for two reasons. First, writing is based on conventions that have become part of a language and part of one's mental representation of that language. Being able to transfer specimens from one writing system into another has no more relevance to the issue than being able to say a word backwards, in Pig Latin. Second, the written form is usually fixed and stable, while the spoken aspect of the sign varies enormously—synchronically, diachronically, and within individual speakers according to the social situation. When queried by another speaker on something one has said, a typical response is to spell (or, in Chinese, write out) the form in question, evidencing a broader and, arguably, more basic standard.

I am spending much time discussing what for all intents should be a nonissue not because of any great confusion in the facts or in how these facts relate to each other. Rather, the whole primacy argument seems to stem from two different views of language: a mechanistic view that looks at language from the ground up in terms of sound and a mentalistic approach that puts meaning first and regards the concrete elements through which meaning is expressed as of less importance. Since writing typically maps onto language between these extremes, both schools interpret its role in terms of their own prejudices, either as a secondary tool for expressing "sounds" or as an instrument of "pure" thought. In fact, neither view is accurate. Acknowledging that Chinese characters represent (or are) morphemes does not require partisans of the former view to abandon language, although the early, structuralist identification of abstract language with concrete speech sounds clearly will not suffice. Conversely, aficionados of writing and of Chinese characters in particular should leave their fantasy world and accept that these written symbols, whatever else they may do, are inextricably tied to the phonology that leads to speech and derive historically from the concrete sounds that manifest language.

The conclusion to be drawn here is that formally Chinese characters have no unique extralinguistic features, and claims to this effect are empty. The symbols are neither pictures that represent reality by mimicking its physical characteristics, nor (one step removed) ideograms depicting aphonic universal concepts. Like all other writing systems, they are an alternate means of expressing spoken languages. Faced with the need to record their ideas and transmit them through distance and time, East Asians took the path taken by every literate culture and tapped into natural language, on which their writing system fully depends.

What distinguishes Chinese character writing from others is the level at which this mapping relationship takes place. While they are largely dependent on sound for their physical shapes, the characters' precise relationship to sound is mediated by the meaning of the symbol as a whole. But is this so unusual? We have seen that English spelling and probably all alphabetic writing in principle is also based on the meaning of the larger unit over which the rules apply. It is neither possible nor, for reasons already given, even desirable that the spoken and written representations be entirely derivable from each other. All that need happen for the system to function is for the totality of the construct—the meaning set and its two representations together—to be unique.

One might ask, if the two types of writing systems work similarly (on this level of analysis), what hidden advantages do Chinese characters offer to compensate for the greater number of principal units one must master? Or to phrase the question differently, what does the user gain by being unable to apply his or her knowledge of one medium to make reasonably accurate inferences about the constitution of the other? The short answer is, nothing. Chinese writing, lacking a systematic relationship between symbol and sound, or even an efficient protocol for describing the structure of its units, places an enormous burden on the user in comparison to alphabetic systems.[10] Later I shall address arguments that attempt to justify this burden in linguistic terms. Although these claims will be disputed, they take place within the framework of linguistics and hence can be reasonably (if wrongly) entertained. What cannot be taken seriously are misguided attempts to invest Chinese characters with formal qualities that place them outside the realm of language and hence beyond criticism based in linguistics.

6. Learning and Literacy

IF OPINIONS ARE MIXED on what Chinese characters represent, they are also divided on their usefulness as a tool of learning. Westerners who have studied languages that use Chinese characters are typically put off by the need to learn thousands of symbols simply to read and write a language. In their view, mastering a separate sign for each basic concept wastes time that could be spent acquiring substantive knowledge. Instead of using language to learn, East Asians are wasting their youth and resources learning about language. Notwithstanding their efforts, the system's inherent difficulties predispose those societies using Chinese characters to low literacy rates and other maladies, especially among the young, who are expected nowadays to become literate in spite of it all. Creativity is snuffed out by the task of memorizing endless rules that lead nowhere. Science fails to take root. Liberal ideals are lost on the mass of people whose reading skills are inadequate and who have been conditioned by the writing system's difficulty into believing that the minority able to master Chinese characters is also better able to govern.

While a few East Asians might agree with these criticisms, most would wonder what the fuss is about. Are not several of the countries that use Chinese characters world models for literacy, technical expertise, and economic development? Conversely, are illiteracy, dropping out of school, teenage suicide, alienation, conformity, intellectual stagnation, and political despotism unknown among the alphabet users of the West? Many East Asians would also argue that the difficulty of learning Chinese characters is exaggerated both absolutely and relative to English with its chaotic spellings. Chinese characters presented as undifferentiated blocks may appear numerous and complex, but the number of characters needed in practice is limited to a few thousand, and these are made up of only a few hundred repeating components. Learning these components is a simple task for someone growing up in an environment where they are seen everywhere. Moreover, the high learning curve means less effort is required to master subsequent accretions. Mastering an alphabet gives one knowledge of two or three dozen symbols and not a clue about the language's vocabulary. Investing in Chinese characters, in contrast, gives the user important information about how the language structures meaning, which makes acquisition of high-level vocabulary a relatively easy task. Far from being an obstacle to literacy, the characters, by this argument, give East Asians an inside track to learning.

A third view, which helps explain how such widely divergent interpretations can be held at all, claims that a writing system itself has little effect on literacy and learning by comparison with other factors such as motivation and access to learning resources. This claim is undoubtedly correct and, coupled with the near impossibility of defining, measuring, and comparing literacy across cultures, frustrates any results-oriented approach to evaluating Chinese characters as a learning tool. The problem must be studied from the inside out, as it were, by examining what the characteristics of the system logically imply for its functioning and utility. Accordingly, this chapter begins by addressing the basic question of "how many of what" must be studied to master Chinese character–based writing. We will then consider how the learning task is influenced by these requirements and how this task in turn *may* affect literacy overall. Finally, we will examine the important theory that learning the language's morphemes qua characters gives East Asians a leg up on students schooled in alphabetic scripts.

Some Preliminary Considerations

How many Chinese characters must be learned to achieve literacy? The question seems simple enough, particularly to users of alphabetic scripts, whose experience predisposes them to imagine the East Asian systems as finite, albeit large, sets of units. In fact there are at least three variables framed in this apparently innocuous question, any one of which frustrates a clear-cut answer.

The first problem we encounter is specifying literacy in what. One would think, at the very least, the focus could be narrowed to "literacy in Chinese," or "literacy in Korean," but even here the boundaries are nebulous. Japanese, by assigning indigenous words (*kun* readings) to Chinese characters, have over the centuries come to think of a large part of the character set as their own. A mechanism exists in theory, if not always in practice, for Japanese to distinguish characters that are part of the Japanese writing system from those used in Chinese and Korean. There is, however, no such mechanism for Korean. In Korean, Chinese characters designate only borrowed Sinitic vocabulary. Even though this accounts for more than half of the lexicon, use of the characters exclusively with Sinitic loanwords has caused Koreans to regard the characters as foreign and not part of their linguistic heritage, despite half a dozen good arguments that can be made to the contrary.

Paradoxically, this failure to "adopt" Chinese characters as their own coupled with the absence of any technical device (such as *kun*) to identify particular characters as part of the Korean set have left the entire stock of characters used *in* Chinese open to Korean writers, who have no reliable standard for distinguishing what is Chinese from what is properly Korean. More important, the mentality for making this distinction is not there: it is all foreign, so why draw a line? The characters, in a sense, are a direct pipeline into the Chinese language, a feature that has annoyed Korean scholars on both sides of the fence, including reformers eager to implement an all-*hangul* script and conservatives trying to limit character use in Korean writing to enhance its viability.

What of the Chinese language itself? Surely concrete boundaries exist here? But it raises another set of problems. Unlike English, which in its spoken forms can be segregated into mutually intelligible dialects, what passes for "Chinese" today in fact are a half dozen or more mutually unintelligible languages. Each of these Sinitic languages has its own unique system of phonological contrasts, important grammatical distinctions, and, most significantly for the present discussion, large lexical differences as well. Although English dialects vary in word choice, too, the differences have no immediate impact on the writing system. Words are still spelled with the same twenty-six letters. In Chinese, however, differences in vocabulary (morphemes) translate directly into different characters, which, depending on the language, can number in the hundreds. One can eliminate (ignore) the problem of "dialect characters," as the Chinese and Taiwan governments currently do, by restricting the definition of "Chinese" and the characters that go with it to one of the recognized standards, namely, the Northern variety centered on Beijing. But these unique, language-specific characters are just the tip of the iceberg. Here is why.

Non-Mandarin Sinitic languages typically preserve aspects of the ancient language lost in the current Beijing standard. This conservatism may apply less to vocabulary than to other parts of the language, particularly in a language like Shanghainese, whose eighty million speakers populate one of China's most dynamic economic and cultural regions, and who bring this spirit of innovation into their language.[1] In many cases, however, the non-Mandarin Chinese languages make more liberal use than spoken Mandarin of morphemes that have roots in the older literary standard, for which recognized characters already exist. While marginal or nonexistent in the Beijing speech of today, these morphemes did have a role in the language that preceded the national standard and still do in the minds of a few hundred million speakers who acquire Mandarin as a second language. For both of these reasons, characters used with these morphemes cannot be separated from the national standard as readily as characters devised solely for a particular non-Mandarin language (which are often based directly on the sounds of that language). They remain part of the standard repertoire or, more accurately, achieve more centrality in the written standard than they would in Mandarin-based writing alone, adding to the number of characters in the inventory.

What is true on the synchronic level is even more of a problem diachronically. Old English words have strange spellings. If the words are very old, they are not English. They are Latin, Greek, or indigenous terms whose original forms can only be hypothesized by specialists. No present user of English feels obligated to learn the old forms of these words as part of his or her synchronic lexicon, much less the ancient languages of which these words were a part. The distinction between present and past states of the language is fairly clear. This is not true of Chinese, at least insofar as the units of its writing system are concerned. Being shielded for the most part from the visible effects of sound change, Chinese characters come down through the centuries intact, giving the false impression that the language itself is little changed. Anyone who has tried to read ancient texts knows better: characters have different meanings, and the syntax is scarcely recognizable. But the characters, or many of them, are at least recognizable and have known meanings and pronunciations in their present-day usage.

The apparent continuity between the present and earlier states of Chinese is reinforced in practice by the insatiable penchant Chinese have for using aphorisms, whole phrases, and literary allusions from the past. If this is true of Chinese speech, the tendency of Chinese to imitate earlier styles in writing is stronger than most Westerners, including many of those schooled in the language, can imagine. For example, I recently reviewed a Chinese proficiency exam administered to people whose business involves frequent use of the language. The reading part of the exam consisted of five "contemporary" passages. The first two were fairly straightforward. The third passage was a reprint of an essay by the late Qing–early Republican era intellectual Yan Fu (1853–1921), written decades before the modern vernacular movement had started. I was able to read it in the few minutes given because I had, by coincidence, studied Yan Fu as an undergraduate and remembered the passage. When I asked the native Chinese examiners why it had been included in a test of modern Chinese, I was told it had reappeared in an issue of *People's Daily*. The fourth selection, as nearly as I could tell, was a eulogy written by a literary critic in memory of a deceased poet. The less said about it the better. I am still trying to figure out what the fifth passage meant. No one I have spoken to seems to know, either. This, I repeat, constitutes the core of a *modern* Chinese proficiency exam given to people whose salaries and careers depend in part on how well they score.

The inability of Chinese writers to distinguish clearly between modern and premodern states of the language, which, I argue, is a product of the character writing system, was identified early on by such proponents of writing reform as Lu Xun (1881–1936) and Hu Shi (1891–1962). These same reformers seem to have been unaware how much their own writings were influenced by the stylistic patterns about which they complained. In order to demonstrate their erudition to peers or to claim the authority of tradition, Chinese writers must search for the "right" character or phrase with the exact nuance of meaning, even if it means using forms whose currency is questionable. If you want to embellish a text, you need to enrich its vocabulary. And in a writing system based more on morphemes than on words, this means using more characters. There is no way in principle to avoid it, and given the lack of any clear, sound-based distinction between past and present usage, there is no reason to avoid reaching into the language's history to resurrect forms that other languages would have left dead.

Assuming one can identify the language under consideration, the second question we need to confront in determining the number of characters required is, literacy in what field? Chinese pharmacology? Korean history? Japanese literary criticism? The question is relevant, because unlike in an alphabetic systems, where the vocabulary of different areas of knowledge is spelled out with a few dozen repeating elements, counts of Chinese characters "in use" vary widely according to the types of materials surveyed. Concepts and artifacts peculiar to particular areas frequently require their own characters.[2] Although compounding and semantic reinterpretation handle much of the burden, expansion of knowledge entails a concomitant growth in the number of morphemes used to express that knowledge. As long as Sinitic morphemes are monosyllabic, there is no theoretical limit to how far the inventory of characters can expand. Granted, no one needs to be literate in all fields of knowledge. Nor does an alphabetic script absolve its users from the need to learn vocabulary. Both of these objections, however, are beside the point in terms of the present inquiry, which is aimed at determining the number of primary orthographic units a user must learn to access vocabulary that is available through speech with no additional investment in the mechanics of speech.

A third conceptual problem in determining the parameters of character-based literacy is the fact that character "learning" is rarely a black and white issue, either in terms of a user's ability to remember given units or in the types of skills one needs to function adequately. These problems are not wholly shared by users of alphabetic scripts, even by readers and writers of English, where bizarre spelling rules put learners at a disadvantage relative to what is needed for other phonemic systems.[3] To begin with, people rarely forget the individual letter forms of an alphabet. The set is small, and the units constantly repeat. Although spelling can be problematic, written forms can generally be coded with some accuracy and decoded with great reliability, from or into something recognizable in speech. The two types of skills are complementary and mutually reinforcing. This is hardly true of Chinese characters. Although hints about a character's pronunciation can sometimes be obtained from its phonetic component (if the character has one and it can be identified), the process is hit-or-miss.

More important, it works only one way in Chinese, when it works at all: knowledge of a morpheme's pronunciation cannot be used to produce the corresponding written form or even a part of it. Thus, assuming one already has command over the substructures that make up most characters ("radicals," phonetics, and hundreds of other elements), there is little or nothing available from speech to instruct the user in how to assemble these components. The units of the two media, written and spoken, are only marginally coordinated. There is very little mutual reinforcement, which means that characters, once learned, are easily forgotten or can be recalled only in part, for example, the meaning is remembered but not the pronunciation, or vice-versa, or something is remembered that may approximate the pronunciation. Or the shape of the character is forgotten entirely.

These problems afflict all users of Chinese character–based scripts, even those highly educated, to an extent that is difficult for literate people operating outside that tradition to appreciate.[4] It is not enough, therefore, to speak of the number of characters that need to be "learned," when the learning that takes place is so marginal by comparison with what is achieved for less effort with alphabetic scripts. This gap is especially noticeable in productive skills. Ignoring the separate question of production in the languages per se and focusing only on the mechanical ability to reproduce written units, it is generally expected that when users of alphabetic scripts learn to recognize a word they will also be able to write it. There is no deliberate pedagogical distinction made between the two skills. Not so in China, Japan, and Korea. Educators, acknowledging the difference between being able to recognize x number of characters and being able to reproduce the forms from memory, have prudently opted to focus on the former skill and maximize return on the time invested. "Literacy" is not viewed so much as the ability to read and write one's language as it is just the ability to read it.

Effects of Inventory Size on Literacy

The above factors—the system's theoretical open-endedness, the difficulty of specifying where one language ends and the other begins, the marginal value of many characters to their users, and the limited degree to which many characters are learned—account for the disparity in estimates of Chinese characters "in use." Still, some attempt must be made to describe the learning task in figures, and a good place to begin is by tracing the growth of the system through time.

Inscribed bones and shell markings dating from the latter part of the second millennium B.C., show about 2,500 distinct graphs, 1,400 of which have been identified as precursors of later forms (Coulmas 1989:92). In A.D. 100, China's first known dictionary, the *Shuōwén jiězi*, was compiled; its 9,350 characters represent nearly a fourfold increase in the size of the inventory over some 1,500 years. By 1716, 1,600 years later, the compilers of the *Kāngxī zìdiǎn* saw fit to record 49,030 characters in what became the standard Chinese dictionary for more than two centuries. If 1,995 variant forms are omitted, the total stands at 47,035 different characters, another fivefold increase over the same period of time. Wieger's view that 34,000 of these are "monstrosities of no practical use" (1915:7) apparently was not shared by lexicographers who compiled the *Chung-hua Ta-tzu-tien (Zhōnghuá dàzìdiǎn)* in 1916, which contained some 48,000 characters "including a great many which have been invented since the *Kāngxī zìdiǎn* was compiled" (Teng and Biggerstaff 1971:131). The *Chung-wen Ta-tz'u-tien (Zhōngwén dàcídiǎn)*, which appeared in thirty-eight volumes between 1962 and 1968, held the record at 49,905 characters until eclipsed by the recent appearance in the People's Republic of China of *Hànyǔ dàzìdiǎn* which has nearly 60,000 entries. Estimates of the total number of Chinese characters ever used from antiquity to present (including variants and "dialect" characters, but not the Vietnamese *chữ nôm* characters, which fall outside that tradition) range up to 80,000 (Samuel Martin 1972:83).

These enormous figures are cited to illustrate that there is no theoretical limit to the number of primary units in the character writing system. Moreover, nothing in principle prevents Chinese writers from reaching back into history to use these characters when the need or whim arises. Of course, practical limits do exist, as evidenced by the necessity for publishers to establish limited character fonts.[5] These are the best guide to the number of Chinese characters "in use," since the publishers operate under market incentive. Commercial codes, industrial standards, entries in modern dictionaries, material surveys, and expert estimates are also useful in determining the size of the current inventory. Chinese, which uses a greater number of characters than Japanese or Korean, will be examined first in Table 3.

Eliminating the high (9,312) and low (4,250) figures in Table 3 gives a simple average of 6,904 characters, which falls within the 6,000 to 7,000 span that Zhou considers "the natural limit of human memory of logographs" (1991:7). This figure represents the number of characters generally in use in Chinese society as a whole, subject to the limitations described above. Of course, "literacy" means different things to different individuals, whose needs and tastes vary. My best estimate, based on two and a half decades of dealing with the language that began with a meticulous count of all new accretions, is that a passive knowledge of 4,500 characters, or two-thirds the number "in use," allows readers to get through most types of materials, although proper names can still be a headache. So-called common use characters, which have a legitimate role in pedagogy, should not be confused with the number "in use" or even with the number of characters needed for literacy. The fact that a smaller number of frequently used characters accounts for 98 or 99 percent of a character text still means the reader must consult a dictionary four or five

Table 3
Characters Currently Used in Chinese

Number	Source
6,807	PRC's 1965 standard font (modified)[1] (Chen Mingyuan 1981:43)
6,000–7,000	Average kept by printers in PRC (Zheng Linxi 1955:22)
7,500	Maximum kept by printers in Taiwan (ibid.)
6,763	PRC national standard GB2312-80[2] (Liu Yongquan 1991:10)
5,401	Taiwan's *Standard Exchange Code for Characters in Use*[3] (Zhou 1987b:11)
7,000	PRC's "Table of Characters in Contemporary Use"[4] (Ohara 1989:143)
7,773	*Mathews' Chinese-English Dictionary*[5] (Harvard University Press)
7,000–8,000	Average for twenty popular dictionaries (Zhou 1961:327)
7,000	Xīnhuá zìdián. (PRC, 1971) (Zhou 1987:11)
7,331	*A New Practical Chinese-English Dictionary* (Liang, ed., Taiwan, 1971)
8,085	PRC's *Standard Telegraphic Code*
9,312	Taiwan's *Chinese Telegraphic Code*
4,250	Survey of materials[6] (Liu Shih-hong 1969:46–47)
6,000	Survey of materials[7] (Kim Min-su 1973:326)
6,400	Survey of materials[8] (Lin Lianhe 1980:135)
6,000–7,000	Estimate by Karlgren (1949:14)
7,000	Estimate by Zhou (1987:22)

[1] Jointly designated by the Chinese Committee on Writing Reform and the Ministry of Culture. The list originally had 6,197 characters but publishers suggested an addendum of 610 characters for scientific vocabulary.

[2] "Code of Chinese Graphic Character Set for Information Exchange (Basic Set)," issued by the National Bureau of Standards in 1981. Supplementary sets of "special use characters" add another 14,276 characters to that number, for a total of 21,039 characters.

[3] An additional 7,650 "secondary use" characters bring the total to 13,051.

[4] Published in 1988 jointly by the National Committee for Language and Script Work (successor to the Chinese Committee on Writing Reform) and the National Office of Newspaper Publishers.

[5] Revised in March 1943. Originally R. H. Mathews, *A Chinese-English Dictionary Compiled for the China Inland Mission* (Shanghai, 1931). Variant forms of the "same" character are not counted.

[6] Liu cites counts done on a wide range of materials in 1920 and 1930.

[7] Kim is summarizing the results of "a dozen or more counts" on Chinese from the 1920s to 1970s.

[8] Based on a sample of 21,660,000 characters taken in 1976 from materials on politics, literature, art, science, and technology.

times for each page. This level of knowledge constitutes literacy of a very limited sort.

Estimates of the number needed for an "active" command over the writing system, defined as the ability to write a symbol from memory for the morpheme one intends, are meaningless. On the one hand, the figure is more idiosyncratic than for reading, since a writer's production is apt to reflect personal tastes even more than what the same person reads. Whereas many people read for pleasure and their choices encompass a variety of genres, most people do not write any more than they have to, in any culture. When they do write, themes generally are limited to the requirements of one's profession, and the content to a large degree is driven (without the writer necessarily being aware of it) by what one knows how to write.

On the other hand, the number of characters a Chinese "must" be able to write equals the number of characters in use, in the same sense that writers of English must be able to produce (by hand or by finding the right key) each letter of the alphabet. Both constitute the primary units that must be handwritten or keyed in the respective systems. One might call this comparison unfair, since the units represent different levels of language—phonemes and morphemes—but that misses the point. In the present context, only two types of units can be significantly compared. One is the number of basic symbols writers must be able to produce to have control over the inventory. The Chinese figure can be reduced by defining components of characters, instead of whole characters, as the graphemes of the system, but only at the cost of adding rules that specify how these components combine for each character. And unlike alphabetic scripts, where rules governing the assembly of letters duplicate in principle the sound of the larger unit, little or no such outside knowledge is available to tell the person who wants to write a character how many of which components go where. Knowing which rules get applied in what order to assemble which of a thousand or more components, but not being able to derive this information from larger linguistic facts means that the focus is still on primary units—6,900 of them.

The other comparison that can be made is on the level of words. Here spelling rules must be added to the twenty-six physical forms to account for the competence one needs to write in an alphabetic script. Does this mean the character user enjoys an advantage, since only some 6,900 forms are needed, in comparison to ten times that number to accommodate the lexical units of a language written alphabetically? Not unless one wishes to maintain—against common sense and the existence of seventy-thousand-plus-entry *pinyin* Chinese word dictionaries—that the size of the Chinese lexicon is coterminous with the number of characters. Characters, as I have pointed out, represent or are morphemes, which can be words but more commonly are parts of words. This fact is lost on many people because written Chinese lacks overt markers for word division. But the words are there, buried in the text, and if that is so then there must be, as in alphabetically written languages, rules for assembling the primary units into words, that is, "spelling" conventions in Chinese, too. Although almost never couched in those terms, a person writing in Chinese can no more write *和適 *héshì* for the word 合適 *héshì* than an English writer can write *sootable* for *suitable*. Both languages, English and Chinese, require users to memorize rules for the production of written lexical items that are word-specific and cannot be generated from a knowledge of the word's sound alone. It is hard to see any advantage Chinese offers here to compensate the writer for having to learn how to form some 265 times as many basic symbols.

This numerical disparity, already quite large, is multiplied by stylistic variants. Many alphabets use uppercase and lowercase letters, both printed and cursive. Thus, strictly speaking, students of English must master 104 different forms, some twenty of which (about ten letters in each style) differ from the other case in size only. Although Chinese has no equivalent for the uppercase and lowercase distinction, there are two cursive styles—*xíngshū* ("running" style) and *cǎoshū* ("grass" style)—which are used today for all but the most formal types of writing.[6] The two cursive styles actually form the boundaries of a continuum, with the "running" style distinguished from the standard *(kǎishū)* printed style by connecting strokes that are kept apart in the standard, and the "grass" style, as its name implies, continuing this same tendency while eliminating whole components besides.

In English, the shape of cursive letters can vary, depending on their immediate environment. The variation, however, affects only fifty-two elements, and the brevity of the letters limits the scope of personal creativity. In Chinese, many times that number of units are affected, and given their original complexity, the margin for innovation is substantial. Not all characters have both cursive forms, and not all cursive forms are necessarily based on the same standard character, in either its traditional or its simplified form. Moreover, the replacement of character parts is not always one-to-one. A printed component may have several cursive equivalents, or vice-versa. Although many dozens of rules can be used to describe these relationships, in the final analysis a given character's cursive forms are peculiar to the individual character, which is another strong argument for treating characters—not components—as the system's primary units. On the concrete level, the real task Chinese face is learning how to form and recognize an inventory of shapes that more than doubles the number of characters in use, a task not appreciably eased by conversion rules that apply across the system.

There is more to it. Although Chinese has no equivalent to uppercase and lowercase letters, it does have two sets of printed forms, one "traditional" and the other "simplified" (see Chapter 9). In an effort to relieve some of the burden of writing, the government of the People's Republic of China three decades ago sanctioned a list of 2,236 simplified replacements for the traditional *kǎishū* forms previously regarded as standard. Since many characters in this "First Batch" of simplifications corresponded to cursive forms already in use, much of the reform simply amounted to approving some existing shapes and abolishing their more complex equivalents. Other simplifications, however, either lacked a well-established precedent or were made out of whole cloth, with the result that people trained entirely in one system became unable to read materials written in the other. This outcome does not impede literacy in any one country, but it is a problem for a growing number of people whose circumstances require that they read both systems, including many Chinese overseas and those engaged in international business.

In terms of unique shapes, the ratio of forms to be learned in English and Chinese thus stands at about 80 to well over 10,000, offset by the fact that some fraction of the 6,900 or so characters in use represent "free" morphemes or words. It doesn't seem like much of a bargain.

How do Japanese and Korean shape up? Here other considerations apply, beginning with the important fact that both languages "mix" the characters with their own all-phonetic scripts or, in Korean, can ignore the characters altogether. The result is fewer characters "in use." That said, it should be mentioned again that character use in both languages, depending on the types of materials and editorial policy, can jump well above the normal figures cited below. The theoretical limit is represented by the number of entries in large *kanwa* (Chinese to Japanese) or Korean *hanja* (Chinese character) dictionaries. Although these are nominally bilingual dictionaries, they are not strictly viewed this way.

The numbers in Table 4 yield a simple average of 3,120 characters "in use" in Japanese, less than half the number used in Chinese. The figure grows in sources that are deliberately exhaustive. For example, the Japan Industrial standard (JIS) adds a "second tier" of 3,388 characters, bringing the total to 6,353. Again, this is roughly half the 13,051 characters included in the two tiers of Taiwan's *Standard Exchange Code for Characters in Use,* which is a comparable compendium. Ueda Kazutoshi's *Daijiten* (Tokyo, 1971), which lists characters that are identifiably part of Japanese, has 14,924 entries, or fewer than half the number recorded by the largest Chinese dictionaries.

Although the number of characters "in use" in Japanese is half that of Chinese, getting by in Japanese seems to require mastering a higher proportion of that inventory. I find 4,500, or two-thirds, of the characters in use in Chinese adequate for most reading in that language but I need most of the 3,100 characters "in use" for comparable reading in Japanese. This is probably because marginal characters used in Chinese for low-frequency terms that the reader rarely needs correspond in Japanese to indigenous vocabulary normally written in *kana.* Proportionately more use is made of the characters that are used in Japanese.

Table 4
Characters Currently Used in Japanese

Number	Source
3,542	Okazaki (1938:62)[1]
2,935	*Kojien* (rev. ed., 1969)[2]
3,505	Saiga (1971:104–105)
3,000	Suzuki (1975:178)
3,213–3,328	Kondo (1977:118)
3,000	Sasanuma et al. (1977:547)
3,200	Kato (1979:66)
3,000–4,000	Sokolov (1981:17)
3,000	Ono (1982:65)
2,300–2,500	Matsuda (1985:37)
2,965	JIS Kanji Code (Ohara 1989:144)

Note: Figures are based on counts or expert estimates except where noted.

[1] Okazaki's figure is based on a sample of 447,000 characters that appeared in five Tokyo and Osaka newspapers. Season of the year and types of news were taken into account in making selections. While indicative of prewar usage, the figure falls far short of the seven to eight thousand characters Coulmas (1983:188) reports were available fo use in pre-1946 Japanese newspapers. The gap helps illustrate the thesis that the number of characters "in use" means different things to Japanese and Koreans than it does to Chinese. Both of the former, especially Koreans, have access to the entire Chinese lexicon, which allows potential use to skyrocket. Conversely, neither of the former, Koreans in particular, *must* use the characters, so actual use is held to half or less the number needed for literacy in Chinese. Koreans and Japanese in principle can choose between writing a word in characters or writing it in the indigenous phonetic script. Chinese choose between writing a word in characters or not writing it at all.

[2] Shinmura Izuchi, ed. (Tokyo: Iwanami Shoten). This is the standard Japanese-language word dictionary, equivalent in status to *Webster's Third International.* Entries are in *kana.* A chart of 2,935 characters "in use" is appended.

Figures for character use in Korean are harder to calculate. They range from zero to many thousands, depending on how the situation is viewed. To begin with, unlike Japanese, who are expected to write the characters they read, most Koreans once out of school can go through the rest of their lives without writing a single character. For example, I once went into a post office in Seoul with a registered letter addressed in Chinese characters to send to Taiwan. Procedure required that the address be copied by a clerk into a ledger, something neither the person serving me nor any of his coworkers could manage.

This story is typical of what one finds in Korea today. Highly educated Koreans, unless they have undergone special training in Chinese or in their own *hanmun* tradition, are often embarrassed when asked to write Chinese characters. It is not a natural act. If you write the character first, a Korean will generally recognize it, be able to pass judgment on it, add a stroke or two, or, having been prompted, rewrite the character in what he or she thinks is the correct form. Generating the character from scratch, however, is another matter. Rather than an indictment of present orthographic practice, the ability of Koreans to excel in today's competitive world without writing Chinese characters is a clear tribute to the superiority of the *hangul* script and speaks for its potential to replace the mixed script entirely in the South, as it already has in the North.

What about reading Korean? Here the problem gets tricky. It was thought for decades that North Korea had abandoned Chinese characters entirely, since they do not appear in any of that country's publications, including even sophisticated technical works where Sinitic terms predominate. As discussed in Chapter 3, we now know that the ability to read all-*hangul* texts is enhanced by latent familiarity with some three thousand Chinese characters, reintroduced into the North Korean educational system, among other reasons, to help readers get a better psychological grip on the phonetically impoverished Sinitic terms that account for so much of the language's higher-level vocabulary. Dismissed by supporters of the mixed script as "false *hangul*," the practice of using a knowledge of Chinese characters to assist in reading all-*hangul* texts makes it nearly impossible to count characters in use, since the characters are "in use" but on a different level. "Use" also takes on a different meaning in the context of South Korean materials, particularly newspapers, which print a Chinese character for the first appearance of a word or morpheme and *hangul* for all subsequent appearances, or vice-versa, allowing the reader to associate the two even though one may have had no prior exposure to the character.

Of course, one can count actual appearances of characters and cite expert estimates, as we have done for the other languages. The numbers in Table 5 average out to about 2,100 characters, some 1,000 fewer than in Japanese. This is only 300 characters more than the 1,800 taught in South Korean schools, which in conjunction with their all-phonetic *hangul* option arguably prepares people better for life in society than the Japanese system does, where the gap between the number taught and that needed (1,945 versus 3,100) is much greater. The negative side is that, lacking any overt device for identifying Korean characters as such, the number used in some specialized works can run up rather quickly, from the several thousand characters used in Korean history texts to a theoretical limit represented by Chang Sam-sik's *Tae Han-Han sajon* (Large Chinese-Korean Dictionary, revised edition, Seoul, 1975) of 41,386 characters, each of which is duly glossed with a Sino-Korean pronunciation!

Table 5
Characters Currently Used in Korean

Number	Source
2,000	1967 newspaper publishers' guideline
under 2,000	Pak Chong-so (1968:104)
1,500–2,000	Nam Kwang-u (1970:7)
2,503	Survey by Nam (1979:8)
2,364	Survey by Yi Yong-baek (1979:196)

The purpose of this chapter is to provide an "inside-out" look at how East Asian character-based writing may be affecting literacy. We are now able to make a preliminary judgment on the basis of two factors: innate complexity, as determined by the number of primary units, and the extent to which the features of the writing system match one's experience with the spoken language. The assessment will be meaningful only if expressed in comparative terms.

Alphabets typically use about two dozen units arranged serially. In the best of circumstances, each unit maps onto a particular phoneme that makes up part of a word's underlying phonological representation. The phonetic realization of each letter-phoneme is determined by applying a limited number of rules based on effects generated by the immediate phonetic environment, rules that are known to every native speaker. In the worst case—probably English—the twenty-six or so letters have multiple sound equivalents, and the number of rules governing the relationship increases. Nevertheless, there are severe constraints on what sounds a given letter can represent. Equally important, the progression of letters and phonemes follows the same serial order. Although the exact relationship between writing and sound is determined at the word level, the letter-to-sound correspondence is generally close enough to allow minimally trained readers to pronounce unfamiliar written words with great accuracy and to spell unfamiliar words with enough accuracy for communication. The "fit" between the two media is fairly close.

Chinese characters, as we have seen, number somewhere between two and seven thousand, depending on the language and on one's personal requirements. Their relationship to the sounds of the language are highly irregular. Although a practiced reader can sometimes postulate a sound for an unfamiliar character that may approximate the correct sound in speech, the connection, where there is one, is based on syllables, that is, phoneme combinations. Nowhere do the components of a character offer any hint—in their structure or layout within the character—as to what the phonemes of the sound might be or the order in which they progress. In terms of the relationship between symbol and sound, the reader, at the very best, is dealing with a large and cumbersome syllabary. The basic level on which the match between speech and writing occurs is higher than in an alphabet, meaning that the advantage to be gained through transitivity between the two media is diminished. In *writing* characters, the gain one gets from being able to speak the language approaches zero.

Put simply, in terms of number of units, the figures speak for themselves. In terms of the connection between writing and speech, the difference between English and Chinese is the difference between a principled and an unprincipled mess.

Hidden Structure as a Mitigating Factor

Besides these direct measures of complexity—the number of units and proximity to speech—several other factors peculiar to Chinese characters affect the relative ease or difficulty with which the system is learned. I have said there is no connection between the number, shape, and ordering of a character's components and the phonemes that make up the character's sound. In the preceding chapter I also laid to rest the myth that Chinese characters in and of themselves provide any patent indication of what they mean. In the final analysis, the individual character as a whole is the only reliable guide one has to the sound and meaning of the morpheme represented.[7]

I do not mean to deny that the characters have structure and that much of it is motivated. Were this not true, the system could not have been created, much less be learned. A good deal of this structure is or was patterned after sounds, a fact that not only grounds the system in the mainstream of orthographic development, but also provides a link to speech without which the system would be unmanageable for most humans. This function is achieved through "phonetic" elements, which are found in about 85 percent of all characters and account for most of the system's hidden structure. There are also so-called radicals ("signifiers," "aphonic determinatives," or in Chinese *bùshǒu*, lit. "head components"), which play a very limited role in identifying what category of meaning the morpheme was thought to belong to at one time. How does this structure facilitate learning?

The first point to keep in mind in answering this question is that "motivated" is not the same as "useful." It is one thing to note that such-and-such a combination of strokes appears in more than one character with the same or a similar sound, or with some common semantic attribute. It is quite another to assert that the user perceives the connection or for that matter even identifies the structure. What is evident to the specialist engrossed in these details may escape the user's attention entirely. This is all the more likely when specialists themselves cannot agree on what constitutes a given character's "radical" or "phonetic" (if the character has either), or for that matter on how many radicals and phonetics there are.

Assuming that some kind of agreement exists between users and lexicographers on what a radical or a phonetic looks like, and assuming further that this knowledge can be related to salient facts about the language, the next obstacle is locating these elements. Certain "rules" facilitate the task. If the character can be dissected into two familiar components, one on the left or top and the other on the right or bottom, chances are they constitute the radical and phonetic, respectively. Which means a character like 切 (qiē, "to cut"), made up of two repeating elements 七 and 刀, has its radical on the left and its phonetic on the right? No, it's the other way around. The 月 "moon" or "flesh" (which one is it?) on the left of 騰 (téng, "to leap") is its radical? Wrong again. It's 馬, the "horse" below and to the right. How about 麻 (má, "hemp")? Surely 广 (radical no. 53), which is both over it and to the left is the radical, leaving two "trees" 林, pronounced lín, as the phonetic? Sorry! The whole thing is a radical (no. 211). Come to think of it, which 木 in 林 is the radical? An irrelevant question; the character means "forest" and quite obviously is a "compound ideographic" character, which has no phonetic element, anyway.

The game could be continued for many pages. Just how many pages is suggested by a chart in the back of Mathews' Chinese-English Dictionary that lists 830 "characters having obscure radicals," from an inventory of 7,773. That is, 11 percent of the time the radicals are "obscure" by a lexicographer's standard. What about the poor stiff using the system? Andrew Nelson in his widely used Japanese-English Character Dictionary tries to reduce some of the guesswork by reassigning different radicals to characters, within the framework of the Kangxi 214 radical system, and ends up moving "about 12 percent of the characters . . . out of their traditional places" (1962:9). Notwithstanding his more "logical" arrangement, an enormous amount of space is taken up in the dictionary by dummy entries that refer the user, who looked it up the old way, or his or her own way, to the "proper" entry. The point in all of this is, if you cannot find the "radical" (and by extension, the phonetic) when you are looking for it in a dictionary, how much benefit for learning or actual use do you get from the connections these components are supposed to have to the language? Discovering (or postulating) relationships does not mean they are being used.

If these remarks apply to recurring elements in general, they apply most strongly to radicals. Nothing illustrates their essential arbitrariness better than tracing their course through time. In Shuōwén jiězi (A.D. 100), 540 radicals or allegedly meaning-bearing elements were identified. When the Kāiyuán wénzi was published in 753, the number of radicals so identified had fallen to 320. Now if these elements are truly part of characters because of what they mean or imply, how can they just disappear? By 1615 when *Cíhǎi* was first compiled and a century later when the "standard" *Kāngxī zìdiǎn* appeared, the number had fallen still further to 214. At present, there seems to be no standard in China; radicals number from 189 to 250, according to the particular dictionary. What we have here is not a semantic "component" at all, but a device, for lack of a better one, to index dictionaries. And if their motivation is so arbitrary, what can be said of their usefulness?

This observation is supported by psycholinguistic experiments conducted by Tsao and Wang on Chinese readers' ability to identify characters viewed only in part. They found "that the upper halves of Chinese characters are read more correctly and rapidly and hence must carry more information than the lower halves; similarly, the right halves are read better and contain more information than the left halves. These results are independent of reading direction." Number of strokes was the main factor in identifying the top halves, which have an average of 42 percent more strokes than the bottom. Although there are fewer strokes in the right halves than left, the right contained what phonetic cues were available, which is what made the difference. Identification of radicals "was not found to be an important factor" (1983:361–362).

This finding supports a hunch I have had for some time. Rather than using one's knowledge of a radical to learn or facilitate recall of a character's meaning, it would appear that users typically work backward to identify (or justify) the radical from what they already know of the character's meaning. "Radicals" are useful chiefly because they are recurring stroke combinations that can be memorized and used as such. It is not what they are or what they represent that makes them useful, but simply that they are. They exist and thus offer some hidden structure in what would otherwise be a sea of chaos. More important, in those characters where the radical-phonetic distinction applies and is evident at all, they tell the user how much of the character to ignore to find something that *is* arguably useful, namely, the character's phonetic.

As we have noted, Chinese early abandoned pictograms as the primary model for making new characters in favor of a phonetic approach that tied the system more closely to the language itself. This involved using characters to represent different words with the same or similar sound, using parts of characters for the same purpose, or (what amounts to the same thing) affixing different "radicals" to a character to distinguish homophonous words that may or may not have begun as the same word. Although regularized during the Qin dynasty and to a lesser extent in the People's Republic of China's writing reform, the relationship between symbol and sound has over time become skewed far worse than even English users would tolerate. Nevertheless, one uses what is available, and enough symmetry remains to make the learning task, in practice, more efficient than memorizing a completely unique symbol for each accretion.

How many phonetic elements exist? The count varies with the criteria used to identify them, which in itself gives some idea how marginal the support is that they render by comparison with what users of the worst alphabetic scripts take for granted. According to Wieger, J. M. Callery counted 1,040 such phonetics,[8] which Wieger reduced to 858, using what he called more "practical" criteria (1915:14). Soothill, whose analysis is used as a starting point by DeFrancis (1984a:97–115), isolated 895 phonetics.[9] Zhou Youguang, defining a phonetic in the broadest terms as what remains in a character after the "radical" is eliminated, ended up with 1,348 (1978:177); later he gave a much smaller figure of 545 "sound elements" (1991:22).

Estimates of the phonetics' usefulness vary even more, reflecting the number of elements chosen for evaluation, criteria for fidelity, the number of times a given structure repeats in different characters as a phonetic, and whether one views usefulness as a function of how well the isolated corpus represents all syllables in Mandarin or simply of how often the phonetic elements can be relied on to indicate a given syllable. DeFrancis' calculation that phonetic elements give useful information about the sound of 66 percent of the characters is higher than other estimates (1984a:109); the figure gives a better idea of what the system potentially offers than what users are actually getting out of it and is meant, I believe, to establish the validity of the character-as-syllabary hypothesis, which it does.[10] Zhou, using different criteria, rates the usefulness of phonetics in modern Chinese from 39 percent to 17 percent, depending on whether tone is a factor (1978:173). Tsao and Wang give a rock-bottom figure of 20 percent (1983:358).

Complicating this whole exercise is the same sort of problem we encountered with "radicals," namely, users must be able to find these ill-defined elements within the character (when they exist at all) and identify them with a sound that matches or approximates the morpheme's real sound for any kind of "useful" transitivity to take place between the two media. The procedure is made more maddening by use of multiple phonetics for the same sound, multiple sounds for the same phonetic (as in English orthography, multiplied many times), and by incomplete "specification" (if we can use that term) of the sound. One can classify phonetics into three types: "(1) those that indicate the same syllable (including tone) wherever they occur; (2) those that indicate the same syllable except for tone wherever they occur; and (3) those that indicate critical features of a syllable, but not always the same" (Coulmas 1989:103). Unfortunately, classifying them in this manner means nothing if one cannot determine through inspection which "type" one is.

"Useful," however, has another aspect. The presence of repeating, internal structures in and of itself, regardless of what sounds they may or may not relate to, makes learning and recall less difficult in practice than would be the case if the two to seven thousand different characters had nothing in common. So perhaps the number of forms to be learned is closer to one thousand. And these forms can, some of the time and in some useful fashion, be correlated with speech sounds. This factor would reduce the roughly 1 to 100 advantage that alphabet users enjoy to something on the order of—1 to 10? Using the most charitable criteria, the comparison still remains highly unfavorable to Chinese characters. Are there other factors that might improve the balance?

Alleged Superiority of Chinese Characters for Learning

As far as I am aware, only two types of linguistic arguments worthy of the name have asserted the superiority of Chinese characters as a learning tool and, incredibly, as a shortcut to literacy. Oddly enough, the arguments apply to both the low and high ends of the learning process. The former asserts that Chinese characters, being more "concrete," are more easily grasped by children. As Gleitman and Rozin point out, an alphabetic script confronts the learner with two novel facts simultaneously: (1) the notion that writing represents language and (2) the abstract concept of phonemes represented by letters (1973a:451–452). By eliminating the latter problem through use of Chinese characters, learners are said to progress more quickly toward mastering the basic concept of reading. The other argument is generally associated with Japanese linguist Suzuki Takao, but it has been advanced in one form or another by supporters of the character script in all countries. It asserts that by learning morphemes, either through the *kun* readings of characters or just through the characters themselves, students make an investment in the language. The payoff supposedly comes later in the relative ease with which character-literate readers master high-level vocabulary. This argument is appealing, since it seems to satisfy human expectations that hard work of any kind will be rewarded. The former argument as well has an attraction to teachers in the alphabetic tradition frustrated by the difficulty many children have learning how to read. The two arguments together, if valid, constitute the best pedagogical case that can be made for Chinese characters and would go far to redress the patent disadvantages of the character writing system described above.

   The problem with the introduction-to-reading-through-characters thesis is that neither of the groups whose independent work has been cited in support of it ever made the claim for which they are credited! Quite to the contrary: both specifically denied that their experiments had anything to say about learning the characters as a writing system. What was shown, in the one case, was the relative ease with which beginners are able to learn writing through syllables and, in the other, the benefits that can be obtained by attributing meaning—something the children are already familiar with—to these larger-than-phoneme-size units. Both techniques are well known to reading psychologists in the West and have been used to good effect in the past in teaching alphabet-based literacy. Although Chinese characters represent both syllables and meaning, the number of units quickly becomes intrusive and erases what gains are realized through a token sample.

Specifically, Rozin et al. selected some thirty Chinese characters "for their ability to fit together to form a wide variety of English sentences" and taught them to nine reading-disadvantaged second-graders "directly in their English translation" (1971:1264). No effort was made to connect the characters with the Chinese language. The children were merely taught to associate an English word with each character and asked to read sentences. The experimenters found that "children who had failed to master the English alphabet sounds in over 1 and one-half years of schooling immediately understood the basic demands of the task and were able to read (simple) sentences in the first 5 or 10 minutes of exposure to Chinese" (p. 1266). Rozin et al. concluded from this that "some unit intermediate between the morpheme and phoneme—for example, the syllable—might be more suitable as a vehicle for introducing reading" (p. 1267). Nothing was said about the superiority of Chinese characters per se. Instead they noted that boredom had overcome the children by the time all thirty characters were being used. They specifically rejected the characters as a learning tool for the simple and obvious reason that they are not "productive," in other words, knowledge gained from learning some characters cannot readily be transferred to others.

In the other experiment, Steinberg and Yamada used a small number of *kanji* and *kana* in a learning task involving forty-two Japanese children ages three to four. The researchers discovered after a number of trials that the children were able to learn *kanji* words more quickly than individual *kana* syllables and concluded that "it is the variable of meaningfulness that is producing the higher scores for *kanji* recognition" (1978–1979a:97).[11] As Steinberg and Yamada later acknowledged, "Nowhere do we say or imply . . . that the *kanji* system as a whole is easier to learn than the *kana* system as a whole" (1978–1979b:670). Their only claim was that individual *kanji*, whose meanings are known to the subjects, can be learned more easily than meaningless syllables in *kana*. Tzeng and Singer, who reviewed the experiment, were quick to note that whatever implication meaning has for learning, nothing can be said on the basis of the experiment in favor of using Chinese characters to introduce this benefit, since only a trivial number (two *kanji* and two *kana* per subject) of characters were used. Beyond this, the characters begin to resemble each other, rendering the technique less effective (Tzeng and Singer 1978:665). Again, the numbers take over long before genuine benefits come into play.

The second major pedagogical argument in favor of Chinese characters has been called "semantic transparency" from its basic tenet that characters provide a window to the meanings of words (Suzuki 1975). The claim has three aspects. The first of these was articulated in 1895 in the

April–May issue of *Waseda bungaku* by Tsubouchi Shoyo (1859–1935), who pointed out the advantages that learning a word's constituents has for acquisition of high-level vocabulary. Words do not exist independently, according to Tsubouchi, but share interrelated structures, and one's ability to learn a language is related directly to one's appreciation of these relationships. This claim in its later appearances has been dismissed by Ho Ung (1971:28) and Roy Miller (1977:58) as "etymology," the implication being that the phenomenon has no practical significance, although it seems to me that its value is self-evident. Certainly people, in most cases, do not trace a word to its historical roots to learn its current meaning. Still, history has left an enormous amount of regularity in the lexicon, which all users at some level of consciousness exploit in learning and manipulating vocabulary. One can no more avoid perceiving and cataloging morphological relationships than one can relationships in phonology and syntax. Although one can question (as I shall later) the extent to which these relationships can be usefully exploited and the wisdom of specifying morphological relationships directly and obligatorily, one cannot deny their importance generally, with or without Chinese characters.

The second aspect of the theory, needless to say, is that the above process works better with characters. According to this view, Western languages written alphabetically are "opaque" to their users, since there are fewer clues to a word's morphological structure. By contrast, the character-literate East Asian is well acquainted with word constituents, because the characters break them down precisely and because the user has learned the morphemes individually or through their appearance in other Sinitic compounds. Each morpheme, thanks to the characters, has its own "memory tag" that is more distinct than what one sees in words written phonetically (Suzuki 1987:16). Meanings of words therefore "do not have to be remembered one by one" (Tao 1957:117). They "need not be studied to be understood," since the meaning of the whole can be deduced from its parts (Oh 1971:43). Another alleged dividend is the accuracy characters lend to word acquisition: by seeing the morpheme in different combinations, one gradually learns its exact meaning, which in turn translates to a better understanding of subsequent words, and so on (Nam 1970:10). Some even claim that the characters, in the long run, save time because in learning characters one is also learning a part of the language (Yu Pong-yong 1974:162).

In view of the ability East Asians allegedly have, through their knowledge of Chinese characters, to acquire a vast store of high-level vocabulary relatively painlessly, Kato Hiroki and others see a direct link between the characters and Japan's industrial success (1979:66). Kato suggests there is no relationship between the ease with which a writing system is learned and its value or utility. He claims the converse is often true, as evidenced by Japanese readers' awareness of "what the structural elements of a word mean concretely," an awareness that enables them to learn more words than

Westerners with their alphabetic scripts can ever hope to. To illustrate his point, Kato assembled ten "technical terms" from a book about Leonardo da Vinci that educated Westerners can barely guess at, provided *kanji* translations for the terms, and went on to claim that any Japanese with a high school education could figure out the meanings of every item on the list (pp. 67–68). The implication is that what can be guessed at more successfully can be learned more easily. Since Kato's method embodies some of the fallacies that apply to the "transparency" argument in general, a closer look at his comparisons is called for.

Some of you may share my ignorance of a few of the English terms in Table 6, so I will supply their definitions from *Webster's Third International Dictionary* (1971) juxtaposed to what a Japanese reader can be expected to understand from the Japanese.

	Webster's	Translation of Japanese
1.	steps to an altar	steps to an altar
2.	type of rock used by Romans	striped rock
3.	additional name (used by Romans)	additional name
4.	pictorial represention in terms of light and shade	means of contrasting brightness and darkness
5.	(mantelet) a movable shelter used by besiegers	portable shield used to fend off projectiles
6.	slope used for defense against attack by people firing from ramparts	sloping embankment
7.	stone-throwing weapon	machine for throwing stones
8.	precious stone	essence of jade
9.	transversal part of a cruciform church	spirit veranda
10.	related to the principles of architecture	structural; (adj. for) system of knowledge

There are several problems with the comparison, the first being that the methodology is spurious. Kato scanned a book, deliberately selecting obscure words that an English speaker is unlikely to know, so that his method prejudiced the result. Second, three of the Japanese expressions are not words at all—they are phrases or definitions and have no place in the comparison.[12] Since Kato does not give a source for the Japanese terms, there is some question about their authenticity. Only four of the terms (nos. 2, 6, 7, 8), for example, are listed among the seventy thousand

Table 6
Some English Terms and Their Japanese Equivalents

1.	predella	祭壇の階段
2.	porphyry	斑岩
3.	agnomen	添名
4.	chiaroscuro	明暗對照法
5.	mantlet	携帶用彈丸よけの盾
6.	glacis	斜堤
7.	mangonel	投石機
8.	chalcedony	玉髓
9.	transept	神廊
10.	architectonic	構造上の，知識體系の

Source: Kato 1979:67–68.

compounds in *Nelson's*. Third, many of these words are obsolete in English. Five of the ten were rejected by *Word 2.0* software. Some are of Latin or Italian origin, which relates to my comments earlier in this chapter about distinguishing one language and one era from another. If English speakers should know these words, then all 47,035 characters in *Kāngxī zìdiǎn* should be included as part of the Japanese learner's task. Kato can't have it both ways. Finally, the reader will have noticed that the Japanese terms do not give the exact meanings. That is, the meaning of the whole is not necessarily evident from the sum of its parts, which, as I shall discuss below, makes the "transparency" phenomenon more of a liability than an asset.

The theory's third aspect is articulated by Suzuki Takao and applies only to Japanese. According to Suzuki, Japanese learners reap a further benefit from the dual readings many characters have in Japanese. Japanese children acquire basic vocabulary words through speech that by and large correspond, individually and in level, to the indigenous *kun* readings that are given to *kanji*. Then they go on to learn the characters associated with these readings. At this time, a second set of readings for the characters is introduced—the *on* or Sinitic equivalents—so that for each character learned, the user now knows a fixed concept and two levels of expression: one popular, the other learned and used in higher-level compound words. These latter words, according to Suzuki, are instantly accessible and constantly reinforced by reference through the characters to the words' more plebeian indigenous counterparts. English readers, by contrast, cannot analyze a word's components with nearly the same facility because the alphabet does not tie the two levels together and because in many cases there is no popular (Anglo-Saxon) equivalent for a learned (Greco-Latin) morpheme (1975:88–89).

To demonstrate the difference, Suzuki compiled a list of over one hundred such *kun-on* correspondences, where the two readings represent the colloquial and learned "manifestations" of a single concept, and matched them where possible with their English equivalents. Some of them are given in Table 7. While the meanings of the learned *on* morphemes are transparent because of a Japanese reader's prior knowledge of the *kun* words, the Greco-Latin words cannot be related in any principled way to their popular equivalents. They must be learned separately, one by one, which according to the theory puts non-Japanese at a disadvantage in acquiring higher vocabulary. Suzuki applies the claim to scientific and technical terms in particular, and asserts that the phenomenon has contributed to what he believes is Japan's greater success overall (1987:48–53).

The above theory constitutes the outstanding claim for the superiority of the character writing system. In view of the importance many writers attach to it, we shall spend the last few pages of this chapter addressing these propositions. Although superficially attractive, the theory has several major flaws, beginning with its claim that the phenomena described are uniquely or even especially advantageous to Japanese.

Suzuki has built his contribution to the theory on the premise that each character has two types of "phonetic realizations," corresponding to the usual gap between common and learned vocabulary, and that the

Table 7

Colloquial *(kun)* and Learned *(on)* Readings of Selected *Kanji* with English Equivalents

頭	atama/tō	head/capita, cephal-
犬	inu/ken	dog/canine
木	ki/moku	tree/arboreal
上	ue/jō	above, over/super, hyper
雲	kumo/un	cloud/nebula
天	ama/ten	heaven/celestial
小	chiisa(i)/shō	little, small/minor, micro
固	kata(i)/ko	hard/dur-, -dure
來	ku(ru)/rai	come/veni-, -vene
見	mi(ru)/ken	see/visi-

Source: Adapted from Suzuki 1975.

meanings of the two are semantically equivalent. According to Morioka Kenji's calculations, however, of 3,474 characters now in use, only some 56 percent have both *on* and *kun* readings (1973). Sokolov's figures, based on readings allowed for the 1,850 *Tōyō kanji* are even lower; 789 have the Sinitic *on* readings only, leaving just 1,061 characters to carry this alleged quality through the corpus of learned Sinitic compounds (1970:104). The distribution is skewed even further in the compounds themselves, where the benefits of "morpheme transparency" are supposed to come into play. As Iwada Mari notes, although it is common for at least one of the members of a two-character compound to have a (latent) *kun* equivalent, the other character often has no common or approved *kun* reading at all (1982:189).

Even in ideal cases where both members of a Sinitic compound have *on* and useful *kun* equivalents, it is still difficult to see any advantage conferred on Japanese that literate Chinese do not share or enjoy even more fully. Suzuki's theory, where it works at all, is based on the assumption that common-use vocabulary, corresponding to the *kun* readings of characters, is absorbed through speech, then later applied to understand the meaning of the same characters in higher-level compounds, despite the fact that the characters are read with a different—Sinitic—sound. But if this is the case, it must be even truer for Chinese, where all vocabulary, however commonplace, is theoretically represented by characters, which go on directly, with no change in pronunciation, to form the components of the language's higher-level compounds.

We have demonstrated that the phenomenon under discussion is not unique to Japanese, but we have not adequately addressed the theory's second proposition, that characters enable learners to grasp high-level vocabulary more easily and with greater accuracy. As it turns out, this part of the theory is also plagued by contradictions, which when analyzed depict the actual role of the characters much less favorably.

According to Choe Hyon-bae, we do not learn words, even Sinitic words, by analyzing their constituent morphemes; we learn them as whole units, no matter what the characters mean individually (1946:82). Whatever the logic underlying their assignment might have been originally, the synchronic user does not know the meaning of a word because he or she knows the characters. Such a user consults a dictionary instead, and then, if he or she bothers at all, imputes meaning to characters based on what may or may not be an accurate understanding of their role in the word itself. Users do not, in normal practice, proceed from recognition of a word's components to the meaning of the word as a whole. In fact, one cannot predict the nature of a compound from its elements much better in language than in chemistry. Karlgren notes that there are combinations "in which one or both members are simpler words with such a wide range of meaning that it is far from obvious which application is appropriate" (1923:87).

Even where the morphemes have specific meanings, there are innumerable cases where the sense of the compound is so far removed from the logical sum of its components as to make this feature useless.

Moreover, given the fact that the meanings of the characters may have no direct relationship to the word's meaning or may even be misleading, one cannot just dismiss them as exceptions while claiming the benefits of "semantic transparency" where it does work. If the character representation helps the reader when the morphemes bear an obvious relation to the whole, then they must affect the user adversely when they do not. It is worth noting, by contrast, that with phonetic writing, although the "transparency" of genuine morphemes is maintained when the component-whole relationship is well motivated, one is not deceived in cases where the motivation has been lost; the user simply ignores it, not being required by the nature of the writing system to draw extravagant conclusions.

This observation leads to a subtle, but potentially more devastating criticism. A literate speaker of Chinese, on hearing an unfamiliar word, may ask, "Which x?" or "What are the characters?" not because the person necessarily wants to write the word, but because one feels instinctively that however detailed an explanation of the word's meaning may be, one does not really know the word until one also knows which morphemes are used in its composition. This constant referral by speakers of East Asian languages to a word's morphology is so pervasive that it can hardly be dismissed as curiosity. According to Pak Chong-so, analyzing Sinitic words into their constituent morphemes cannot be avoided and follows from the fact that all parts of a Chinese compound are supposed to have meaning (1968:46).

There are at least two corollaries to this endemic inquisitiveness engendered by the character writing system that may be having deleterious effects on one's ability to use language in its proper function. On the one hand, there is a tendency among literate East Asians to confuse recognizing the written character components of a Sinitic word (or, similarly, tracing to its characters the syllables of a spoken word) with understanding the word itself, when in fact no such understanding has been achieved. The user literally does not know that he or she does not know the word, having become satisfied that he or she does know all there is to know about the word. The other harmful side effect of overanalyzing a compound is that one tends to see less, more, or something other than the meaning of the word itself. As Yamada Hisao has suggested, the presence of visible word components, each with their individual meanings, tends to weaken the cluster itself and to confuse the reader who is concerned only with the meaning of the whole (1987:64–66, 95).

A final criticism brings us back to our original contention that Chinese characters, far from facilitating learning, make literacy in principle much harder to achieve than it is for users of alphabetic writing systems.

Chinese characters over time tend to accumulate a host of meanings, which in an alphabetic tradition are treated as separate morphemes if a big enough semantic gap develops to obscure their common origin. The "new" morphemes in turn are listed alphabetically as individual dictionary entries, and the separation is complete. Unneeded baggage from the past is discarded, and users get on with the business of applying language synchronically to the needs of life.

Unfortunately, this is less true of Chinese character–based systems, where the visual distinctiveness of the symbols tricks users into believing that serviceable relationships exist between one of the character's meanings and another when such may no longer be the case. To illustrate this point, Paul Serruys assembled a group of commonly used Chinese words, each sharing the character 經, even though the words have no apparent synchronic relationship (1962:72–73). Although all are reducible to a single etymological core, this fact is irrelevant to contemporary Chinese users, who in the act of learning the meanings of words are encumbered by an artificial analysis that brings words together that should be kept apart. Whatever benefits users of Chinese characters may get from their "transparency"—and these benefits are far fewer than supporters have claimed—must be weighed against the disadvantages I describe here.

Chinese Characters and Literacy

It has become fashionable in some circles to assert that Chinese and English, all appearances to the contrary, differ little in the degree of obstacles they present to literacy.[13] The argument, at its best, runs as follows: English and all alphabetic systems require their users to learn spelling rules for every word in the lexicon. Although there are few symbols to learn, mastering an alphabet does not provide any sense of the language's morphology. This knowledge, which is essential to literacy, is available only implicitly and must be built up, for the most part subconsciously, over a long period. Chinese, in contrast, contains a great deal of structure that is invisible to Westerners unfamiliar with the conventions and on which users depend to facilitate acquisition. In terms of effort, the task is not unlike that of students learning how to spell English. If the efforts are not exactly comparable, then character users at least are rewarded later by the greater insight they have into the language's morphological structure. In any case, what counts more in determining literacy than the writing system itself are the social and economic conditions prevailing in the society where the writing system is used, so why argue?

While it is not my intent to defend English spelling (partly morphophonemic and partly arbitrary) or to dispute the overriding importance of nonlinguistic determinants of literacy, it seems self-evident that if the latter are held constant, the society with the more efficient writing system has an advantage. Some writers, most recently James Unger (1987:83–95), have sought to infer the efficiency (or lack of it) of the Chinese character–based scripts in part from what they believe to be their observable effects on society. In my view, this approach will always be subject to counterclaims that point to similar maladies within alphabet-based cultures. Looking instead at what the system itself necessarily implies can yield more objective insights, and this is the approach I have followed here.

The first such factor, and the one that stands out immediately, is the enormous difference in the number of units that must be mastered, a difference that is not attenuated by the characters' internal structures enough to affect the comparison. A second measure of efficiency—arguably more important—is how closely the writing system matches the language itself, and here the characters do not fare very well, either. Even in the worst alphabetic systems, users can rely largely on their knowledge of a word's spoken sound to understand or reproduce a written equivalent. The knowledge behind this maneuver is enormous, but it is for the most part free. Character users have nothing comparable. The "radicals," as we have seen, are almost totally useless as bearers of information. Although phonetic components can give hints about pronunciation, the relationship is haphazard, incomplete, contradictory, and unidirectional. Proposing this "system" as the equal of English, even in terms of the match it has with the language, makes no sense at all.

About the only area where character writing can be said to enjoy a better fit with its spoken counterpart is morphology. This fact is seized by admirers of Chinese writing as evidence of its latent superiority, although, as I have tried to show, the effects of this phenomenon are more harmful than the benefits it supposedly brings. Overspecifying the components of a word leads to a less-than-perfect grasp of the word itself, which is to say, less command over the units that count most in the day-to-day use of the system. The overwhelming pressure put on the learner and user to focus on morphemes, or what the system pretends are morphemes, to the exclusion of the word has other deleterious effects on literacy, namely, the erroneous belief of Chinese writers "that all they need do is connect two Chinese characters together and people will understand it" (Li Xingjie 1987:27), when the most they are doing is guessing at it.[14] If this is the "precision" characters lend to the grasp of high-level vocabulary, one can only wonder how East Asian societies have done as well as they have. Certainly, there is nothing in the nature of Chinese characters or in their relationship to the languages using them to account for it. We can only conclude on the basis of the foregoing that the effects of Chinese characters on literacy and learning have been uniformly negative.

7. Reading

UNTIL RECENTLY, linguists believed that "meaning-based" Chinese characters and "sound-based" phonetic scripts were processed by readers in different ways. Readers of alphabetic and other types of phonetic writing were thought to recode written symbols into their corresponding sounds, and then go on to interpret these sounds with the same mechanisms used for processing speech. Although details varied from one model to the next, the common assumption was that readers make direct use of the phonological information available to them to build up a representation of a word's sound prior to accessing its meaning in their mental lexicon. This hypothesis was attractive because it assumed shared reading and speech comprehension mechanisms and also because it accounted for certain clinically observed phenomena such as subvocal speech and some types of data in latency experiments, which I will discuss below.

Conversely, it was supposed that the paucity of phonetic clues in Chinese characters caused readers to process these scripts differently. East Asians, unable to use phonology that is not manifested or is manifested only minimally, were believed to serendipitously bypass this stage and move on directly to higher comprehension mechanisms (Oh 1971:33; Nakada 1982:34; Tien 1983:12). Meanwhile, other experiments seemed to show that East Asians were using the right part of their brains to read Chinese characters, while everyone else in the world (including Japanese and Koreans when they read *kana* and *hangul*) was using the brain's left half. The discovery was taken as support for the theory that character scripts and alphabets are processed differently, since it seemed to localize the two types anatomically. It also reinforced the notion that Chinese characters have supralinguistic qualities inasmuch as they appeared to bypass the brain's left hemisphere, which is the locus of linguistic activity.

Now if these descriptions of how Chinese characters and alphabetic systems are read look, respectively, like the "ideography" versus "language as speech" arguments encountered in Chapter 5, it is for good reason. Whether the issue involves structural relationships or functional processes

153

like reading, both arguments proceed from the same flawed premises, and both fail to take into account the fundamental interplay between meaning and sound that occurs with both alphabetic and character writing. As we shall see, readers of alphabetic scripts do not normally access meaning through sound or sound images, and readers of character scripts do not process texts without the use of phonology. Although the above views are no longer held by specialists, their legacy lives on among those intent on showing some positive attributes of Chinese characters to compensate for their obvious disadvantages.

How Phonetic Scripts Are Read

In order to assess the utility of Chinese characters in terms of what they offer the reader, we must first understand the psycholinguistic processes associated with alphabetic scripts, as a basis for comparison. What exactly goes on in a reader's mind when encountering a sample of his or her native language written in a conventional alphabetic system? This topic has stimulated a great deal of research, which has yielded answers that will surprise many, particularly in light of the stereotypes described above. Accordingly, I will spend the next several pages looking at how readers process alphabetic writing before discussing the analogous problem with Chinese characters.

At least four different theories have purported to explain English language reading and, by extension, reading of phonetic scripts generally (Foss and Hakes 1978:332). The first of these is the "subvocalization hypothesis" which holds that a reader converts graphemes or groups of graphemes into subvocal speech and literally listens to the auditory image generated. This model handily accounts for the presence of silent speech in most, perhaps all, styles of reading. Another attractive feature is its economy. Since aural and reading comprehension, according to this theory, depend on the same mechanism, no separate apparatus need be proposed for the latter.

A second hypothesis holds that readers convert grapheme input into "systematic phonemes," which are passed on as such to higher comprehension mechanisms. This is not subvocal speech per se, but an abstract phonological stage between surface phonetics and syntax through which all incoming and outgoing signals must pass, according to one model of language. Like the subvocalization hypothesis, this formulation is able to preserve the notion of a primary phonological aspect in reading inferred from some types of experiments, while avoiding some of the first model's demonstrable fallacies. Both theories, however, share the same basic hypothesis that readers must first change print into a phonological code before access to the stored lexical item can be accomplished.

A third theory known as "direct access" claims "readers are able to go directly from the graphemic representation of the printed word to the lexical representation in their mental dictionary" (Foss and Hakes

1978:332). There is no phonetic intervention between first perception of print and lexical access (although, as we shall see, the appearance of sound at a later stage can be posited without damaging the basic postulate). One advantage of this theory is its universality. Another is its ability to accommodate high reading speeds allegedly beyond that possible with either of the first two theories.[1] On the minus side is the model's costliness. According to Foss and Hakes, the theory requires "two independent paths to the lexical item . . . and that two separate connections between the visual and auditory stimuli and each word must be established" (1978:333).

A fourth alternative called "dual access" combines one or both of the phonological theories with the third theory of direct access. It has two versions: one maintains that an experienced reader of an alphabetic script shifts from one method to the other depending on the quality of the stimuli, word familiarity, or any number of personal, unquantifiable factors. The other version is more deterministic. Described by Kleiman as "a parallel horserace" (1975:327), the model depicts simultaneous processing of the same stimuli by both visual and phonological routes. Since direct visual access is faster, this hypothesis ends up supporting the direct access model for "ideal" conditions and some type of phonological recoding when conditions are less than ideal, for example, with unfamiliar words or difficult passages.

Besides these methodological models, readers employ two strategies to operate these models. There is the "plodder," on the one hand, who processes text piece by piece, and the "explorer," on the other hand, who seeks confirmation of guesses made in advance of the stimuli (Rozin and Gleitman 1977:59–62). Although the plodder strategy is usually associated with one or both of the phonological recoding methods, while the explorer strategy appears with direct access models,[2] this need not be so. A direct access model could stipulate that readers process all stimuli, in serial order, whether or not each item is important to the discourse's overall meaning. Conversely, an efficient decoder could extract only what information is needed to provide an unambiguous phonological key to items in the lexicon.

Although all of these models have been criticized from one perspective or another, few scholars would claim that any one of them can account for all types of reading. Disagreement focuses instead on what is the normal or preferred means of skilled readers. Under such circumstances, the arguments for direct access and against either or both phonological theory seem to be more convincing. Many can be cited:

1. Laboratory experiments show that words are recognized more quickly and accurately than individual letters (Gunther 1983:356). This phenomenon, known as the "word superiority effect," is the opposite of what should occur if sounds, sound images, or the abstract phonemes from which sound images are generated are used to access lexical items. A coun-

terclaim, based on an experiment that shows pseudowords (meaningless constructions that conform to the phonological rules of a language) and nonwords producing the same effect (Baron and Thurston 1973), has been shown to be invalid for failing to take into account the difference between basic and derived words, the latter requiring more time to process (Gunther 1983:361). That pseudowords themselves are processed more quickly than nonwords can be attributed to the visual perception of orthographic regularity. There is no need to postulate phonological processing.

2. Pseudowords learned as spoken forms take longer to process when first encountered in print than do pseudowords learned as written forms. No such difference should appear if speech or phonemic recoding is used to process the latter. This gap, moreover, disappears as the reader gains visual familiarity with the first group of forms, those learned through speech, indicating transition to a more direct form of processing (Rozin and Gleitman 1977:71).

3. If written symbols were normally treated to some form of phonological recoding before lexical access, then anyone trained in the use of a general phonetic notation could immediately read transcribed texts so written, with a speed and degree of understanding comparable to what occurs when reading a language in its regular script. This, of course, does not happen. Text transcribed from one phonetic system to another seems strange, and reading slows. Even if we assume that lexical units are represented in the mind by strings of systematic phonemes, the transcription should have no effect on how quickly the text is processed, since the reader would already be skilled in moving from phonetic to phonemic representations by virtue of his or her competence as a speaker.

4. Whether a reader ever uses the strings of systematic phonemes hypothesized for speech is also open to question. In an experiment conducted by M. J. Cosky at the University of Texas in Austin, subjects were shown words containing either three or four phonemes, and their response times between display and first vocalization were measured. The assumption was that if phonological recoding occurred, more time would be needed for words with more phonemes. However, no such difference was measured (Foss and Hakes 1978:339).

5. The phonemic recoding hypothesis is based on the identification of English orthography with the phonemic structure alleged to underlie spoken forms, but this assumption may be invalid. There are too many instances where the orthography and hypothesized underlying form fail to correspond, necessitating the addition of ad hoc rules that detract from the model's simplicity (Brewer 1976:539).

6. According to Smith, "Not more than six or seven unrelated items . . . can be held in short-term memory at any one time" (1983:27). This factor severely limits the length of words that can be processed, phoneme by phoneme, in the recoding model. Even if, as Gough suggests, "the

abstract phonemic representation is assigned the first lexical entry that can be found" (1976:516), removing the need for all letters of the stimulus to be processed, a reader would have to make the identification after the first five or six letters, which is impossible for many of the items one encounters in print.

7. As with speech perception itself, one can assume the units operated on and stored in short-term memory are longer than single letters (or their corresponding sounds) if subvocalization—not phonemic recoding—is the method employed. This assumption resolves the above contradiction, but opens the door to others. For example, readers who encounter a word that is not immediately familiar are known to sound out the word, letter by letter, until enough data are registered to identify the stimulus with an established lexical entry. Only then do they pronounce it with confidence. But if that is the case, how did the reader use sound to access the word in the first place?

8. Subvocal speech, in any case, does not normally appear as a verbatim account of the text's phonology. Instead, words are slurred, pronounced partially, or left out altogether depending on the difficulty of the text (Gibson and Levin 1975:342–345). If the reader depended solely on subvocalized cues, the information source would be scanty indeed.

9. Of course, there is little or no such information available to nonhearing readers, who read nevertheless. It is true that many congenitally deaf people do not learn to read well. But the fact that they read at all is proof that phonological recoding is not a necessity. By the same token, there are no large differences in the reading performance of nonhearing children who have been taught to articulate (and energize these articulations during silent reading) and those who have not (Conrad 1972:233).

10. Both the subvocalization and phonemic recoding hypotheses acquire much of their formal attractiveness by positing shared use of existing speech mechanisms. Such theories look less appealing, therefore, in the light of clinical evidence of pure agraphia occurring without aphasia of speech. Moreover, according to Marcie, "The disorders of writing which appear with these lesions which produce aphasiacs do not parallel the disorders of speech. The features of writing disorders cannot be automatically inferred from speech disorders and the reverse can also be true" (1983:409).

11. The functional independence of the two mechanisms is also implied in our ability to retrieve meaning from written homophones (that are not homographs) in real and experimental situations. Expressed the other way, substituting nonhomographic homonyms (e.g., *reed* and *read*) for the correct word in a text will decrease performance, which should not happen if phonological recoding were the only method operating.

12. By the same token, we routinely detect misspelled words, even where the pronunciation is not affected, for example, *werk* for *work*, not-

ing that the word does not "look" right. Conversely, a phonological recoding model cannot explain how readers sometimes fail to notice typographical or spelling errors where pronunciation *is* affected (Brewer 1976:539).

13. Phonological recoding is also at a loss to explain how bilingual subjects will often translate spontaneously when told to read, verbatim and as quickly as possible, a text composed of words and phrases in two languages. If readers were changing print directly into subvocal speech, they would "simply vocalize the subvocalization" (Foss and Hakes 1978:332). Nor can it explain how many of us read foreign languages with great fluency, yet fail to understand the simplest spoken sentences. If both depended on the same mechanism, facility in one medium would transfer to the other.

14. Most damaging—to the phonemic recoding hypothesis in particular—is the existence of nonalphabetic character scripts. Whatever theory of underlying phonemic representation one proposes for spoken Chinese, there is no convenient way of transferring these postulates to the character script. While the subvocalization hypothesis as applied to Chinese is less palpably absurd, one assumes a lot (as will be discussed) by claiming that speech recoding is the only or even preferred route to written Chinese lexical items.

15. A final criticism applies to methodology generally. According to Smith, "Almost all the experimental work that has provided the conceptual basis for outside-in [i.e., letter > recoded sound > meaning] theories of reading has been done . . . in unmotivated laboratory situations" (1983:60). While this may be equally true of the experimental data used to support direct access, most promoters of the latter theory concede that phonological recoding does occur, but only in atypical situations, the laboratory setting itself being one example. The abnormal environment predisposes readers to a fallback strategy, namely, recoding.

The Direct Access Model of English Reading

Taking these arguments into account, it is difficult to concur with the view that readers of English employ phonological recoding as the only or even the preferred method of lexical access. Although there are problems with the direct access theory, too, they are fewer and can be resolved.

First, as mentioned, is the model's costliness. If we reject shared use of reading and speech mechanisms, alternative addresses (phonological and graphic markers) must be posited for each lexical item. This hypothesis not only wastes neurological storage capacity, it also puts an excessive burden on the learner, who, having learned ten thousand words, is unable to use this knowledge in any principled way to read word number 10,001 (Foss and Hakes 1978:333). Another problem is that many words are encountered in print only once every few years, leaving little opportunity to establish direct pathways to the less frequent entries (Rozin and Gleitman 1977:67). This latter objection, although hard to test, does seem to be a fair indictment of direct access to the extent that the model applies to whole words only. However, if we can assume provisions in our linguistic competence for morphemes, that is, for parts of words, either as standing lexical items or as the recurring residue of parsing mechanisms, there is no reason not to apply these provisions to a reading model in which large components are also processed as wholes and recombined in some parsimonious fashion to access larger entries. Many of the less frequently occurring words could be accounted for in this way by a direct access model, without assuming individual links to all words and all of their morphological derivations.

In other words, the analogy of a mental "lexicon," acting as interface between meanings and symbols, with the usual dictionary as exemplified by the use of such terms as "mental dictionary" or "lexical lookup" should not be taken literally. No reasonable hypothesis of the lexicon's organization can overlook the probability of extensive subdivisions and lateral connectivity between word components. The likelihood that this is actually the case is evidenced in psycholinguistic experiments that "support a model of lexical organization that represents words in morphologically decomposed form" (Burani et al. 1984:342). Moreover, there is solid laboratory proof that the lexicon can be accessed either by whole words or by root morphemes (ibid.: 351). This mechanism allows us to retain the direct access concept of words apprehended as visual wholes at the same time it eliminates the first of the two objections to the theory, since it is apparent that readers can use their prior knowledge of the lexicon's morphemic structure to good effect on new vocabulary by accessing these smaller units as the need arises.

Some room for accommodation can also be found in the composition of the links themselves. As will be discussed, there is no need and probably no justification for the assumption that the visual pattern or even most of the information associated with it is important for direct access. "Some characterization of an overall pattern" may be enough (Brooks 1977:148–149). This requirement would reduce the amount of learning needed for any one lexical item, rendering the infrequency argument less potent. But there is still the other problem: however much these codes are reduced or abstracted, one is still associating unique nonacoustic representations with the myriads of units that presumably are accessible as units through speech-based codes.

There are two ways to handle this objection. The first involves putting it in perspective. As discussed above, the spellings of English words number in the tens of thousands and are learned individually, not by the application of sound-to-spelling correspondences, which generate a correct spelling less than half the time (Smith 1983:99). If we can remember the sounds of fifty thousand or more words, their meanings, rules for use, and spellings for each entry, then the need to store visual patterns for these words seems less excessive by comparison. The other approach focuses on the differences between investment cost and long-term gain. If direct access is the faster method, economy favors it over other models where the cost is paid in perpetual installments through inefficient reading. Taking these factors into account, we should conclude with Fowler (1981:185) that both phonological and orthographic information are contained in the same lexicon. It is interesting to note that this psycholinguistic formulation coincides with our earlier, structural description of the word-morpheme as a unit consisting of meaning on the one side with both phonetic and graphic addresses on the other.

Direct access has also been criticized for assuming, naively, that one can move uninterruptedly from print to "meaning." We have met this problem before in connection with ideographic theories of character writing, and its use here is open to the same types of criticism. Fowler, for example, observes that since word meanings are useless for sentence comprehension outside of their grammatical context, one cannot claim that a reader goes "directly to meaning." "What a reader has to do, directly or not, is go to words—that is, lexical entries" (1981:184). Reed likewise criticizes the notion that one can extract meaning directly, noting that if this were true, we could utter "canine" upon seeing "dog" (1970:289). His definition of reading as "the identification of *linguistic forms* from strings of written configurations that represent them" is consistent with our finding in Chapter 5 on the structural representata of character forms.

The above applies to the meaning half of the linguistic equation. What of the internal representation itself? Here, too, the direct access theory has been naive in at least two respects. On the one hand, while the passage from first perception to word identification may be "direct" in the sense that it is beyond cognitive control, a series of intermediate stages can be and likely are involved that render the model as complicated as the phonological recoding models with which it competes. As Banks et al. have noted, "The only truly direct model of visual perception is template matching," which cannot account for rapid recognition of different orthographic styles (1981:139). Nor is overall word shape especially helpful (Gibson and Levin 1975:197; Carrol 1976:10). According to Rozin, "Readers show almost normal word recognition abilities and almost normal reading rates when faced with materials in which the orthography severely distorts the normal shape of words" (1978:415). Note also that the concept is hard to apply to Chinese characters, which in principle all have squarish shapes.

Rather than posit word detectors that mirror stereotyped images, a more realistic hypothesis is a prior stage of processing that converts raw data into representations of the relationships existing among the stimulus' component features.[3] This processing applies to the internal features of the printed word at least as much as to the word's external configuration. At this point, however, it becomes difficult to avoid asking: if we concede the significance of the visual structures inside the profile, can we ignore the likelihood that the components being operated on are the letters themselves? I do not believe that we can,[4] although it should be emphasized that there is a world of difference between this process and phonological processing. To begin with, not all letters are of equal importance to word recognition; while this is also true of individual sounds, I know of no studies that correlate the two. Second, while recognizing the role of letter-icons, the model allows that readers derive word-specific information from the spatial relationships between these letters, which cannot be correlated in any useful way with intersecting speech formants or whatever imaginary distances obtain between shapeless systematic phonemes. Letters and their positions with respect to each other function as distinctive graphic forms, not as carriers of sound or any other type of abstract speech code. Their inclusion in the direct access model enhances its plausibility although, as we have seen, the only thing "direct" about it is its ability to function without sound.

This last statement needs to be qualified. The main elements of support for phonological recoding—and against direct access—are vocalization reflexes that persist even in silent reading. They are detectable electromyographically and from phonologically oriented errors that occur in some types of visual recall tasks. For example, experiments using strings of paired word sets have shown lexical decision to be impeded in pairs that do not rhyme, even though spelling is the same except for the initial letter (Foss and Hakes 1978:336). Rubenstein et al. in a well-known paper titled "Evidence for Phonemic Recoding in Visual Word Recognition" (1971) concluded from latency tests for English and three types of nonsense words that legal (pronounceable and orthographically regular) nonsense words elicited longer delays than either type of illegal nonsense words, presumably because the latter types were rejected at once when they failed to pass through an early phonological recoding stage. Other evidence comes from nonhearing readers, who can recognize a large number of individual words but often cannot process connected text as well as hearing people (Gibson and Levin 1975:501). Similarly, hearing subjects trained deliberately to suppress vocalization read easy materials with comprehension but stumble badly over more difficult texts (Laberge 1972:245).

Such examples have been taken as evidence of a prior stage of phonological recoding, although nothing of the sort is necessarily implied. At least three different questions need to be answered before the appearance of phonology by itself can be used to demonstrate the validity of either recoding model. These questions, which are not specifically addressed by the above arguments, are (1) Is the phonological recoding optional or obligatory? (2) What is its purpose? and (3) Where in the process does the phonology appear? Some clinical findings shed light on the first problem. Marshall describes certain brain-injured subjects who must assign a phonological value to a string of letters to reach meaning and others who cannot use phonology to access meaning, but derive meaning nevertheless (1976:114). This latter group, according to Marshall, includes (1) Subjects who cannot read nonsense syllables, (2) Subjects whose errors are often semantically similar to the stimulus, (3) Subjects whose errors are (almost) never nonexistent lexical forms, and (4) Subjects whose semantic misreading of the stimulus is sometimes preceded by a (partially) erroneous visual analysis of the stimulus.

Another example of meaning being accessed without the use of phonology is given by deep dyslexics who can read content words but not homophonous grammar words, for example, "witch" and "oar" but not "which" and "or" (Marshall 1976:114). Obviously these subjects are using some other, nonphonological, method to reach the lexical items. More evidence against phonological recoding as an obligatory device was provided by Kleiman in a series of experiments carried out on college readers (1975:328–330). The first involved making lexical decisions with and without concurrent shadowing tasks on pairs of words of three different types, labeled graphemic (heard-beard vs. grace-price), phonemic (tickle-pickle vs. lemon-demon), and synonymous (mourn-grieve vs. bravery-quality).

The subjects pushed buttons marked "true" or "false" to indicate whether the words had identical letters after the first letter in the graphemic tests, whether they rhymed in the phonemic tasks, and whether the words had similar meanings in the synonymy tasks. Response times were measured. The shadowing, which involved having the subjects repeat aloud a series of digits that they heard, presumably would occupy the subjects' phonological processing mechanisms and interfere with the lexical decision tasks to the extent that they depend on the same mechanism. The results of this experiment were striking. Whereas shadowing produced a mean latency of 372 milleseconds for the phonemic trials, only 120 and 125 milliseconds were required for the synonymy and graphemic decisions, indicating that phonological recoding could not have been employed and hence can hardly be obligatory. To guard against the possibility that the graphemic decisions were made via recoding (which would apply, by extension, to the synonymy trials also), a second experiment using phonemically similar and dissimilar homograph pairs (blame-flame vs. couch-touch) was conducted with and without shadowing, on the premise that recoding on the nonshadowing trials would facilitate decisions for the first group of words relative to the second. This happened as expected for the nonshadowing trials. For the shadowing trials, however, mean reaction time increased by the same amount for both phonemically similar and dissimilar groups, which should not have happened if recoding had been employed (ibid.: 331–332).

Kleiman's first two experiments involved data obtained on isolated words (or word pairs). There was no requirement that these words or their meanings be integrated into larger structures as happens during reading, which raised the possibility that the nonappearance of obligatory, prelexical phonological recoding was the result of an artificial setting. Kleiman's third experiment therefore controlled for this possibility by using longer, five-word strings, some meaningful and some nonsense, in addition to the usual single words. He found that "the average shadowing effect on the acceptability and phonemic decisions was significantly larger than the average shadowing effect on the graphemic and category decisions" (1975:335). That phonological recoding operates on phonemic decisions was known from the first experiment (and predictable in any case). However, its operation in acceptability decisions suggests that phonology does have a role in "normal" reading, as other tests also indicate, but that its role is not that of lexical access, as proposed by recoding theories.

If phonology is not normally used to access English words in reading, where does it come into play? We know from tests, from recall errors, and from the fact that input itself occurs over time that reading comprehension is not instantaneous. Some type of storage buffer, probably short-term memory or a form of it, is necessary to hold sentence components that have been addressed in focus until enough information has been accumulated for parsing mechanisms to operate that lead to comprehension. There is universal agreement on the need for this stage, and there is a general consensus that the code used here can be either visual or phonological, the latter predominating as difficulty increases.[5] This mechanism not only explains the appearance of phonology in a model that specifically discounts its necessity, it also accounts for the greater difficulty nonhearing readers and others who are not using phonology have in comprehending strings of connected discourse, even while understanding the individual items.

If phonological recoding does not or need not occur before accessing lexical items, where in the process does it occur? The only other possibility is after lexical access, when the item with its associated information including its phonological code has already been addressed by the "direct" visual method. This hypothesis makes a lot of sense. It explains, for example, why real words can be read aloud faster than nonwords, even those that conform to correct orthographic and phonetic patterns: the former are accessed visually then read off, while the same attempt to access the nonwords, failing, gives way to the alternate device of prelexical phonological processing (Venezky 1972:7; Goodman 1976a:483; Banks et al. 1981:148).

Having found a role for phonology within direct access, we have eliminated the last obstacle to accepting this hypothesis as a model for reading alphabetic texts. The process seems to go as follows: pieces of text corresponding to letters or clusters of letters—individually, in sequence, or separated—are visually apprehended. They are then subjected to a feature analysis. The icon that results—a reduced, abstracted representation of the physical stimulus—is matched with the corresponding graphic address of a morpheme, word, part of either, or larger unit in the lexicon. The activated address, with or without its attendant information, is stored in short-term memory by the same "visual" code or by a phonological code obtained after the item has been accessed. Parsing mechanisms then operate on the stored string, which is cleared from short-term memory when the comprehensive structure (or some abstraction of it) is passed on to the same higher mechanisms used to comprehend speech.

Although direct access may be the most plausible model, we have not established that it is the only method for reading alphabetic texts. The main flaw that we saw in prelexical phonological recoding models was that they cannot possibly function obligatorily, as has been claimed. Nothing was said about the suitability of recoding as a practical alternative, however, and on this point—the co-use of a variety of methods (dual access) and strategies—most scholars agree (Gibson and Levin 1975:471; Gleitman and Rozin 1977:36; Glushko 1979:678; Gunther 1983:366). As mentioned at the beginning of this chapter, however, there is real disagreement on the specific blend of methods employed. On the one hand, there is Rozin and Gleitman's view of the "average adult reader [who] does a substantial amount of phonological processing of the print, converting individual letters or letter sequences into some covert phonological form enroute to meaning" (1977:132). At the other extreme, we learn that "the hypothesis that speech recoding is used normally by mature readers to determine the meaning of words in text should be laid to rest. There is some evidence against it, and every piece of evidence seemingly for it is better attributed either to processes of recoding that occur after meaning is determined or else to paradigm-specific strategies that are unlikely ever to be used in reading" (Banks et al. 1981:167). Berry's characterization is even more radical:

"The way in which a fluent reader identifies words has little or nothing at all to do with phonology; the sound-spelling relationship is not of critical importance. An extreme conclusion to be drawn from this view is that the alphabetic principle is irrelevant for reading. The fluent reader reads English or French or German efficiently only insofar as he treats the written language as if it were ideographic" (1977:10).

I believe that the key to this problem lies in distinguishing between what is "normal" for readers to do and what they do under "ideal" circumstances. Direct access seems to work best under these latter conditions, where the reader is free of distraction and processing clear text on a familiar topic. Just how often these conditions obtain for the average reader, however, is an open question, assuming an average reader can even be identified. Among those questions that can be answered, it seems clear enough that readers of alphabetic scripts need not translate through sound or through any other kind of speech-based code, nor need they in practice treat the letters of print as anything more than components of visual wholes that distinguish one word from another by their different physical configurations at least as much as by the sounds they happen to represent.

The Role of Sound in Reading Chinese

We have come some distance from the "common sense" view of reading described at the beginning of this chapter as it pertains to phonetic scripts or, at any rate, to their most widely used specimen. Practiced readers of English, without being aware of it, use two methods to access meaning: the "direct" visual method, through which lexical items are accessed by a sight-based code, and phonological recoding whereby the reader translates visual input into a speechlike or speech-based code prior to lexical access. Skilled readers use both types for normal reading, the former when rapid cognition is desired, the latter under conditions of interference. What methods are available to readers of Chinese character scripts? Fortunately, we need not spend much time reestablishing the validity of direct access for Chinese because, as stated at the beginning of the chapter, this view is not disputed and the only alternative—phonological recoding as an obligatory process—is highly implausible. Although the likelihood that this process occurs optionally cannot be dismissed a priori, it cannot possibly be required, or we could not explain how a character can be understood whose pronunciation has been forgotten or never learned, or how readers are able to distinguish the meanings of homophonous characters.

Our task with the character scripts, then, is to ascertain whether sound plays any role in their processing at all. It was long believed there was no such role and that readers managed through visual processing alone. This belief was not confined to lay persons. According to Tzeng, Hung, and Wang, "Many reading researchers have argued that since an ideographic [*sic*] language has printed forms that do not contain information about pronunciation, people must be able to read without speech coding" (1977:623). Later research, beginning with Tzeng's own, has shown that this is not always true. Using character lists designed to encourage phonetic interference in recall tasks, Tzeng et al. were able to establish the use of phonological recoding at some stage in the reading process. Their argument that recoding occurred after lexical access seems to have been inferred from the paucity of phonetic clues available and from demonstrations that phonological recoding occurs after lexical access in English. Conversely, the interpretation given by Mae and Loritz to another experiment showing phonological involvement in character reading—that "word recognition strategy" is phonological (1977:345)—almost certainly confuses postaccess short-term memory coding for its prelexical counterpart. Summarizing what evidence is available on this point, Paradis et al. agree that tests demonstrating the operation of phonological processes with character scripts "tell us more about short-term memory than about . . . reading" (1985:28).

To this extent, reading Chinese characters parallels what we found to occur "ideally" with phonetic scripts. In both cases, the lexicon is accessed by a "visual" code. The corresponding phonological code is subsequently added as an aid to short-term memory, as a requisite to further processing, or as both. In neither script type is prelexical phonological recoding obligatory, although it can happen optionally under a variety of circumstances with phonetic scripts. Can it also happen optionally with the characters?

Gleitman and Rozin claim that fluent readers of English "recognize thousands of syllables and whole words as units and that they characteristically analyze unfamiliar words in terms of syllabic rather than phonemic chunks" (1977:474). Glushko states similarly that English "readers use larger and more specific units of orthographic and phonological structure" than single phonemes and letters (1979:677). If this is true, there can be no objection in terms of numbers to the hypothesis that Chinese readers have learned to do the same thing with the syllable-size units of their own script, without regard for the direct symbol-meaning association. If the Chinese character writing system can be viewed formally as a syllabary, it makes sense that the system should also be able to function as a syllabary.

Many who read Chinese have had the experience of assigning a correct subvocal pronunciation to a character during reading, then erroneously associating that character's meaning with another of the same sound with a resulting loss of comprehension. This same type of processing is also likely to occur with marginally familiar characters for which "visual" pathways have not yet been established. Conceivably, there are other cases where the only item retrieved from a lexical store is the character's standard pronunciation, which in combination with the sounds of surrounding morphemes is enough to identify the referent. To a native speaker who thinks in the language he or she is reading, a strong hint of the character's pronunciation may be enough to elicit the morpheme when context has already limited the possibilities to a narrow set.

The most plausible conclusion to be drawn from these cases is that both methods—direct access and phonological recoding—are available to readers of Chinese character scripts just as they are to readers of English and other phonetic scripts. That is, the "dual access" model applies to both script types with equal validity. Where differences do arise is in the propensity of a given script to foster processing of one type or the other, although even here the critical distinction seems not to be "morphemic" versus "alphabetic," but the particular correspondence between sound and symbol. For example, in Chinese, where the relationship between symbol and sound is less principled, Treiman et al. (1981) found subjects relying almost entirely on "visual" processing to make truth judgments on sentences where falsity could be masked with homophones. English readers in the same experiment were more consistently misled by the homophone sentences, indicating their greater reliance on prelexical phonological recoding. At the other extreme is the Korean *hangul* script, where the relationship between pronunciation and symbol is entirely regular. Although Choe

(1970:54–57) and Ho Ung (1974:54) claim that *hangul* words can be processed "directly" by experienced readers just as the characters can, Pak contends that, because of the regularity between symbol and sound, readers cannot avoid using sound to reach meaning (1968:32–33).

Both claims await verification. If experiments with other phonetic scripts—and on particular words within a writing system—are any guide, however, Pak's characterization will not be far off the mark. Evidence is accumulating that for writing systems that follow pronunciation closely, choice of method is correspondingly constrained. According to Packard, "the more principled the relationship between sound and symbol, the more likely it is that readers will be aware of the principled nature of the relationship, and accordingly, the more likely it is that phonological information will play a part in lexical access" (1987:385–386). If this is the case, it may be that the question to have asked at the beginning of this chapter is not what differences exist between the processing of phonetic and character-based scripts, but where on a continuum bounded by these two methods particular writing systems belong.

One final consideration will help put this issue into perspective: even if it were possible to identify a "normal" method (or mix of methods) for reading the units of a given script in isolation, in practice the psychological processes operating within the same time frame are so numerous and complex that the basic norm is reduced to a meaningless abstraction. According to DeFrancis, readers of Chinese "pick and choose" their clues from among "(1) the graphic structure of the characters, (2) the information provided by the phonetic if there is a useful one, (3) the hint that might be provided by a radical, (4) punctuation and other typographical information, (5) the immediate environment of each character and the larger grammatical patterns in which it occurs, (6) knowledge of the subject matter" (1984a:169–170). Taking these factors into account, it would not be surprising to discover more variation in method among the users of a given script, at different times and under varying circumstances, than between the respective norms for English and any character-based writing system (if norms could even be established).

The Right Brain–Left Brain Dichotomy

The major fact that emerges from the foregoing discussion is that there is nothing "special" about the way people read Chinese characters, and hence nothing to be gained here, either, to compensate for the many disadvantages that their use entails. Chinese characters and alphabetic scripts are read by a mixture of the same two methods involving "direct" processing of the printed forms with phonology literally added on as an afterthought, and, alternatively, by pre–lexical access phonological recoding. Moreover, it is highly likely that for both systems these two processes operate in tandem to enhance speed and also as a redundant backup to guard against mistakes from either pathway. The final question is, how does one reconcile the hypothesis that the same mechanisms are used for reading character and phonetic scripts with evidence of right hemisphere involvement in Chinese character recognition, in contrast to use of the brain's left hemisphere for reading phonetic scripts and for linguistic activity generally?

Not only is this bicameral phenomenon observed between script types, it also occurs within writing systems that use a mixture of phonetic and character representation. In Japanese, Hirata and Osaka found a left hemisphere superiority for individual *katakana* words and symbols (1969); Hatta later found the same for *hiragana* (1978). These findings were replicated by another experiment (Endo et al. 1978) that compared random shape recognition with recognition of two-syllable *katakana* nonsense words: regardless of which hand was used (a function of hemispheric dominance), reaction time for the tachistoscopically presented items was shortest for shapes in the left visual field (governed by the brain's right hemisphere) and shortest for *kana* in the right visual field (i.e., the brain's left hemisphere).

Similar results were obtained for Korean *hangul*. Endo et al. tested thirty-three Japanese and Korean-Japanese subjects with two-syllable nonsense *kana* and single *hangul* syllables (1981). The Korean-Japanese subjects had been taught to read pronunciation from *hangul* symbols but could not understand their meanings. As expected, the Japanese demonstrated a right visual field (left hemisphere) superiority for *kana*, which were part of their everyday linguistic repertoire, and a left visual field (right hemisphere) superiority for the *hangul*, which were completely unfamiliar. The Korean-Japanese subjects, however, while showing the same tendencies for the *kana*, demonstrated a significant right visual field (left hemisphere) advantage for the *hangul* as well. A similar experiment (Shimizu and Endo 1981) involving recognition of nonsense *kana* and *hangul* syllables by Japanese showed the same respective right visual field–left visual field bifurcation regardless of the subjects' handedness. The left visual field (right hemisphere) advantage for *hangul* disappeared when the subjects were taught their pronunciations and meanings.

These and similar experiments conducted with alphabetic writing systems demonstrated that the brain's left hemisphere dominates the processing of phonetic scripts. But how valid is the opposite claim that characters are processed in the brain's right half? As mentioned at the beginning of this chapter, tachistoscopic experiments conducted by Tzeng et al. (1978) and Hatta (1977, 1978) with single-character stimuli in both Chinese and Japanese show strong right hemisphere participation in the recognition process. Tzeng et al. replicated these results as part of another experiment,[6] but subsequently asked the important question of whether these findings are related in any significant way to what actually occurs during reading.

Since individual characters in Chinese refer to morphemes primarily and to words only when the morphemes themselves are words, "the perceptual unit in reading may be much larger than the single characters" that formed the basis of this and other experiments (1979:500). Tzeng tested the new hypothesis on two-character words, resulting in "LH [left hemisphere] dominance, a complete reversal of the previous experiment." A third test, based on multiple-character words that required fast decisions to deny possible use of phonology, replicated the second (ibid.:501).

The same reversals from right to left hemisphere dominance occurred with multiple-character stimuli in Japanese-language experiments. Sasanuma et al. carried out tachistoscopic studies using fifty sets of *kana* pairs and fifty *kanji* pairs, all meaningless as pairs. A right visual field (left hemisphere) superiority was found for *kana* as predicted. For the character pairs, however, a small, statistically insignificant left visual field (right hemisphere) preference appeared, which was far short of the strong tendency evidenced by single-character and nonlinguistic materials in earlier studies. The authors hypothesized that "some kind of phonological activities may accompany the *kanji* processing" even with nonsense words (1977:551–552). Hatta's experiments with two-character stimuli used naturally occurring character combinations instead and obtained results even more striking: a significant right visual field (left hemisphere) preference, which Hatta also interpreted as a function of the *kanji's* "phonological aspects" (1978:55–57).

Neither Hatta nor Sasanuma specified whether the alleged phonological involvement resulted from pre- or postlexical recoding. Elman et al. conceded the possibility of phonological involvement but added that the observed right visual field (left hemisphere) effect for two-character words may stem from "the analytical skill of the left hemisphere" (1981:410). They also introduced a new variable: abstractness. In their own experiments with *single*-character stimuli, Elman et al. found "no significant difference for visual field," which contradicts earlier studies that showed a right hemisphere preference for individual Chinese characters. What they did find was a significant correlation between visual field and the abstractness of the word represented, the right hemisphere performing poorly on abstract items. Earlier studies had neglected to control for this variable. Stimuli were usually concrete nouns, which prejudiced the experiments in favor of the right hemisphere.[7] Summarizing these and other laterality experiments, Paradis et al. concluded that "the only pattern that has consistently emerged across a variety of studies is that two-character word stimuli written with any type of script will produce a RVF advantage" (1985:32). Tzeng et al. reached the same conclusion from the Chinese data, that "the locus of the cerebral lateralization cannot be on the logographic symbols per se" (1979:500).

Pathology also fails to support the belief that character and phonetic scripts are processed in different hemispheres of the brain. According to Paradis et al., "There is no clinically documented pattern of greater impairment for *kanji* with right hemisphere lesions and greater impairment for *kana* with left hemisphere lesions" (1985:166). Rather, correlation of impairment with locus of lesion suggests that both types of script are handled primarily by the left hemisphere, *kana* in the left temporal area and *kanji* in the left parieto-occipital area (ibid.:159).

Even this distinction may be artificial, however. The left temporal area, which houses the auditory cortex and one of the brain's two language centers,[8] is responsible for primary auditory processing. It also handles semiprocessed visual stimuli sent in from the occipital lobe "for more abstract kinds of processing" (Hooper and Teresi 1986:37–38). The use of this area with *kana* for phonological processing is entirely consistent with this region's function. That character input can bypass the temporal area without a loss of understanding only confirms what we have established above in connection with "direct access," or "visual" processing of writing systems in general: that "conceptual meaning is directly connected to the visual recognition of the character and the corresponding linguistic acoustic image follows" (Paradis et al. 1985:159). Equally important for our overall thesis that there are direct, functional links between meaning and sound, on the one hand, and between meaning and its written representation, on the other, is the phenomenon of brain-injured patients who can read *kanji* aloud without understanding them. Speculating on the cause, Paradis et al. observe that "since *kanji* have both a phonemic and an ideographic dimension, what is evoked from a *kanji* has both a phonemic and conceptual element (a morpheme), and either can be selectively impaired" (1985:160). This statement—an explanation for observed clinical phenomena—coincides with the structural description offered in Chapter 5 for the triad relationship between sound, character, and semantic referent.

My basis for suggesting that any anatomical distinction between writing systems may be artificial, however, is not the propensity of character processing to avoid the temporal area (at least for lexical access), but rather the probability that the activation of this area for *kana* words was paradigm-specific and hence atypical. As Paradis et al. noted, the *kana* stimuli used in tachistoscopic and other types of experiments "are nearly always transcriptions of words that normally appear in *kanji*, and are therefore visually unfamiliar representations, for which a visual route would not be expected to exist" (1985:20). Had the *kana* been naturally occurring words and apprehended as such (which is less likely to occur in experiments than in reading connected text), there would be no more reason for processing differences to arise here than between characters and the "visual" processing of phonetic scripts.

Failure to control for this variable led to the same erroneous conclusion in a number of other studies as well. For example, Stroop tests of color naming showing different processing methods for characters and *kana* are invalid for the simple but compelling reason that color terms are normally written in characters (Paradis et al. 1985:22). Hink et al.'s reported confirmation of laterality differences between characters and *hiragana,* for all its technical sophistication, may have the same flaw (1980:456). Finally, there is Marshall's criticism of Sasanuma and Fujimura's (1971) experiment comparing recognition performances of two groups of aphasics, with and without apraxia of speech (1976:124). Although *kanji* performances were comparable, the group with apraxia of speech scored worse than those not afflicted when the same words represented by characters were spelled in *kana.* But since these latter stimuli were not naturally occurring units, the subjects had to use phonological recoding, and those with the speech handicap were correspondingly disadvantaged. When natural *katakana* nouns were used, the performance differences disappeared.

To summarize, the notion that Chinese character scripts are processed in the brain's right, or "intuitive," "holistic," "synthetic" half, in contrast to phonetic writing systems, which are known to be processed in the language-specialized areas of the brain's left or "logical," "analytic" half, cannot be supported. Neither clinical studies on patients with physical brain impairments nor lateralization experiments on normal subjects show any hemispherical differentiation by script type, provided the symbols of the latter are recognized as naturally occurring linguistic units. The right hemisphere becomes involved only when the brain perceives shapes that cannot be identified with familiar symbols of a writing system or when the symbols do not correlate with their usual referent, because the normal orthographic convention is violated or the symbol is less than the normal perceptual unit. Otherwise, linguistic processing of Chinese characters is entirely straightforward. The brain treats these symbols, apprehended by the reader as units of a written language, to the same types of processes used to extract meaning from writing that is more overtly phonetic. Here, as in other aspects of reading, there is nothing absolutely unique that distinguishes Chinese characters from alphabetic and other phonetic systems, and certainly nothing that accrues to their advantage.

The Nonuniqueness of Chinese Writing

Our review of the psycholinguistic properties of Chinese characters as pertains to reading and recognition shows other interesting parallels with phonetic writing, beginning with the psychological reality of these graphic representations for literate users of a language. Neither in English nor in any of the character script languages can direct "visual" access be explained without assuming an internal, graphic counterpart to the abstract phonological representation of lexical items. We have seen that these graphic and phonological representations are independent of each other functionally, just as we earlier saw them to be structurally, their primary link being the relationship they share with the semantic and syntactic representata of the word itself. Neither can be considered "primary," either in the formal sense discussed in Chapter 5 or in the functional, psychological sense described here.[9]

There are implications here for problems to be discussed in subsequent chapters. First, we must reject on both structural and psychological grounds the criticism that characters are deficient for failing to "represent" the sounds of a language directly. No practical orthography does. The primary function of any writing system, from the standpoint of the practiced reader, is to make lexical meanings available in a form appropriate to the medium, which is visual, not auditory. In this respect, English and the character writing systems function similarly. A second point is the alleged functional directness with which characters convey meaning. We have shown this to be a misconception, absolutely and relative to what happens under the same "ideal" circumstances with phonetic writing. In neither case is meaning apprehended directly from print. Rather, both types require the intermediate processes of icon formation, reduction, and image matching, which in balance may be no less complex than prelexical phonological recoding. Either way it is hard to see how the character scripts offer an advantage over alphabets in this regard.

On the contrary, some distinct drawbacks can be discerned. A major one is the less principled (unprincipled) relationship of the characters to sound, which is used in significant ways by readers in "normal" if not "ideal" circumstances. Another is the nature of a character's complexity. According to Carrol: "In a nonalphabetic system, recognition of characters depends on the total configuration of parts. In an alphabetic system, skilled recognition of words depends not so much on the recognition of individual letters as on the recognition of the total configuration of letters" (1972:106). In other words, reading in either system begins with visual apprehension of discrete components, their individual significance being not what phoneme they may or may not represent, but their graphic distinctiveness with respect to other symbols in the inventory and their spatial relationship to the other concrete units that appear. Such configurations must be learned individually for both systems, Chinese character and alphabetic, which in principle seems to equate the two types in terms of difficulty—until we consider the nature of the parts that make up these wholes.

English words are formed through the serial ordering of units from a pool of twenty-seven (the letters of the alphabet plus a blank space), the most complicated having only a few strokes. Chinese characters, in the usual case, consist of a two-dimensional, largely unprincipled arrangement of components that are more complex individually than English letters and are drawn from an inventory of hundreds. An alternative analysis could reduce the tokens to a few dozen, but at the cost of a corresponding increase in the number of rules governing their ordering. The complexity is there, one way or another. I shall argue in the next chapter that there is a need for this complexity, which in the long run is self-generated. For the present, however, it should be clear that if we consider only the end points of these writing systems, without regard to specific features of the languages underlying them, an enormous amount of complexity has been applied to realize the same—or probably less—psychological utility as that provided by alphabetic scripts.

8. Appropriateness to East Asian Languages

THE BEST ARGUMENTS for Chinese characters revolve around what many see as their "appropriateness" to Chinese language and by extension to the Sinitic vocabularies of other East Asian languages. Chinese itself, with its alleged "monosyllabic" structure, is regarded as uniquely suited to a form of representation whose units are one syllable long. Since the serviceability of a writing system is measured by how well it fits the language, what more could be asked? Also, by focusing on meaningful units, the characters are said to eliminate a major deficit in the Sinitic parts of East Asian languages, namely, their poorly differentiated phonetic structures. Because of its many homonyms, Chinese vocabulary—by this argument—cannot be reliably distinguished through speech or through a phonetic writing system based on speech. But since Chinese characters "transcend" speech, users distinguish by sight words that cannot be distinguished by sound. Finally, this same supralinguistic quality allegedly enables characters to bridge the differences between China's many "dialects," enabling people all over China to read the "same language." The conclusion drawn from these arguments is that what counts is not the writing system per se, but how well that system matches the concrete reality of the language, in which case Chinese characters are said to score high.

The above can be called the "enlightened" view of Chinese writing, held by many linguists, East Asian and Western, who have taken the trouble to analyze the character writing system in terms of what it is asked to accomplish.[1] Unfortunately, these arguments, while valid on one level, share the same basic flaw of confusing the remedy for a problem with its cause. In the first place, I shall argue below that Chinese is not "monosyllabic," perhaps even less so than English. Multisyllable words are the norm in Chinese, and the only reason it appears otherwise is the morphosyllabic writing system, which enforces an artificial analysis of a word's constituents while masking or preventing the emergence of phonetic interaction across syllable boundaries. Similarly, claiming that Chinese characters are useful because they distinguish homonyms is, quite simply, putting the cart before the horse. Homonyms are a problem in Chinese and Chinese-based vocabulary because the characters let people coin words that cannot stand on their own phonetically or that are not words at all, but written abbreviations of words. Lacking any incentive to write the full representation of a word that can be understood visually through some fraction of its components, Chinese writers over time evolved a set of conventions that worked for the written medium but ignored the conflicting requirements of speech. Phonetic ambiguity was the result.

By the same token, the "unity" that Chinese characters allegedly impart to the language by allowing speakers of different "dialects" to read a common written language turns out to be an illusion. These so-called Chinese dialects have less in common than the Romance languages of Europe, meaning that speakers of nonstandard Chinese (some 30 percent of the Han population) are not reading their own language or even a common language, but what is to them a Mandarin-based second language written in Chinese characters. Granted the characters allow non-Mandarin speakers to read segments of written Mandarin in their own regional pronunciations. But, far from unifying Chinese, this practice only perpetuates differences that would have been leveled out long ago under the influence of a phonetic script. Again, the cause of a problem is mistaken for its cure. I shall argue in this chapter that the "appropriateness" of Chinese characters to Chinese is solely a function of the effects this writing system has had on the language. Or, put another way, the only good thing to be said for the characters from a linguistic point of view is that they "solve" certain problems that their own use has created.

"Monosyllabic" Chinese

There is a popular notion that the words of Chinese are made up of single-syllable units. This belief owes its currency to three factors: (1) The classical style of writing, which still predominated earlier in this century when Western scholars first became interested in Chinese, was until recently given more weight in the training of China specialists than the colloquial language itself. In classical Chinese (a written language that has no spoken counterpart), a one-syllable-one-word paradigm really was approximated. (2) Chinese dictionaries are for the most part still arranged by characters, leading users to assume that these single-syllable graphic forms correspond to what one normally finds in dictionaries, namely, words. (3) There is a lay misconception that if characters are more than letters and have meaning, then they must represent words, and that these "words" are all one syllable long. Noting that Mandarin has fewer than 1,300 distinct syllables, various authors have gone on to associate these two "facts" about the language and have concluded erroneously that Chinese have restricted vocabularies, cannot understand each other in speech, and have trouble with abstractions (Gleitman and Rozin 1973b:497; Bloom 1981; Logan 1986; Tezuka 1987).

Thus the allegation that Chinese is monosyllabic is based not on the language as it is spoken (and, presumably, internalized by its speakers), but rather on the way the language was and is conventionally written. By identifying the syllable-sized units of written Chinese with words instead of with morphemes, people began to believe mistakenly that the language itself is monosyllabic. According to Zhou, monosyllabic words account for just 12 percent of the contemporary Chinese lexicon (1987b:13). DeFrancis reckons about 5 percent of the two hundred thousand words in a modern dictionary are monosyllabic (1984a:187). These figures apply to the lexicon as a whole. For running text, DeFrancis estimates Chinese "as only 30 percent monosyllabic as against 50 percent for English material written in a style comparable to that of the Chinese" (1943:235). Zheng gives a higher figure of 40 percent monosyllabicity for Chinese texts (1957:50), while I find English text nearly 60 percent monosyllabic. Clearly, the notion that Chinese, absolutely or even relative to other languages, is made up of monosyllabic words is untenable.

In his book *The Chinese Language: Fact and Fantasy,* John DeFrancis devotes a chapter to exposing what he properly calls "the monosyllabic myth," which some scholars have mistakenly applied to Chinese and to Sinitic words in other Asian languages. Although the concept is no longer defensible, the term "monosyllabic" is susceptible to another interpretation that is more consistent with the facts. Looking not at words but at the morphemes of Chinese, we find that they do by and large correspond to single syllables, and in this special, restricted sense the language *can* be considered more or less monosyllabic (Hockett 1951:44; Li Fang-kuei 1973:2; French 1976:103; Ohara 1989:85). Sinitic words are not monosyllabic, but the fact that most of their morphemes are has had an important impact on the formation of vocabulary.

No language can get by today with only a few thousand monosyllabic words. However, if each of the monosyllabic morphemes of a language has its own unique graphic sign that shields the morphemes (in some cases artificially) from attrition and draws attention to their existence as units, then there is no need for words to exceed *two* syllables in length, since, mathematically, the format can accommodate millions of word-length expressions. By focusing attention on the morpheme and making possible the preservation of a one-syllable-one-morpheme relationship, Chinese characters enabled the language to evolve in such a way that its concepts can be and usually are expressed in one- and especially two-syllable words. There was no need for a more complex morphology to come into play, since such words find their natural application in writing or in the discourse of groups sensitive to a particular context.

Not only do Chinese characters make possible a lexicon of one- and two-syllable words, they strongly inhibit the formation of words that exceed this length. This is not to deny the existence of multisyllable words entirely. The process of compounding has its own dynamic that involves more than the need to create structural distinctions. Two-syllable words are expanded and further defined by morphologically productive affixes,[2] or they become fused into longer expressions as aphorisms or compounds. Yet despite what would seem like natural causes for their development, multisyllable terms are still relatively scarce. According to Chen Mingyuan, words with three or more syllables account for just 2 percent of the text in contemporary Chinese writings, whether the subject is science and technology or everyday topics (1980:69). Hai Ying gives a figure of 3 percent (1980:150). A similar impression is gained by inspecting the regular columns of words in Chinese character dictionaries and even in *hangul* dictionaries of Korean, where the progression of two-syllable words is only occasionally interrupted by longer entries. How can this be explained?

One reason may be the Chinese propensity for symmetry and balance. But this phenomenon could as easily have resulted from the influence of the language's morphology and syntax on behavior. Another factor is visual redundancy. There is already a great surplus of graphic information in a written two-character expression, so why use more than necessary? A third explanation invokes principles of semantics. Given the autonomy of thousands of single-syllable, meaning-bearing elements that the use of Chinese characters has made possible, a combination of two such units is the most natural semantic configuration, encompassing both the root-modifier format and the fusion of complementary or antithetical concepts. Extending these basic patterns by the addition of a third or fourth morpheme has more to do with the requirements of syntax than semantics.

Incredibly, another reason for the ubiquitousness of the two-syllable format may be a shortage in the modern language of genuine one-syllable words! I have argued that the number of syllables needed for high-level vocabulary in Chinese is fewer than in European languages because the syllables are given an additional (and from a strictly phonetic point of view artificial) level of redundancy through the character script. This redundancy, however, applies only to the language as it is written, which may be the usual habitat for that segment of the lexicon but is hardly so for the bulk of everyday concepts that must be communicated verbally. And as differentiated as the written forms of Chinese syllable-morphemes are, the phonetic qualities that separate them are few indeed. Statistics compiled by Gao and Yin show 1,280 spoken syllables for standard Mandarin compared to 4,030 for English (1983:70). Equally important, this difference arises not because of a relative shortage of phonemes, but from restrictions on the use of these phonemes within the syllable (there are, for example, no consonant clusters and only three consonant endings), which makes the Mandarin syllable appear even less differentiated. Because there are fewer phonetic distinctions within the syllable, basic concepts, which are the logical candidates for single-syllable expressions, are also represented by compounded two-syllable words to a surprising degree, just to insure phonetic intelligibility.

What conclusions can be drawn from the foregoing? Most basically, that Chinese language is not monosyllabic, and hence the argument that single-syllable graphic units are its most appropriate form of representation is wide of the mark. Absurd as it sounds, it would be far easier as things stand now to argue for a writing system that uses bisyllabic units. What *is* monosyllabic about Chinese is its morphology, but this can be directly attributed to the effect Chinese characters have had on the structure of morphemes. Claiming for this reason that characters are more suitable than a phonetic script to write the language is equivalent to praising heroin because it "happens" to satisfy a user's addiction. If there were no need to ascribe meaning to every syllable, a polysyllabic morphology would have emerged long ago.

Morphemes versus Words

One need not subscribe to the thesis presented here—that the Chinese writing system, more than any "inherent" typological factor, is responsible for the language's monosyllabic morphology—to appreciate that Chinese look at their language not in terms of words at all, but in terms of morphemes. This apparently innocuous difference has had profound effects on the structure of the Sinitic lexicon and, as we will see in later chapters, on the ability of East Asians to mechanize writing and make other adjustments required by modern times. What is involved here is an entirely different mindset. One need only consider how few Westerners know the term "morpheme," which has no direct relationship to their alphabetic writing systems, to appreciate the fact that until recently Chinese did not even have a word for "word." Just how poorly this latter concept is held is evidenced in the habitual use by Chinese—including some with doctorates in linguistics—of zi (written character) for ci (word), even in referring to units of the spoken language. Since the focus of standard Sinitic (although not the nonstandard Chinese "dialects") is clearly more on morphemes than on words, Chinese characters, which represent morphemes, are regarded by many as the most appropriate way to write the language.

In fairness, it must be acknowledged that "word" has been one of the trickiest terms for linguists working with any language to define. Structural linguistics, with its outside-in view of language, has failed to provide any commonly accepted definition of the term, which surprises most people who feel intuitively when they use the term "word" that they and their listeners know what it means. Linguists, with some embarrassment, have ended up accepting a definition of word that is anathema to this speech-oriented discipline, namely, that a "word" is something one finds written between two blank spaces. But this empirical observation makes a lot of conceptual sense. What at any given time is a word in a language is not something linguists can ascertain on the basis of phonological characteristics alone, but is rather a social convention that must be made or discovered. This discovery process is precisely what writing systems that have word division force on literate users of the language. Words have to be "coined," that is, willfully manufactured and then ratified through a concrete mechanism that shows that the neologisms enjoy widespread acceptance. Word division in writing provides this mechanism.

However, this is only part of the story. Spoken languages, like any open-ended system, are constantly changing as different speakers seek to adapt their linguistic habits to a dynamic physical and psychological environment. This is as it should be. Concepts serviceable today eventually lose their relevance or validity, and it makes no sense at all to pretend that linguistic conventions once agreed on can or even should continue in perpetuity. Obviously, they do not, or I would be speaking some form of proto Indo-European, and my southern and northern Chinese colleagues would understand each other. However, no language is worth much (or even imaginable) if its conventions—including what it recognizes as concepts—are not shared by a wide body of users long enough for them to act on these shared assumptions and create a culture in which to live. Some balance must be reached between linguistic growth and conceptual chaos. Although any conventional writing system will help formalize a language, only those systems that incorporate word division can exercise a stabilizing effect on the flux between what different speakers of the language at different times regard as its finished concepts.

Morphemes, by contrast, are relatively easy to define: they are the smallest meaningful units of sound. But they are not sufficiently distinct in meaning or stable, and they cannot stand by themselves in transmitting information (Xie Kai 1989:17). Users still have to combine morphemes into words, and although this process of word formation occurs in Chinese as in any language, there are important differences. On the one hand, because Sinitic morphemes are identified by their own unique signs, they tend to remain "morphemes" longer than they should. In non-Sinitic lexicons, when two or more morphemes combine to form a word, the rationale for selecting the particular morphemes can often be inferred later from the meaning of the word and what users know about how the particular sounds relate to the meanings of other words. This is especially true if the language is written in an alphabetic system where spelling tends to be conservative. Eventually, however, the original motivation is lost to all but a small body of professional etymologists, the remaining users having better things to do with their time and language than to contemplate why a word means what it does. Character-literate East Asians, for their part, are denied this luxury; on some level they are forced by the nature of their writing system to associate meaning with every syllable long after semantic change has erased the original connection—assuming the connection was logical to begin with—and to this extent fail to grasp the totality of the new concept.

On the other hand, the absence of word division in Chinese writing, the need for which is obviated on the textual level by the fact that the characters are already providing a semantic analysis of the discourse, means there is no reinforcement of or check on what users do regard as words. This phenomenon is usually presented in positive terms by proponents of Chinese characters as "word-building power," whereby one can combine Chinese "characters" (morphemes) into an unlimited number of new concepts. It also lets some Chinese believe that one need master only a few thousand characters to grasp the whole of the language, unlike foreigners who must learn tens of thousands of units.[3] The problem with this morpheme-dominant practice of word formation is that "words" are produced that are not words at all, in the usual sense of rating an entry in a dictionary or even being known to a significant minority of users. Writers assume that if they choose appropriate characters, readers will probably get the idea, more or less, of what they intend.

Not surprisingly, these same habits are reflected in the composition of dictionaries. Students of alphabetically written languages can generally expect to open a dictionary and find unknown words that they encounter in speech or writing. However, fantastic as this may seem, the student of an East Asian language (including Vietnamese, which has not shaken its Chinese-style fixation on morphemes) beyond a certain level can usually count on the unknown combination *not* being in a dictionary, neither a bilingual dictionary nor one in the target language. The situation is so perverse that I sometimes feel guilty when I do find a combination I am looking for. More often than not, if the word is there at all, it is only because it was coined as a translation of a borrowed Western concept. Usually I end up doing what most East Asians do, and piece together the meanings of the two morphemes for a general idea of what is meant and try to convince myself that I understand it even if I do not.

If words are a language's finished concepts, it is difficult to see how anything that subverts the role of words could be beneficial to a language and its users. Yet, as we have seen, Chinese writing does this in two ways: by encouraging users to focus on a word's parts instead of on the whole and by allowing people unlimited license to make up "words" with no social sanction. The result is a collection of relatively amorphous units (morphemes) that dominate the written language and to a great extent the psychology of its users, and a reduced role for actual words in the language. Again, one can claim for this reason that the characters are more "appropriate" to the language in its present state, although the declaration seems rather vacuous.

The Homonym Problem

One of the most commonly cited—and misunderstood—justifications for Chinese characters is that they "eliminate" the so-called homonym problem in Chinese and the Sinitic lexicon in general. The thesis runs as follows: Chinese and Chinese-based vocabulary, more than that of other languages, include many words that sound the same. Not only are the number of syllable types in Chinese and in the Sinitic parts of Japanese and Korean few, the "monosyllabic" structure of these languages makes it inevitable that the same sounds and sound combinations will carry an unusually high number of meanings that cannot be reliably distinguished by phonological features (written or spoken). Fortunately, Chinese characters, being tied to meaning, are available to disambiguate this phonetic homogeneity. Words that sound alike at least do not look alike, meaning that East Asian languages, thanks to this "visually oriented" writing, are free to acquire vocabulary despite their phonetic handicap. Once again, Chinese characters save the day.

Plausible as this argument sounds, the statistics and rationale behind it as it applies to Chinese are spurious, and I include it here only because it is raised so often in the procharacter literature by East Asians who do not distinguish morphemes from words, and by nonspecialists in the West who accept their arguments at face value. The usual ploy is to consult the index of a large character dictionary, note the number of single-character entries under a given syllable—which can be in the dozens—and assert that the languages obviously need to be written with Chinese characters because phonetic representation would make the meanings of these sounds indistinguishable. However, as we have already noted, the number of single-syllable *words* in Chinese is less than in many alphabetically written languages. Even for sounds like Chinese *yi* and *shi*, where the inventory of characters is especially large, single-syllable morphemes that can stand alone as words are few. Almost all of these entries are bound or semibound morphemes that do not appear as isolated units in the spoken language.

What must be counted if statistics are to be meaningful are homophonous *words*. Using pinyinized Chinese, that is, Chinese written in a style appropriate to the phonetic writing system where the units are or should be words instead of syllable-size morphemes, Wen Wu found 11.6 percent of Chinese words to have homonyms, compared to 3.1 percent for English (1980:120). Zhou reports that in a Chinese dictionary of 60,000 words, some 4,000 or about 7 percent of its entries have homonyms; for a 120,000 word dictionary, the homonyms increase to about 6,000 or 5 percent (1987:13). Although high by Western standards, the figures are hardly alarming, since nothing has been said yet about frequency, the effects of context, or the phenomenon of "related meanings" in alphabetically written languages, which skews the comparison. In practical terms, Zhou calculates that the homonym problem in modern standard Mandarin reduces to about 1 percent. In an earlier study, Chen Wenbin counted 2,196 homophonous Chinese words from a corpus of 30,000.[4] Of that number, only 82 (39 sets of) polysyllabic words and 164 (70 sets of) monosyllabic words required differentiation.

These figures are a far cry from the impression one gets hearing about thirty-nine different Chinese "words" pronounced *shi*, forty-nine pronounced *yì*, and so forth. Another factor that makes the homonym "problem" in Chinese seem worse than it actually is relates to the etymology of homonyms in general and the impossibility of distinguishing them from their close cousins: polysemantic words. According to Sampson, the distinction "is essentially a historical one: when a given phonological shape is used for more than one meaning we say that we have distinct homophonous words if we know that at earlier stages the words were entirely separate, but we have a single polysemous word if the various meanings can be shown to have developed out of one original sense" (1985:155). Although polysemy exists in Chinese, particularly among its monosyllabic words, the incidence among polysyllabic Chinese words is lower than in Western languages because of restraints imposed by the character writing system. There is a limit to the meaning that can be logically imputed to the sum of two or more character-designated morphemes. Moreover, as meanings drift through time, Chinese tend to assign (or fashion) new characters for the changed sense, which technically yields "homophony" instead of polysemy. It seems likely that if all the meanings of polysemantic words in English or other alphabetic languages were counted and added to the number of words that pass as homonyms in those languages, the total would approximate the number of "homonyms" in Chinese; it would at least make the problem seem less formidable.

These points are raised to demonstrate that the so-called Chinese homonym problem involves much more than counting homographic dictionary entries and making cross-language comparisons on that basis. One can even question the assumption that homophony itself is bad. As Shi Xiaoren (1983:58) and Ao Xiaoping (1984:21) point out, there is nothing intrinsically wrong with the phenomenon. It is an economy measure common to all languages, and it would not happen if people did not feel that using longer units or a greater number of phonemes was more difficult than sharing meanings over a smaller number of representations. The question is how much homophony is desirable, a certain amount of it evidently being indispensable. I suspect that what lies at the bottom of the incessant carping about how Chinese, because of its "homonym problem," could not be understood if written phonetically is a deep-seated realization that if the characters did disappear, users would be forced to adjust to a new and unwanted regimen. They would have to use words that are words and abandon the undisciplined, self-indulgent practice of creating them arbitrarily.

I am more sympathetic to analogous claims about phonetic ambiguity in the Sinitic parts of Japanese and Korean, which can be attributed to special circumstances surrounding their adaptation. For nearly two millennia, non-Chinese languages on China's periphery have shared Sinitic vocabulary freely, in a manner known to all of the world's languages. Until recently, the direction of this "borrowing" had been largely from Chinese to Japanese, Korean, and Vietnamese, although the latter languages—most notably Japanese—have reversed the process and for the last century and a half have been coining new terms from Sinitic morphemes that are adopted by all four languages.[5] As a result of this borrowing, more than 40 percent of Japanese, 50 percent of Korean, and at least one-third of the words in Vietnamese are based on Sinitic morphemes, according to Liu (1969:67). These figures apply to everyday vocabulary and are lower than other researchers' counts that take in a wider corpus. For example, Sokolov claims 60 percent for Japanese, with the range for actual use varying between 10 and 80 percent, depending on the topic (1970:98). Ho Ung claims 60 percent (1974:44), and Oh claims 90 percent for some types of Korean materials (1971:26). Helmut Martin notes that in formal Vietnamese the ratio of Sinitic words can reach 50 percent; for newspapers it goes much higher (1982:32).

In general, the share of Chinese-style words in these non-Chinese languages increases with formality and difficulty of content, which is to say, Sinitic terms dominate those environments where style and subject matter make them the least predictable. One would think that the emphasis would be on maintaining phonetic distinctions between these word forms, but the opposite is more nearly true. Since most of the terms refer to higher-level concepts, the expectation was they would be identified through writing, where phonetic characteristics matter less. Accordingly, there was less pressure to avoid homonyms and near homonyms. Another, more important reason for the homophony can be traced to the dynamics of borrowing. When a language "borrows" terms from another, it typically adapts the words' sounds to its own phonology, which is never a perfect match. The borrowing language cannot add distinctions to the sounds of the terms it is borrowing, but it can and does ignore phonological distinctions that its own system is not equipped to handle. In the case of international Sinitic, this means dropping the tonal features that help distinguish one Chinese syllable from another.[6]

Just what this meant for the Sinitic vocabulary of Korean and Japanese is evident in the following figures. From an inventory of thirty-six initial and six syllable-final consonants totaling 3,877 different syllable types in sixth century A.D. Chinese, the number of syllables in modern standard Mandarin fell to 1,280, distinguished by twenty-two initial consonants, two final consonants (three, including the Beijing dialect's -*r*), and four phonemic tones. Korean speakers, for their part, have 1,096 syllables at their disposal (Yi Kang-ro 1969:44), which increases to 1,724 if we count written syllable types, hundreds more than in Mandarin even with the tones. This inventory seems to give Korean an advantage, until we realize that only four hundred or so different syllables are used for Sino-Korean. If this were not bad enough, most of this vocabulary is expressed in Korean as two-syllable compounds, even more than in Chinese, because of the availability of indigenous single- and multi-syllable words to handle the day-to-day concepts. The result is significantly more homonyms. Nam counted 22,983 Sinitic homonyms and 4,077 of mixed origin among the 91,825 entries in the Hangul Society's *Kukŏ sajŏn* (Korean Language Dictionary) (1970:11). Pure-Korean homonyms numbered only 3,120.

For Japanese the situation is even worse. Not only were Chinese tonal categories leveled, the phonetic reduction that occurred when these words were borrowed and their subsequent erosion through time have left just 319 sounds (*on* readings, including bisyllabic morphemes ending in *tsu, chi, ku,* and *ki*) for the 4,775 character-morphemes listed in Nelson's dictionary. Even this figure understates the problem, because many of these sounds have one character only, while others accommodate more than one hundred. Samuel Martin noted that the Japanese syllable *kō* corresponds to "at least 38 different (Chinese) syllables, some of which already represented more than one morpheme in classical Chinese" (1972:99). More than 180 characters are identified with this sound alone. Even with compounding the numbers are still formidable. Korchagina counted twenty-four words pronounced *kōkō*, twenty-three pronounced *kōshō*, eighteen *kōtō*, and fourteen *kōchō* in a modern Japanese-Russian dictionary (1977:43), adding that "the allegation of certain linguists that homonyms are an imaginary problem that exists only for linguists can hardly be applied to the Japanese language" (1975:52).

Other sources of homonyms are attenuated classical expressions in the modern colloquial language and extensive abbreviation—a practice that Zhou called the "monosyllabification of polysyllabic words" (1961:300). These abbreviations appear in technical terms and other types of new vocabulary that are shortened for convenience after the concepts take root in society, in names for organizations and institutions where the first or most significant characters for each word in the name are singled out to represent the whole, and, especially in Chinese, in the use of pithy, shortened slogans generally of a political nature. Although abbreviations make sense from the point of view of the reader, who, thanks to the characters, is inundated with a surplus of graphic information, the same morphemes that make up these abbreviations lose most of their redundancy, both absolutely and with respect to other expressions in the language, when spoken aloud. What began as graphically and phonetically distinct words collapse into homonyms or near homonyms ("paronyms") as reductions are made based on the requirements of writing that have no direct connection with the information-bearing requirements of speech.

This brings us to the heart of the problem. If a word's intelligibility is a function of its distinctiveness and predictability, then Sinitic vocabulary, because of the way it is formed and expressed, falls short in both respects, transforming what began simply as an abundance of homonyms into a genuine homonym "problem." With respect to distinctiveness, historical factors, the mechanism of borrowing, and most important, the use of a writing system in which graphic redundancy does not translate into anything remotely equivalent in speech have created an enormous number of terms with the same "external" phonetic characteristics or, what is just as bad, terms that differ in sound only minimally, by squeezing half or more of the languages' words into some 10 percent of the phonetic forms available to represent them. Homonyms are only the most noticeable effect of a phenomenon endemic to the Sinitic corpus as a whole, that is, its lack of phonetic distinctiveness overall.

The other factor—predictability—scarcely fares better. Goodman has shown that readers' ability to predict words from context can be as important for understanding as what actually appears in print (1976b). Cryptanalysis throughout much of its history was based on this same principle: that context severely constrains what can or cannot appear at any given point in a discourse and still make sense. If a printed form has a dozen or more meanings (or is missing from the text entirely), readers can often figure out what is intended on the basis of expectations induced by the surrounding text. In Chinese and Chinese-style writing, however, certain factors work against this. Since Sinitic terms are able to function in different grammatical environments without overt changes to their form, readers are less able to use this feature to predict what types of words can appear (Korchagina 1975:48; Yi Ul-hwan 1977:65). Guesswork is further constrained by a shortage of what can be called "serial redundancy." By comparison with alphabetic writing, Chinese character texts focus a disproportionate amount of their informational cues on individual graphemes, making it possible (or, from the standpoint of aesthetics, necessary) for writers to cut back the number of units introduced in the whole text, classical Chinese and modern newspapers being extreme examples. The result is that the information value of each remaining unit rises and the units become less predictable.

If Sinitic vocabulary lacks distinctiveness and suffers more than comparable terms in Western languages from shortage of context, what of the remaining determinant of a word's predictability, its familiarity to users? Here is the major cause of the problem that passes, with only partial justification, as the result of a surplus of homonyms. Readers of all-*hangul* Korean texts, for example, who because of the absence of Chinese characters are forced to rely entirely on phonetic information and context, are not encumbered so much by homophony per se (i.e., confusing one word with another) as they are by the inability to identify any meaning at all for the string of symbols given. In some cases this phenomenon can be dismissed as insufficient exposure to the word in phonetic form, whether spoken (where the vocabulary appears less frequently) or in texts, where it normally appears in characters. In this case, the user knows the word but is not used to its phonetic representation. Elsewhere, the sequence may not be a word at all, in the usual sense of being known to a majority or even a significant minority of educated users.

One can argue that none of this matters as long as the representation is in Chinese characters—but that is my whole point. Homonyms, near homonyms, and the shortage of grammatical and stylistic conventions for distinguishing them in the beginning had nothing to do with the features of the languages themselves and everything to do with the way these languages came to be written. As I have pointed out, the ability of characters to designate most concepts without reference to sound[7] has enabled the morphemes that they represent to be combined into words on the basis of their semantic values alone. There was no need to take phonetic intelligibility into account when the expectation was that discrimination would be accomplished through Chinese characters. According to Sokolov, "In creating Chinese or Chinese-style words little or no consideration was given to the need for distinguishing the words by sound." Rather, they were formed with the tacit understanding that their use would be restricted primarily to the written medium. The characters allowed phonetically deficient words to come into the language, and as long as these terms exist, there will be a need for characters (1970:97–98).

Neverov points to the high combinatory potential of Sinitic morphemes, which facilitated word formation and made this portion of the lexicon the first choice for a quick solution to the problem of introducing Western concepts. In forming these words, attention was paid only to the accuracy of the result; pronunciation played no role at all (1977:240). Korchagina's argument—that because characters can be used without ambiguity, the usual pressures leading to homonym discrimination do not come into play—comes closest to the present thesis. "In this way, the characters themselves ought to be regarded as the indirect source of homonyms in the Japanese language" (1977:44).

How the source of a problem can be regarded by supporters of the character script as that problem's solution escapes all logic. Rather than praising Chinese characters for their "appropriateness" to East Asian languages, it would be better to blame them for what they have done.

Transitivity across Languages

Next to homonym discrimination, the advantage most commonly claimed for Chinese writing is its supranational, supradialectal function, which allegedly enables speakers of different East Asian languages and "dialects" to communicate without knowing each other's speech. According to this argument, character-literate Chinese, Japanese, and Koreans can read materials written in any of the three languages by virtue of the characters' functional independence from sound. Although the symbols may be pronounced differently, they mean the same thing to any East Asian who has learned the system, it is claimed. Members of this "Chinese character cultural sphere" are thus better equipped than users of "sound-based" alphabetic systems in the West to exchange information and cope with the demands of today's international society. What is true of countries within East Asia, by this argument, also holds true within China for the same reason. Chinese characters, being tied to meaning more than to sound, are said to transcend "dialectal" variation inside China, thereby "unifying" the language and its speakers. Finally, literate Chinese, because of the ability of characters to mask differences in sound, are also said to be able to read Chinese written millennia ago based on what they know of the language today. In sum, what seems like a complicated and cumbersome system on one level is believed by some to make sense from a broader perspective.

I will try to show that these claims for the most part are fanciful fabrications, and that most of the success that the characters have in bridging different languages and "dialects" is also achieved with alphabetic writing. Let us begin with the former assertion: that Chinese characters allow literate users of Chinese, Japanese, and Korean to read each other's languages. It is tempting, though poor scholarship, to dismiss this claim up front by pointing out that if such were the case, there would be no need for governments to maintain separate pools of Chinese, Japanese, and Korean translators at enormous expense or to separately recruit specialists whose function is to read newspapers and technical works in these languages. Similarly, I and many of my colleagues in academe whose interests lie primarily in one of these three languages could happily have saved the years of effort it took to acquire a reading knowledge of the others. Although isolated words and segments of character text sometimes achieve the cross-language transitivity claimed for the system as a whole (such as occurs with the "international" vocabulary shared by alphabetically written European languages), anyone who has taken the trouble to learn more than one of these East Asian languages will find the notion of literacy in one equating to literacy in another simply laughable.

More than any actual performance factor, what gives credence to this claim, I suspect, is the tendency of Westerners to lump whatever differs from their own culture into a common bin, abetted by certain East Asians' naive or willful assertion that characters are characters, and what can be understood in China can be understood everywhere else in East Asia. In fact, nothing could be further from the truth. As described in Chapter 4 of this book, Vietnam long ago left the "Chinese character cultural sphere" and is using an alphabetic script. Chinese characters today have the same status in Vietnam as they have in the United States, namely, as decorative items and as a script for the country's Chinese-speaking minority. They have no present role in the language or in the linguistic psychology of its users. This fact is bemoaned by advocates of the character script in other Asian countries, but it is not something I have ever witnessed the Vietnamese themselves to be concerned about. For someone long inured to the vagaries and outright nuisances that accompany the use of Chinese characters, it is almost surrealistic to observe people of the same Confucian culture going about their lives *using* their language instead of being absorbed by it.

But there it is nonetheless: an East Asian society rebounding from decades of colonial rule, war, and socialist economics, blissfully unaware of its "benighted" status in the eyes of East Asian traditionalists. Vietnamese is able to borrow the international Sinitic terms coined elsewhere in East Asia just as alphabetically written Western languages share new vocabulary with each other. But the similarities between Vietnamese and character-based East Asian languages stop there. Words are spelled in Vietnamese, not drawn. Dictionaries, personal names, book titles, company listings, products, and geographical locations are cataloged in alphabetical order and are immediately accessible to any literate speaker. Text is composed on a computer screen directly; there is no dancing between an intermediate form of representation and units that may or may not correspond to what one actually wants to write. If Vietnamese are suffering through their non-use of Chinese characters from cultural deprivation or any linguistic maladies occasioned by an alleged breakdown in "transitivity," someone had better tell them. It won't be me.

What of the other areas of East Asia where Chinese characters form part of the repertoire of literate speakers? The most obvious problem with the transitivity thesis is that the character "system" used in the different countries is not the same, not even in its externals, owing to independent reforms. According to Virginia Chen, of 2,295 characters simplified in China, 309 in Japan, and 502 in Singapore, "only 178 original characters were simplified in all three countries. Of these 178 characters, only 48 were simplified in identical manner" (1977:64). Seventy of Japan's simplified characters have no counterpart in China, and only sixty of them have the same forms as China's. In Singapore, seventy-eight characters were simplified differently from their People's Republic of China equivalents. In Taiwan and South Korea none of these changes—neither Japan's nor China's—found their way into the standard inventory.

These variations in the forms of characters used by different East Asian countries are apparent even to Westerners not trained in the languages or writing systems. But there is more to the problem. Long traditions of independent use, particularly in Japan, have led to characters being used in one country that have little or no application to the language of another, or to the same characters used with different meanings. The effect of these absolute discontinuities is amplified by practical differences, resulting from government-backed limitations in some countries on the number of characters in use and the availability of *hangul* in Korea and *kana* in Japan, which have erased hundreds of "shared" characters from the inventory of most of their potential users. The results of these differences are striking. Highly educated Chinese on both sides of the Taiwan Strait, unless they have learned the other's system, stumble badly when trying to read each other's writing and often can make no sense of a passage at all. Japanese and character-literate Koreans fare even worse than mainland Chinese with materials printed in Taiwan, have virtually no capability with materials printed in the People's Republic of China, and enjoy less success with connected discourse written in each other's language than a literate English speaker has with French.

Even if the forms of the characters did not vary, individual tokens were shared more widely, and they had the same primary meanings in different languages, Chinese characters could not enable East Asians actually to read each other's languages because the languages themselves are different, in both grammar and morphology. Typologically, Chinese has less in common with Japanese and Korean than it has with English. And although Korean and Japanese may have some kind of genetic affiliation, they are communicably as different now, for example, as English is from German. Reading connected discourse in any of these languages is a function of linking the meanings of words (a large percentage of which are indigenous) according to unique grammars, and there is no way Chinese characters or any system of writing can mask these differences.

Assuming a character-literate East Asian in one country had made the effort to learn the different character forms used in another, it is true that he or she would be able to understand segments of discourse written in the other language. But this phenomenon—whatever its actual utility—has less to do with the writing system itself than with the fact that the languages share a lot of common vocabulary. The proof lies in the extremely poor cross-language transitivity achieved by the characters when they are used to represent indigenous words in Japanese *(kun)* as opposed to borrowed Sinitic terms *(on)*. In other words, Chinese characters give literate East Asians approximately the same facility with each other's languages as Westerners enjoy with cognate vocabulary written alphabetically in their languages, namely, a glimpse into the meaning of a text, which, depending on the reader's background, familiarity with the subject, and ability to reconstruct different character forms, may or may not be enough for some rudimentary understanding.

Ironically, Chinese characters, through their artificial support of moribund Sinitic morphology, their incompatibility with nontraditional word forms, and their reinforcing the notion that writing must be based on syllable-sized units, may be inhibiting cross-language transitivity by restricting the importation of international vocabulary that would otherwise be expressed in an alphabetic system shared by all. Despite complaints from cultural "purists," new terms based largely on English sounds are being borrowed individually into Japanese, Korean, and even Chinese on a scale that decades ago few could have imagined. These words now number in the tens of thousands, but because of the way the writing systems are constituted, they remain entirely opaque in one East Asian language to literate users of another. Rather than promoting cross-cultural communication, the character-based writing systems increasingly are standing in its way, making the languages themselves less relevant to a significant number of their own users.

Unification of Chinese "Dialects"

If transitivity of Chinese characters across languages turns out to be something less than what the system's advocates claim, what about the Chinese "dialects"? Surely one cannot deny the unifying effect Chinese characters have on disparate speech forms within China? Well, as with many other features attributed to Chinese characters, this claim will not hold up to a rigorous analysis either. Unless one trivializes the claim by reducing it to "psychological unity" or, as I shall discuss below, "unity by default," Chinese characters are not much better at bridging linguistic diversity inside the world's most populous country than they are at unifying languages outside China, and for the same reason: what many call "dialects" of Chinese are not dialects at all, but different languages with less in common than the Romance languages of Europe.

Before getting deeper into this discussion, however, I need to emphasize that for some eighty million or more people living in China the "transdialectal" feature claimed for Chinese writing cannot apply even in theory, because they speak non-Chinese languages written in alphabetic or indigenous systems.[8] Although they are relatively few in number, non-Han peoples dominate half of China's geography and because of their history and culture are far more likely to dissociate themselves from Beijing's laws and standards than Han non–Mandarin speakers living in the south. The irrelevance of Chinese writing to those very people who from the central government's point of view are most in need of it makes the argument that "Chinese characters unify the country" seem rather silly.

If we ignore this inconvenient phenomenon and focus on the speech of China's Han population, we find a collection of at least seven or eight mutually unintelligible varieties that in any other context would be called "languages," but which are "dialects" in China, in part for political reasons and in part because of a problem with the translation of the Chinese term *fāngyán*. The political motivation for claiming that these distinct varieties constitute a single language is fairly obvious: it is easier to govern a country in which the majority believe they are speaking one "language" (whatever the linguistic reality) composed of several "dialects" instead of several related languages. The terminological problem, however, is genuine. For millennia, Chinese used the word *fāngyán* ("local speech") to refer both to nonstandard forms of Chinese and to non-Chinese languages spoken within or around China. No distinction was made between a language and a dialect; there was standard Chinese spoken in the political capital and *fāngyán* spoken elsewhere. Later, under the influence of Western linguistics, Chinese began using the word *yǔyán* to translate "language" and *fāngyán* as a standard translation for what is known in the West as "dialect." But since nonstandard forms of Chinese were already called *fāngyán*, these mutually unintelligible non-Mandarin varieties became "dialects" of a Chinese "language."

Recognizing the problem, DeFrancis (1984a:53–67) and Mair (1991) proposed translating *fāngyán* respectively as "regionalect" or "topolect." This solves the technical question, but it leaves nonspecialists with the impression that Chinese is a "special case," when there is nothing special about it. Here is the reality. On the basis of linguistic criteria such as the development of Ancient Chinese voiced initial consonants, palatalization of velars, tonal registers, and certain morphological conventions, supported by the degree of intelligibility and native speakers' own intuitions, Chinese and Western linguists distinguish seven or eight major varieties of Chinese.[9] There is "North," or Mandarin, spoken in the northern, central, and southwestern parts of China with some 679 million native speakers;[10] Wu spoken by 81 million people on the east coast focusing on Shanghai; Northern and Southern Min spoken by 39 million people in Taiwan, Fujian province, and throughout Southeast Asia; Yue or Cantonese, used by 48 million speakers in the south; and three transitional varieties including Gan (23 million), Xiang (46 million), and Hakka (35 million), spoken respectively in Jiangxi, Hunan, and widely scattered pockets throughout the south. How are these varieties to be classified?

To answer this question at least four factors must be taken into account: the degree of mutual intelligibility, the underlying linguistic causes for the intelligibility or lack of it, how the Chinese situation fits into taxonomies used elsewhere in the world, and how Chinese speakers themselves feel about the problem. The first factor—degree of intelligibility between the major varieties of Chinese—can be dealt with easily: there isn't any. One of my strongest early impressions as a student of Chinese in Taiwan was that "Chinese" did not always work. No matter how hard I studied the "national language,"[11] there were large groups of people who could not understand me and others who could exclude me from a conversation by switching to some other variety that did not seem like Chinese at all. The situation did not change as my Mandarin improved, until I was finally led some twenty years later by curiosity and frustration deliberately to study Southern Min, an experience that reminded me uncannily of my high school days as an English-speaking student of Latin.

Before this, however, I had wised up to the reality of "Chinese," befriended a series of Wu speakers, and begun to have some fun of my own learning that variety and using it to annoy Mandarin and Min speakers who had no idea what we were saying. And although these experiences prepared me intellectually for my first known encounter with Cantonese (Yue), it was still upsetting to discover that nothing I had learned of the other varieties of Chinese would serve me here. The *fāngyán* was incomprehensible, as it is to all Mandarin, Min, Wu, and other native Chinese speakers born outside a Cantonese-speaking area, as evidenced, for example, by the Mandarin-speaking Chinese who uses English to order from a Cantonese-speaking Chinese waiter in the United States.

Dialects or languages? Let's look at another aspect of intelligibility. Early in my studies I discovered that the Taiwanese who *could* understand the Beijing Mandarin I was learning in school and who professed to speak the "standard language" spoke it in a funny way. Though we understood each other, my interlocutors failed to make certain phonemic distinctions that I had been taught to expect and occasionally used grammar that did not accord with what was in my textbook, although it was easy to figure out. When I tried these street forms in the classroom, I was "corrected" and informed they were not standard Chinese. A more advanced student with a bigger heart told me (to the enormous discomfort of our Beijing-born teacher) that these forms were not wrong but the difference between the Southern Mandarin spoken in Taiwan and the northern variety that passes for the national standard. But at least I was being understood! My first exposure to Southwestern (Sichuan) Mandarin was trying but also manageable. Although colleagues report they have encountered backwoods Mandarin varieties that are unintelligible to standard Mandarin speakers, these cases are exceptional. In the aggregate, Mandarin-speaking China looks very much like the mosaic that characterizes the English-speaking world with its distinct though usually intelligible dialects. Excepting one remarkable incident involving the numbers four and ten (they are segmentally homophonous in Southern Mandarin) that I would rather forget, I have never suffered any consequences that can be attributed to Mandarin speech differences, although there have been lots of laughs. This situation contrasts with the inability of speakers to communicate anything between the major varieties.

The same situation is characteristic of other, non-Mandarin forms of Chinese. On my bookshelf are textbooks of "Amoy Hokkien" (Xiamen Min) spoken in southern Fujian province and parts of Southeast Asia. It seems to have much in common with Taiwanese Min, and I understand parts of it despite my poor background in the latter. Next to that are two series of textbooks compiled by the Defense Language Institute titled *Chinese Cantonese* and *Chinese Cantonese (Toishan)*. The two varieties are sufficiently distinct to warrant separate treatment, but not so far apart that one cannot be understood by a native speaker of the other. I discovered with some embarrassment that the same applies to Wu. After studying for three years what I thought to be Shanghainese with a tutor from Ningbo, I tried it out one day on a woman from Shanghai. Peals of laughter ensued, after which she informed me, tears still in her eyes, that I was speaking "like a hayseed from Ningbo." But, again, I was being understood, in contrast to a Mandarin-speaking Chinese along for the show who had no idea why the Wu speaker was laughing. So what do we call *these* differences? Dialectal? If so, what does that make the larger groups that cannot be mutually understood and within which these dialects are subsumed?

The linguistic factors that account for unintelligibility between the major varieties of Chinese are sometimes dismissed by proponents of the one-language view as "mere" differences in sound. In fact, the differences encompass much more than phonology, but let's explore this aspect of the claim anyway using as an example the Shanghainese dialect of Wu, which impressionistically and in terms of linguistic features differs less from Mandarin than either Min or Yue does. Consonant phonemes for Mandarin (Kratochvil 1968:25–28) and Wu (Jin 1985:4) are shown in Table 8.

Shanghainese stops *(t, t', d)* are dental and Mandarin stops *(t, t')* are alveolar; conversely, Shanghainese affricates and fricatives *(ts, ts', s, z)* are analyzed as alveolar by Jin, while their Mandarin counterparts *(ts, ts', s)* are dental. Jin's alveopalatal consonants are treated as palatals by Ramsey (1987:92), but none of this is particularly significant. The important distinction is not where these sounds are articulated, but rather that there are three sets of affricates and fricatives in Mandarin and only two sets in Shanghainese. More important, Shanghainese has eight voiced consonants that are entirely absent in Mandarin (*ng* is used only as a final in Mandarin) and uses a glottal stop for Ancient Chinese *-p, -t, -k* endings, which were lost in Mandarin.

Vowel differences are also considerable, as depicted in Table 9 (which includes individual vowel phonemes and those that appear in diphthongs, triphthongs, and before consonant finals). The Shanghainese retroflex (apical) vowel *ï* is treated by Jin as an upper high back unrounded vowel, different from the apical vowel ʅ, which is pronounced with the tip of the tongue instead of the blade. Perceptually the two sound very similar, although Norman locates it farther back (1988:201). The two Mandarin vowels ʅ and ɭ in fact are one phoneme, with the former value realized after *ts, ts', s* and the latter after *tš, tš', š*. Since Shanghainese *ï* appears only after *ts, ts', s, z*, the difference is one of distribution. Other distinctions are more important, such as a front high-mid/low-mid contrast in Shanghainese not made in Mandarin and the presence of two rounded mid vow-

Table 8

Shanghainese and Mandarin Consonants

	Bilabial	Labio-dental	Dental/alveolar	Alveo-palatal	Palatal	Velar	Glottal
Stop							
Voiceless unaspirated	p		t			k	[ʔ]
Voiceless aspirated	p'		t'			k'	
Voiced	[b]		[d]			[g]	
Affricate							
Voiceless unaspirated			ts	tš	(tɕ)		
Voiceless aspirated			ts'	tš'	(tɕ')		
Voiced				[dž]			
Fricative							
Voiceless		f	s	š	(ɕ)	h	
Voiced		[v]	[z]	[ž]			
Nasal	m		n	[ny]		[ng]	
Liquid			l				
Semivowel	w				y		

Note: Unique Wu phonemes are in brackets [ ]; phonemes unique to Mandarin are in parentheses ( ).

Table 9

Shanghainese and Mandarin Vowels

	Front		Central		Back	
	Unrounded	*Rounded*	*Unrounded*	*Rounded*	*Unrounded*	*Rounded*
Plain						
High	i	ü				u
High-mid	e	[ö]			(ɤ)	o
Low-mid	[ɛ]		ə	[ɘ̈]		ɔ
Low			a		(ɑ)	
Retroflex						
High	(ɿ)		[ï]		(ʅ)	
Mid			ɚ			

Note: Unique Wu phonemes are in brackets [ ]; phonemes unique to Mandarin are in parentheses ( ).

els in Shanghainese that sound strange to a Mandarin speaker. Several of the Mandarin vowels appear only in combinations with other vowels and consonant finals. Shanghainese entirely lacks these descending diphthongs and triphthongs, but the number of its vowel phonemes is much higher.

What really distinguishes the two systems are tones. Beijing Mandarin has four, including (on a scale of 1 to 5) high level (55), mid rising (35), a tone that begins mid, drops, then rises (214), and high falling (51). Tone sandhi (changed values that result from contact with other tones) is fairly simple, the most important instance being the change of the dipping tone to a rising tone before another dipping tone. Shanghainese has five tones, but nothing equivalent in contour to the dipping tone in Mandarin. Four of its five tones are spread over two registers, that is, two rising tones (24) and (35), and two essentially level tones (23) and (55). The remaining tone (42) is similar to the falling tone in Mandarin but less abrupt. Although a few of the tonal contours approximate each other, the similarities are mostly fortuitous, and no useful connections can be made between elements of the two systems. In Shanghainese, basic tones are largely determined by the syllable's segmental phonology, according to the presence or absence of voiced initials and the glottal stop ending. In Mandarin, tones are distributed across syllable types much more evenly. Finally, tone sandhi in Shanghainese applies universally, not just to restricted combinations, and operates through complex rules across word boundaries.

I submit that these "mere" differences in phonology are as marked as what obtains between different European languages. They would be even more striking if we had compared Mandarin with a more southern variety like Min or Cantonese, with seven or eight tones, a full range of final consonants, nasalized vowels (in Min), and other features that make them distinct. Of greater concern in the present context, however, are vocabulary differences, the magnitude of which is often obscured by cross-variety linguistic studies of phonological differences, which focus on cognate terms, by casual students of non-Mandarin Chinese who want to know the pronunciation of a word they know in Mandarin and by the fact that these nonstandard varieties, being out of the country's cultural mainstream, tend to adopt Mandarin terms for their higher-level vocabulary. Anyone who knows a non-Mandarin variety or who is familiar with the psychology of its speakers will admit that these "high-level" terms—for the most part—are simply grafted onto the body of indigenous words and given new pronunciations. Although an educated, bilingual native speaker of a non-Mandarin variety can usually come up with a plausible pronunciation in the target speech for a Mandarin word, everyone involved knows that the exercise is bogus, either because another word or way of saying the same thing exists already or because the concept itself is not central to the community of speakers.

What *is* central is the day-to-day vocabulary that, by virtue of its uniqueness, is stigmatized as "colloquial" when in fact it constitutes the language's very core. This fact became apparent to me immediately in my studies of Wu, as my tutor and I searched in vain for characters to transcribe recorded specimens. Often the character was one that had dropped out or had never been part of Mandarin, or that appeared only in literary texts. Other times we ended up inventing characters or borrowing them from Mandarin on the basis of similar sounds or meanings. In retrospect, the activity was not unlike what scholars believe happened when characters were first being formed and applied to the archaic language. When I complained to a colleague who was working with a Hakka dialect, he just laughed and showed me a long list of his own homemade characters. Both Wu and Hakka include so many indigenous words, particularly in their core vocabularies, that the Mandarin-based character writing system was not very applicable no matter how we tried to bend it.

How much do they diverge? According to R. L. Cheng, about 5 percent of the morphemes in Taiwanese "have no appropriate, established Chinese characters to represent them. Since many of these morphemes are high frequency function words, in a written Taiwanese text they account for as much as 15% of the total number of characters" (1978:306). Cheng's statistics, while no doubt valid, understate the problem since many of the "established" characters that can be applied to Taiwanese are peripheral or nonexistent in modern standard Mandarin. Moreover, these morphemes—shared or not—often do not combine in the same way to form words. One cannot simply take morphemes or a combination of them from one Sinitic variety (or the characters used to write them, if there are any) and expect to produce anything intelligible to a user of another. All of which is to say, the words themselves are different. The extent of these differences can be appreciated by examining Ruan's (1979) *Táiwānhuà rùmén* (Introduction to Taiwanese), especially pages 62 to 108, where some two-thirds of the words listed have separate Mandarin glosses. Similarly, Qian Nairong's (1989) *Shànghǎi fāngyán lǐyǔ* (Colloquial Shanghainese) lists 282 pages of unique Shanghainese terms that are not in Mandarin or have different meanings!

Citing estimates by Chinese linguists, DeFrancis reports "the differences among the regionalects taken as a whole amount, very roughly, to 20 percent in grammar, 40 percent in vocabulary, and 80 percent in pronunciation" (1984a:63). The last two figures are reasonable, but I suspect the grammatical differences are understated because of the difficulty in Chinese of distinguishing lexical features from syntax. Cheng, for example, states that 50 percent of the so-called function "words" in Taiwanese differ from those in Mandarin, a statement that seems to tell us more about the two varieties' respective grammars than about differences in vocabulary alone (1981). How these function words function can be described by rules analogous to what is called "grammar" in Western languages. What seems to play an even greater role in Chinese is a phenomenon loosely defined as "patterning." Ramsey puts his finger on this in the following passage:

> Some differences between Cantonese and Mandarin grammar are very subtle. Almost any Mandarin grammatical pattern can be used in Cantonese and be understood, but such locutions are often not idiomatic. Typically, a sensitive and forthright native speaker will say of such Mandarinisms: "You *could* say it that way—that sentence pattern exists in Cantonese—but actually that's not the way we say it, we say it this way: . . . ." A colloquial Cantonese discourse always has a number of patterns that would sound peculiar in Mandarin. (1987:105)

Assuming rough equivalency in the amount of structure needed in any language to show relationships between concepts, the challenge becomes one of finding this order in languages where it is expressed less overtly. Function words provide part of this structure in Chinese, as does patterning, which can be thought of as a larger body of grammatical rules whose domains are individually narrower. Both devices exhibit marked differences across major varieties of Chinese, especially between standard Mandarin and the nonstandard southern languages. A third grammatical device— word order—also differs from one variety to the next, such as the reverse order of direct and indirect objects in Mandarin and Cantonese, and the placement of certain adverbs in Cantonese. It is hard to imagine a word order difference more striking than use of the *ba*-construction in Mandarin, which changes a sentence's structure from subject-verb-object to subject-object-verb but is not used in Cantonese.

There are profound linguistic reasons for the mutual unintelligibility that exists between major varieties of Chinese, reasons that go well beyond what is commonly thought of as different ways of pronouncing the same morphemes. How does this situation compare with that of other major speech communities and with the taxonomies used to describe them? Most linguists familiar with the classification problem acknowledge that the major Chinese varieties differ from each other at least on the order of the different languages of the Romance family. History confirms this observation: most of the Chinese varieties separated from their common proto-forms by the eighth or ninth century A.D., which corresponds to or predates the emergence of the Romance languages from Latin. It would seem, therefore, a simple matter to project the taxonomy used to describe concrete linguistic differences in one part of the world to another, that is, to apply the two words "language" and "dialect" consistently and either start calling Spanish and Italian two "dialects" of the Romance "language" or, if that seems inappropriate, stop calling Min and Mandarin two "dialects" of the Chinese "language."

One way out of the dilemma is to call into question the legitimacy of the terms in general by noting, for example, the smooth transition in degrees of intelligibility between Italian and French through border areas (in technical terms, the nonconvergence of linguistic isoglosses). But one need not pretend that one language stops where another starts to recognize—as do the speakers of languages themselves—distinct *cores* of Parisian French versus the Italian spoken in Rome, or Beijing Mandarin versus Shanghai Wu, across which there is no appreciable communication. By shedding the fiction that the major varieties of Chinese are "dialects" instead of languages, other inconsistencies are rectified and the whole taxonomy falls neatly into place. On one end of the scale, what look for all the world like dialectal differences within Mandarin, Wu and, for that matter, each of the major Chinese varieties really do become dialects instead of— what? On the other end, Chinese (Hànyǔ) can take its proper place as a language group within the Sino-Tibetan family, along with what the government of the People's Republic of China officially recognizes as that family's other groups—Tibeto-Burman, Miao-Yao, and Zhuang-Dong— eliminating a badly skewed (and very suspicious) distribution that accords no subdivisions whatsoever to Hànyǔ, which is used by the overwhelming majority of the family's speakers, but defines the other three groups in detail down to the branch and language level (Mair 1991).

Another way to avoid acknowledging that "A" is "A" is to reject linguistics, symmetry, and objective criteria altogether and rely instead on political boundaries or the subjective notions of the speech community (however that may be defined). The first of these latter two "criteria" can be dismissed, since it would require Han Chinese either to call Tibetan and Chinese one and the same "language," because they are genetically related and fall at present within the same geopolitical boundary, or to agree to Tibetan demands for political independence—a choice no Han Chinese would enjoy making. This is not sophistry; it only looks stupid because the idea of using national boundaries to determine linguistic categories is inherently unsound. The fallback argument would be, "Well, we really mean the Chinese spoken inside China." But this does not work either, since it forces us—if consistency still matters—to rename Miao-Yao and Zhuang-Dong "languages" instead of "language groups" because they are also spoken primarily inside China, which is a bit hard to swallow. The whole rationale for calling Chinese a "language" comes down, it would seem, to simple wish-fulfillment. Chinese is a language because certain of its speakers want it to be, and if objective criteria get in the way, who cares?

It is tempting to explore why this last "factor," as it were, is taken seriously by some Western linguists who would oppose such muddleheadedness in their own technical specialties but are willing to allow it here on a grand scale for China. Part of the reason, I believe, is sympathy with the Beijing government's efforts to unify China on its own (or any) terms, abetted by the same sort of cultural relativism that has found its way nowadays even into the hard sciences. Add to this sympathy China's never-ending insistence on being viewed as a "special case" where universal criteria do not apply, along with the pressure it can put on its own scholars to support this perverse view, and one comes up with a fair picture of how the single-language myth is maintained. But do the Chinese really accept the myth themselves? We do know for certain (1) that Chinese are highly aware of the linguistic differences between them; (2) that this is especially true of non-Mandarin Chinese speakers, who are taking new pride in and a fresh look at their own native vernaculars, embellishing them with such refinements as dictionaries, textbooks, formal instruction, writing, media exposure, and legal status, which in the lay view are associated with different languages (Hannas and Edelstein 1994); and (3) that most Chinese are not equipped to deal with this terminological problem anyway, since their word *fāngyán,* as we have seen, glosses over the language versus dialect distinction.

Returning to the purpose of our inquiry, if the major varieties of Chinese are not "dialects" at all but different languages, then Chinese characters should not be any more able to transcend the differences between them than they can those in the different East Asian languages, which in fact is the case. We have seen that the Chinese languages differ not just in pronunciation but also in vocabulary and grammar, and that these differences are realized through unique morphemes (or unique uses of shared morphemes) for which characters do not exist at all, do not exist in Mandarin, or are used with different meanings and functions. Consequently, character texts in Cantonese and (where available) in Taiwanese are largely unintelligible to Mandarin readers. Many characters are completely unfamiliar; others are recognizable but make no sense in context. This occurs where conventions exist for writing the non-Mandarin variety in characters. Actually, most of these languages have no established writing system and hence lack even the possibility of being understood by readers of other varieties.

The failure of the character writing system to provide Chinese speakers trained in one variety with the means to read other, non-Mandarin varieties exposes the transitivity thesis as a sham. Oddly enough, this view is not disputed. When people claim Chinese characters "transcend" the "dialects," they are usually not even thinking about how literate Mandarin speakers use their knowledge of characters to read non-Mandarin Chinese. What they really mean is that characters allegedly help non-Mandarin speakers read Mandarin. But if the feature does not work in one direction, how can it work in the other? The only explanation for the ability of some non-Mandarin speakers to read Mandarin-based character texts is bilingualism, pure and simple, that is, they have taken the trouble to learn Mandarin (the language, if not its spoken form) and the character writing system that goes along with it. Thus, in a very twisted sense, the characters do "unify" Chinese by denying some 275 million non-Mandarin Chinese speakers literacy in their own native languages and forcing them, by virtue of its being the only sanctioned orthography in China, to learn the language of the politically dominant group.

What applies to the character writing system across languages also applies across time. Character-literate Chinese are no better equipped to read ancient Chinese texts than they are texts written in other East Asian or Chinese languages, for the same reasons: major differences in vocabulary, grammar, and style that make older states of the language mostly incomprehensible to anyone who has not had special training. I recall my first trip through Taiwan's National Palace Museum and the exasperation I felt when, after years of intensive study of the modern written language, I was unable to decipher inscriptions in the classical style written no more than a few hundred years ago. My companion, a well-educated native speaker, could not provide much help. Every year American students with native Chinese skills enroll in a classical Chinese course and end up doing no better (often worse) than classmates without their modern Chinese background. Not only are the underlying languages (or language states) different, the inventories of shared symbols used to write them often have different meanings, erasing what little "transitivity" even this knowledge provides.

Synchronically or diachronically, the notion that Chinese characters offer literate Chinese a bridge across linguistic boundaries is pure fiction. One could even argue that its effect is the opposite. By allowing non–native speakers to read Mandarin-based texts with nonstandard pronunciations, the characters are reinforcing the differences that they are supposed to eliminate.

Chinese Characters and the Lexicon

The goal of this chapter has been to assess the appropriateness of Chinese characters to East Asian languages by examining claims to the effect that the characters accommodate idiosyncratic features of these languages better than other types of writing and hence are worth using despite their many shortcomings. Our analysis has shown that these claims either are vacuous (the "transitivity" of characters across space and time) or confuse the cause of a problem with its solution (monosyllabic morphology and too many homonyms). In addition, we have seen that the acclaimed "word-building power" of character-based morphemes, while offering East Asians a means to cope with the expansion of new concepts, has had serious side effects, namely, words that cannot be distinguished phonetically and the use of "words" that are not words at all. This "power" of Chinese characters to create new terms, seen in another light, is simply a system run amok, unchecked by the ordinary requirements of phonetic intelligibility and popular sanction.

The ability of character-morphemes to combine freely as single-syllable units into new terms and of the system to assert itself (until very recently) as the dominant paradigm in word formation has had other con-

sequences germane to the present inquiry. An analysis of these consequences will further support the thesis that the "appropriateness" of
Chinese characters to the languages is merely an ex post facto rationaliza-
tion of effects produced on the languages by the characters. In other words,
Chinese characters "fit" East Asian languages by virtue of having molded
them over the centuries in all aspects—phonology, lexicon, and even syntax—according to the writing system's own peculiarities, in particular, its
requirement that morphemes be one syllable long and that all syllables have
meaning. Not surprisingly, this one-syllable-one-morpheme alignment is
largely what one does find in a written passage of modern standard Mandarin and in the Sinitic lexicons of other East Asian languages. But it is not
characteristic of the way these languages were and almost certainly is not
how they will be in the future.

Research into early states of Chinese and into certain types of premodern colloquial literature shows a language made up not only of polysyllabic words, but also of polysyllabic morphemes. Although many of the
latter were borrowed into Chinese from non–East Asian sources, some portion of them either were indigenous or were adopted so early in the language's history as to make the distinction between borrowed and native
vocabulary meaningless. Just how much the spoken language was characterized by polysyllabic morphemes we will never know, since expressing the
language in writing meant reducing these units to a form compatible with
the medium, so that each written syllable-sized unit had a meaning of its
own that could potentially stand by itself. When the language failed to correspond to the requirements of the writing system, Chinese simply reanalyzed the term so that it would consist of as many morphemes as it had
syllables and characters representing it, and used one of the new single-syllable morphemes for the whole, either as a "word" by itself or in new polysyllabic combinations with other single-syllable morphemes.

Evidence of this process is found not only in the disposition of foreign
polysyllabic loanwords, but also in the lexicons of non-Mandarin Chinese
languages, which are characterized to a remarkable degree by polysyllabic
morphemes, especially in their colloquial vocabulary. Because most of these
languages never had much (or anything) to do with Chinese characters,
they were never exposed to their "monosyllabification" effect. Since these
languages are based almost entirely in speech, even when they are written
or glossed with characters for textbooks or linguistic studies, their polysyllabic morphologies are maintained. This morphology is seen, for example,
in the cooccurence of two or more characters that are not used individually
in other compounds and in the use of dummy characters (often with the
"mouth" radical) that do not show up elsewhere and were clearly contrived
to represent a single-morpheme polysyllabic word. Unlike in modern Mandarin, where polysyllabic words are often the result of recombining single-
syllable morphemes (in some cases just to make the words intelligible in

speech), many polysyllabic words in non-Mandarin Chinese were so from the start. Their relative immunity from the monosyllabification process plus the fact that they tend as a whole to reflect earlier states of the language better than Mandarin suggest rather strongly that Mandarin is the anomaly—not the other way around. Chinese characters over time imposed their own order on the standard language that used the system for its "representation," generating by their own logic the conditions that make written Mandarin, as it is now constituted, amenable to morphosyllabic writing.

The deceptive ease with which one-syllable meaningful elements, each supported by its own unique written symbol,[12] could be thrown together without regard to the phonetic result to form new concepts or represent borrowed ones also had an enormous impact on the structure of the Korean and Japanese lexicons, although here the molding mechanism was different. In Chinese, the characters became "appropriate" to the language by fostering a monosyllabic morphology that matched the system's unique requirements. In the other East Asian languages, they accomplished the same thing by enabling Sinitic roots to outcompete indigenous morphemes and morphological processes and to emerge as the predominant word-building units. As the Sinitic morphemes took hold, the character writing on which the morphemes depended became necessary not only for social reasons but absolutely to insure that texts would be intelligible. The languages in effect became Sinicized, having lost a good deal of what was their own, in fact and in principle, through displacement and then through neglect.

If this competition had been fair, one could hardly quibble with the characters' success. But two factors skewed the field so badly that the indigenous morphologies had no chance to develop as viable alternatives. On the one hand, there was the enormous prestige China and the Chinese language had enjoyed since the Tang dynasty in countries on China's periphery, which would have been enough to establish Sinitic loans and the writing system in these languages whatever their actual utility. On the other hand, with a head start of a millennium or more, Chinese characters were already available to serve the needs of these developing languages and hence became a quick fix both as direct loans and as morphemes that could be assembled on the basis of meaning alone, without having to stand the test of phonetic intelligibility. The indigenous morphemes, which were intelligible phonetically, were longer, less malleable, and could not compete in the written medium, which was where most of the innovation was taking place. When efforts began during this century by linguists in Japan and especially Korea to reestablish the indigenous morphologies for the sake of national pride and to make the written languages phonetically viable, their creations were spurned by the public either for being too long or—a far worse sin—for looking like fakes.

There is nothing in the indigenous structure of Japanese or Korean that lends itself to representation by Chinese characters. What compatibility does exist between these languages and character-based writing is a function of changes brought about directly or indirectly by the writing itself. There are clear signs, however, that the incestuous process of using and reusing the same phonetically depleted Sinitic morphemes to form new words has broken down. Although Sinitic morphology still plays a role, it must now compete with Western loanwords written in *katakana* and *hangul* as direct, phonetic borrowings. Even in Chinese, the incidence of sound-based, polysyllabic borrowing seems to be rising and is forcing itself into the written language through a subset of characters used for their phonetic values alone. As sound-based media develop technologically and their use becomes more widespread, the pressure for these languages to adjust will intensify, rendering Chinese characters and traditional Sinitic morphology anachronistic and eliminating what vestiges of "appropriateness" still remain.

Part 3 FORCES FOR CHANGE

9. The Chimera of Reform

WE HAVE SEEN in the first several chapters of this book that users of Chinese characters everywhere have sought by one means or another to transform this cumbersome writing system into a serviceable artifact. In China, these efforts led to radical "simplification" of character shapes, elimination of some forms through phonetic borrowing, and creation of an alphabetic notation that is taking some heat off the characters by acting as a de facto orthography in places where the latter are completely unsuitable. Japan introduced its own simplified forms and attempted to limit the number of characters in daily use. In Korea, reformers also experimented with limitation schemes or replaced Chinese characters outright with their own phonetic writing. The best that can be said for a century of writing reform in China, Korea, and Japan is that the character orthographies were tidied up somewhat. Only in Korea, which reached outside the character system and its shortcomings, was a fundamental breakthrough achieved.

There is a reason why reform of Chinese character–based writing has produced and will continue to produce unsatisfactory results. Whereas alphabetic systems derive their complexity largely from facts speakers already know about their languages, the complexity needed to drive character-based writing is contained within the system itself. For alphabetically written languages, knowing the language means knowing a good part of the writing mechanism. Unfortunately, this is not true of character-based systems. Lacking well-motivated connections with sound, the characters must depend on their own intrinsic structure to differentiate meaning, which cannot be appreciably reduced ("reformed") if enough redundancy is to remain in the system for it to work. As a result, every effort to reduce complexity in one sphere merely transfers the complexity to another, giving the appearance of progress but in fact only shifting the problem around between different aspects of the system.

This phenomenon—the cycle of robbing Peter to pay Paul—is most apparent in reforms that target character shapes, but is also manifested through a series of paradoxes that frustrate efforts to lower their numbers.

Even in Japanese and Korean, where character use is limited, their availability in principle prevents the emergence of viable alternatives by obviating the need for a change in the underlying language and the way it is used. History shows that using a limited number of Chinese characters invariably leads to the use of more, leading in turn to new demands for another reduction in an endless cycle that goes nowhere. Ultimately, East Asians must choose between the morphemic, character-based systems, more or less as presently constituted, and systems founded more solidly on phonetic principles.

The Five Paradoxes of Character Limitation

The two most obvious drawbacks to Chinese character-based writing and those most commonly targeted by reforms are the large number of individual tokens and the complexity of their shapes. While conceptually distinct, the two categories tend to merge when analyzed. For example, one can reduce the number of characters in use by dropping the form of one and assigning its meaning and sound to another character. This action can be regarded as a change in form, especially if the two morphemes are etymologically related. Conversely, simplifying individual forms entails the progressive loss of distinctions between members of the set, the limiting case being merger of different forms into the same character, which reduces their total number. Although I will deal with these two problems separately, one should not lose sight of their interrelatedness.

Character limitation programs in China, Japan, and Korea have taken the form of prescriptive lists meant to apply to society as a whole, introduced through public agencies and the compulsory education system. Although the lists are generally called "guidelines," reformers through their governments are usually able, in the beginning, to enforce some degree of compliance from the public media and even among private publishers. Particular mechanisms vary. In some cases, society is encouraged to use only characters that appear on an officially sanctioned "common use" list. Other lists prescribe which of two or more competing forms of the "same" character should be treated as standard and which should be abolished. Still others identify replacements for existing characters, contrived through a variety of techniques to be discussed below. Selection is typically done on the basis of frequency; just like the letters of an alphabet, some characters appear more often than others, providing one handy measure for deciding their relative importance. More sophisticated lists take other criteria into account, such as combinatory potential, the structures represented, types of materials on which the frequency counts were based, and in Chinese whether all of the standard language's syllables are represented. Political factors can also play a role in determining which characters are included on the list and the order in which they are learned in the public schools.

In Japanese and Korean, reformers technically have the option of replacing unwanted characters with their phonetic equivalents in *kana* or *hangul.* Although this simple expedient often involves unforeseen complications, at least it remains an option. China has not been as fortunate. Since there are still no provisions in Chinese orthography for mixing characters with phonetic *(pinyin)* text, changes to the inventory are effected entirely within the confines of the system itself. This process allows some latitude for cleaning up the system, for example, by eliminating variant representations of the same morpheme. But for the majority of the tokens, abolishing the character means abolishing the morpheme itself or marginalizing it (with respect to the orthography) by writing it with a different character and letting the reader decide from context which morpheme is intended. The third choice for Chinese is to relegate the character-morpheme to an indeterminate status outside the recommended list of "common use" characters, not really abolishing it but not sanctioning it either, rather hoping the character will go away of its own accord—which is not an altogether unreasonable expectation, because if knowledge of a form is lost, people will lose the concept or find another way to express it.

In the final analysis, however, tinkering with the writing system in Chinese entails changing the language itself, if a substantial reduction in the number of characters is to be achieved while the system maintains its identity as a morpheme-based script. This observation leads to the first of five paradoxes that pertain to character limitation, namely, that the enterprise is fundamentally at odds with requirements imposed on the language by its speakers.

Here is why. Chinese users (albeit influenced by the script itself) have found it expedient over the course of time to express a certain portion of their vocabulary in single-syllable words that are morphemes and the remaining words in compounds made up of the same or other single-syllable morphemes. Although the number of genuine monosyllabic words in Chinese may be less than in some Western languages, it is still larger from the reformer's standpoint than the number of tokens that can be included in a practical writing system, particularly when the bound morphemes are also figured in. There is simply no way the two requirements—an adequate number of morphemes to express all the concepts Chinese speakers wish to express and a significantly reduced character set—can be harmonized as long as the units of the writing system are keyed to discrete morphemes.

If it is impossible to reduce the number of characters used in Chinese significantly without stripping the language of its vocabulary, then are there, at least, practical limits to the size of the inventory that can be drawn up to cover most exigencies? There are characters, for example, that a scientist considers important, but that a farmer or classical scholar may not bother learning, just as there are words in English that some people use and others do not. Conversely, there are characters that form a part of every user's repertoire. If the latter tokens can be identified, would it not be possible if not to prescribe then at least to describe the boundaries of a general list whose membership would be far fewer than the total number of units in use?

The logic behind such a "common use" character list is sound: for decades researchers have known that a relatively small number of characters accounts for most of those used in a text. Statistics compiled by the Mass Education Movement of the 1920s, for example, show 78 characters accounting for half of all simple reading materials, 352 characters for 70 percent, and 1,169 characters for 91 percent of most texts (Rawski 1979:3).[1] DeFrancis, using 900,000 characters of running text, found the 100 most common characters accounting for 47 percent of the text, and the 1,100 most frequent characters making up 90 percent (1984a:108). In 1952, the Chinese Ministry of Education compiled a list of 1,556 common use characters based on their appearances in school primers, surveys, and statistical reference works. Combinatory potential was also figured in (Zhang Renbiao 1955:116). The list was then checked against nine different types of current publications totaling 30,000 characters. Its first subdivision of 1,017 characters was found to accommodate 90 percent and the total list 95 percent of all characters appearing (Cao et al. 1955:107–108). The percentages rise to 99.8 (Yi Xiwu 1955:67) or 99.9 (Cui 1985:58) with a list of 4,000 well-chosen characters.

Based on such figures, common use lists have been drawn up with subdivisions that allow the user to prioritize his or her studies. To this extent, the enterprise is helpful, especially in education. A problem develops, however, when people reinterpret this foundation as a ceiling and lament the fact that the program has "failed" because certain people at times exceed what has become the "limit." Choe Hyon-bae cited two reasons why such lists cannot succeed as limiting devices (1946:87). First, there will always be people who confuse literacy with the ability to use obscure characters. As these people vie with each other to display their erudition, standards are driven up to the point where form becomes more important than content. This phenomenon is not confined to East Asia. Western academic, journalistic, and bureaucratic writing is replete with examples of high form masquerading as substance. In East Asia, the characters just add another dimension.

His second complaint is more to the point. Choe claims it is impossible to determine beyond a certain number what are "commonly used" characters, since they differ according to one's profession and interests. This statement relates to scale and to the list's philosophy, since it is clear from the foregoing statistics that a large number of characters indeed are shared by all users. However, after the first thousand or so, usage begins to follow the subject matter of the text (Chen Mingyuan 1981:47). This bias can, to some degree, be eliminated by plotting frequency distributions of characters over texts of different topics.[2] Invariably, though, some groups of users are excluded or the character set becomes larger until it approaches a natural limit corresponding to the total number "in use." This brings us to the second paradox of character limitation: as the number of tokens increases, the additional increments, while representing a progressively heavier burden, are less valuable to a larger number of users.

We can draw the following conclusions about the utility of common use character lists: they are essential in education. They probably help reduce the number of characters in use, totally and as encountered practically, by serving as a guideline for writers and editors. They cannot function in Chinese, however, as an overall standard without depriving users of access to words or forcing people to learn characters that are irrelevant to their individual needs.

How effective is the other device, that of proscribing individual characters, as a means of reducing their total number? Seven such techniques can be identified, including (1) eliminating graphic variants of the same character, (2) merging characters with the same sound and similar meanings, (3) merging characters by removing "radicals," (4) replacing a character with its homonym, (5) assigning two or more readings to one character, (6) using a phonetic orthography in the character text, and (7) changing the word itself.

As mentioned above, the first of these techniques—eliminating graphic variants—can also be treated as simplification of form, since with very few exceptions the variant chosen is the one with the simplest structure. Known in Chinese as *yìtǐzì* ("different form characters"), both characters of a set designate the same morpheme, making one of them superfluous. Lu identified six types of *yìtǐzì*, including characters with a slight difference in the number of strokes, those with the same radical but a different phonetic, those with the same phonetic but a different radical, variants that use the same components in different positions, forms that allow the addition of another radical, and well-established simplified forms (1955:90). Some sets still used in Taiwan contain several variants, for example, three different forms for the word *yān* ("smoke"), three forms for the morpheme *jī* ("track, footprint"), and so forth. Besides adding to the number of characters to be learned, they confuse the user by permitting structural deviations in some cases that are not generalized throughout the system. Another type of inconsistency allows two or more radicals to be interchanged in some characters but not in others. There were 170 to 180 of these pairs in use prior to January 1956, when the government of the People's Republic of China issued a list of "adjustments" that eliminated 1,055 variants of 810 basic forms, without affecting the morphemic nature of the writing system (see Chapter 1).

By contrast, the next three limitation techniques are all forms of phonetic substitution that transcend the one-character-one-morpheme principle. As discussed in Chapter 5, the meanings ascribed to individual characters, while generally reducible to a common core, expand to varying degrees depending on the particular morpheme and the environment in which it functions. Phonetic substitution as a character limitation technique acts by increasing the range of permissible semantic drift and finally by ignoring the constraint entirely. The first of these devices is quite innocuous. Characters with the same sound and similar meanings are merged; all but one form (usually the simplest) are eliminated, with the surviving form covering all meanings. A variant of this technique merges characters with overlapping and etymologically related meanings by removing their identifying radicals. Both practices usually have precedents in popular usage.

The second type of phonetic substitution technique also involves removing radicals but is distinguished from the first in that the semantic relationship between the characters is no longer visible. This process simply reverses the historical process by which the more complex form was created. In the past, as the number of meanings represented by a character grew through semantic extension and phonetic borrowing, many units were given a radical, a semantic gloss of sorts, to designate the more specialized meaning. In the reforms, the character loses the radical and returns to its original shape. In another sense, the technique mimics a countertrend also observed historically: the elimination of characters representing specific morphemes and the accretion of these meanings to other characters fully or partially homophonous. This process differs from the so-called borrowed sound class of characters described in Chapter 1, in which morphemes with no written representation accrued to homophonous characters, and demonstrates the essential dynamic governing the system's development since early times, namely, the conflicting demands for iconicity,[3] on the one hand, and the user's everyday need for simplicity, on the other.

Zheng Linxi made an interesting point in this regard. Unlike some other early Chinese writing reform advocates, Zheng did not deny the historical utility of adding radicals to distinguish different morphemes (1955:57). It was necessary, he argued, when the written style was largely monosyllabic and a clear national standard did not exist. However, modern colloquial (*bái-huà*) writing, with its emphasis on polysyllabic words, eliminates the need for these graphic distinctions, allowing phonetic substitution to proceed whether or not the meanings of the characters are similar or related.

The third and most controversial form of phonetic substitution is replacement by homonyms. Here the original meanings of the characters play no role in determining which characters are merged with which others. Sound is the only relevant factor. The technique, if carried out consistently, would result in an inventory of only about four hundred characters, the approximate number of syllables (minus tone) in Beijing Mandarin. Although the nature of the script is altered, there is no other way to reduce the number of tokens in the system substantially unless one is prepared to introduce a phonetic subsystem (which this becomes in the limiting case) or savage the lexicon.

The problem with all forms of phonetic substitution, and homonym substitution in particular, is that the characters cease functioning as semantic indicators, becoming in Shtrintsin's words "simply a conventional designation for phonetic units—syllables" (1972:320). If taken far enough, the technique exposes the system to all the problems one would encounter with a phoneticized script, without the latter's advantages. One is still using a minimum of four hundred units, and probably three times as many to include tone. Clearly there is nothing gained here. Yet if the technique is not followed with complete rigor, a situation develops that is worse still. Karlgren described it in this way: "A small number of such cases of borrowing could of course not create any great disorder, but assuming that they became hundreds the practice might lead to a completely intolerable uncertainty as to what the graphs in the sentence really meant; whether they had their original, concrete meaning, or whether they stood as phonetic loans for something else" (1949:12).

For example, some reformers would use the character 于 *(yú)* for all syllables with this sound. Taking into account only those used for the surname *Yú*, there are at least six possibilities: 于, 俞, 余, 虞, 喻, and 禺. Obviously, this substitution would lead to problems that would have to be addressed through other devices. But at least the representatio n would be consistent. If, instead, two or three characters with this sound were chosen, ostensibly to smooth out the transition to purely phonetic writing,[4] readers would wonder if the syllable was being designated or the morpheme. But if no characters are eliminated by phonetic substitution, there is not much one can do to reduce the inventory. This is the third paradox of character limitation, namely, a significant decrease in the number of characters can be achieved only through phonetic substitution, which unless taken to its limit—reduction to a syllabary and abandonment of the system—creates more complications than it resolves.

It is useless to object that the learner would not face these difficulties, because sooner or later he or she would begin to ask why certain characters can be used for all appearances of given sounds, others for only some, and still others only when the sound has a certain meaning. If this situation is confusing for a speaker of standard Chinese on which the substitution conventions are based, nonstandard speakers would find it hopeless. As mentioned, characters homophonous in one dialect are not necessarily so in another. The nonstandard user would therefore be tasked with learning variant readings for the same characters according to their meaning in context, on top of the other complications.

This resembles the fifth technique for eliminating characters, whereby two or more readings are assigned to the same character as a means of reducing the overall number of characters. In a sense, all phonetic substitution is a variety of this technique, since it increases the polysemy of a character. Instead of learning one core meaning for a symbol, users learn several. It is hard to see what is gained here, since any savings from a reduced inventory is offset by the need to remember multiple meanings for each character (Kaizuka and Ogawa 1981:378). If this is true of phonetic substitution, it is even more of a problem when the polysemy is compounded by phonetic differences, such as those included in the People's Republic of China's second list of simplified characters released in 1977 but rescinded almost immediately. In addition to wider use of phonetic substitution, the plan also introduced the concept of "two readings to a character," eliminating in principle the iconic relationship between symbol and referent with no clear gain in overall utility.

Of particular interest is the relationship of this technique to character limitation in general. When reform of the Chinese writing system first began in earnest after 1949, one of the items targeted for change was the phenomenon known as "broken sound characters" (pòyīnzì), where a given character represents two or more morphemes each read differently. It was felt at the time that this practice complicated the writing system by disrupting the regular one-to-one paradigm. As a result, between 1957 and 1962 more than 1,800 variant readings for characters were abolished (Chen Mingyuan 1981:42), which restored the paradigm for all but a few cases, making the system "simpler." Then, fifteen years later, another plan was hatched, which in the interest of simplicity sought to reverse the effects of the previous reform!

This phenomenon—the fourth paradox—demonstrates the essential flaw with character limitation, namely, that reforms tend to be circular. Problems solved in one area only lead to new problems in another. Whether one focuses on the units of the character script or the relationships between these units and their referents, one is simply transferring problems from one area to another with no reduction in the character script's overall difficulty. Nothing illustrates this fact better than the next theoretical technique for lowering the number of characters in Chinese: substituting *pinyin* spelling directly in the text for difficult or unusual characters. Although controversial from an aesthetic standpoint, the proposal itself is not extraordinary, since it parallels the conventions used for Japanese and Korean, which get by with half the number of characters needed for Chinese. The idea at one time seems to have generated some interest in the People's Republic of China (Cao 1955b:82), and it survives today in pilot programs for elementary education and in weird proposals that combine the "semantic" part of a character with *pinyin* spelling in place of the character's traditional "phonetic."

The problem with this approach—and with similar practices in Korean and Japanese—is that the very characters that the technique is designed to eliminate are the ones most needed to disambiguate phonetically vague vocabulary. This is the last, and most significant, of the five paradoxes frustrating character limitation schemes. As discussed above, one of the strongest arguments for character writing is that the symbols add redundancy to a phonetic system that has not developed enough contrasts to identify many of its words unambiguously. Since whether a word is "ambiguous" or not depends as much on frequency, familiarity, and context as on the structure of the word itself, it follows that less common words, with their less frequent characters, are the ones for which character representation is most needed. "Obscure" characters are obscure only because the morphemes and words they represent are themselves uncommon, making these the least desirable candidates for phonetic representation. Conversely, the more common characters can be dispensed with more easily, because they represent words that users are used to hearing!

The problem can be avoided only by changing or eliminating the word itself, which is the last of seven techniques available for reducing the number of characters. As was true of the first technique (abolishing variant character forms), there is some potential here for cutting out fringe characters, particularly those used in place names, classical expressions, and monosyllabic technical terms (Pu 1973:357), although it is questionable how much of this will reach the average user. If the technique is pursued vigorously, one ends up either robbing the language of its vocabulary or, in Chinese, increasing the burden placed on a shrinking stock of indigenous morphemes, which from a phonetic standpoint are already saturated with meaning. One cannot continually make up new vocabulary from the same set of monosyllabic morphemes without adding to the number of homonyms and near homonyms in the language. This final technique brings us back to the same old dilemma: as long as the representation is in characters, change of any sort always entails substituting one set of problems for another. It is a perfect example of a zero-sum game.

Character Limitation in Japan

As in Chinese, character limitation in Japanese begins with the observation that although a certain total number of characters are in use, fewer than that number account for most of the usage. According to Saiga, the most common 1,500 characters account for 96 to 97 percent of all appearances of characters in contemporary Japanese magazines (1971:107–108). Two thousand characters increase the coverage to 98.5 to 99 percent. Okazaki, in a careful survey conducted more than a decade before the postwar reforms, found 1,900 characters accounting for 98.45 percent of the text (1938:68). Raising coverage to the ninety-ninth percentile, however, meant adding three hundred characters to the inventory, and so on, with increasingly smaller returns. Since no amount of additions, practically speaking, will cover all appearances of characters in an unregulated system, Japanese reformers asked themselves why not restrict usage to those characters most needed?

Such attempts to limit the number of characters in Japanese started more than a century ago. Brigitte Muller, author of a study on the 1946 *Tōyō kanji* reforms, compared twenty-four Japanese common use character lists that appeared between 1872 and 1966 in the form of decrees, proposals, or guidelines for actual use. She considers it remarkable that "in most cases the number of characters lies between 1,850 and 2,600" (1975:57–59). It is also notable that the arithmetic mean of 1,995 characters, distilled from over a century of proposals, corresponds so closely with the number of characters chosen for the *Tōyō* (1,850) and *Jōyō* (1,945) lists that govern modern usage. This mean is some 60 percent less than the total number in use and, in view of Okazaki's statistics, probably close to the optimum number for a list of this sort.

The chief difference between the Japanese concept and "common use" character lists devised for Chinese is that the *Tōyō* list was intended as a prescribed maximum. Characters not on the list were, for government publications, simply proscribed; there was no need to specify which particular characters outside the list were to be avoided—they all were. There are two reasons, linguistically speaking, why the Japanese were able to devise such lists, whereas the Chinese could not. Because of *kun* "readings" and multiple-word representation, a given character in Japanese covers a greater part of the lexicon than in Chinese. Not only do characters participate in the representation of *kango* (i.e., Sinitic) compounds; they also, by virtue of their identification with native words, represent a significant part of the indigenous lexicon as well, either individually (with *okurigana*) or in combination with other characters also read in *kun*. In Japanese, more words are covered by fewer characters.

The other reason why a prescriptive list is conceivable for Japanese is because users, in theory, can write the balance of the vocabulary in an established phonetic subscript. Proscribed characters are simply replaced by the *kana* spelling of the underlying word. It is important to note that this option of writing at least part of the text in phonetic symbols is more viable in Japanese than in Chinese (if Chinese had the technical means to do so) because in Japanese writing, unlike Chinese, the same Sinitic morphemes are not simply rewritten in a different script or used over and over to form new or substitute vocabulary. This does happen when *kango* words are directly transcribed, whereupon the potential for ambiguous homophony is even greater than in Chinese. But it need not happen for many of the affected characters, because one is not rewriting the character per se, but the word or words that the character designated, many of which are indigenous and less apt to cause confusion when expressed phonetically.

The presence of indigenous, non-Sinitic vocabulary in Japanese also gives its users the option of replacing *kango* words whose characters have been proscribed with native equivalents that are less ambiguous phonetically. Or the Sinitic words can be replaced with Western borrowings. Chinese, too, can and does borrow Western vocabulary directly, using the characters as phonetic symbols to represent the sound of the word, but the technique is cumbersome and the results are awkward. In Japanese, by contrast, writing foreign loanwords is not only practicable, it is the main function of the *katakana* subscript. The practice has become so ubiquitous that, in the opinion of many Japanese, it now causes more problems than it solves, although I suspect that most of the complaining is based more on nationalist feelings than on linguistic principles.

In addition to the above phonetic techniques, other practices evolved both to compensate for the *Tōyō kanji* list's shortcomings and to minimize dependence on the phonetic option, particularly where this involved transcribing existing *kango* compounds. One such technique involved finding synonymous or nearly synonymous words whose characters had not been proscribed and that are homophonous with the original. The fact that this can be done at all gives some indication of how serious the problem of homophonous ambiguity is for Sinitic words in Japanese. The practice has been applied not only to monosyllabic morphemes, but to bisyllabic words as well. Finally, Japanese also compensates for lost characters by substituting other characters still on the list or by replacing the word either with a *kango* synonym or by one newly created.

One problem with the *Tōyō* list concerned the "readings" that a complementary law enacted in 1948 allowed for sanctioned characters. Even among the Japanese who support character limitation there were those who maintained that restricting the number of words assigned to each character unnecessarily reduced their expressive potential (Saiga 1971:116). Recall that multiple readings was cited above as one of two reasons why a character list this short could be conceived in principle. The response of many writers, accordingly, was to ignore the 1948 directive and continue using (implying or otherwise indicating) proscribed readings, which may have expanded the range of those characters that were sanctioned, but hardly encouraged respect for the program generally. In fact, the reform seems to have satisfied no one. Strong supporters of character use feared it was the first step toward complete elimination. Those favoring abolition maintained that it would become the perpetual standard. Those advocating reduction as an end in itself complained that the methods for selecting particular characters were illogical (Kim Min-su 1973:327).

The main problem with the list, however, has less to do with its composition or interpretation and more with the fact that many Japanese simply do not feel comfortable writing Sinitic compounds in *kana*. Although a number of devices were employed to escape this dilemma, the ratio of *kango* in high-level materials is so high that the choice really comes down to writing in characters that may not be on the list or spelling the word out in *hiragana*. This much was acknowledged by the government: the 1973 revisions to the *okurigana* and "readings" lists stated that these measures apply to laws, public documents, newspapers, magazines, broadcasting, and so on. The scientific, technical, and literary fields were conspicuously exempted. In May 1968, a report to the general assembly of the Kokugo shingikai (National Language Council) by a committee set up to investigate national language policy likewise recommended more leniency in the areas where these standards apply.

The result of this backtracking was the *Jōyō kanji* list of 1981, which was significant not for its 5 percent increase in the number of characters, but for abandoning the fiction that a legal ceiling could be established at all. As was true of "common use" character lists in China, Japan's own experiment demonstrated the usefulness of a list for general education and, probably, as a standard against which flagrant overuse could be measured. But as a device for limiting the number of characters in use, the program had no lasting effect.

Character Limitation in the Koreas

If character limitation is frustrated in Chinese by the cyclical nature of the problem, this is only slightly less true of Japanese and, as we shall see, Korean. Although these latter two languages have at their disposal phonetic subscripts that in theory enable them to break the chain of dependence on Chinese characters, in practice they continue to rely to a greater or lesser degree on the characters. The problem is endemic to the languages themselves. As noted above, a large part of the Japanese and Korean lexicons are made up of Sinitic loanwords that were brought into the languages through Chinese characters or with the expectation that the characters would be available to support these words with enough redundancy to compensate for their lack of phonetic distinctiveness. One can certainly write Sinitic words in *kana* or in *hangul,* but whether words so written can be understood clearly is another matter entirely. The only guarantee that phonetic writing will work is to use words that can stand on their own phonetically in a text. This means finding substitutes for ambiguous words, while allowing the inventory of Sinitic terms to shrink to the point where the remaining words are distinct by virtue of being fewer in number.

Unfortunately, as long as the characters exist, there is less incentive to change the language that evolved with them. Limiting the number of characters does nothing to change the basic problem of phonetically ambiguous Sinitic vocabulary, because most of this vocabulary is made up of polysyllabic terms whose morphemes are common enough to escape the proscription. Moreover, admitting characters in principle is tantamount to acknowledging their availability as tools to disambiguate confusing terms. Users get accustomed to having this solution at their disposal, are less inclined to avoid phonetic ambiguity, and sooner or later as a community lose sight of what the limitation scheme was supposed to accomplish. Some ask what sense it makes, for example, to write one part of a Sinitic compound with a character and the other part in *kana* or *hangul*, since everyone knows what the missing character is anyway. Other users, writing for their peers in academia or the arts and sciences, having mastered their language's high form, quickly tire of inventing unnatural sequences to avoid proscribed characters and persuade themselves that the reform, after all, was never meant to apply to *them*. Faced with the necessity of changing linguistic habits that have their roots in the core of the language, society opts for the easier path. The list of approved characters, at first honored in the breach, is soon not honored at all. What was once intended as a cap on usage is watered down to mere guidelines for compulsory education.

Even getting rid of the characters entirely is no guarantee that the cycle of dependence can be broken immediately. Although stricken from society on one level, people still know the characters, their sounds, and what words they represent, and they use this knowledge in significant ways to compensate for the characters' visible absence. The phenomenon is well-known to Koreans, who have even given it a name: "false *hangul*." It means a text written completely in *hangul* but intelligible only to people with a solid grounding in Sinitic morphology, obtained through a knowledge of Chinese characters, that enables them to "see through" the phonetic text to the "characters" (i.e., morphemes) that are intended. While the extent of this phenomenon may be exaggerated by those opposed to reform, it is unquestionably true that knowing characters helps the user identify the language's morphemes, no matter how they are written, and allows one to make educated guesses in cases of phonetic ambiguity. Those lacking this background are disadvantaged with respect to the language as it is now constituted.

So the characters disappear, and several things happen. Antireformists, armed with test results biased by the fact that the tests are based on transcribed mixed script (characters and *hangul*) text instead of text written to be understood in all-*hangul*, claim the younger generation is losing its ability to deal with the language. The reformers who abolished the characters, of course, are to be blamed. The antireform group goes on to accuse—this time with some justification—the reformers of hypocrisy in demanding that the younger "*hangul* generation" achieve literacy in all-*hangul* without the knowledge of Sinitic morphology that makes these texts legible to the older group who engineered the reform. But the matter does not stop here. Lacking visible props, the language begins to change, and these changes are reinforced by younger writers whose marginal familiarity with characters forces them to evolve new vocabulary and stylistic devices that make the underlying language less character-dependent. These changes, however, provoke a reaction from the older generation who, accustomed to the types of clues the characters provided, claim now that they cannot read the new, authentic all-*hangul* writing, partly because of the reforms and partly because of the changes in the language itself.

Linguistic habits change slowly, but the frustration and problems both sides experience are immediately evident. There are other issues besides. Although Chinese characters are proscribed in the media, in government publications, and in compulsory education, college educators faced with the task of preparing students for a competitive world ignore the reform and assign texts in the mixed character-*hangul* script. Students aided by supplementary texts and prompted by their own drive to succeed learn to recognize (if not write) enough characters to master the texts and graduate. The group then carries this knowledge of characters and Sinitic morphology into society, establishing what the antireformists call (again, with some justification) a two-tiered social structure made up of those fully literate in all of the language's genres and those whose reading skills are limited. Whatever the long-term benefits of the reform may be, its immediate results become less palatable to a sizable segment of society.

People start learning characters on their own. Parents pay tutors to teach their children Chinese characters, while publishers offer remedial textbooks promising a working knowledge of characters for so many hours of study. "Experimental" instruction in Chinese characters is given, allegedly after regular school hours, in certain junior and senior high schools; the students are tested, their scores are compared with those of students educated in the all-*hangul* curriculum, and the superior performance of the experimental group is publicized. Newspapers start using characters again, at first in parentheses after ambiguous Sinitic terms (instead of avoiding the term), then later in the text directly. A call goes out from ad hoc groups to reintroduce the characters in limited number into the compulsory educational curriculum, and the motion succeeds. The characters are taught not as Korean, mind you, but as a foreign language, as a sop to the reform movement, first 1,300 characters, then 1,800 characters, and in college, for all practical purposes, without limit.

This scenario exactly describes what happened to South Korea's attempts to eliminate Chinese characters. It is, in essence, the same cycle described earlier in this chapter, writ large. Because of the unique relationship that has lasted for centuries between language and writing in East Asia and, in particular, the fact that this relationship is relatively independent of sound, radical changes in the writing system made through reform cannot occur without inducing distortions elsewhere in the system. Reform is difficult to sustain, because the immediate dislocations are more evident than the long-term gains. One cannot just limit the number of characters in Japanese and Korean to less than the natural number in use because the operation, besides being inherently contradictory, does not address the core factor that makes the characters worth learning. Nor can they be eliminated easily at one stroke, because the world will not sit still for a decade or two while the societies using Chinese characters stagnate intellectually and economically until the transition to a new and better system can be effected.

This last hypothesis is authenticated by information that has come to light on North Korea's radical move to proscribe Chinese characters outright. As described in Chapter 3 of this book, North Korea in 1946 undertook to replace its mixed character-*hangul* writing system with an all-*hangul* script. Sure enough, some three years later all publications in the country, including technical works, were appearing without Chinese characters. Except certain textbooks, all books, newspapers, magazines, and written communications in general are now in all-*hangul,* in contrast to the situation in the South, where Chinese characters are used in everything but novels and popular literature. The success of the North Korean reform has led some people to conclude that the only element needed in the South to eliminate the characters is political will.

The solution, as it turns out, was not that simple. Although the North's publications are in all-*hangul,* evidence began to emerge decades ago suggesting the North Koreans had come to the same conclusion reached by South Korean linguists on the need to learn Chinese characters during the transition to make their all-*hangul* system work. Between 1959 and 1972, a series of textbooks was published, ostensibly for *hanmun* (classical Chinese), which reintroduced more than three thousand characters in the educational curriculum. The selection of characters and the context in which they are presented makes it clear that they are intended for modern Korean readers. North Korea at first sought to justify the measure on political grounds, as preparation for reunification with the South, where the characters are still used (Kim Il-song 1964:5–6), and as a necessary foundation for translating classic Korean books (ibid. 1966:7). By 1970, however, the country's Great Leader was admitting that the all-*hangul* reform had caused severe dislocations. In Kim's preface to the *Kukhanmun tokbon* he stated, "During the time of all-*hangul* education the people were unable to understand Korean concept words, and the fact that their mental abilities were declining was viewed as a problem." Kim's observation echoed similar complaints made in South Korea by educators opposed to the all-*hangul* reform on the basis of its debilitating effect on students' ability to learn high-level Sinitic terms (Yi Sang-un 1973:120).

Both Koreas grasped early on that changes in the writing system could not be effected without adjustments to the character-dependent Sinitic lexicon. And although these changes would, in principle, evolve by themselves over time, the abrupt nature of the reforms required that immediate measures be taken to offset the imbalance between what people could be expected to understand given the level of redundancy the characters provided and the amount of information the new system was actually providing. In the North, linguists elaborated a set of guidelines to purge the language of troublesome Sinitic terms, which included finding replacements for Sinitic terms in the indigenous lexicon, limiting the application of Sinitic terms to specific semantic domains so that context would be more helpful in distinguishing them, creating new words from the native stock of morphemes, and discouraging use of Sinitic terms that are not words or not truly part of the Korean language (Choe Ho-ch'ol 1989:197–198). Meanwhile, South Koreans were busy compiling five volumes of substitute terms for Sino-Korean words, some of which were based in popular usage, others created out of whole cloth on the basis of what linguists imagined would have happened had the indigenous language been free to develop without Chinese and Chinese characters (Pak 1968:41; Choe Hyon-bae 1970:12).

The problem with these "native" replacements was that no matter how well motivated they were, they are, essentially, *fakes* imposed from the top down and as a result were rejected by the mass of users. Language, especially spoken language, is quintessentially a social process and does not respond well to artificial adjustments, let alone wholesale attempts to change its structure. Another contradiction, endemic to the enterprise, was a lack of standards for deciding what constituted ambiguous Sinitic vocabulary and what part of it was phonetically viable. What sense did it make, South Koreans asked, to replace a well-established and unambiguous Sino-Korean word like *pihaenggi* ("airplane") with the artificial native "word" *naltul?* A similar reaction occurred in the North, as evidenced in Kim Il-song's 1966 speech, where he warned against replacing Sinitic words for its own sake.

As in the South, North Koreans also had to acknowledge that language is not something that can be engineered by a handful of scholars (Ko 1989:28). Although reformers can set goals and erect the basic structures and mechanisms through which these goals can be achieved, the idea that one can undo in a night what Chinese characters did to these languages over centuries is no longer considered viable. The trick, it seems, is to sustain the movement away from characters long enough for alternative practices to emerge and take hold, without causing insufferable disruptions, and to keep the process on track against the criticisms of people opposed to change for reasons of culture and personal convenience. It is not an easy task.

The Futility of Character "Simplification"

Paralleling efforts to lower the number of characters in use were reforms aimed at reducing the complexity of their forms. Chinese reformers believed that by reducing the number of strokes in individual characters and ironing out what they felt to be inconsistencies, they could help the average user learn, write, and remember the characters more easily. The utility of character-based systems would thereby be enhanced in perpetuity, or for however long it took to replace them with phonetic scripts. To the extent that simplification involved merging distinctive elements, the process would have the desirable effect of weaning users away from their dependence on morphemic representation. Finally, it would demonstrate to skeptics that existing conventions could be modified, also helping pave the way for phonetic writing (Chen Guangyao 1955:70; Cao 1955a:36; Zheng 1957:40).

Another justification for altering standard character shapes was that these changes had already taken place. The only element lacking was official recognition. As the evolution of Chinese characters demonstrates, suppletion by popular, simplified forms had been the norm from earliest times. Reduced versions would come into use, be denied sanction by the political authorities, then, depending on the attitude of the next group of rulers, replace the older more complex shapes as the new standard. The great seal forms that were standard before the Qin dynasty were succeeded by the simpler, contemporaneous small seal characters endorsed by the Qin when it came to power, and so on, through the clerical and standard characters (see Chapter 1). According to Qian Xuantong (1887–1939), 70 to 80 percent of the popular simplifications in use in this century before the People's Republic date from Song and Yuan (960–1368) times (Kaizuka and Ogawa 1981:356). Since experience had shown that popular forms cannot be displaced and since the existence of alternate styles only increases the burden on users, the obvious expedient seemed to be to sanction the shorter forms and discard their more complicated counterparts.

Accordingly, the People's Republic of China's first "Character Simplification Plan" of 1955 and 1956 involved little more than shifting recognition from one set of forms to another. Creativity was exercised only in the sense that the Committee on Writing Reform had to decide which of the existing short forms would be adopted and which particular characters would be affected. There were 515 characters changed in this manner, in four installments through 1959 (Fu Yonghe 1981:23). In addition, fifty-four simplified *elements* were designated to replace components of other "complex" forms, which extended these modifications through the system at large. Later, in 1964, another set of regulations was issued that stipulated that ninety-two elements that stood previously as independent simplified characters could also be used to replace components in other characters and that forty reduced forms that had been allowed only as components could now stand alone (Seybolt and Chiang 1978:10). Here is where snags began to develop.

It is one thing to recognize some five hundred reduced forms that writers have been using anyway. But by sanctioning simplified components, reform authorities were obliged to extend these paradigms throughout the whole system, creating new forms for which no popular precedent had existed. In all, 2,236 characters were affected, some 30 percent of the total inventory of characters in use and about 1,700 more than (3.5 times) the number of popular simplifications. One immediate result was that millions already literate in Chinese had to start anew building fresh associations in their minds for vocabulary that had previously been taken for granted, that is, processed "visually." By the same token, those just learning to read were denied ready access to materials published before the reforms went into effect. Chinese readers also lost much of what marginal ability they did have to interpret headlines, proper names, and segments of text in other Asian languages.

A second result was that nonstandard speakers found phonetic categories skewed. Residual connections with sound, which users employ to good effect in identifying or processing characters, are based, where they exist, on ancient sound categories. Although sound change through time affected the Sinitic languages differently, most of these changes can be traced to common antecedents, so that users of any Chinese language were able to derive from the characters meaningful clues that applied to their own spoken variety. When the characters were simplified, however, all of this changed. The reason, presumably overlooked or ignored by reformers, can be traced to the fact that two of the devices most commonly employed to simplify the characters—homonym substitution and replacing complex components with ones that have the same sound but fewer strokes—were based on their phonetic correspondences in Mandarin. Collapsing these ancient graphic distinctions deprived non-Mandarin Chinese speakers of what few motivated links the writing system had with the sounds of their languages, causing—for 30 percent of the Han population, at least—a clear loss in utility.

The third consequence was even more important. Having exceeded their original mandate, reformers were free to interpret on their own the course that evolution would have taken had users been as enlightened. What followed, inevitably, was a "second" (actually, the third) group of simplified forms that made even greater use of phonetic substitution than the original scheme. First advanced in 1977 in draft form, the proposal was withdrawn the following year in the face of widespread criticism that there were too many new forms and too few distinctions between them. As with the 1955–1956 plan, the new plan included both new simplified characters and sixty-one reduced forms that could be used as components to simplify other characters outside the list by analogy. Adding these to the 853 characters specified would have yielded a total of some 4,500 simplified forms, about double the number changed by the 1964 reform and more than most Chinese were ready to accept (Seybolt and Chiang, 1978:10–11; Cheng Chin-chuan 1979:48, 1983:2–3).[5]

What did the Chinese get for their trouble? The short answer is, the average number of strokes needed to write Chinese fell by about 16 percent. Prior to reform, stroke count averaged eleven to twelve strokes per character, depending on the number of characters included in the sample.[6] Since the characters targeted for change were, by and large, more complex, the savings realized for the 2,236 characters affected were considerable: average stroke count was reduced from fifteen to about nine (French 1976:117).[7] These figures, however, are not representative of the system generally, since the changed characters are not the most common. Focusing instead on the two thousand most frequently used, we find the count dropping from 11.2 to 9.8 strokes, for a savings of 12.5 percent. The figure rises to 16.2 percent (9.15 to 7.67 strokes) for running text, which is probably the best gauge of the reform's overall effectiveness (DeFrancis 1984a:260).

If the 16 percent figure seems lackluster, further analysis gives cause for even less enthusiasm. The reform gets off to a very bad start epistemologically with its assumption that top-down planning produces a more efficient system than what emerges from the natural order. Had the reform's scope been limited to the endorsement of existing practices and the removal of impediments favored by the elite, this objection would be nullified. However, the state's involvement on a minor scale led at once to changes that lacked social sanction and precedent. No one seems to have asked why, if it were desirable for substitutions to be extended analogically through the entire inventory, this had not already occurred. Nor was much thought given to justifying the selection of particular forms with any kind of outside standard. Simply claiming a reduced form has popular currency is not enough, since many hundreds exist that were not chosen.[8] Moreover, there were no clear criteria for deciding which characters would be replaced or how many strokes a character needed to qualify as a candidate (Jian 1957:140).

If we drop the pretense that the Chinese reforms from 1964 onward were the fruits of "mass" action, a plausible case can be made for the need to deal ad hoc with individual characters. The reason lies in the relationship of characters and their components to particular sounds. There is enough regularity in the system as it existed to make trying to preserve it worthwhile, but not enough for a noncontradictory solution, and this made guidelines of any sort difficult to apply. For example, if one proceeds from a rule that phonetic series should be preserved as indicated, one ends up endorsing sets that have no synchronic motivation, that no longer sound the same. But if current sound (in Mandarin?) is used as the criterion, the situation becomes even messier. The same phonetic "components" often have multiple sounds, many sounds are "represented" by more than one component, and a given component can sometimes be read one way as a phonetic element and another way as a character. The only way all of these inconsistencies can be regularized is to rebuild the entire system from scratch—in which case, why bother with the characters at all?

Considerations such as these may help explain the committee's willingness to operate without standards but hardly justify their ambivalence toward the basic question of what, precisely, was being simplified. Were individual units the target, or was the system as a whole? That the two are not the same is illustrated by the following example: if the single character pronounced *de* (a marker of attribution or modification) were reduced by a stroke or two, the effect would be felt by all users 6 to 7 percent of the time that they moved their pens. In contrast, replacing a complicated but uncommon character like 鑫 *xīn* (a word used in names, with the connotation of good fortune or profit) with its homonym 欣 saves sixteen strokes but is not likely to be noticed by many readers in a lifetime (Wang 1980:101).

A more fundamental concern is "the implausible judgment that the most important factor determining the efficiency of Chinese script is the number of strokes involved in the graphs" (Sampson 1985:160). There are two problems with the notion that stroke reduction equates to greater efficiency, the first being apparent in the example of 鑫 *xīn* above. With twenty-four strokes, the character is clearly a candidate for replacement by the usual criteria. Closer examination shows, however, that it is made up of three occurrences of the same component 金, which happens to be a common "radical" known to any elementary school student. The components that make up its replacement 欣, by contrast, are less common both absolutely and in this configuration, and probably pose a greater psychological burden on the user than the original version. This same reasoning can be applied to many of the so-called complex characters that were simplified.

The second flaw in this interpretation is its neglect of the reader. Granted there is probably something to be gained for the reader by removing some of the clutter that comes with traditional "complex" forms. But this advantage is negated by the relative lack of distinctions available to identify discrete symbols. As the number of strokes is reduced, individual characters tend to resemble each other. This point has been made before by many observers (Serruys 1962:92; Kaizuka and Ogawa 1981:378; Coulmas 1983:243; Sampson 1985:160), and we need not belabor it here. An interesting corollary is that the indistinctiveness of simplified forms seems to have affected memory, too. According to Fu Yonghe, forms containing half the number of strokes are written incorrectly more often than the original "complex" character, owing to greater similarity between the "simpler" form and other members of the set (1981:24).

This indistinctiveness also applies to the identification of traditional subdivisions within the character. Serruys has shown that in "modern simplified characters, both radical and phonetic elements are equally reduced, without keeping them clearly distinguished, to the extent that it is no longer possible to distinguish from the structure of the new character which part is phonetic, which one not" (1962:92). As a consequence of fewer strokes, standard components necessarily take on more phonetic functions, or at any rate are perceived by the learner as doing so. Serruys goes on to list several examples of structural inconsistencies that result from the reforms of 1956 to 1964 that lead one to believe that in seeking one form of simplicity the reformers sacrificed another. It is useless to object that the original system was also imperfect, since the removal of these inconsistencies was part of the project's justification. As was the case with reduction in number, tinkering with the characters' forms succeeded only in shifting the difficulties from one part of the system to another.

We must conclude from the foregoing that character simplification in China has not benefited the reader or the learner to any appreciable degree and may even have caused a loss of utility. Ironically, the reform does not seem to have done anything for writing, either. Printing is still done character by character, and a few less lines on a typeface makes no difference at all to printer or machine. With regard to handwriting, the truth is no less blatant: people had been using many of these forms before, so how precisely have they benefited? One might argue that mainland and Singaporean Chinese no longer need to write the longer, traditional forms. But except in school, where did they ever? The "masses" are still making their own choices from among the large, unsanctioned inventory of popular forms, which is where the vitality of the system has always been. There is no reason to believe that people pay any more attention in their own writing to official standards now than they ever did. To the extent that conformity *can* be exacted, the whole spectacle becomes *déjà vu*.

Japan's Simplified Characters

In comparison with the Chinese reforms, character simplification in Japan was a modest undertaking. The *Tōyō kanji* list of 1,850 characters published in 1946 included 131 simplified forms. They were expanded to about three hundred by the 1949 law on character shapes. Unlike the Chinese simplifications, which sought to reduce writing effort, these changes appear to have been aimed only at standardizing the inventory. The savings, theoretically, would come from the need to memorize only one set of forms. Consequently, simplification in Japanese for the most part involved shifting endorsement from one existing form to another with fewer strokes. Analogic modifications were not vigorously pursued, and phonetic substitution (of components) seems to have played no role at all.

If we look at the proportion of characters involved, just 17 percent of those approved for use were affected,[9] which translates into 10 percent, assuming 3,100 units in use. Thus, not only is the absolute number of simplified characters used in Chinese greater than in Japanese, they also account for about three times more of the inventory. Add the fact that the abridgments in Chinese are, as a rule, more radical, and one begins to appreciate how far the two systems have diverged, particularly from the viewpoint of a Japanese trying to read Chinese. There is little likelihood that any sincere effort will be made to bring the systems back into alignment, since many of the changes in Chinese make no sense at all to a Japanese.

Three factors account for the relative lack of enthusiasm Japanese have shown for character simplification. First, the architects of the postwar reforms were not as interested as the Chinese in improving the utility of the characters over the long term. The main thrust of their efforts was directed at limiting the number of characters in use, in preparation for replacing the characters with an all-phonetic script or as a tactic for forestalling major changes. A second reason was the existence of the *Tōyō* list itself. Number and stroke counts aside, the chief difference between the simplified characters approved by the Japanese government between 1946 and 1949 and the program endorsed in the People's Republic of China a decade later was the latter's addendum of simplified components, which could be used to modify other characters not specifically listed. Although the Japanese lists lacked this provision, it was obvious enough to those familiar with the old system which of the "complex" components had changed. Should these changes be extended to other characters? In China, questions such as this led to the 1964 General List, which analogized the changes to 1,754 new characters. In Japan, however, the analogies could not be made because these other characters officially did not exist! True to its principles, the Japanese government has steadfastly refused to adjust the shapes of extralegal characters, which would be tantamount to recognition. This is another reason why the number of simplified forms remained low.

A third probable reason is more intriguing, since it relates to the validity of the enterprise generally. We noted above that some specialists believe simplified characters impair recognition because there are fewer distinctions. In the late 1930s, the Japanese government conducted some careful surveys of students' ability to write characters after six years of schooling, as part of a study to find ways and justification for simplifying the character-based script. The results were startling. Performance was found to vary according to how recently the character was learned and the character's frequency. When these two factors were controlled, stroke count was found to have no discernible effect on the ability of students to remember (Okazaki 1938:39). To the extent that form affects memory at all, it was found to apply only to the ability of students to analogize from the structure of one character to another. When analogy was impossible, as with characters like 乏 *bō* ("meager, destitute"), performance was poor despite the low stroke count. More recently, Paradis et al. made the same observation that the "number of strokes per se may not be a sufficient or even acceptable measure of complexity, in that groups of strokes may form familiar subpatterns" (1985:9).

We may draw two conclusions: firstly, it was meaningless to lower the stroke count for its own sake. Second, the "complex" characters in Japanese and Chinese, with their greater redundancy and internal consistency, may have been the better bargain.

Evolution and Reform

I have argued that positive reform of character-based writing in Chinese is a zero-sum game, since improvements in one area reappear as problems in another. Even in the case of the non-Sinitic languages, government-mandated restrictions on character use were also found to be problematic. It is impractical to reduce the inventory of characters to less than the natural number in use, because doing so splits the representation of hundreds of Sinitic compounds into half phonetic–half character hybrids, imposes a static "solution" on a dynamic system, and does nothing to solve—indeed, it fosters—the basic problem that makes learning Chinese characters necessary: poorly distinguished word shapes. Moreover, as long as the characters are available, people will use them in their intended fashion to disambiguate words, depriving themselves of the incentive needed to look seriously for other ways around the ambiguity. However, eliminating the characters altogether by fiat can result in so many immediate problems that the writing system breaks down, or appears to, in the eyes of many whose patience with reform is outweighed by their eagerness to get on with their lives with as few inconveniences as possible.

Does this mean there is no prospect for change? Not at all. I am skeptical about reform as an absolute mechanism for change, but I have said nothing yet about that other engine of development: the natural, decentralized, "spontaneous" evolution of society adapting to new pressures. In the following chapters I will argue that the influx of Western words into East Asian languages is overwhelming the capacity of indigenous writing systems to absorb them, rendering traditional morphological processes obsolete, and redirecting users away from syllables as primary units and toward phonemes. These structural and psychological changes, which are probably irreversible, are erasing the concrete, linguistic conditions that the characters created and on which they depend. Western vocabulary is doing, in effect, the same thing to East Asian languages that Sinitic vocabulary did more than a millennium ago, namely, bending the language to meet its requirements.

Meanwhile, as the languages themselves undergo structural change, another powerful element is providing the venue through which these changes can be expressed, refined, and distributed throughout communities of users. Computers, once regarded as technology's answer to the palpable drawbacks of writing in Chinese characters, are forcing East Asians to develop new conventions based on words and letters, which is leading to full-fledged alphabetic writing. This writing in turn will compete with and ultimately drive out the character scripts. As that day approaches, we can probably expect state-sponsored reform movements in the opposite direction—toward preserving the traditional writing systems—which will have as little effect as the preceding set of reforms.

10. Language, Speech, and Writing

THE FORMAL RELATIONSHIP between writing and speech has been debated by linguists for nearly a century. One school of thought treats writing as derivative of speech and maintains that writing's true and only function is to represent speech sounds. In this view, speech represents (or *is*) language, and writing in turn represents (or should represent) speech. The contrary view asserts that writing and speech both represent language, that the one does not (even should not) necessarily derive from the other, and that neither form of language is "primary." Not surprisingly, linguists disposed one way or the other to Chinese characters generally agree with the view of writing that supports their prejudice. Those who see little linguistic value in the character systems claim that since Chinese characters do not represent the sounds of speech, or in any case, do so very poorly, the characters are deficient to that extent. Others, who support Chinese characters on linguistic or cultural grounds, argue that the system—any writing system—has no business "representing" speech, since written units tie into language on a higher level.

I am well aware that many colleagues who share my low view of Chinese characters do so, in part, from their conviction that "language is speech" and that writing is (or should be) derivative of speech. This is one possible interpretation of the relationship between language, speech, and writing, and although there are problems with the way the proposition has been formulated and understood, it is far more tenable than the pre-Bloomfieldian paradigm that treated written language, and writing in general, as the primary object of linguistic inquiry. It is still superior to the misguided notion that language can exist in any practical sense independently of speech. However, it makes little sense to go on demanding adherence to the Bloomfieldian dictum when large numbers of scholars who might be sympathetic to the arguments against Chinese characters made here and elsewhere are likely to be unimpressed by what they believe to be a simplistic view of how writing maps onto language. Worse, as long as alternative theories are available, such as the view that holds that both writing and speech are concrete manifestations of one abstract language or, more radically, that the two are not even representing the same language, scholars disposed for reasons of their own to defend Chinese characters will be able to cite these paradigms in support of their view, just as those who oppose the characters claim support from *their* paradigm. Meanwhile practical reform gets nowhere.

I will not presume to resolve in a few pages the long-standing dispute over the connection between language, speech, and writing, which linguists and other specialists have devoted entire careers to examining. Nevertheless, it does appear that the argument to a large degree rests on the confusion generated by false premises and loosely defined concepts. The first of these is the failure to distinguish between historical and synchronic relationships. As DeFrancis has pointed out, although writing emerged from speech, it later developed a life of its own that makes it "both more and less than speech."[1] What is true historically and ontogenetically is not necessarily true of a system's functioning. Another problem is the Bloomfieldian identification of "speech" with "language." Although intended to establish speech as the primary substance of language, the prescription can be and has been interpreted to mean that speech is the whole of language. This latter concept has since been rejected by linguists operating within the framework of a speech-oriented discipline, but its legacy continues to add needless confusion to an already perplexing topic. Finally, as a reaction against the language-is-speech axiom, another group of scholars in their eagerness to rehabilitate writing have gone too far in the other direction by implying that speech (more precisely, phonology, the precursor to speech) and writing enjoy coequal status with respect to language. Although true in the sense that both represent language, the paradigm fails to take into account the necessary role phonology plays in the structure of language and its functioning on all levels, and the fact that writing's role here is entirely optional.

I hope that these remarks and those that follow will help clarify the framework for debate on the relationship between language, speech, and writing. But for present purposes, absolute agreement on this matter is unnecessary. Those who hold the view that language is or is primarily speech and that writing synchronically derives or should derive from speech will have no trouble rejecting Chinese characters for lack of a theoretical justification. Instead, this chapter is addressed to people who support the other proposition—that writing and speech are both concrete expressions of abstract language—and who may, accordingly, be tempted to regard Chinese characters (wrongly) as no more of an aberration from the ideal than phonetic systems. If it can be shown that Chinese characters fail to meet common expectations even in terms of this alternative theory of writing, then the theoretical underpinning for the characters, as it were, would vanish entirely.

The present chapter begins by discussing the relationship writing has with language and with speech, and the different interpretations linguists give to this relationship. I will then demonstrate how the notion that writing and speech are parallel manifestations of language contrary to expectation offers no more linguistic support for Chinese characters than the Bloomfieldian notion of language as speech. That done, I will try to show why efforts to make Chinese-based writing stylistically more speechlike cannot succeed, given the nature of the character script, and what this fact means for East Asians. This applies to writing on the functional level. Formally, my task will be to demonstrate why phonetic scripts, which are supposed to represent sound, also do a better job than Chinese characters in the semantic arena. Finally, I will argue that writing and language have an enormous influence on each other, and that this relationship may be breaking down the cycle of dependence between East Asian languages and character-based writing.

The Relationship between Language and Writing

Underlying the debate over the efficacy of Chinese characters versus phonetic alphabets are concerns about how writing in general represents language and about how both language and writing relate to speech. The linguistic axiom that speech is paramount over writing in its relationship with language has at least three sources. The first is its chronological primacy. Although true writing, defined as a visible representation of spoken language, has existed for fewer than five thousand years, speech is believed to predate writing by tens of thousands of years and is regarded by anthropology as one of humankind's defining characteristics. The chronological primacy of speech is also manifested in the fact that every writing system, Chinese characters included, has tried in the course of its historical development to connect itself in one way or another with the sounds of the language it sought to represent, and did not develop, even on its own terms, as the visual expression of a language until this essential link with sound was completed. Chronologically speaking, the argument that speech is primary is incontestable.

A second reason for maintaining that speech is primary, as noted in Chapter 1, is its indispensability for human language. Although there are hundreds of languages that have no writing at all, there are no human languages that are not or have not been spoken. Even more basically, although one can devise writing systems for languages lacking them, the notion of devising a system of phonological contrasts for a language is simply absurd—the language either has one, or it does not exist. The phonological elements of language and the psychological apparatus that leads to their concrete realization in speech are part of every human language. Although different from one language to the next, their role and position in the universal hierarchy of linguistic structure is the same, in contrast to writing, which maps onto language at different levels according to particular conventions.

Phonology, moreover, plays a necessary role in language's internal processing. We do not think in terms of letters or characters, but do think habitually with the same sound traces that find their way into speech. Sound traces also play a role in short-term memory, particularly in preparing written discourse. If writing were primary, or even structurally coequal with speech, one would expect traces of the former to appear as a precondition for verbal expression or, at least, as the precursor to writing in short-term memory. In fact, the opposite is true. It is not only abnormal but virtually impossible to rely on a visual short-term-memory code long enough to get more than a word or two on paper, and even then phonation still fights its way into the process. Although writing, once established, develops a life of its own and becomes equal to speech in the sense that both serve as concrete expressions of language,[2] its role is far less significant in terms of a language's structure. Functionally, although writing is a highly useful appendage, it is not, like speech and the mechanisms behind it, an absolute necessity.

The third source of the primacy-of-speech argument, however, has less to do with linguistics than with the intellectual environment in which the paradigm emerged. Here, in my view, is where problems developed. Armed with linguistic facts alone, language scholars during the first half of the twentieth century had ample basis for establishing speech as the paramount representation of language and writing as a device of somewhat less importance to language and to scholars investigating language. Unfortunately, linguists, for reasons to be discussed, drove writing out of the discipline entirely, marginalizing it and the scholars who embraced it. In so doing, they allowed errors to creep into their own paradigm, in particular the misguided notion that speech is the whole of language, while laying the groundwork for a countermovement committed to the same types of overstatements made in the reverse.

Several factors were responsible for the early-twentieth-century linguists' unwillingness to treat writing seriously. When linguistics was establishing itself as a science, the scientific community was dominated by a physics that accorded the mantle of "science" only to those disciplines whose data were amenable to measurement. Although this paradigm was eventually superseded in the natural sciences, its strength was still felt in praxeology, the sciences of human action, in the belief that if something could not be quantified, it was not science.[3] This belief led to the rejection of all phenomena that did not fit the paradigm, that is, could not be expressed in numbers, which in practice meant focusing on the simplest elements in a chain of events, "reducing" complex systems to the sum of their identifiable constituents, and ignoring whatever could not be explained in these terms. Psychology had behaviorism, which tried to explain all mental phenomena as a function of preset responses to external stimuli. Linguists, eager to join the ranks of what passed then as science, followed suit by elaborating a discipline that tried very hard to base itself, similarly, on the smallest concrete elements (or what they thought were concrete elements) at their disposal: sound phonemes. Higher linguistic phenomena not suited to gross measurement were dismissed as "mentalistic" and not part of the new discipline's "data."

These early linguists seem to have grasped that the study of writing's relationship to language leads inevitably to higher levels of language that could not be usefully treated within their new paradigm. All practical writing systems are built to greater or lesser degrees around linguistic meaning and cannot be described in terms of sound alone. There were other reasons why linguists looked on writing with disfavor. Concerned with an ideal state and less involved in portraying sound per se writing also seemed to epitomize the prescriptive enterprise from which linguistics had just broken free. For decades, language study had focused entirely on written texts, and ancient texts in particular. The move against writing in part was a reaction against this earlier paradigm.[4] Moreover, when the new axioms were being set down, linguists in the United States were immersed in the study of Native American languages, most of which had no writing system. Their attention necessarily shifted to sound, the immediate target in the study of any unknown, unrecorded language.

All of these factors conspired to push writing and written language off center stage, where it did not belong, and then off the stage entirely, where it does not belong either. The upshot was yet another paradigm shift toward writing, which addresses the more egregious oversights of the language-is-speech axiom, but at the same time has exposed linguistics to some far-fetched ideas about how writing should represent language or, worse, how it need not represent spoken language at all. Our present concern is that the new paradigm, by reacting against the Bloomfieldian concept that writing represents "speech," has lent support to the untenable notion that writing need not even approximate speech, in other words, to the idea that Chinese characters in their relationship to language are no better or worse than phonetic alphabets. Who were the scholars responsible for these paradigm shifts, and how did their ideas play out in practice?

Ferdinand de Saussure, the founder of modern linguistics, was one of the first to reject the prescriptive, text-based view of language. In the process, he defined the relationship of writing to language that was to guide mainstream linguistics for half a century. According to de Saussure: "Language and writing are two distinct systems of signs. The only reason the second exists is to represent the first. The object of linguistics is not defined by the combination of the written word and the spoken word; the latter constitutes its only object" (1916/1974:45). There was no need for de Saussure within the framework of his system—which distinguishes abstract language from its concrete representation—to relegate writing to a secondary position. Indeed, some would argue that his scheme should have led him to posit both writing and speech as concrete representations of language. As Scinto points out, "In wishing to distinguish language *(langue)* from the facts of speech *(parole),* de Saussure must insist that there is no necessity for sound, a physical substance, to be part of *langue*" (1986:9). But de Saussure, confusing abstract phonology with its concrete substance, felt that sound is natural to the system itself. So did Edward Sapir, who in his widely read work *Language* (subtitled *An Introduction to the Study of Speech*) stated: "The written forms are secondary symbols of the spoken ones— symbols of symbols" (1921/1949:20).

Leonard Bloomfield, who founded American structuralism, was emphatic in his insistence on the primacy of speech. According to Bloomfield, "Writing is not language, but merely a way of recording language by means of visible marks" (1933:19), which is true in itself, but falls short by failing to describe speech in similar terms as the audible representation of language. Jakobson and Halle, in their *Fundamentals of Language,* however, explicitly denied that speech and writing are different representations of language. Instead they viewed speech phonemes as primary elements on which the graphemes of writing are based, the latter being supplemental and "parasitic" (1956:17). Charles Hockett, another guiding light in the development of linguistics, described the relationship as follows: "The linguist distinguishes between *language* and *writing,* whereas the layman tends to confuse the two. The layman's terms "spoken language" and "written language" suggest that speech and writing are merely two different manifestations of something fundamentally the same. Often enough, the layman thinks that writing is somehow more basic than speech. Almost the reverse is true" (1958:4).

Some exceptions to the antiwriting paradigm did emerge, even before structuralism fell prey to another theory whose tenets were intrinsically less hostile to writing. H. J. Uldall's contrary formulation was one of the earliest and most consistent. According to Uldall, neither speech nor writing is primary in a logical (versus chronological) sense; rather, both express or manifest the same underlying language (1944:11–16). In this model, "the orthographic units and the units of pronunciation correspond to, or, better, are functions of the same units of content." Dwight Bolinger's views were similar. In his landmark article "Visual Morphemes," Bolinger argued that the existence of homonyms (that are not homographs) and spelling irregularities sufficed to prove "that writing can exist as a series of morphemes at its own level, independent of or interacting with the more fundamental (or at least more primitive) vocal-auditory morphemes" (1946:333). Moreover, he found it hard to justify the notion that speech is primary in a culture where most new vocabulary is acquired through print. Bolinger recommended that we "revise the dictum that 'language must always be studied without reference to writing' [in] recognition of a shift that has taken place in the communicative behavior of literate societies" (p. 340).

I. J. Gelb was another exception, whose monumental work *A Study of Writing* by itself went far to establish writing as a respectable subject of inquiry. Gelb agreed "entirely with the linguists who believe that fully developed writing became a device for expressing linguistic elements." That is, writing is not "writing" without language. He did not, however, confuse *language* with *speech*. For Gelb, "the general statement that full writing expresses speech should not be taken to mean that it expresses nothing else but speech. . . . The existence of . . . 'visual morphemes' that is, forms or spellings which convey the meaning only in writing, shows clearly that writing can sometimes function as a means of communication separately and in addition to speech" (1962:13–15).

Even more significant for the reinterpretation of writing's role in language was the eclipse of structuralism. From the late 1950s onward, linguists became increasingly attracted to a model of language that distanced itself deliberately from surface phenomena, relying instead on the intuition of native speakers toward an utterance's "well-formedness" for clues to its underlying structure. This shift rehabilitated writing without meaning to. While avowedly descriptive, the emphasis placed by generative grammarians on rule writing and on the correctness of sentences began to resemble—in substance though not by design—the sort of thing done by prescriptive grammarians before the structuralists had come to the forefront. At the very least, the specimens accepted for analysis more closely resembled those found in edited texts than the casual, disjointed speech one hears and uses daily.

While American generative grammar was paving the way for the resurrection of the direct role of writing in language, some European linguists were already arguing for its "coequal" status with speech, both logically in terms of its relationship to language and in terms of its importance in the overall scheme. Hjelmslev (1961) maintained that language is purely a schema, which is empty not only of concrete realization on the level of expression, but also of material content as such. Writing, therefore, is a different form of the material substance for realizing the same universal scheme. Motsh (1963) similarly defined natural language as a "grammar," its system of representation being a "phonemic component" or a "graphemic component," depending on the substance. Amirova argued that "no type of writing is directed only at a reflection of the phonological system. The history of the evolution of writing shows that . . . words, parts of words, and even sentences" figure into the meanings of graphemes (1977:117). To Amirova, the "correlation of spoken and written language is realized . . . on the level of the structural-functional modeling of linguistic thought, with a very complicated system of links that runs through the whole hierarchy of linguistic structure" (p. 38).

Meanwhile, some American linguists, and psycholinguists in particular, were interpreting the concept of generative grammar, which distinguishes a language's "surface structure" from its "lexical representation," to mean that the latter can be realized either in speech or in print, depending on whether phonological or orthographic rules are applied (Gibson and Levin 1975:180–181). In moving from abstract structures to surface representation, generative grammar had no necessary commitment to the form that the representation has to take. Both writing and speech could manifest the body of rules that govern the outcome. As Goodman describes it: "Writing and oral language are alternate surface structures with the same underlying deep structure. . . . Phonological rules produce a signal which is an oral sequence. Orthographic rules produce a signal which is a graphic display" (1982:26). Both "represent alternative encodings of the same meaning. For the proficient reader, written language becomes parallel to speech and not a secondary representation of it" (1970:103).

One aspect of this alternative formulation is that it departs from the view that speech "is" the language. That the concepts are not coterminous is suggested by the existence of the two words themselves. Julia Falk explains the difference:

> *Language* and *speech* are not synonyms. Speech is a concrete, physical act—the production of specific utterances containing particular words arranged in particular ways and expressed by means of certain sounds. Language is a mental phenomenon, a body of knowledge about sounds, meaning and syntax which resides in the mind. This knowledge can be put to use, of course, but the speech, or writing, that results is merely a representation of the language—it is not the language itself. (1973:12)

Later Falk restates this idea in terms that parallel de Saussure's dichotomy between *langue* and *parole*: "Speech is actual language behavior, subject to interference from many nonlinguistic factors. Language, on the other hand, is a body of knowledge that resides in the minds of human beings—the linguistic competence of the speakers of a language" (ibid.: 20).

Writing theorists working outside the framework of generative grammar came to the same conclusion about the relationship between an abstract language and its representations. Wrolstad asserts that "comlang—our basic organization of language—handles language on an abstract level independent of its expression in either of the language systems" and that the latter both "approach this basic control directly—through clear channels" (1976:12). More recently, Vachek proposed accommodating de Saussure's "concept of a formal, insubstantial *langue*" with the proven existence of independent "norms" by interjecting a "spoken norm" and a "written norm" between *langue* and "spoken utterances" and "written utterances," adding that "from the synchronistic viewpoint de Saussure's distinction of the spoken norm as historically primary as opposed to the written norm as historically secondary is for their function evaluation beside the point" (1989:108).

In other words, the phylogenetic and ontogenetic primacy of speech does not, in this view, privilege the latter with respect to its formal and functional relationships to language. Both writing and speech "constitute complementary systems of language norms" (Scinto 1986:2), each manifesting language in its own way according to the particular requirements levied by nature on the two media. The possibility of a parallel functional relationship of writing and speech to language, for those languages that have writing and for their literate speakers, is further supported by neurological evidence (cited in Chapter 7 above) showing that selective impairment of one route has no necessary effect on a literate person's ability to access meaning through the other route. The human brain has found it expedient to "hard wire" two separate pathways to linguistic meaning, neither of which depends absolutely on the other, much as society has evolved two parallel but separate mechanisms to communicate the same abstract body of knowledge.

This new formulation corrects the mistaken notion that language and speech are one and the same thing, which was never part of de Saussure's system to begin with, and rehabilitates writing as a respectable subject for linguistic inquiry. Regrettably, it also opens the door to a host of implausible interpretations and paradigm-specific nonsense. As an example of the latter, generative grammar, with its emphasis on abstract rule writing, has led its main practitioners to make some rather astounding assertions about the basis for English orthography, at the same time it diverted a generation or two of scholars from what many believe is linguistics' primary business: the study of concrete human behavior. Also, the notion of coequal representation, while valid on one level, ignores the fact that language, even for literate speakers, is designed around a phonological code that has applications on several tiers of the linguistic hierarchy and is therefore intrinsically more a part of language than is writing (or, strictly speaking, the code that precedes writing). And from coequal representation, it is a short step to the belief, fraught with bad consequences, that writing need not connect with phonology to be valid and, finally, that any written representation is as good as another.

To summarize, speech and writing both represent language and in this way parallel each other. The elements that lead to concrete speech form a large and necessary part of the abstract body of knowledge called language. Writing, by contrast, is an accessory. Unlike the precursors to speech whose mechanisms are fixed and universal, writing systems map onto particular languages by convention. Since phonology permeates the language hierarchy, writing by *any* convention must take account of these preexisting contrasts in forming its own particular set of relationships and in this sense depends on the speech mechanism—although not on "speech."[5] The system, perhaps, can best be characterized by paraphrasing Orwell: in terms of their relationship to language, writing and speech are equal, but speech is a lot more equal. Or we can drop the silly "primacy" argument altogether and let the facts, as I have tried to do, speak (?) for themselves.

The Difference between Writing and Speech

If writing and speech both manifest the same (or, in some schemes, similar) abstract body of knowledge, then what exactly is writing representing? Where does it link up with this body of abstractions that range from linguistic meaning[6] down to the phoneme?

We can begin by rejecting the notion that writing—in any system—is (or should be) a mirror image of speech.[7] Although the two systems may be *logically* equivalent in their relationship to language, functionally and structurally they are different—otherwise why have two systems? Looking at the functional differences, we note that writing typically involves a greater range of topics than speech and hence is less predictable (Sampson 1985:177). Writing, according to Stubbs, is likely "to contain relatively more lexical (content) words and fewer grammatical (structural) words. . . . Since lexical words are less predictable (there are many more of them in the language), the information content of written language is correspondingly higher and less predictable" (1980:111). An extreme example of this is list making, one of the earliest forms of writing, which has no parallel in speech despite the importance of lists, catalogues, and this entire genre to civilization.

Topics common to writing, moreover, are often too complex for speakers to manipulate and depend for their realization on linguistic structures that cannot be generated or interpreted simultaneously. As Chafe points out, in writing "we have time to integrate a succession of ideas into a single linguistic whole that is not available in speaking. In speaking, we normally produce one idea at a time" (1982:37). Writing "can be reflected upon, altered, and even erased at will. . . . It gives the writer power to manipulate time. Events that occurred in the past or that may occur in the future can be evaluated, organized and changed. . . . Such control over time is completely beyond the scope of spoken language or of thought that remains 'in the head' " (Smith 1983:82).

The result is a text that is both more consistent and more demanding than what is normally found in spoken discourse. However, by way of compensation, written texts, "need not be attended in the order presented. (They) can be read faster or slower, reread, skimmed, scanned for isolated words or phrases, read only in parts omitting large sections" (Stubbs 1980:103). In sum, the procedures governing both production and interpretation of written texts vary from those used in speech, according to the requirements that people and nature have levied on the medium.

Moreover, a written text must be intelligible on its own terms. While speaking, people make continuous use of paralinguistic (intonation, repetition, pauses, juncture, stress) and extralinguistic (facial expressions, pointing, arm waving) devices to ensure that their messages are being correctly interpreted, a condition more or less guaranteed in a dialog. None of these is available to the writer, who must in addition overcome constraints caused by what Martlew calls "the lack of an immediate and shared context" (1983a:301).

In other words, the style of written language is also conditioned by its need to span distance and time. Because of its relative permanence, a written text is prepared on the assumption that its readers may not share the idiosyncratic linguistic habits of the writer qua speaker. To accommodate regional and temporal variation, a written standard evolves that is more resistant to pressures for change than speech. Writing, accordingly, becomes more formal, both in the literal sense and in the usual meaning of something strict and definitive, which language users look to for guidance. This fact disturbs many observers, professional linguists among them, whose own training and mental outlook have predisposed them to regard spontaneity as the engine of development, and it is certainly true that excessive attachment to prescriptive norms has done nothing to further the utility of language in either of its forms. Nevertheless, it is senseless to decry the difference per se between spoken language and written language, because no matter what interpretation one gives to these differences, they are occasioned in the final analysis by the different requirements to which the media are subjected. As Haas has noted, "The more nearly a written text approximates to the structure of speech, the fewer distinctive advantages of writing over speech" (1976:206). Merging the two styles fully would benefit no one.

As a consequence of these particular requirements and because the permanence of writing lends itself to greater scrutiny, written texts are distinguished by a tidiness and accuracy that in speech would be considered affected, if intelligible at all. Writing must be "legible, grammatical, explicit, and unambiguous in a more rigorous way than is required in speech" (Martlew 1983a:300). It is also more concise. Whether brevity in writing is considered "good style" to avoid what Koestler called "the deadening cumulative effects of saturation" (1964:336) or because the characteristics of the medium make this compression possible, or for economic reasons, or simply because talented writers have established this as the norm, good writing in any language is associated with a conciseness that does not normally obtain in speech.

These functional differences explain why writing cannot mimic speech—either in its style or, as we shall see, in its level of representation. If writing had to follow speech, the obvious question to ask is, whose speech? The Chinese linguist Y. R. Chao, who was tasked with devising a national spoken standard, used to say, only half jokingly, that he was the only standard Mandarin speaker in China. The point is, no writing system can mirror pronunciation, because speech sounds are highly individualistic, while the whole purpose of writing is to transcend the personal differences caused by space and time.

That variation can be accommodated at all within a "phonetic" writing system is the result of two factors. The first of these is the existence of underlying lexical representations for words that (we presume) do not vary much between users. Although the underlying forms are related to print by one set of rules, the phonetic representations derive from another set, making it possible for different speakers to share common vocabulary without compromising their own habits or learning what amounts to another language. Second, when a word acquires a recognized spelling, it also takes on a characteristic shape that relates to its meaning, regardless of how that shape is pronounced (or mispronounced) by individuals. As the example of English illustrates, users are more willing to accept complex orthographic rules and irregularities than changes to the overt graphic representation.

Writing, therefore, maps onto language at an abstract level, unlike speech sounds, which are entirely concrete. No matter how concrete one tries to make a writing system, some level of abstraction is needed even for representation at the segmental level.[8] Practically speaking, the "sound" that is provided by most "phonetic" scripts has already been abstracted up to the level of the phoneme or morphophoneme, which gives important clues, unavailable to the listener, about the semantic structure of the discourse. Moving up one level, we note further that a phonetic "notation" becomes a "script" only after its symbols have been applied conventionally to every word in the language (Zhou 1961:243). That is, the true function of a phonetic script is not to spell out sounds, but to identify morphemes and words.[9] Most phonetic orthographies, whether alphabetic or syllabic, are keyed to language at the level of finished lexical units and hence offer readers a semantic analysis of the text that is not provided in speech.

The Discontinuity between Chinese Characters and Units of Speech

In view of the foregoing, it is impossible—on a first level of analysis—to fault Chinese characters for "failing" to represent speech, either stylistically or in terms of its units of representation. No writing system, phonemic or otherwise, maps onto speech sounds, either in the naive sense of actually "representing" phonetically the sequence of phones uttered by a speaker or in the sense of one system being entirely specifiable in terms of the other. With regard to the first case, as we have seen, any writing system that is more than an explicit model of wave shapes is already doing more than representing speech. It is providing input one or several stages removed from the stimuli that reach our ears. As Charles Read puts it: "The phonetic segment, or phone, is an abstraction from the acoustic event, being a segmentation and categorization of it. . . . Similarly, the phoneme is more abstract than the segment, since phonemes are further categorizations of segments on the basis of their physical similarity and distribution" (1983:144). Written units, as such, represent higher linguistic units. They are oriented by design to abstract constructs that cannot be deduced directly from physical speech events, but must be inferred. Chinese characters simply raise the abstraction one level higher.

In the second case, as we have seen in connection with the relationship between spoken and visible morphemes, it is impossible to derive the units of writing (spellings) from speech or the units of speech (pronunciation) from writing, with 100 percent accuracy, even in the most phonetically rigorous writing systems. English requires no comment. In Russian, where the fit between symbol and sound is much more regular, just five of the alphabet's thirty-three letters correspond to one sound only (Sokolov 1977:80). Even in Korean *hangul,* a "scientifically" devised writing system that has undergone periodic spelling updates, one cannot move from sound to spelling unless one knows what the sound means. That is, the two media, spoken and written, are linked primarily by the fact that they both represent the same language and incidentally because the connection with that language necessarily involves a certain amount of congruity between the two structures. Where exactly the primary link lies is hard to determine. Amirova, whose own research focuses almost entirely on "phonetic" writing systems, believes "it is possible that the unification of spoken and written language takes place on that level where thought processes enter into the phase of [their] realization as signs and make their appearance in communication" (1977:35), that is, at the very apex of the language hierarchy, about as far removed from the concrete, physical level of speech as one can imagine.

The fact that the units of one system cannot be derived from the units of the other system can, of course, be attributed to history: speech sounds change, and writing is slow to catch up. In this connection, DeFrancis' (1989:205) critique of Chomsky and Halle's (1968:49) fanciful thesis that English orthography—appearances notwithstanding—is an "ideal" representation of the language's underlying structure is right on the mark. But the fact that users tolerate such a wide divergence between the two media strongly implies the operation of other, practical considerations. Some of these were mentioned in the preceding section, such as the need for writing to span distance and time, which cannot be accomplished with a speech-based transcription. Others relate to the physical nature of the media and the way they are delivered, in particular, the relative permanence of writing, and the availability of paralinguistic devices in speech, both of which affect the intrinsic levels of redundancy needed to communicate a message. Moreover, as we have already argued in connection with the morpheme, it may not be desirable in terms of a user's overall communicative competence that language expressed in one medium be translatable, unit for unit, into the other medium, if for no other reason than the fact that a merger of the two would reduce the total redundancy available in the system to users, making it impossible to use one medium as a check on the other in cases of ambiguity.

We shall return to this theme presently in what I shall describe as the "tutorial" effect the two media have on each other in the minds of literate users. For now, however, it should be apparent that attempts to criticize Chinese characters for not representing concrete units of speech make little sense in a world where their only competitor, namely, "phonetic" scripts, also "fail" to do so. As we have seen, characters map onto language at an abstract level—the morpheme—and in so doing provide the reader with text that has already been analyzed to a significant degree. The same symbols are also providing a representation of sound, albeit holistically, and in this sense carry out the same functions as those accomplished by phonetic writing. The two types of systems would appear, in a formal sense, to be similar: neither maps onto "sound" primarily, and in neither case can the units of one medium be derived from the other.

There are, however, two crucial differences. One is the matter of degree to which the two types of writing distance themselves from speech. I have maintained that some amount of separation between the units of the spoken and the written media is desirable, in fact, is a concomitant of the existence of two venues, and that this separation entails the impossibility of specifying the units of one exactly in terms of the other. But when the synchronic motivation between the units of the two media is, for all practical purposes, lost entirely, as in the relationship between Chinese characters and the units of speech, the media no longer reinforce each other on the representational level. Rather than serving as a mutual check, restraining—in theory if not always in practice—either of the two from drifting too far from the shared norm, while at the same time informing speakers of the rough parameters of the one representation on the basis of the other, Chinese characters and Chinese speech go their own separate ways with impunity, cheating the user of most of the cues that would allow the media to support each other. It is not just a matter of having to learn two very different representational systems. The inability in Chinese of one medium to inform the other cannot help but affect linguistic performance as a whole.

Second, although Chinese characters are functioning like the writing systems used with other languages by providing both a semantic analysis of the discourse not available in speech and (holistically) the sounds of the language, there is a major difference in the way this is accomplished. Phonetic writing normally uses two particular devices to represent language: (1) graphemes, which give a fair to accurate picture of the sound in terms that resemble (if not replicate) the basic units used in speech and (2) spelling conventions that together with word division provide a semantic breakdown of a text. Each device has its own distinct function, and as a result, the system acquits itself well in both respects. By contrast, Chinese character-based writing employs just one device—the character itself—to provide both semantic and phonetic information and does a lousy job in both areas. Sound is indicated at the syllable level by the configuration of the unit as a whole,[10] which is to say, in no practically motivated fashion. Reinforcement between the two media is almost wholly lacking. Semantically, the characters provide just enough information to lessen the need for word division, but not enough to get the user beyond morphemes and into the language's finished lexical units.

The Relationship between Written and Spoken Discourse

Thus although Chinese characters cannot be criticized for failing to represent speech, they can be held accountable for failing to provide the types of information users require from writing generally and for the enormous gap they create (or allow) between the written and spoken media, which exceeds by a wide margin the distance needed for the linguistic system to operate efficiently. This gap applies not only to their methods of representation at the unit level, but also stylistically, at the discourse level.

I have explained why writing styles in general cannot be made to follow speech and why this is not even desirable. Nature imposes different requirements on speech and writing, which must be fulfilled through the arrangement of different types of material substances, acoustic and graphic. Redundancy needs at the surface level vary for the two media. Since writing is more permanent than speech, writers are also held responsible for expressing their thoughts in a more logical, or at least more grammatical, fashion that is beyond what most writers as speakers are able to emulate. People do not write the same way they talk, and for good reason. It makes no more sense to merge the two media styles at the discourse level than it does to demand that they coincide on the level of representation.

It is, however, in language users' interest that the distance between written and spoken discourse be restricted to what is needed for the two media to function, so that the language expressed in one medium nurtures and informs language used in the other. One obvious example is the ability to use vocabulary learned through print in speech. Another is the increased fluency one realizes through greater exposure to a language in both of its forms through access to different but complementary structures—a fact demonstrated by language pedagogy's highly effective multimedia approach. This is the "tutorial" effect alluded to above. Different but complementary representations of the same underlying code interact to create a more diverse, resilient, and viable product than would obtain through development along either of the two tracks.

The importance to a language of having two media is emphasized by writing theorists, who point to the beneficial effects writing has on language. According to Vachek, "Clearly, a language community which has not yet developed its written norm has not yet developed the latent possibilities of the language to the full" (1989:20). While not absolutely necessary, writing facilitates a language's acquisition of extended vocabulary and the complex grammatical structures that relate physically distant components of a proposition into a single coherent thought. What applies to phylogeny is also true of ontogeny. Wrolstad states, "Literacy acquisition is the child's introduction to an understanding of what constitutes the rules of language organization. . . . Reading research is discovering that most children enter school in a state of cognitive confusion regarding the components of a language" (1976:20). Smith is also of the opinion that "our ability to understand (highly abstract) language is simply a by-product of our being literate. Only because of our experience in reading can we make sense of abstract speech, which in its form is more like writing than everyday spoken language" (1983:82). Speakers with the best mastery of a language's forms typically, though not exclusively, are those who are literate in the language.

The foregoing observations demonstrate the critical role writing has on the development of language and on the mentality of a language's users. While it is amusing and to many even comforting to imagine the simple joys of living in an oral culture, the plain truth is that neither such societies nor the individuals they comprise have any hope of competing in today's complex technological world against groups whose linguistic competence is shaped, expanded, and informed by written language.

Let's look now at the other side of the equation, at the effects speech has on writing. Although people can learn to read a language without any oral or aural competence, reading comprehension improves dramatically as spoken skills are acquired. Moreover, it is almost impossible for someone to write competently in a language without being a fluent speaker of that language. This point relates to individuals. On the macro level, the results of a written medium that is not informed by an oral component are appalling. One of my most vivid recollections of graduate school involves an incident that occurred in a class in historical linguistics. The professor, an MIT graduate and disciple of Noam Chomsky, was giving a thumbnail description of generative grammar as a foundation for one approach to understanding language change. The reader will recall that generative grammarians, with their stress on the well-formedness of linguistic data, concern themselves with the type of language people associate more with writing than with speech. One student who had been quiet most of the semester became visibly agitated as the lecture went on, until he finally asked if the model had anything to do with language as it is actually organized in people's heads. When the professor asked why, the student responded, "It can't be this way. It's too much like death!"

One example of what happens when language gets divorced from speech, that is, when the locus of mentation is informed solely or even predominantly by writing-based codes, is medieval Europe, where writing was done in Latin and people spoke in something else. Progress as it is usually measured came to a standstill until the two media reconverged into single languages. Closer to our concerns is classical Chinese, a language that through most or all of its history had no spoken counterpart, but that until recently was the only sanctioned vehicle Chinese had for writing (non-Mandarin speakers still have none). While an immense body of literature was produced, much of it was insipid and almost all of it unimaginative. The language seems neither to have inspired nor to have been inspired by the sort of creative impulse that can transform society. It was only when China's literati, in private moments and under Buddhist influence, experimented with writing styles that approximated the vernacular that genuine creative works began to appear (Mair 1994). Classical Chinese served symbolically and intrinsically as a vehicle for maintaining the status quo. Recognizing this fact, Chinese reformers in the early part of this century sought to replace this stultifying vehicle with one closer to the present vernacular, although these efforts were not fully successful for reasons to be discussed below.

The Problem with Chinese Character–Based Discourse

Writing and speech each in its own way enhances a language's development. Writing provides depth and coherence; speech adds richness and life. The two media complement each other by virtue of their distinctiveness, reinforce each other in the minds of literate speakers, and enable the community of users to fuse the elements of literate (logic, rigor, planning) and oral (fluency, spontaneity) cultures into one coherent, dynamic, and adaptive tool. Although writing and speech differ representationally and stylistically, and although both benefit from these differences, there is a limit to how wide the gap can be before these benefits cease to operate. That limit is surpassed when texts written in the language are no longer intelligible when read aloud. This was the case in East Asia until recently and is still characteristic of much of the writing that is done there.

Scholars disagree over whether early Chinese speech and writing ever were united. Karlgren (1949) believed that the terse, telegraphlike style of the Chinese character texts handed down to us was paralleled millennia ago by a spoken style that was roughly equivalent. Although they are incomprehensible when read aloud today, the richer phonology of Archaic Chinese may have made the monosyllabic words reflected in these texts distinctive enough to be intelligible. However, research conducted by Boodberg (1937), Serruys (1959), and Kennedy (1964) shows that by the time the earliest texts were written, the spoken language already possessed a large number of bisyllabic terms that the writing did not reflect. This finding is consistent with Creel's belief that "the language of the old texts" did not represent the speech then current, but was "regarded as a separate discipline," distinct from the rules and styles governing speech (1936:124–125).

Whichever theory is correct, from Han times onward, the written idiom had as little to do with modern, colloquial Mandarin as Latin texts had with the spoken Romance languages of Renaissance times. Chinese wishing to read the script of high culture or write in an acceptable manner had to acquire what amounted to a second language. Not only was the grammar of classical Chinese unfamiliar to Chinese as speakers, good style demanded that writers express themselves not directly through words, but indirectly through allusions to passages in the classical litany with which readers were expected to be familiar. The result was a sketchy text, where "adequate guiding details" are routinely omitted (Karlgren 1923:91). While all writing to some degree functions in this matter, it seems that nowhere else was the elliptical style of classical Chinese approached.

From about 1918, reform advocates in China began agitating for a writing style patterned after the spoken idiom. Known as the *báihuà* or "colloquialization" movement, these efforts eliminated the worst excesses of the classical tradition, but they were never able to institute a style that was fully intelligible phonetically. As DeFrancis has noted, despite all efforts to encourage use of a genuine colloquial style, modern *báihuà* "is so riddled with classical remnants that it is incapable of simple phonetic transcription" (1985:11). Karlgren observed similarly: "If we transcribe a few passages with ordinary letters, and try to read them, we are left at a nonplus. Some of it reads well enough, but it fails as soon as we get to abstract and scientific terms, etc., cultural terms in general" (1926:160).

No amount of persuasion could cause Chinese writers to perform the unnatural act of adding more redundancy to a text than what most readers need for comprehension. Given the nature of the Chinese character writing system, it is not only bad taste but a definite nuisance to write out full expressions like 時候 *shíhòu* "time," 已經 *yǐjīng* "already," and 事情 *shìqíng* "matter," when 時, 已, and 事 by themselves are sufficient. This accepted, symmetry alone demands that graphic redundancies that can be eliminated from other words disappear, until a point is reached where the text cannot be understood when read aloud or written phonetically.

Just as one cannot intelligibly transcribe texts written under the constraints of one medium directly into another system with different requirements, neither can writers be expected to follow criteria that have no relationship to the system they are using. When they do, the effect is ludicrous. Any fluent reader of modern Chinese who has had to read a speech transcribed verbatim in the character script can testify to the numbing effect so many extraneous cues has on one's consciousness, but these same texts written out in *pinyin* seem natural and normal. These examples are just another way of saying that the style of writing Chinese is determined largely by the character script itself.

The same contradiction between Chinese characters and phonetic intelligibility has characterized the literary traditions of Japan and Korea. Under the influence of Chinese texts, the early unity between the language of Heian period (794–1185) novels and spoken Japanese disappeared by the middle of the Muromachi period (1338–1573) (Habein 1984:58). As was true of Chinese, there were two causes for the gap between spoken and written discourse, namely, the conservative nature of writing abetted by the inclination of Japanese writers to follow authoritative models and the particular traits of the character script. The latter factor's contribution has been aptly described by Sansom: "In so far as the script remained ideographic or logographic, not only could the written language not easily imitate the spoken language, but also, conversely, the spoken language could not freely incorporate words and locutions which the written language was able to take over from Chinese with little or no change" (1928:520).

Words and entire Chinese grammatical constructions were carried over intact into Japanese writing through the *kambun* tradition, which because of their abbreviated structure could not be assimilated into the spoken medium. Even at the end of the Edo period (1600–1868), when *kambun* had lost its authority, the mixed *kanji-kana* script used for most types of formal writing continued to suffer from a surfeit of Sinitic words, which compressed the style unnaturally, making it unintelligible when read aloud.

Conservatism, the other factor, manifested itself in two ways. First, serious writers avoided the colloquial style because it lacked prestige. Despite the availability from the early Edo period of a popular, all-*hiragana* style used in illustrated texts, "the tradition of writing in classical styles was so entrenched for writers of education that they thought that writing in the spoken language was too unsophisticated" (Habein 1984:69). The second way in which conservatism divided the two media was by failing to reflect changes that occurred naturally in the spoken language over the course of nearly a millennium. According to Sansom, this "difference can be summarized by saying that the spoken language, by phonetic change and by simplification, lost a good deal of its agglutinative and synthetic character, while the written language retained most of the grammatical apparatus which the colloquial discarded" (1928:65).

Consequently, by the early Meiji period there was a wide divergence between spoken and written styles, the latter based largely on obsolete grammar and a preponderance of borrowed (but not necessarily assimilated) Chinese vocabulary (Thranhardt 1978:44; Twine 1983:115). As part of the effort to simplify written Japanese, reform advocates, beginning with Maejima Hisoka in 1866, proposed that in addition to vocabulary changes and greater reliance on *kana*, the gulf between the way people write and speak be reduced *(gembun-itchi)*.

Although a number of such programs were enacted, real progress did not occur until the end of the Second World War, when the Japanese government officially endorsed a writing style based on speech, as specified in a *Handbook of Official Language Use (Kōbun yōgo no tebiki)* adopted in December 1946 (Muller 1975:126–130). The reforms narrowed the gap between spoken and written Japanese to a greater extent than similar efforts did for Chinese, without the verbosity that characterizes Chinese texts that imitate the spoken style. The reason is easy to pinpoint: with phonetic subscripts at their disposal, Japanese writers get by with fewer characters and, the fewer characters used, the more the style resembles speech. Although there will always be a difference between the way people write and speak, no matter what system of writing is used, the character script encourages differences in excess of what is normally encountered, because the individual symbols convey so much more information to the eye than their phonetic equivalent does to the ear.

The same phenomenon applies to modern Korean. Texts written in the mixed character-*hangul* script are, as a rule, more terse than those composed entirely in *hangul*. It is impossible to argue, as one plausibly could with Japanese, that this terseness is caused by a desire on the part of writers and publishers to conserve space (although the choice of using the mixed script itself may be), since in Korean the same brevity is achieved by writing the Sino-Korean morpheme with its one-syllable phonetic equivalent, which in *hangul* also appears as a single unit. The problem is such words are not sufficiently distinctive in *hangul* without adequate context, which can be reduced if characters are the medium.

Nowhere are these differences better illustrated than in the early, all-*hangul* "translations" of Korean classic works, which were little more than transliterations of the character text and hence nearly incomprehensible. Nam cites the similar case of an all-*hangul* textbook, rendered as such for senior high students directly from its original mixed script version, and claims that neither he nor a famous literary critic could read it (1970:62). Whatever merits the respective orthographies have, it is clear that the styles that accompany their use are different and that the style used with the character script deviates more radically from the spoken norm.

If we factor out tradition, it is apparent that the reason for the truncated, abbreviated style of Chinese character texts lies in the nature of the writing system itself. Because of a character's inherent complexity, which enables it to refer unambiguously to a particular morpheme, there is no need to specify in writing the additional morphemes that a word might have for the concept to be understood in speech. Not only is there no need, it is superfluous to do so. As mentioned above, it is impossible for an experienced reader of Chinese, when reading a transcribed speech or even a close translation of a foreign work, to escape feeling that there are too many cues on the page, that many of the characters could be eliminated, and that by doing so the task of sifting relevant from extraneous information would be much easier. Character texts, accordingly, when written as such, seem to carry the principle of conciseness much further than texts written phonetically, a fact cited by supporters of Chinese characters as proof of their superiority.

But is this really the case? Or is the claim based on a confusion of categories? While it is true that character texts seem more concise, we obtain this impression from the paucity of phonetic information that accompanies the decipherment of successive symbols. Graphically all the characters do is distribute the required amount of information over different parameters: instead of encoding it serially, the characters provide the visual data in compressed chunks. Either way, the redundancy needed to convey a given amount of information is present. In terms of the number of visual cues available, there is no reason to believe that one system is more economical or concise than the other.

This point helps explain why the stylistic gap between character text and speech is greater than that between text and speech in languages written phonetically. Although writing in either system yields a style more concise than speech, the compression in both cases is carried out according to the characteristics of the graphic units employed. For the one type of system, an intelligible phonetic aspect is preserved by virtue of the fact that the letters roughly correspond in number and order with the phonemes that appear in the word's spoken equivalent; the complexity of the two are comparable. One can use shorter words, longer words, fewer words, or words uncommon in speech, but as long as the medium is expressing words, the compression itself will be effected outside the word boundary. This fact puts a limit on how far the text, when read aloud, can vary from what would appear in speech.

Character systems have no such restrictions. A character carries a phonetic code that contains far less complexity relative to speech than the complexity of its form relative to the requirements of writing. Since this latter criterion is the only one that matters, there is an incentive for users to choose morphemes whose visual forms by themselves contain all the information needed to establish their meaning, whatever their currency or intelligibility happens to be in speech and whether or not the unit even corresponds to a full word. While it is probably too much to claim that individual writers, when they sit down to do a piece, are influenced by considerations of visual redundancy directly, the evolution of the style itself must have been governed by such factors.

The style appropriate to writing (in any system) is not the same as that needed for speech. Both media impose their own generic requirements. While this would seem to be an argument in favor of character scripts, where the gap between writing and speech is typically wider, this gap is not accompanied by any practical gains that accrue to character users. On the contrary, some distinct disadvantages can be attributed to a system that encourages stylistic variation in excess of that required by the different media. There is, moreover, a logical limit to how far the autonomy of writing and speech can be extended. After all, they both are supposed to manifest the same language, and when the lexical forms, their types of inflection, and the order of arrangement common to writing and speech cease to enjoy significant overlap, it becomes hard to justify calling the two aspects of one language.

The Effects of Chinese Writing on Language

As long as writing is done in characters, the gap between speech and writing will exceed the boundaries within which the two media can usefully inform each other. The effect is a degradation of users' ability to manipulate the language or, viewed from a different angle, the failure of the language—if, indeed, we can speak of a single language—to develop fully as an integrated whole. There are other, more concrete ways in which Chinese characters influenced the languages using them, which in my view have been more significant than the influence on language of speech itself.[11]

I have noted that Chinese characters represent (or are) morphemes, but perhaps I have not sufficiently emphasized that they also represent syllables. The usual explanation is that the characters map onto morphemes, and the morphemes are one syllable long; ipso facto the characters also equate to syllables. This is putting the cart before the horse. If Chinese characters, for systemic reasons or by convention, equated to morphemes only, how could we account for the fact that when polysyllabic loanwords are brought into Chinese directly, they are reanalyzed (often artificially) as having as many morphemes as there are syllables in the word, even though the word may originally have been made up of only one morpheme? There is no reason why Chinese has to do this, as evidenced by the Japanese practice of assigning polysyllabic morphemes (*kun* readings) to single Chinese characters. The conclusion seems inescapable that the characters, besides representing morphemes, are also identifying syllables.

This is to say, the connection between syllable and morpheme in Chinese does not owe its existence to anything in the spoken language. Indeed, there are excellent reasons for spoken Chinese to have rejected this one-to-one formula, beginning with the fact that there is not enough phonetic information in a Mandarin syllable to distinguish the unit—in speech—from dozens or even hundreds of morphemes with the same sound. Nor is there any phonetic reason why Chinese would go to the trouble of reinterpreting foreign concepts into segments that correspond to one-syllable morphemes, when the word could otherwise be brought into the language and pronounced as it is, within the limits of Chinese phonology. Finally, although this point is largely impressionistic, Chinese languages such as Shanghainese that have no recognized writing system of their own seem to have in their indigenous vocabularies a number of stable polysyllabic morphemes that in Mandarin would, through processes described in Chapter 5 above, have been redefined as monosyllabic components. Although it is too much to say that Chinese characters made standard Chinese "monosyllabic," they did impose on the language a monosyllabic morphology that was not characteristic of the ancient language.

Other features of Chinese writing also affected the language. As noted above, a language's vocabulary is enriched by writing as well as by speech, and this was no less true of Chinese. In alphabetically written languages, however, when new words are introduced through writing, a connection with speech is maintained by virtue of the way the words are represented in script. Both media, despite their different requirements, depend on a one-dimensional serial redundancy to convey information. Although mapping relationships vary, the phonetic intelligibility of the written representation is preserved, since both the writing and speech provide (by and large) the same sequence of phonemes. If a word can be understood in phonetic writing, it can also be understood in speech.

This is not the case with Chinese. In standard Chinese, there is no built-in link between intelligibility in one medium and in the other. All that is necessary is for the word to make sense in the medium through which it is introduced, that is, in Chinese characters, whose graphic redundancy has no analog in speech. As a consequence, there is no guarantee that words that are understood in writing can also be understood when spoken. The problem is exacerbated by the fact that the characters, while restricted to one syllable, are individually representing a full morpheme, which means that two of the character-morphemes joined together are normally sufficient to convey all of the information needed to distinguish *in writing* one concept from tens of thousands of others. The result is a lexicon composed largely of bisyllabic words, a circumstance that never would have occurred if speech had been the controlling factor in the lexicon's development.

What one ends up with phonetically, therefore, is an unrelieved collection of two- and one-syllable words that make perfectly good sense when written but are often ambiguous when spoken. One would think, in light of the ubiquitousness of this format, that the language would have evolved a large number of syllable types to compensate for the small (and uniform) number of syllables in words, but in fact the opposite is true. In standard Chinese, which is the only major Sinitic language with a sanctioned and well-developed writing system, phonetic reduction of syllable types has proceeded much more rapidly than in most of the other Sinitic languages. Mandarin today has lost four of its six syllable-final consonants and in some styles of speech is well on the way toward losing its initial consonants too.[12] The language has just 1,300 syllables, four hundred if tone is not counted. Granting the importance of sociolinguistic factors in promoting and sustaining sound change, it may be that the availability (in principle) of Chinese characters as a differentiating device enabled Mandarin speakers to proceed more quickly along these lines.

This recalls the discussion of the Chinese concept of "word," or more accurately, the absence of it. As I mentioned earlier, Chinese are acutely aware of *zì* (written Chinese character), but the notion of *cí*, which is supposed to mean "word," is not widely held even among literate speakers, including some with graduate degrees in linguistics, who use the word interchangeably with *zì* when they use it at all. While surprising at first, the lack of a shared concept for "word," paralleled by the absence in Chinese of well-defined words, is just one more effect the writing system has had on the language and the psychology of its users.

As Wrolstad (1976:20–24), Olson (1982:159–160), and others have pointed out, "word" is a visible language concept, not a part of oral culture. There is nothing physically identifiable in the speech stream comparable to what speakers, especially literate speakers, regard as words. Linguists have wrestled with the problem, only to end up defining "word" as "that which appears between two white spaces in print." However, this decidedly nonoral description of "word" makes a lot of sense if we keep in mind the proposition that one of writing's functions is to provide a semantic analysis of the language that is unavailable in speech and beyond the vagaries of idiosyncratic interpretation. Words, in other words, have to be discovered and ratified by the body of users through a concrete mechanism that speech does not provide. In alphabetic systems, this task is accomplished by spelling and word division.

In Chinese, there is no provision in the character-based orthography for word division, nor need there be, since the characters already offer a semantic analysis of the text several levels beyond the surface representation in speech. As a result, generations of Chinese have learned to think in terms of morphemes, syllables,[13] and the written units representing them—but not in terms of words (Xu 1987:42). This way of thinking has led to the Chinese practice of arbitrarily stringing together characters (morphemes) to make whatever "words" an individual writer wants, whether or not the constructs have any currency or any hope of being understood by readers. Many stable configurations do emerge, helped by loan translations from foreign languages and the recent appearance of alphabetic *(pinyin)* word-based dictionaries, but by comparison with alphabetic languages, the Chinese lexicon is in a much greater state of flux.

Finally, as I have intimated above, the character script has had an enormous impact on the way the language adopts foreign vocabulary. Three options are available: transliterate the borrowing, using characters whose sounds roughly approximate the target; match the foreign word's morphemes with semantic equivalents from the indigenous stock; or create a new morpheme (and character) that sounds like the foreign word and has some semantic relationship. An example of the last is the morpheme *yóu* for "uranium" written as 鈾 with a phonetic element normally pronounced *yóu* and the semantic component used with metal. This option is not very common today. Polysyllabic transliterations, until recently, were not as popular as they might have been, because the Chinese feel obligated by the nature of their writing system to associate meaning with every symbol and because it seems silly to waste so much graphic redundancy on a single word that may have had just one morpheme in the original language.

The most common word-borrowing technique in Chinese is the second option, known as the calque or "loan translation." The method almost certainly would not be so popular were it not for the character writing system. Since Chinese characters identify particular morphemes, Chinese are more or less forced to insure that what appears in print makes some kind of sense in terms of the units chosen to represent the borrowed concept. What these constructs sound like, however, is irrelevant. This process brings the phenomenon full cycle: while impressing a monosyllabic morphology on the language, the writing system allows these syllables, themselves poorly differentiated, to be thrown together without regard to whether the total result is intelligible to the language's speakers. Although homonyms are generally avoided, "paronyms" (words distinguished only minimally) abound, making the spoken language much less differentiated than it would be if left to its own devices.

How East Asian Languages May Influence Writing

Given the influence that writing, and Chinese writing especially, has on language, one cannot help but wonder if the effect might work both ways. Chinese writing has shaped the Chinese language and the Sinitic vocabulary of other languages because, primarily, it was the only system available. Even Japanese *kana* and Korean *hangul* bear the historical—and to a large degree functional—legacy of the characters. Furthermore, the prestige of Chinese language and culture throughout most of the period when these other languages were developing was such as to force the Sinitic paradigm on these less sophisticated languages, which came to be despised even by their own educated speakers. This situation, in turn, reinforced the Chinese belief in the superiority of their linguistic conventions. There was no cultural reason for anyone to doubt the efficacy of Chinese characters. As long as the locus of innovation was in East Asia, there were no technical reasons either for changing the writing system, since progress in the real world was expressed through character-based concepts.

Neither of these conditions apply today. Not only is alphabetic writing well known in East Asia, most younger Japanese, Taiwanese, South Koreans, and many educated Chinese are intimately familiar with the mechanics of phonetic writing by virtue of their training in English. Moreover, alphabetic writing is being used increasingly in East Asia as an alternative script or notation for writing the indigenous languages, for example, Japanese *romaji* telegrams, Chinese *pinyin* elementary school primers, and phonetic computer inputting in all of these languages. It is even making its way directly into character texts to represent acronyms and words as they appear in the original language. In terms of the linguistic competence of users and, increasingly, the conventions of the writing, there is no longer an absolute need for language in East Asia to be expressed in Chinese characters or character-based writing.

Culturally, East Asia and China in particular have been groping for a new identity for over a century. What passed decades ago in Japan and passes today in China under the rubric of "modernization" is nothing less than an all-out effort to acquire the technology, institutions, and material culture of Western civilization.[14] This same trend has its immediate linguistic counterpart in the tens of thousands of loanwords brought into Japanese and South Korean in *kana* and *hangul* through direct phonetic borrowing,[15] and indirectly into Chinese through loan translations. Significantly, the importation of Western (English) vocabulary into East Asian languages has gone beyond what is needed to express new concepts; these forms are now displacing established everyday terms, both nouns and verbs, and are working their way into the grammar, even though there is no apparent linguistic need for borrowing on such a scale. If language reflects culture, it is clear that the Sinitic model's time has expired.

These changes to East Asian languages are putting enormous pressure on the traditional character-based writing systems to cope. Partly for linguistic reasons (one cannot keep using the same overworked, phonetically impoverished Sinitic morphemes indefinitely) and partly for cultural reasons, Chinese seem to be more willing than before to use characters to transliterate foreign borrowings—a formula that is largely inescapable in rendering the foreign place and personal names that form an increasing part of Chinese speakers' repertoires. However, the system is poorly equipped for these phonetic renderings. The phonetic content of each symbol, as I have already described, is small by comparison with the graphic redundancy available. Far more distinctions are made in print than are needed simply to convey sound. Moreover, since the characters convey sound holistically, there is no possibility of modifying the representation at the segmental level to better accommodate the original sound of the borrowing. In fact, owing to the near absence of syllable-final consonants in Mandarin, the original word is often rephonologized into something with twice as many syllables as it originally had, pushing the amount of surplus graphic redundancy in the Chinese expression to an absurd level. Chinese *speakers* meanwhile, particularly those with some training in Western languages, have no reason to pronounce every syllable of the transliterated monstrosity, when the original word is available to them as speakers. Thus the gap between spoken and written Chinese becomes even wider.

Japanese and (to a lesser extent) Korean suffer the same type of problem because their phonetic writing systems are syllabic and cannot easily reflect subsyllabic distinctions in the borrowed Western word. What happens, especially in Japanese, is the *kana* representation gets impossibly long and is a nuisance both to read and pronounce. Users, accordingly, clip off the transliterated word's last few syllables, which may make the word easier to write and say, but aggravates the homonym problem, which is already severe. Just how desperate the situation has become is illustrated by the Japanese linguist Hashimoto Mantarō's effort to popularize a convention he calls *shōkun* (*kun* readings for the Shōwa era) that involves writing the semantic equivalents of Western borrowings in Chinese characters, and pronouncing the characters with their truncated, *kana*-inspired borrowed Western sounds. For example, English "high technology" gets shortened to *haiteku,* but is written with the characters 高技 ("high technology"); the reader looks at the *kanji* and supplies the reading *haiteku.* Hashimoto acknowledges that the Sinitic pronunciations (particularly in Japanese) are too few and thinly spread to accommodate the influx of new vocabulary, but also sees that the writing system with its present conventions cannot accommodate much more phonetic borrowing. Something has to give (Hashimoto, 1987).

I have gone to some lengths in this chapter to show how East Asian writing has affected the East Asian languages, but I have yet to suggest that the relationship should work both ways. The languages are not infinitely malleable. Besides the effects of writing, they also have to respond to changes brought about by culture and to be shaped by the requirements of speech. Furthermore, the gap between writing and speech is already wider than is needed for the two media to function and is approaching the point where they do not inform each other—they are not representing the same language. This tension coupled with the availability of romanized writing as an alternative to the character-based scripts may be preparing the way for the latter's demise. The process will be hastened as other factors, to be discussed in the following chapter, cause East Asians to solve the technical impediments to alphabetic writing.

11. Computing with Chinese Characters

TECHNOLOGY'S CUTTING EDGE is two-sided. While enhancing our ability to shape nature, technology also highlights defects in mechanisms whose limitations were not universally recognized. Progress is served in both cases.

The present chapter explores the relationship between Chinese characters and computers—the most recent in a millennia-old series of technical innovations for recording language. I begin by examining how well computers have fulfilled their predicted role of eliminating gaps in the ease with which alphabetic and character texts are generated and processed. The practical consequences of a large character set whose units lack a well-motivated design will be assessed as they apply to computer storage and output, and to various types of character input schemes. The result of this interplay between modern technology and one of history's oldest forms of writing will startle many.

Overview of Chinese Character–Based Computing

A few years ago, I was chatting with a younger Vietnamese-American friend who was interested in learning about Chinese writing. I explained the six "types" of Chinese characters, their connections with Chinese syllables and morphemes, the use made of characters by Koreans, Japanese and, historically, by Vietnamese, and how the system developed in these countries. When I finished talking, his first question was not how do the characters affect learning and literacy? or can Chinese and Japanese read each others' writing? or some other of the usual questions that have preoccupied over-forty students of Chinese characters. He simply wanted to know, "How do you get these things onto a computer?"

Indeed, how? Before we get wrapped up in details, let's stand back and try to get a perspective on how this question has evolved over time. Some twenty-five years ago, when personal computers were first being marketed, many people who used East Asian languages saw computers as the "great equalizer," which would do for Chinese characters in text processing the same thing that photocopiers and facsimile did for characters in text reproduction and transmission. The reason why alphabetic writing was more convenient than character writing, why it could be typed, printed, telegraphed, and telexed more easily, it was argued, had nothing to do with any intrinsic flaws Chinese characters might have and everything to do with the fact that the system was being pressed to conform to existing, alphabet-based technology. What was needed was new technology that took the character system as a given, instead of the other way around. Computers were to be the source of that technology, the invention that would give Chinese characters a new lease on life.

How did this prediction pan out? For reasons already apparent plus a few more that will soon become evident, computers are becoming the pro–Chinese character camp's worst nightmare. One of the problems, endemic to each of the many "catch up" schemes hatched in East Asia, is that the target refuses to stand still. When Chinese character supporters were first proclaiming the potential of computers to erase the gap with alphabetic scripts in text generation and processing, personal computers were not much more than modified typewriters with limited memory capacity that allowed some basic text editing. Today they are extensions of our lives— and, for all intents, our minds. Not only have computers facilitated our relationship with the real and psychological worlds, they have changed the nature of these worlds so that what began as means toward ends are now, for better or for worse, ends in themselves. For hundreds of thousands of people, computers are their entire lives. For many millions more, their development, manufacturing, programming, sale, use, and repair constitute a large and growing chunk of their livelihoods. Life is becoming, in many ways, a function of information processing.

Computing speed on personal computers is approaching and may even have exceeded what users can comfortably handle, which is to say, the speed of thought itself. Early PCs took what seemed like an eternity—two or three seconds—to execute basic commands. Current alphabet-based word processing programs running on inexpensive, commercially available hardware carry out most of their functions nearly instantaneously. Delays of the sort that plague character-based programs are unconscionable to someone accustomed to the luxury of alphanumeric word processing. While the difference between waiting a few milliseconds and a few seconds may seem marginal in comparison to the difference in the time it took three decades ago to type a page of alphabetic text and to write the text in Chinese characters by hand, the tempo of society as a whole has also quickened, making the penalty for delay more costly.

Applications have also increased exponentially. The generic home and office PC, which used to be limited in use to word processing and record keeping, was even a decade ago being used for high-speed communications, database retrieval, automatic editing and desktop publishing, computerized instruction, scientific management, machine translation, model discrimination, and artificial intelligence, and with high-level programming language (Chen Mingyuan 1980:65). This growth in the number of computer applications serves to amplify the performance differences associated with the languages and writing systems the computer is required to deal with. As Unger put it, the inefficiencies of character writing will increase "as the scope and number of computer applications grow" (1987:8). Computers, in other words, are not putting the two script types on an equal footing, as proponents of character writing systems had hoped. To the contrary, they are accentuating the gap.

Paralleling the rise in computing speed and applications is an increase in the ease with which these systems can be operated, made possible through their connection with natural language. This process is simply a replay of what happened millennia ago, when writing itself was first being developed. What began as an independent means of modeling reality through different (nonspeech) media ran into practical barriers as its own complexity put it beyond the reach of nonspecialists to whom the medium could potentially be of service. The solution, in both cases, was to tap into the structure of an existing semiotic system that all humans had already mastered—natural language—and to adapt the new medium to the nature and requirements of that system. Today, not only computer use, but programming as well is being done in natural language. As this connection intensifies, benefits accrue to those users who through their conventions of writing have developed distinct mechanisms for identifying the units of language unambiguously on two levels—phonetic and semantic—mechanisms that (not coincidentally) correspond to the basic requirements for any type of high-level computing, namely, defined units that make the notion of a syntax possible and a consistent linear protocol for specifying the configuration of these units.

This latter requirement will be discussed in the last two sections of the present chapter under computer input. Our immediate focus is on the need for regular units as a basis for computing. Thanks to alphabetic writing, Western languages have, for the most part, a clearly defined set of finished concepts—words—identified by Liu Yongquan and others as the "basic unit in any information processing system" (1991:10). Word boundaries, which are not always apparent to speakers qua speakers, have been elaborated and ratified by the community of users through the orthographic convention. This means that for users of Western languages, there are already (1) a set of units on which a program can operate and through which the program itself can be described; (2) agreement between the user and the system on what these units are, imply, and how they are constituted; and (3) a high likelihood that these conventions are known by other potential users. All of these prerequisites for efficient computing are available by virtue of the literate tradition that has grown up around

Western, alphabetically written languages. Spelling checks, grammar checks, on-line thesauruses, automatic text editors, database searches, electronic mail, and machine translation all depend on widespread agreement on the language's words, an agreement that users of alphabetic languages simply take for granted.

Character script users are not as privileged. The "word" is a written language concept peculiar to alphabetically written languages that use word division. East Asian languages lack explicitly defined words because the characters are already providing a semantic analysis of the discourse string (albeit an incomplete one), obviating the absolute need for word division. Thus the concept of the word is weak in East Asia and until recently was absent altogether. Words are not available a priori for computerized processing of character-based scripts because they are not part of the scripts' tradition and hence not in any definitive sense part of their users' repertoire.

This does not mean East Asian languages have no words—clearly they do, or the languages could not function. Nor does it mean that users of alphabetic systems are in total agreement on what constitutes word boundaries for each element in their lexicons. As long as languages are spoken, there will always be a gray area of indeterminacy as a language and its speakers adapt to a changing environment. What Chinese and Japanese lack is not words per se, but any common means for identifying words and ratifying these choices throughout the body of users. Of course, lexicographers can and do compile word-based dictionaries in *pinyin* and *romaji*, which serve as standards for the languages and as a basis for computing. But the process is often prescriptive and arbitrary; it lacks the legitimacy of conventions established from the bottom up by users in their everyday orthographic practices. Moreover, lexicographers themselves are uncertain about how to treat some constructs in these languages—whether a sequence is one long word or two or more shorter words, whether it should be considered part of the language's grammar or an independent word— because there *is* no logical basis for deciding. Custom is the determining factor, and in East Asia there is no such custom.

At this point one might wonder, since written Chinese and Japanese texts do not use word division, why not simply input the texts as they are? Why force an analysis of the text that is not in the original as a precondition for processing the language in computers? There are two good reasons why. First, although there are several ways to get Chinese character text into a computer and onto a screen (some five hundred or more ways, as it turns out), there is little that can be done with this information beyond basic word processing, and even this application is severely limited by comparison with what users do routinely with alphabetic texts. Machine translation, database searches,[1] automatic text editing, and anything else that relies on syntax cannot be done without words, because without words there is no syntax. Of course, there are programs available that parse a string of characters into its syntactic components and attempt to decide along the way what words are implied. These interactive programs periodically invite the user to confirm the accuracy of the computer's guesses and provide opportunities for hands-on correction. The procedure takes time, wastes storage capacity, and, worst of all, ties up the user's thoughts in the mechanics of the operation. This is the dark side to the vaunted "word-building power" of Sinitic terms: having no defined word boundaries and no clear means of ratifying individual creations, East Asians make up whatever "words" they want, in defiance of one of the most basic requirements for mechanized writing, as the term "word processing" itself signifies.

The second reason why character texts cannot be input as is, without word division, is that (as we shall see later) the most efficient means of getting Chinese characters on screen is by typing them in phonetically. This process in turn requires that users make decisions on word boundaries to aid the computer in deciding what characters match up with the phonetic input. Even this method is no guarantee the correct characters will be selected, but it helps make an impossible task more manageable. Here the operation comes full circle: to input Chinese characters into a computer, most users have to figure out what the words are and then try to spell the words to get the machine to display a string that may or may not correspond to what the user wants to write. In other words, inputting character texts means going through, willy nilly, all the procedures the user of an alphabetic script employs in the course of generating a final product, just to get an intermediate representation. This hardly seems like the "equality" that the designers of the technology had envisioned.

Computer Storage and Output

The lack of conventions for word division and the absence of universal standards for managing character scripts in general have had a devastating impact on computerized language processing in East Asia. For a long time, East Asians have gotten by, thanks to their character-based orthographies, without making decisions on what constitutes their language's finished concepts. Westerners, meanwhile, to make their alphabetic writing more serviceable, had to elaborate rules for distinguishing words. They committed themselves to a long-term process of analysis and decision making that created substantial consensus on how to segment the basic units of discourse. This result, in turn, both encouraged and made it possible for them to extend the process to larger semantic domains. Having reached agreement on words, users moved on to identify through punctuation basic grammatical structures (phrases), completed thoughts (sentences), and rhetorical units (paragraphs). For alphabet users, it was more than a matter of convenience. As the conventions for punctuation became established, writers were forced by those conventions to structure their discourse explicitly, creating an identifiable framework that machines, with no implicit knowledge of the discourse's meaning, could seize and manipulate.

East Asian writers until recently were under no such requirement. Not only do character-based texts not segment words, they are not very well punctuated, either. Premodern Chinese character texts were not punctuated at all. This does not mean that classical texts did not have cues for identifying the components of a discourse. But these cues are ambiguous; readers require years of practice to be able to infer where the discourse breaks. Many students of classical Chinese would argue that most of the difficulty in understanding classical texts can be attributed to the absence of punctuation, that is, clear signs to the reader concerning which elements get processed with which others.

Although texts in the four major East Asian languages today are punctuated, much of it seems to be done as an afterthought. Run-on "sentences" that continue for a dozen lines or more are common. Some Korean newspapers have even given up on sentences and now use periods only at the end of paragraphs. Even modern Vietnamese writing, which is alphabetic but lacks *word* division per se, is often plagued with ambiguities caused by inadequate punctuation that confuse well-educated native speakers trying to figure out what goes with what. While some of the problem can be charged to the relatively late appearance of punctuation in East Asia, I am more inclined to suspect that the character script, or its legacy, is to blame. To repeat: there is no syntax without words, and to the extent that the words are ambiguous, so is the fabric that holds them together.

People can live with ambiguities, but machines cannot. As engineers of East Asian language machine translation systems have discovered, it is far more efficient to do some up-front editing of the Asian language texts— segmenting words (or what the system has been told to recognize as words), grouping phrases by adding punctuation, and breaking up run-on sentences—than to write programs that try to do this automatically or, worse, just to feed the text in and try to make sense of the result. But this is, essentially, the basic problem that all character-based text processing is faced with: trying to get computers to do for East Asian languages what Westerners have worked out for their languages over the course of many centuries, simply to get the Asian language text into a form suitable for further processing. Granted, system designers can use phonetic, semantic, and grammatical criteria to come up with a fair idea, much of the time, of what the language's words probably should be. But what good is it? Rules to operate a program are not the same as conventions shared by a body of potential users.

The absence of shared standards on how to manage East Asian writing systems has affected the development of the East Asian computer industry as a whole. Unger notes that in Japan, users expect computer manufacturers to sell appropriate software with their own hardware as a way around the lack of conventions (1987:73). This "solution" is a complete reversal of the situation in the West, where software manufacturers, operating with shared assumptions on how the language is constituted, have developed industry-wide computing standards so well established that they are able to dictate how the hardware itself is to be built. Meanwhile Japan, which leads the other East Asian countries in indigenous software development, continues to build programs "on an ad hoc, special-purpose basis" (Unger 1987:71). The result, according to Unger, "is that sophisticated, high-quality software is rarely encountered outside the organizations that write their own. As a consequence, Japanese computer users have nothing against which to judge the quality of the software available to them unless they travel overseas or tap into international data networks" (Unger 1987:74). Again, what was supposed to have lifted East Asian writing out of the Dark Ages seems to be pushing it further back, relatively speaking.

The same contradiction also shows up in two other areas of computing: storage and output. As computer speeds quicken and memory increases, it is easy to overlook the burdens that a large character set places on storage and representation. These burdens are especially apparent in the monumental problems posed by character input, which have taken up most researchers' attention. However, the cost of manipulating character text even after it gets into the computer are considerable and, as Unger has shown, will always be greater than for alphanumerics (1987:129). This cost applies not only to the initial outlay in yen, yuan, and won, but also to time wasted in perpetuity as the cumbersome equipment and software needed to support Chinese characters lumbers on. "Lumbers," of course, is a relative term, since character-capable systems move much faster than they did even a decade ago—although it does not feel that way. For someone accustomed to alphabet-based computing, the difference seems like an eternity.

Unger describes the problem less impressionistically: "Any one of these operations—retrieval from memory, memory management, and physical output—may require only a few milliseconds in any one particular instance, but their cumulative effect can be substantial" (1987:68). And the problem only gets worse as the size of the character set increases. The "Information Exchange for Chinese Character Codes—Basic Set (GB2312-80)," which is the standard for all Chinese-language computers in the People's Republic of China, has 6,763 characters on two levels: 3,755 plus 3,008. According to Zhou, the set provides for better than 99.99 percent of all usage (1987b:11). Nevertheless, the designers found it necessary to add 14,276 "special use" characters to cover other contingencies! Taiwan's "Standard Exchange Code for Characters in Use," enacted in 1982 and published in 1986, is much the same: there are 5,401 "first-level" characters, and another 7,650 added for special uses, yielding 13,051 totally.

Japan's JIS-C6226 standard specifies 2,965 characters for the first tier and 3,388 for the second, giving a total of 6,353 characters.[2]

Now, according to Ao, some 80,920 bits are needed to encode 6,400 characters (1984:5), the minimum needed for basic computing in Japanese and about half of what is required for Chinese. However, a two-byte/sixteen-bit code yields only $2^{16} = 65,536$ possibilities, which is still far short of what is needed for Chinese—a three-byte code must be used (Becker 1984:96), which increases the demands made on the system exponentially. Compare this with the 416 bits needed to encode the fifty-two uppercase and lowercase letters of the English alphabet, and you get a fair idea of the magnitude of the problem.

If storage and retrieval are complicated by the need to provide for ten thousand or more basic units, output is also problematic. In 1985, China's National Standards Office promulgated guidelines for 15×16 and 24×24 dot matrix character shapes. The former resolution is used mostly for computer screens and the latter for printed output. Although both are much larger than the 5×7 or 7×9 matrices that alphabetic scripts can get by with, there are still 138 characters on the GB2312-80 list of 6,763 that will not fit into the 15×16 matrix, which accommodates a maximum of eight vertical or horizontal lines (Feng 1992:22). Accordingly, a year later 32×32 dot standards were approved. But even this matrix is not enough for print-like quality, which for a standard size (no. 5) character requires at least 108×108 dots of resolution. This number grows to 576×576 for newspaper headlines (ibid.: 20).

Nonphonetic Input of Character Text

Figures such as these make it impossible to write off the difficulties of Chinese character–based information processing with comments like "the computer can handle it." Although it is certainly easier to generate a long character text by computer than by hand, the only comparison that counts is the relative one of how computing with Chinese characters stacks up against the speed, versatility, and applications computers make available to users of alphabets. In this sense, it is fair to say that the situation from the Chinese user's perspective has not improved at all in the past century. Although the specific equipment has been updated, the different principles underlying both orthographies have not changed, so that the performance gap is and will always be there. Nowhere is this gap more evident than in data input.

The story begins in 1867, when the first usable English-language typewriter was invented, revolutionizing the production of information and decentralizing control over text-based knowledge. We complain about the QWERTY keyboard, but the invention was such an incredible boon to the Western world that Ho Ung, a leading Korean advocate of writing reform, later identified the lack of a practical *hangul* typewriter as one of Korea's most pressing problems and the impossibility of building a simple device for Chinese characters as the latter's worst flaw (1974:108). True to form, the first Chinese "typewriter" was not invented until 1913, nearly fifty years later, and in Japan. Not only was the equipment late in arriving, it was impossibly bulky, expensive, and inefficient. The machine itself without stand and peripherals weighs twenty-five kilograms and has a surface area of about one square meter, most of which is occupied by a "keyboard" of 2,400 characters. Another five thousand characters are kept in boxes (Zhang and Li 1980:80). To type a character from the basic matrix, the user hovers over the set with both hands locked on controls that guide a pivoting clamp along two axes; when the clamp has been positioned over the correct character, another hand motion causes it to swing down, grasp the small block, and drive it up to strike the paper in more or less the same way as Western typewriters.

Besides all the physical movements, there is also the task of trying to find the right character. Either their locations must be memorized,[3] or the operator refers to a chart. Just looking at the font will not do—what one sees is an upside down, poorly differentiated collection of minuscule pieces of type. According to Feng, the apparatus takes 160 to 200 times longer to master than a Western-language typewriter (1989:4). Normal speed does not exceed twenty characters per minute or about ten pages per day. Moreover, its cost and complexity prevented it from being diffused throughout the general population. Unlike in Western countries, where touch typing skills are widespread and most middle-class people owned or had access to a typewriter, professional typists in China and Japan were rare. Eyestrain and other job-related maladies put their functional lifespans on a par with uranium miners and Chinese political activists. The machine's worst drawback, however, was that it could not be used to compose original text. Typing Chinese absorbs all of one's concentration and much of one's stamina. It is simply impossible to sit down with a machine such as this and do any creative writing.

I mention this first attempt at mechanizing Chinese character input because its problems parallel in concept and in many details those that beset users of character-capable electronic computers. Although technology has alleviated much of the physical strain, expenses related to Chinese character input—loss of time and, most important, loss of concentration—remain formidable problems that have not been solved in some five hundred attempts over a quarter century. While East Asians busied themselves knocking their heads against this brick wall, Western users of alphabetic scripts, who never had to think about input problems, went on their way devising new computer applications, improving office efficiency in quantum leaps, and using their systems to create text instead of merely transcribing it. Technology, in other words, has not closed the gap; it has only raised the stakes.

As we saw in the example of the Chinese typewriter, once a character has been found and selected, the operation thereafter is not unlike what Westerners used to do with their typewriters. Although the process was slower and the machinery needed to support it much more cumbersome, the two operations paralleled each other in principle. The main difference between typing on a Chinese and a Western-language typewriter was in selecting the items to be typed. Now there is nothing simple about written Western words. They contain at least as much redundancy as is in the spoken language, or the writing system would not work. Typing these words therefore involves a degree of complexity comparable to any of the myriad coding schemes used to input Chinese from a keyboard. The difference, as I mentioned above in another context, is that the rules for ordering keystrokes to input Western words are already known to literate users, so that the operator brings to the system most of the information needed to operate it. The complexity that Chinese characters embody, by contrast, is less principled in its relationship to the spoken language, which means the characters have to be encoded on their own terms unless the input is based on sound. In the former case, the Chinese user must learn some novel, task-specific scheme to input characters that has no relation to anything in the user's linguistic competence (information that the Western user gets for free by virtue of being literate). In the latter case, the user is not typing characters at all, but sounds that have to be converted (or reconverted) into characters, which brings in different kinds of complications.

There is another crucial difference between inputting in alphabetic and character-based systems. Western words break down into a small number of discrete, repeating elements. While users may not always remember how to spell words, no one disagrees on what the elements (letters) of the words are, how they are to be isolated from the word's overall shape, or how they are to be put into a computer: they go in serially, the same way they are written, and (more or less) the same way their corresponding elements in speech are spoken. These facts seem banal to users of alphabetic scripts, but that is the whole point: what we take for granted in manipulating alphabetic text are major and, in a relative sense, unsolvable problems for character script users. Let us examine these character input methods in turn.

Zhou Youguang, writing in 1987, noted there were 450 different techniques for getting Chinese characters into a computer (1987b:7). Feng Zhiwei observed two years later that more than five hundred different input schemes had been devised, dozens of which had found their way into actual systems (1989:6). In 1991, Mair gave a figure of seven hundred for the number of methods that had been proposed (1991b:5). One would think if there was anything natural or even rational about putting Chinese characters into a computer, some type of consensus would have emerged long ago on how this should be done, but new approaches keep coming out, each involving some trade-off between training time and accuracy or speed. This contradiction will never be satisfactorily resolved because of the size of the character set and, more important, because of the haphazard way individual characters are constructed. But let's look anyway at the limiting case—the so-called large keyboards—which input characters directly and do not require that the symbols be decomposed into smaller "units." This setup differs not at all in principle from the design used in Chinese character typewriters: operators are still hunting and pecking from an enormous character set. Although technology has eliminated some of the physical strain, the difference is akin to that between mechanical and electric typewriters in the West. There is no fundamental breakthrough achieved to alleviate the problems inherent in the original device.

For example, a generic "large keyboard" described by Zhang and Li has four hundred keys representing three thousand Chinese characters and other symbols (1980:87). Each key controls nine characters defined by selector keys that are pressed simultaneously. Zhang and Li call it slow, bulky, and expensive. A variant of this system replaces the keys with pen targets, which reduces the overall size with a corresponding increase in eyestrain. As with the mechanical devices, vision is still a limiting factor, because the average user of such a keyboard (not someone trained by the manufacturer for dog-and-pony shows) simply cannot remember the location of each character's key. Even if he or she could, with a "keyboard" this large one still must guide one's finger visually to the proper key, identify where on the key the particular character is located, then press the proper toggle so that the correct character and not one of eight others gets printed or displayed. Touch typing is out of the question. All of this is for three thousand characters, a number that we have seen is barely adequate for Japanese and significantly less than what is needed for Chinese.

There is another problem with this method, which spills over into all of the nonphonetic input schemes to be discussed, namely, that of unit redundancy. When users of alphabetic systems misspell or mistype a word, it is normally recognized as such by the writer or by the computer's software. If spelling errors slip through, it is only because there is enough redundancy built into the word and its surrounding context that the wrong letter does not affect the reader's ability to understand the text. That is, the error is insignificant enough to go unnoticed. The one or two misstruck keys either have no effect on intelligibility or they produce a sequence that is visually so much at odds with what the writer expects that it is immediately rejected. Character input lacks this built-in safety feature. If a user pecking from among the three thousand characters gets it wrong, the result is not a graphic non sequitur, or even something that can be reconstructed by the reader from its other constituents (e.g., *Chimese > Chinese), but a perfectly well-structured, legitimate character that, unless read by an editor, does not *appear* to be an error. Moreover, there is no simple way spell-check software can flush the mistake out. For alphabetic languages, the only thing equivalent is when a misstruck key happens to produce a legal word.

The problem can be described technically in terms of the redundancy of individual graphic units, Chinese characters being some 3.7 times more redundant than English letters. The redundancy of whole English words, while greater than individual Chinese characters, is irrelevant here because an English word needs as many keystrokes as it has letters. Since a given character bears more information than a letter, that much more information is lost if the wrong key is depressed. Redundancy—or in this case, a lack of it—also figures among the problems associated with another major type of mechanized character input, that is, coding systems. There is nothing novel in the approach; assigning a unique sequence of four digits (or three letters) to individual Chinese characters is as old as Morse telegraphy, which in fact is the archetype for this second genre of inputting schemes, which no longer requires a large keyboard. Just as experienced Chinese code clerks memorized Standard Telegraphic Code numbers for the more common characters (and leafed through dictionarylike code books for the numbers they could not remember), users of some types of code-based input systems are expected to learn a number for each of several thousand Chinese characters, so that when the correct digits are keyed in, the corresponding character registers. The problems with this "method" (besides the near impossibility for average users to remember enough of the code for practical use,[4] and the fact that none of this knowledge has anything to do with language or the ideas one is trying to express) are (1) there is no tolerance for error; as with the large keyboard, a mistake anywhere means the whole item is changed; and (2) there is no causal relationship between the code and character to prompt the user's memory. If any part is forgotten, the rest of the code is useless.

Other coding systems have sought to minimize this arbitrariness by linking digits or key sequences with character components or by imprinting actual components directly on the keys. The components can be selected and input in a particular order, or in any order while the computer decides what goes with what. Both types have problems. According to Jack Kai-tung Huang, "There is no reliable definition of what constitutes an element within a character." Sometimes the wrong character shows up, sometimes no character at all. The "method is more of a guessing game than anything else" (1985:21). Some of this confusion can be eliminated, but only at the cost of having users memorize complex rules for identifying what are "components" under what circumstances and inventing more rules to tell the computer how these components are to be reassembled.

The only type of coding scheme that seems to show any merit is the two-stroke method invented by Yamada Hisao of Tokyo University. Endorsed, relatively speaking, by both Becker (1985:29) and Unger (1987:158), the system assigns two keystrokes that the user memorizes to each commonly used character. According to Becker, a professional typist can use it to input 150 to 400 characters per minute, some three times faster than any other method. While useful as far as character input systems go, even this technique has some obvious drawbacks, beginning with the burden it places on memory compared to input with alphabetic languages. It can be mastered by professional typists (which in itself is an enormous contribution), but not by average users who regard typing as a tool for accomplishing other tasks, not as an end in itself. Furthermore, although the system can accommodate most of the commonly used characters in Japanese, its capacity is far short of what is needed for Chinese. Finally, it shares with most other coding systems the same problem of isolating the user from the sounds of the language, that is, from a direct, motivated connection between what is (or should be) in the writer's head and what actually is being typed, making keyboard composition of original text (as opposed to typing from a prepared text) very difficult.

Some hybrid coding systems do attempt to preserve a connection with the language's phonology at the same time they reduce the code's arbitrariness. They typically involve typing in the *pinyin* or some other alphabetic representation of a single character's sound along with some nonphonetic tag to specify which of the many characters associated with that sound is intended. More sophisticated programs arrange these characters by frequency, so that the user can more easily identify the target form. Like all other coding systems, these, too, are time consuming and take the user's attention away from his or her thoughts and the language needed to express those thoughts by introducing extraneous processes. Although the notion of using knowledge that speakers of a language already possess is on the right track, by focusing on individual characters these systems run the same risk as other coding systems of errors caused by a lack of redundancy. They also present an unresolvable contradiction: the user must either memorize a host of nonphonological, character-specific tags to identify exactly which of the homophonous characters is intended or have his or her attention interrupted by the need to pick through a few or a few dozen alternatives, each forcing its own irrelevant meanings onto the user's psyche. Either way, the work gets disrupted.

Anyone who doubts the importance of this problem need only recall from experience with alphabetic scripts how much of a bother it is to concentrate on a text when a mainframe has slowed down or is acting strangely. Even a minor glitch like failing to keep pace with input speed or a shift in response rate is an intolerable nuisance for someone used to normal computerized word processing. Nonalphabetic functions, such as pressing the shift key to change cases, keying in numbers and less common symbols, not to mention functions connected with the "alternate" and "control" keys, are to me at least a burden to be avoided whenever possible. *Anything that interferes with the smooth, continuous input of phonetic text breaks* one's train of thought and slows production. Yet these very anomalies are the norm for character-coded input.

The last type of nonphonetic input to be discussed is optical character recognition (OCR). There are two varieties: one that inputs existing texts and another that accepts original text as it is being written. The former is identical in principle to scanners that input alphabetic text line by line into a computer or onto a disk, with all of their limitations magnified a hundredfold, since the set of units the system must recognize is that much larger. Performance is seriously degraded by such factors as low-quality printing, different character fonts, complex formats (as found in newspapers), and paper of varying quality (Matsuda 1985:42). The other technique involves writing directly with a light pen or stylus in a carefully defined, sensitized area. The computer compares the finished handwritten sample with patterns of characters stored in its memory until a match is found and the character is registered. Now writing Chinese characters in the best of circumstances is no easy task. Fatigue catches up with most writers rather quickly, so to get the job done fast users generally write in an abbreviated, cursive style that is highly idiosyncratic—precisely what OCR systems will not recognize. For the device to work at all, the characters must be neatly and correctly drawn so that the process is labor-intensive, which brings us back to where we started—trying to find ways around handwriting.

There is one more problem with nonphonetic character coding methods that needs to be mentioned. Educators speak too facilely of the distinction between character "recognition skills" and the skills needed to produce them by hand, as if the two were completely independent. In fact, there is much experimental and anecdotal evidence to support a connection between the two types of skills. As one's ability physically to write Chinese characters, stroke by stroke, improves, so it seems does one's ability to recognize them and distinguish one from the other. Conversely, as writing skills deteriorate from lack of practice, so does recognition. Primitive motor skills seem to play a part in reinforcing memory here as in other areas.[5]

If this phenomenon were related to handwriting specifically, literacy would have been lost in the West entirely by now, for most Westerners do their "writing" today on keyboards. But the fact is, typing has reinforced Westerners' "hands on" awareness of the language by virtue of the direct one-to-one correspondence between discrete hand motions and the letters that make up the words. Character coding schemes, as we have seen, have little or no direct physical connection with the structure of the character—certainly none that bears any relationship to the specific motor skills that are exercised in forming characters. Although it seems unlikely, for all of the reasons given above, that nonphonetic coding will emerge as the primary means of processing Chinese characters for a significant part of the character-literate East Asian population, if this were to happen, the technique could lead eventually to a deterioration of users' ability to deal with the characters generally. In other words, the same machines that were supposed to give the characters a new lease on life may contain the seeds of the characters' destruction. In the following section, we will examine an inputting technique whereby this very outcome seems assured.

Phonetic Character Conversion

I described above one type of coding system based on the characters' syllable sounds. Because most Sinitic syllables correspond to several different characters, the technique must be supplemented by other types of coding that delineate which particular character is intended. At a minimum, users must deliberately choose the right character from among the homographs shown on the prompt. Still, there are definite advantages to sound-based input. Feng lists several for Chinese: there is less psychological burden on the user; most such systems are based on *pinyin*, which has been in use for some thirty-five years and is widely known; excepting umlauted *ü*, all *pinyin* letters are found on standard keyboards; and character sounds carry a greater information load than character shapes (1989:21). In our terms, the technique is superior to shape-based coding because it makes use of knowledge that average users already share as speakers of the language. Not only does this convergence potentially eliminate the need to master hundreds of task-specific rules, it also keeps the user's mind focused on the language of the text.

Are there ways to improve this technique? Huang and others have noted that a "continuous conversion algorithm" will convert phonetic input to Chinese characters without word division (knowledge that is not, as yet, widely spread throughout the population of users) by matching input with an internal dictionary, giving priority to longer inputs (1985:9). The automatic selection is also based on stored frequency characteristics, which helps boost accuracy rates to nearly 90 percent. At this point, problems develop. In order to get the accuracy up to serviceable levels, the size of the computer's dictionary must be increased, which slows down the system's operation. There is also a limit to how well a computer can anticipate without additional input from the user which syllables group with which others in forming the string's syntactic units. For phonetic input to be really effective, users must make decisions on what constitutes the input string's words.

There is near universal agreement that practical phonetic conversion depends on inputting words. By increasing the size of the units being entered, the operator cuts down on the amount of ambiguity the computer has to deal with, limiting choices to those characters that correspond to what both the system and the operator recognize as linguistic forms. This practice does not eliminate the homonym problem entirely, especially for one-syllable words, where phonetic input can still result in multiple correspondences. But combined with frequency weighting and context sensitive grammar, choices are constrained severely and are usually limited to the characters that the user has in mind. Yin, for example, cites a correct character conversion rate of 97 percent on Chinese-language text using a program that expands context to sentences and paragraphs (1991:28).[6] This rate is achieved even without indicating Chinese tones, which according to Wu is a waste of time for bisyllabic words and for monosyllabic words is not enough of a help to make a difference (1991:59).[7] Becker describes a word-based Japanese phonetic conversion system that gives no homonym choice 55 percent of the time, and in cases where the phonetic input is ambiguous, the correct characters are in the first display set's (eight items) first position 32 percent of the time (1983:17).

Even these input systems have shortcomings, however. Unger lists several of them: Time can be wasted while the computer figures out what character options to display and while the user shifts focus between the manuscript and the display screen. The user must also anticipate the computer's ability by dividing long character sequences into what he or she thinks the computer has stored (1987:136–138). Becker, whose system contains an automatic parser, notes this same "intractable" problem of Sinitic "long conjoined compounds" (1983:12). The problem results from a lack of widely shared conventions for word division and from the present telegraphlike style of many character texts, which in the interest of economy collapses full forms, runs others together, and leaves out clues that would facilitate segmentation. Special techniques have to be used for proper nouns, especially in Chinese, where characters are pressed arbitrarily into service to represent phonetically an ever-increasing number of foreign terms. In Japanese, there is a problem splitting word strings into their character and *kana* parts, both for inflected words and for those followed by postpositions. Although a complicated program can do a lot of this automatically, it slows the process down. Moreover, these programs "tend to encourage the use of rare *kanji,* unusual readings, and inconsistent *okurigana* that the writer would never think of without prompting from the machine." And the user's "train of linguistic thought" is constantly interrupted (Unger 1987:155).

Finally, for Chinese users there is the added problem of "dialectal" variation. As we have seen, some 30 percent of China's Han population does not speak Mandarin—on which *pinyin* spelling conventions are based—natively, but some other Chinese language entirely. Many of these people resent Mandarin, still others cannot speak it at all, while many more who do speak it do so with a nonstandard accent. Unless they have learned standard *pinyin* spelling, their own linguistic expertise will be of limited value here or maybe even a negative factor. Many or perhaps most Chinese who do speak Mandarin have their own regional pronunciations that must be suppressed to operate the system.

Even more important, all Chinese users, even Mandarin speakers, must learn general rules for Mandarin spelling and word division to input Chinese into a computer effectively using a phonetic standard. Simply relying on one's competence as a speaker (native or bilingual) of a standard language is not enough. This competence must be supported and refined by conventions that (1) allow a speaker/writer to generalize knowledge from particular instances of rule applications to the language as a whole and (2) enable this knowledge to spread throughout the community of potential users. It is difficult for literate speakers of alphabetic languages to conceptualize, much less appreciate, the magnitude of this problem, living as they do in societies flooded with reminders of the basic conventions needed for alphabetic word processing. In China, Japan, and Korea, educated speakers may be aware of romanization rules, having learned them in school, especially as they apply to English. But the linguistic milieu in which they live lacks opportunities whereby the rules can be generalized and reinforced. Worse, there are, practically speaking, no "rules" at all for spelling and word division for much of Chinese. Linguists still disagree on how certain strings should be segmented, on whether tones should be indicated fully, in part, or not at all, and on other critical issues such as word shapes for monosyllabic words. Although spelling is less of a problem in Korea and Japan, there are still differences of opinion on how long Sinitic expressions should be divided and particularly on word division for Japanese, including the treatment of particles and postpositions.

These problems aside, phonetic conversion remains the only efficient input method that ordinary people can learn. Based on an innate knowledge of one's language (or, at least, of a real language), users need not waste time learning task-specific rules that have no application anywhere else in the real world or in the user's own mind. With phonetic conversion, typing speeds for average operators range from 50 to 150 characters per minute; at an average of two characters per word, this is only slightly slower than standard alphanumeric typing. Although there are, as I have outlined, several drawbacks to this technique, the critical difference between phonetic conversion and other types of computer input is this: the user can minimize time lost in look-up procedures and failed searches by anticipating what information the computer needs to convert the *pinyin* or *romaji* input successfully. Not accidentally, this information coincides with what readers need to process a stand-alone phonetic orthography, which is another way of saying that the system works best when users pretend they are not inputting for conversion, but are typing a finished orthographic string.

Central to the problem of phonetic conversion is getting the computer to recognize on the basis of an ambiguous code what particular Chinese characters the user has in mind. This task involves programming the computer to make what amount to semantic decisions, since the correct choice of characters depends on more than the phonetic information that is being provided. Now we are a long way from building computers intelligent enough to understand the meaning of a text and to make informed choices on the basis of that understanding. But what we can do is supply enough clues—in the form of fixed lexical units that match those in the computer's memory, an overall context redundant enough to constrain choices through rules of association, and, very important, a writing style that avoids homonym conflicts—so that the range of choices is limited to a value close to one.

These clues, as it turns out, are precisely what users of alphabetic scripts have worked out through the centuries to make their orthography intelligible to themselves and to others. Just as computers must "infer" the meaning of an input string to make decisions on which character to use to represent it, so must people use the orthographic information before them to infer—in the absence of paralinguistic cues and immediate context—the meaning being conveyed. To accomplish this, mimicking the speech stream with a continuous sequence of graphemes is not enough. Other *semantic* information (morphophonemic spellings, word division, capital letters, punctuation, and so forth) has to be added to make the phonetic representation intelligible. For both people and computers, decisions on meaning require something more than what the phonological representation has to offer.

Measures needed for efficient phonetic-to-character conversion read, accordingly, like a prescription for an effective romanized orthography. Most basically, phonetic conversion needs a well-designed internal word bank to function (Liu Yongquan 1991:13). This requirement implies elaborate and generalized conventions for spelling and word division of the sort that exist among users of alphabetic scripts in the West.[8] Users will discover that the computer works best when it is not asked to find unusual or classical characters (Zhou 1987b:12), so these forms (and the habits supporting them) will begin to fall out of use. Since selection is based on real words with enough currency to have earned a place in the computer's word bank, operators will do their best to anticipate these forms, enter legitimate words, and end the infernal practice of making up words as they go along. Writing style will also change, as users discover that the terse, monosyllabic writing typical of character texts cannot be easily disambiguated by the computer (Xin 1989:36). Finally, as *pinyin*-to-character word processors spread throughout China, they will carry their conventions with them, doing what Chinese characters—despite all the hype and lies—never did nor could do, namely, unify the language. Even more subtly, as Unger points out, typing in an alphabetic code will cause people to start thinking in an alphabetic code and to think of their language in these terms as well (1991:133).

What these processes lead up to should be apparent to many readers by now, but it is of such importance that it bears stating in explicit terms: computers and phonetic conversion software in particular are laying the foundation for the replacement of Chinese character writing in a way that no "positive" reform could accomplish or the designers of character-capable computers ever imagined. One of the main reasons Chinese characters have persisted, next to the weight of tradition itself, is because they bent the languages that use them to conform to their own requirements, creating the concrete linguistic conditions that insured their perpetuation. This was when writing was done by hand, or through crude mechanical devices only slightly more sophisticated. These conditions no longer obtain. The objective requirements of writing in today's world have led to a situation in which users are pretty much forced by economic law to elaborate, generalize, and put into regular use the very conventions needed for alphabetic writing. Probably sooner rather than later East Asians will begin asking themselves: why convert into characters at all when the "intermediate" alphabetic representation already has everything it needs to be understood in its own terms?

This shift should play out in two ways. Since romanized writing is already replacing the character scripts in certain applications, the refinement of orthographic conventions brought about by the demands of computing will be adopted generally and contribute to the efficiency and popularity of phonetic writing. This popularity in turn will lead to more applications, more refinements, and, most important, to changes in the languages themselves. The effects will be cumulative and the process very hard to stop. The second arena will be the world of computing itself. As users become accustomed to romanized text, there is less incentive to run through the hit-or-miss process of trying to convert that text into characters. The user understands it as it is. If the text is to be sent via computer link for soft copy display on the screen of another user, who by virtue of being a computer user already shares these new skills and practices with the text's originator, then why go through the trouble to convert it, especially if the communication is informal chatter between subscribers of a computer net, as much of today's "writing" is?

Computer users are hip. They tend to be on the cutting edge of technological and social change. When the clock runs out, they will have as much use for Chinese characters and the conventions that support them as I had for my antique Ford and the repair bills that supported that. Sometimes we just have to move on.

12. Chinese Characters and East Asian Culture

DISCUSSING EAST ASIA's linguistic culture as a single entity is simply asking for trouble. For starters, different people beginning with the principals themselves define "East Asia" by different criteria. Some would include Mongolia and Tibet, others would question my including of Vietnam, while still others would wonder why the remaining Southeast Asian countries were left out. Even if agreement could be reached on the geography, a full accounting of the area's linguistic culture would have to consider dozens of well-attested minority languages in China and Vietnam, besides the four "major" languages I have chosen to treat. More fundamentally, what sense does it make to group together and attempt to draw inferences about four entirely different languages, three (or all four) of which are not even genetically related and one of which is not a "language" at all but a branch of a language family?

The problem reminds me of the first question I raised in my academic career, in a freshman survey course on East Asian culture. I wondered aloud why the course was being taught, given the enormous diversity there. The professor's response seemed weak to me at the time; he argued that the countries, besides being contiguous, came under Western colonial influence at about the same time and had much of their subsequent development defined by how they individually dealt with that influence. Yet change a few words, and this same logic adequately explains the situation with the languages and why it is admissible to consider China, Japan, Korea, and Vietnam as a cultural whole. Each of these East Asian languages is or was written, entirely or in part, in Chinese characters. Although their responses to the introduction of the character script varied, the four languages and the cultures of the peoples using them were all affected by this fact. All carry a common legacy into the present, even Vietnamese and North Korean, which no longer use the characters. Together they form what many East Asians themselves regard as a "Chinese character cultural sphere" or, as the title of a book suggests, the linguistic culture of the "Chinese character peoples."[1]

East Asia's Linguistic Culture

Character writing in each of these countries began as a vehicle for writing Chinese. It was only later, in adapting itself to the indigenous languages, that idiosyncratic usages emerged. Capitalizing on the preexistence of a highly articulated semiotic system, namely the Chinese language itself, Chinese characters in China early in their development established indissoluble links with speech and in the process became "true writing" (DeFrancis 1989). The system's subsequent development was shaped, for the most part, by two processes: the expansion of its symbols through phonetic borrowing and a countervailing tendency to affix semantic determinatives to identify which morpheme of several with the same or similar sound was intended. Users presumably felt that the effort to disambiguate homographs through context was greater than the effort needed to master a larger inventory of signs tied to discrete morphemes, when doing so simply meant applying one's knowledge of existing phonetic symbols (what DeFrancis calls the "Chinese syllabary") to new symbols that differed only slightly. As a consequence of this latter tendency, Chinese writing was never able fully to shake its morpheme-based typology and develop into a full-fledged phonetic system of writing.

Outside China the system developed in other directions. Under pressure to render place names, personal names, and the indigenous languages' grammatical particles, a restricted subset of Chinese characters came to be used for their phonetic values in Japan. Since there are relatively few syllables in the Japanese phonetic system, there was nothing to prevent Japanese from developing this subset of characters into true syllabaries, based on a limited number of abbreviated characters that could in principle be used by themselves to write the language. Efficient though they are, the *kana* syllabaries were never able to displace Chinese characters in Japan, owing to the latter's high prestige and their suitability for rendering the thousands of phonetically depleted Sinitic words that were inundating Japanese.

Koreans also developed conventions for using Chinese characters as phonetic signs, irrespective of their original meanings. But the systems could not evolve into efficient syllabaries, as they did in Japan, because of the large number of syllables in Korean, each of which needed its own phonetic sign. Although some gains were realized by creating abridged forms for characters used phonetically as grammar particles, the systems were so unwieldy that the Koreans ended up inventing an unrelated phonetic system—*hangul*—that is used as a stand-alone orthography in North Korea and for many types of writing in the South.

The Vietnamese were introduced to Chinese writing even earlier than the Koreans and the Japanese, but the language, which like Chinese lacks grammatical inflection, put less pressure on its users to develop a phonetic character subset. Instead the Vietnamese created new characters and found novel ways to use existing ones to represent the morphemes of their language, many of which were Sinitic in any case. With its large inventory of syllables, Vietnamese *chữ nôm* writing had even less hope than Chinese writing of developing into a syllabary. The system finally was scrapped and replaced with a phonetic alphabet.

The result of these diverse responses by different languages and their users to the Chinese character writing system is an even gradient of adaptations ranging from full, unrelieved use of the characters in China, to nonuse in Vietnam, with all stops in between: the obligatory mixture of Chinese characters with phonetic *kana* in Japan, the optional mixture of characters and phonetic *hangul* in South Korea, and the use of all-*hangul* in North Korea supported by training in the characters to help users through the transition. Even in Vietnam, the ghost of Chinese characters is visible in a phonetic writing system that segments syllable-morphemes but not words.

Granting all of these differences, there are still commonalities to be found in the linguistic culture of the "Chinese character peoples" that can be attributed to their shared heritage. At least five can be identified: (1) the singular difficulty these societies have had adapting changes in technology to facilitate writing and information processing, (2) the effect of Chinese characters on the organization and retrieval of knowledge, (3) the influence Chinese characters have had on literacy, (4) the development of an excessive bifurcation between speech and writing not found in alphabetic cultures, and (5) the effect of Chinese characters on linguistic development in East Asia, isolating users from their indigenous resources while hindering access to an evolving worldwide standard.

We saw in the preceding chapter how Chinese characters have put people using them at a competitive disadvantage vis-à-vis users of alphabetic scripts in the speed and facility with which information can be written and processed. There are two reasons for this disadvantage, both of which lie beyond technology's capability to address. The first is the large number of basic symbols in the Chinese character set, which reform cannot appreciably reduce and which, as Unger (1987) has shown, will always be a factor, relatively speaking, no matter what technologies are applied. The second problem has to do with poorly defined words, which complicates machine processing. The reader will recognize these problems as functions of the same underlying difference between Chinese characters and alphabetic writing that we have encountered in other contexts, namely, the fact that Chinese characters seek to accomplish with one device what most phonetic writing does with two. At the low end, alphabets use a limited number of symbols to represent the phonemes of the language. Input is based on two or three dozen symbols, not several hundred or several thousand. At the high or semantic end, alphabetic systems usually employ a second device—word division, complemented by morphophonemic spellings—to identify finished lexical units, which can be more usefully operated on by computers. Character systems use only one device, the character itself, and hence strike too high at the phonetic level (syllables instead of phonemes) and too low at the semantic level (morphemes instead of words) for machine processing at either end to proceed well.

While technology *can* facilitate East Asian language processing, new applications almost invariably begin to show an effect only after the same innovation has already made life easier for users of alphabetic scripts. This is simply another way of saying that, relative to other parts of the world, this aspect of East Asia's linguistic culture never improves. Whether the technology was typewriters, telegraphy, linotype, computers, or machine translation, East Asians have had to pay a greater price for the same or less utility at a later date. Even in the case of facsimile, earlier (or less expensive) machines lacked (or lack) the resolution needed to transmit clear likenesses of the denser Chinese characters. Bigger characters had to be used, which meant less information per sheet or making do with less clarity. Although institutional users, particularly in wealthier countries like Japan, Singapore, Taiwan, and South Korea, may be able to absorb the cost difference, the locus of scientific and intellectual progress in the information era is becoming increasingly decentralized, from large corporations to small businesses and ultimately to individuals working on PCs bought at their own expense. This cannot help but amplify the cost problem and put East Asians at further disadvantage.

It is also worth repeating in this context the earlier observation that, even in a make-believe world where cost is not a factor, the need to manipulate the more complex character scripts distracts writers from their primary tasks of thinking, getting their thoughts into writing, and putting the latter into a coherent whole that can be understood by others. Here the disparity between alphabetic and Chinese character societies becomes even more pronounced. Keyboard operations with an alphabetic script are mostly automatic. For experienced users, the transition from thought to what appears on the screen is for all practical purposes direct and immediate. Users expect the mechanical aspects of the writing process to happen quickly, smoothly, and subconsciously. They become annoyed when progress is delayed a fraction of a second by a glitch in the software, a busy mainframe, or any number of technical factors that are not part of the typing operation itself. Even editing becomes a highly automated skill through computerized spelling checks, grammar checks, and the physical ease with which segments can be replaced by new text generated with a minimum of intermediate operations.

With Chinese characters scripts, however, delays are the norm. Users are required to make more decisions just to get the basic unit onto the screen. Worse, the process involves mental operations that have no connection with either language or the thoughts being expressed, but only with the physical shapes of graphemes, as if this had anything to do with the meaning or even the language of the text. By contrast, users of alphabetic systems, when they think about these things at all, may subvocalize the spellings of the words they are typing; in doing so they are preserving at least some connection with the language. The distraction (if it is one) occurs within the context of what is in one's short-term memory as a concomitant to writing. With Chinese characters, even if the input is done phonetically, the user must still make decisions on the appropriateness of the characters that are thrown up on the prompt, taking his or her mind away from substantive thinking and into the mechanics of displaying these thoughts. Editors must focus proportionately more of their energy on the mechanical task of manipulating text and less on the intrinsic quality of the piece.

The second problem afflicting the linguistic culture of the Chinese character peoples involves difficulties with the organization and retrieval of knowledge. Alphabets, besides serving as a convenient tool for writing language, also provide their users with an extremely efficient means of ordering knowledge. Files, electronic databases, encyclopedias, directories, indexes, and lists of all types representing much of humanity's efforts to make sense of our physical and psychological universes can be arranged and accessed by a common system that is simple to learn and easy to use. If an object or thought can be named, it can also be ordered. There is no need for people to agree on the object's intrinsic properties and how these should be classified. The classification is done *linguistically* by tapping into a discrete body of knowledge shared by all literate users of the language.

Knowledge is ordered in Chinese character-based societies, but with nowhere near the facility that peoples steeped in the alphabetic tradition take for granted. If characters themselves are used as the classifying medium, users face the immediate problems of deciding (1) what the characters' recognized components are, (2) which of these are relevant, and (3) how are they ordered with respect to each other. These questions apply not to a few dozen shapes, as with the letters of an alphabet, but to a set (if the word "set" can even be used) of several hundred configurations, which besides complicating the decision process puts an enormous strain on memory. Even the best character classification schemes leak. In contrast to alphabets, where the units and their relative order are known, systems used to classify Chinese characters always involve a large, indeterminate area in which final decisions on how certain characters should be analyzed and classified are made arbitrarily by the system's designer, decisions to which users are not privy. Even if the ordering is consistent in its own terms, what good is it if people cannot use it?

The above arguments assume the user already knows the physical shape of the character-unit and knows it well enough to be able to dissect elements from it. This may be true when the character is right there under one's nose, but what if one has to recall the character from memory or has never learned it? While the same objection could be raised in principle to words spelled in alphabetic systems, the marginality of this problem—not knowing a word's spelling—is proven by the fact that most Westerners consult dictionaries not to learn the meaning of a word, but to learn its spelling—in other words, they can use the system without full knowledge of its conventions. In Chinese, how much hope does one have (without consulting a phonetic index) of finding in a dictionary a character one does not know how to write?

Every year I take pains to prevent my Chinese language students from discovering the dark secret that East Asians themselves loathe character dictionaries and will do everything possible to avoid using one, including forgoing knowledge. In East Asia, the standard procedure for learning a character is to ask someone else. Failing that, one consults the phonetic index of a character dictionary, if there is one, if the user knows how to spell the sound of the character, and if the user can then determine which character of potentially dozens with the same sound is the one sought. This can be done if one learned the character before and has simply forgotten it, but it is a real problem if one is learning it for the first time.

But let's assume the user has the character available, either physically or in his or her mind. How is it to be ordered with respect to the two to six thousand or more characters in the inventory? Or, looked at from the other angle, how can one use knowledge of a character's shape to retrieve that symbol from a file? One basic strategy can be called the "brute force" method (by analogy with a procedure in cryptanalysis or computer hacking), which involves no analysis at all. The user simply counts the total number of strokes in the character, then looks for the character within a subset of characters having the same number of strokes. Unfortunately, all this does in most cases is limit the search from several thousand to several hundred, depending on the size of the dictionary.[2] And this is not the end of it. Lexicographers disagree whether certain configurations count as one stroke or two, which means that many times the user's stroke count will not correspond with the lexicographer's. So after plowing through several hundred entries without success, one faces another dilemma: Did I miss it in my first search? Or should I try searching with one more or one less stroke? Or, better yet, why not just forget about it!

For most practiced users, that is, those who have struggled with the system long enough to learn its ins and outs, trying to find a character by its total stroke count is a last ditch method. It is usually more efficient to do some analysis of the character before searching. As I have mentioned, characters in most cases can be broken down into components and subcomponents, some of which reappear with enough regularity to be exploited for indexing purposes. Although a variety of techniques based on different types of analyses have emerged, the most common method is to identify the character's supposed "radical" (Chinese *bùshǒu*); locate it on the basis of its stroke count relative to the other two hundred or so similarly designated components; count the strokes that remain in the character after the radical is eliminated; and then complete one's search by turning to the part of the dictionary where characters with that particular radical are listed, then to the segment that lists characters by remaining strokes, and finally by leafing through the pages, examining each carefully until the character is found. Alternatively, one can carry out the same process in an index arranged the same way, if one's eyes are up to it.

Although this method is an improvement over the brute force method, there are plenty of problems here, too, beginning with the difficulty of identifying the radical. In an attempt to create order in the system, lexicographers have taken advantage of the fact that many characters—some 85 percent of the inventory—were formed by adding a "semantic" component to another character with more or less the same pronunciation. For the present-day user, what these components may have meant in terms of the character's overall meaning is less important than the fact that they can be isolated as components and ordered on that basis. The obvious problems with this approach are, in the first place, the fact that different lexicographers have their own ideas about what constitutes a character's main component. Furthermore, users looking up characters are not necessarily aware of the logic (if there was any) that went into choosing one of several identifiable components as a given character's radical, meaning that the user must first try one hypothesized radical as the basis for his or her search, then another, until the character is found or the user quits in disgust.

This brief description glosses over a host of other problems encountered in trying to find characters that have been ordered on the basis of their shapes. Assuming the radical has been properly identified, there is still the problem of counting the number of remaining strokes "correctly" (i.e., the way the lexicographer did) and then finding the character among many dozens listed. This process can be time consuming even if everything goes as it should. Paradoxically, characters with fewer strokes are often harder to find, simply because there is less material to work with. Sometimes the character itself is a "radical," and one can waste a lot of time trying to find it under this or that component. Other times the paucity of strokes makes the assignment of radicals even more arbitrary, especially when the lexicographer is determined to maintain the fiction that "radicals" are semantically driven throughout the inventory. There is also the problem of variant shapes, which range from subtly to totally different. Some lexicographers take them into account, while others ignore them. Still others deal with them only in part, telling users who have gone to the trouble of finding one version of a character to look it up under a different form—without bothering to give the other form's number, as if the user should be punished for not knowing the "correct" form.[3]

But enough of this lunacy. What East Asians really do, when they bother with dictionaries at all, is to look the character up phonetically. This applies not only to dictionaries, but to the ordering of information in East Asia generally. Nevertheless, there are major difficulties involved in trying to arrange data phonetically, beginning with the fact that, as long as the data is character-based, one cannot derive a pronunciation, much less the correct spelling, from a Chinese character just by looking at it. Unless one happens to know the character's pronunciation already, all one can do in the best of circumstances is make educated guesses as to what it ought to sound like on the basis of its "phonetic" component. By the time one is good enough to do this, one has probably already learned the character anyway, unless it is something obscure that the average user (who has long since lost enthusiasm for the system and its quirks) probably will not bother with.

This basic problem is magnified by the lack of widespread spelling conventions, poorly distinguished phonological systems (a function of the characters' historical influence), and a lack of agreement on what constitutes the language's words even in East Asian countries where phonetic writing is well developed (Do I search the database for the Vietnamese city under "Haiphong" or under "Hai adjacent Phong" or what?). As we have seen above in the discussions on mechanization, humanity's move into the information age, with its emphasis on the storage, retrieval, and manipulation of language-based knowledge, will only inflate the inherent contradictions of Chinese character writing while spreading them through society as a whole, although these same discontinuities are also laying the foundation for phonetic and especially alphabetic writing.

The third aspect of East Asia's linguistic culture I will discuss is the peculiar character-based literacy these writing systems engender. Now literacy is a touchy subject, for many reasons. As I have mentioned in Chapter 6, there are real difficulties in defining it, measuring it, and comparing it across cultures. Although minimal objective standards can be established and then surveyed, presumably with some reliability, how does one measure and compare higher degrees of literacy, that is, society's ability to generate and absorb materials whose content and style is more challenging and on which a society's progress is increasingly based? Although governments for their own reasons tend to be preoccupied with the problem of achieving minimal literacy standards, I believe this question of quality is equally important. The difference between being able, largely on the basis of one's facility with speech, to work through the pages of a tabloid and being able to comprehend serious works of nonfiction is at least as vital to a modern society as the difference between marginal literacy and none.

Shifting the focus from literacy per se to degrees of literacy helps explain the apparent contradiction between my earlier claim that Chinese character scripts hinder literacy and the nearly 100 percent literacy rates claimed by some East Asian countries and supported by casual observation.

No one can deny the proliferation of printed materials in Japan, Taiwan, South Korea, and the coastal areas of China that would not be printed if they could not be sold and would not be sold if they were not being read and understood. The question to ask, however, is literature on what level? James Unger (1987) has marshaled impressive evidence to show that what masquerades as universal literacy in Japan is a facade, and that if one looks more closely at what is being read—pulp fiction, magazines filled with pictures, newspapers whose grammar and vocabulary is highly formulaic, and comic books *(manga)* nearly devoid of writing—an entirely different picture of literacy emerges. While these lower forms of literature flourish, Unger reports that serious publishers in Japan have trouble selling enough books to stay in business.

There is reason to believe that literacy in East Asia is not what it is supposed to be even at the college level. Learning in East Asian universities is largely lecture-based. Unlike students at Western institutions, whose classes meet for one hour, two or three times a week, and the bulk of whose learning takes place through assigned readings, East Asians spend much more of their time attending lectures and absorbing their lessons through speech. Granting that some of this difference may be culture-based, one cannot help but wonder if the difficulty of reaching higher levels of literacy in Chinese character texts had something to do with the cultural difference in the first place. Moreover, textbooks used in East Asian colleges are often not in the country's language at all, but in English. This may be an indictment of character-based learning or simply a reflection of textbook availability. Either way, the upper reaches of literacy in the indigenous languages are not being tested. Finally, after having memorized (not necessarily learned) enough of the secondary school curricula to pass national entrance exams and get into college, it is virtually impossible to be dismissed from college no matter how poorly one performs. No doubt there are cultural factors operating here as well, but one does begin to wonder where, if anywhere, the vaunted literacy in East Asia is being manifested.

What is true of reading also applies to writing. I would be the last to defend American university students' writing, but I am compelled to point out on the basis of what I have seen and heard from East Asian colleagues that the situation there if anything is worse. In the West, generally speaking, what finds its way into print in respectable magazines or through the better publishing houses is usually if not necessarily brilliant, then at least internally consistent and presented in good order. The content (a reflection of prelinguistic thought) may be absurd and the rhetoric (in part a function of taste) awful, but generally the piece hangs together well enough in terms of the language's conventions to "make sense." This is not always or even usually the case in certain types of high-level writing in East Asia, particularly in the social sciences, which put a premium not just on thought but on linguistic expression.

My realization that something might be wrong with the way many East Asians write came slowly and reluctantly. At first I was sure the problem was me. Try as I did, I was unable as a grad student to make any clear sense of some Japanese-language essays assigned to me in an advanced readings course. I began to suspect that something was wrong when, English "translations" in front of me, I still could not relate the meaning of the text to what I knew to be true of the mechanics of Japanese. Finally I complained about it. The professor explained that in Japanese much of the grammar is implied and that if I were more familiar with the culture I could understand it. Fair enough. But wouldn't this problem be even more pronounced in novels, where conceptual leaps of the sort that were bothering me are part of the genre?

Oddly, that was not so. I enjoyed reading Japanese literature and believed I was understanding what I read. At least the language *seemed* to make sense. So why was I reading Dazai Osamu's works with clarity and pleasure, while stumbling over these other, nonliterary works that should have been easier? One hint came from a Japanese history professor, well known for his fluency in both Japanese and English. The professor was translating and editing a compilation of essays on U.S.-Japan relations written by scholars in both countries. One night his frustration came out: "You know, it hurts me as a Japanese to say this, but these Japanese scholars can't write." Puzzled, I asked if he meant articles written by Japanese in English. "No, I mean articles in their own language. This stuff is horrible! I can't translate it, because I have no idea what it means. Frankly, I've had to rewrite entire essays."

Now sloppy writing is not unique to Japan, but a lot of what gets published there, particularly in the humanities and social sciences, would never get past a Western editor. This is also true of writing in Korea, which like Japan boasts extraordinarily high literacy rates. The less said about North Korean writers the better; their writing is too warped by politics to be of any use in this analysis. In the South, the same dichotomy described for Japan seems to hold true: there is first-rate imaginative literature, equal in style and content to anything in the world, and some of the densest, most incomprehensible verbiage in the so-called learned areas that I have seen anywhere. Sinitic morphemes, in *hangul* or in characters, are arbitrarily juxtaposed, with little thought given to whether the "words" they form have any currency. Worse, the higher proportion of Sinitic terms found in these types of works seems to obviate in the writers' minds the need to specify clearly, with grammatical devices, how the terms relate to each other in a sentence. Professional translators of Korean and Japanese receive the highest fees in the business. Although this compensation is nominally due to the difficulty of the mixed-script orthographies, any pro will tell you that the hardest part of the job is figuring out what the writer means in the first place. Translators of Korean and Japanese political, economic, and scientific texts are often forced to guess the meanings of sentences and have been known in desperation to fabricate whole passages.

How can we explain the coexistence in these same countries of some of the world's best imaginative literature with some of the most abysmal "informative" writing? There seem to be two explanations. First, scholars, social scientists, and other members of East Asia's intelligentsia are not, after all, professional writers, whereas those people whose livelihoods depend entirely on the commercial appeal of their writing are. This of course is true of any society, but the difficulty of character-based scripts may exaggerate the skill difference between those for whom writing is an end in itself and those whose writing is concomitant to some other specialty. Second, imaginative genres (poetry excepted) in any East Asian language resemble speech more closely than other types of writing, which tend to be stilted and far less "natural." While this is also true of writing in alphabetic languages, the stylistic differences between imaginative and informative writing in East Asia are more pronounced. As a result, not only are professional writers better versed in the mechanics of expression, they are also writing in a style much closer to the language they speak and in which they presumably think. Meanwhile, others whose skills are less professional to begin with are forced by stylistic conventions to produce tracts that have little relationship to the language they are accustomed to thinking in. Is it any wonder so much of it is incomprehensible?

The fourth special feature of East Asia's linguistic culture is this enormous gulf between the spoken and written languages. In the discussion of the relationship between language, speech, and writing, I pointed out several reasons for the difference between the language expressed in the two media, namely, constraints relating to the media's physical properties, the functional differences between writing and speech, and finally the nurturing effect that the two different modes of expression have on the language and the facility that users have with the language. This last factor is more important than many realize. Just as living organisms have discovered that the vitality of a species can be enhanced by generating offspring through the interaction of two of its members, each with different but complementary genetic codes, so is the versatility of a language improved by channeling that language through two different media and allowing the norms to interact with each other. Some distance must be maintained for the vital interaction to occur; if the two media are expressing the same style of language, we have duplication and some reinforcement, but no *interplay*. If the variation between the two norms is excessive, there is no reinforcement, and the interplay, as it were, has no common focus; it is simply dissipated.

So how does this analogy play out in practice? Scholars have long recognized the role that the shift from writing in Latin to writing in the vernaculars had in the European Renaissance. For the first time in a long time, people were applying the language they thought in not only to speech, but also to writing. The transformation led to a fusion of the spontaneous, creative thought associated with speech-based codes with the discipline and logic that writing encourages by virtue of its permanence, causing profound changes in the languages, the psychology of their users, and the structure of the society supported by them. This principle of media interplay, absent or nearly so through most of East Asia's history, may help explain some features of the area's linguistic culture that go beyond mere literacy.

Students of East Asia and East Asians themselves have long blamed the difficulty of character-based writing for widespread illiteracy and what they viewed as slow social and material progress. Though no doubt valid on one level, these criticisms lose much of their relevance today in the context of East Asia's dynamic economies, huge trade surpluses, and universal education. Instead of gross measures of literacy and wealth, it may be time to consider other, more subtle effects that character scripts are having on the culture of the peoples using them. We must begin by recognizing that there *is* literacy in East Asia. Quality may be a problem, and the price East Asians pay to achieve literacy in these writing systems is almost certainly a problem. But no one can deny that these societies are, after all, literate and that the literacy is widely shared. But is this literacy tied in with speech and thought in any useful way?

Scholars of language acquisition have observed that, although many people become fluent speakers and readers of two or more languages, true bilinguals or multilinguals are rarely able to achieve a high enough level of proficiency in any one language to become exceptional writers and exceptional thinkers. This is especially true of people who were exposed to a second language before an adequate foundation in the first had been attained. Although they do eventually sort things out, for many bilingual people quantity does seem to exact some payment at the extreme edges of the quality scale. There is one language in a person's mind, and another language somewhere else in the person's mind. But instead of supporting each other, they function as separate systems. While bilingualism may facilitate survival in one sense (it has put food on *my* table for years), it does very little for facility in either the one language or the other, or for one's ability to capture and translate prelinguistic thought into a mechanism useful to oneself and others.

The same principle seems to operate between the spoken and written norms of a single language, the chief difference being that, instead of affecting a handful of people, it affects every literate member of society. Just as we have empirical reasons (the Renaissance) to believe that the approximation (not the merger) of written and spoken norms is beneficial to a language and its users, so it would seem that when the two norms diverge too radically, people are deprived of (1) the ability to use much of what they learn in one medium productively in the other, (2) the qualitative improvements one gains from focusing on a single, common means of expression, and (3) the creative-disciplinary interchange, engendered by the two media, which insures that the thoughts one creates are sensible and worth attending to and that they are created in the first place. What I mean, in other words, is synergy.

I have argued in Chapter 10 of this book that, for technical and historical reasons, the gap between speech and writing is greater in East Asian languages than in Western languages written with alphabets. As a consequence, literate East Asians are forced to learn two disparate modes of expression (and for many millions of Chinese, it is two different languages) that do not reinforce each other as they should. Not only may this be having an effect on the ability East Asians have with their languages generally, it may also be responsible, in part, for what many believe is a shortage of creativity in East Asian societies. There is too much distance between the language that one uses to think and the system one has to write in for either of the two to proceed as well as it might.

I will return to this theme in my discussion of psycholinguistic culture. Meanwhile, there are at least two other ways the character scripts may be hindering creativity. One of these I mentioned in connection with machine processing, although the principle has wider applications. East Asians spend far too much time engrossed, physically and mentally, in the mechanics of their writing systems, so that they lose sight of the purpose of their writing and begin to confuse the means with the end. Getting the right characters on a screen or a piece of paper should have nothing to do with the value and validity of the thought that is conveyed, but it accounts for such a large part of the effort that writers (and readers, too?) cannot help but feel that the representation is its own reward. The physical act of writing itself is an accomplishment, so does it matter if it has been said before or if it does not make much sense?

Finally, there is the complaint made by many East Asian proponents of script reform that school children have their creative impulses stifled by the need to memorize hundreds and then thousands of Chinese characters just to be able to read and write. Instead of learning how to think, they learn how to memorize. I mention this argument last because my own observations of American public and parochial education lead me to suspect that if it were not for the Chinese characters, East Asian educational institutions, like institutions everywhere, would find some other way to wreck creativity before it developed in new and dangerous directions.

The fifth and last aspect of East Asia's linguistic culture to be discussed involves the role Chinese characters play in isolating East Asians from their own languages and from the mainstream of international development. We have seen how Chinese characters facilitated the importation of many thousands of Sinitic terms into East Asia's non-Chinese languages. Although this historical process was engendered in the first place by China's regional prestige—which had nothing to do with the language or its particular writing system—it was a simple matter for Vietnam, Korea, and then Japan, having adopted Chinese writing, to bring in large parts of the Chinese language along with it. In fact, the Sinitic terms could not be avoided, since use of the morpheme-based character script implied use of the Sinitic morphemes that they designated. Because it was impossible to draw a line between characters used for the Chinese language and characters used to represent Sinitic loanwords, all Chinese characters and theoretically all Sinitic morphemes became in principle part of the non-Chinese language using the characters. This had several effects.

Since these Sinitic terms represented the artifacts and concepts of East Asia's elite culture, there was little or nothing in the lexicons of the indigenous languages that could compete. Not only were native terms outnumbered, they were also outclassed: even when indigenous vocabulary did exist, educated users preferred the Sinitic terminology, with the result that many established lexical items fell into disuse. As indigenous terms dropped out of the inventory, so did the morphological processes that they supported and some of the grammar as well. None of this is unusual. Patterning linguistic behavior on the elite culture is a universal phenomenon and a prime cause of linguistic change. What makes the East Asian case stand out is that these "borrowings" took place through a writing system that did not require the vocabulary to make any sense in speech, not even in terms of the Sinitic phonology that accompanied it. What were once whole languages, therefore, were split into two widely divergent norms: one that was phonetically comprehensible, based on the remnants of indigenous vocabulary and morphology, along with Sinitic terms that were truly adapted ("indigenized" to use the Korean term *kuksanhwa*) into the borrowing language, and another norm defined largely by universal Sinitic, which depends (at some level) on Chinese characters to be comprehensible and through which the language's informative writing was and is supposed to be expressed.

Japanese, Koreans, and Vietnamese today reading anything of a technical, abstract, or formal nature are reading a language that is neither their own nor, for that matter, Chinese. In some cases, it is hard to call it "language" at all. In those genres where the use of Sinitic vocabulary is especially high—80 percent or more—morphemes are often thrown together without regard for native (or Chinese) grammatical conventions, even when the representation is in *hangul* or the Vietnamese alphabet. The only way the piece can be understood—assuming one can identify the morphemes to begin with—is to treat it like a transposition-enciphered cryptogram, where all the elements one needs are there but must be rearranged to make sense. Do I exaggerate? Try reading a Japanese government policy statement, or a South Korean history text, or a Vietnamese newspaper editorial. Then contrast this writing with the beautiful, flowing, coherent prose one encounters when the subject is less formal and the language more closely approximates the indigenous norm, that is, when it is phonetically intelligible.

These are not the complaints of a disgruntled Westerner. East Asians themselves complain bitterly about the impact Chinese characters have had on their indigenous languages and have backed movements aimed at purging unassimilated Sinitic terms.[4] Some Asians confuse the source of the malady with its cure, claiming they cannot read a text because it has no Chinese characters or too few. Others get right to the root of the problem and argue that the languages themselves have been distorted. This distortion has another dimension, moreover, that goes beyond associations with the languages' pasts. Just as Chinese characters and the Sinitic morphemes that they support have prevented non-Chinese East Asian languages (for that matter, Chinese itself; there are many spoken expressions that never find their way into the literary language because they lack characters) from developing their own culturally unique resources, cutting these peoples off from an important part of their heritage, so do the characters continue to thwart the languages' natural development by hindering introduction of phonetically sound international vocabulary.

I have already discussed the problems with calques or "loan translations" whereby Sinitic morphemes, with or without the characters, are enlisted to represent the semantic "parts" of a borrowed concept without regard to what the combination sounds like after it is pieced together. Increasingly East Asians are bypassing this cumbersome technique in favor of semidirect phonetic borrowing, "semi" because the syllabic, character-inspired indigenous phonetic writing systems still require that a borrowed term be segmented to conform to orthographic requirements not necessarily paralleled in speech. Often the indigenization results in words that are too long, which users trim back by eliminating their last few syllables so that the word neither looks nor sounds like the original.

Now one can hardly fault a language for tailoring foreign borrowings to fit its own conventions. The problem, however, is no East Asian is fooled for a minute about the origins of these terms. Like the Sinitic terms of the past, new borrowed Western vocabulary is well outside the indigenous tradition, and many East Asians are unhappy about this quantum departure from what is left of their own languages. But, worse by far, there is not much linking these terms to anything else in the world, either. With the Sinitic vocabulary, at least, literate East Asians enjoyed as much cross-cultural transitivity as users of Western languages realize within their own cultures. But what do these syllabified, truncated, borrowed Western terms resemble? Certainly not the original international vocabulary, not in speech and not at all in writing.[5] And because each of the four East Asian writing systems—*kana, hangul,* the Vietnamese alphabet, and characters in China—changes the borrowed term differently, there is absolutely no cross-cultural connectivity for this increasingly important part of the lexicons even within East Asia.

Some Aspects of the Psycholinguistic Culture

Such is the legacy Chinese characters bequeath to East Asia's linguistic culture: major problems with the mechanization of writing, problems organizing and retrieving knowledge, the high cost of literacy, written and spoken norms that fail to inform each other, and the isolation of many East Asians both from their own cultures and from an emerging worldwide standard. This picture is a far cry from the idyllic notions many of us have of the "alternative," character-based linguistic culture of East Asia. Nor does it speak well for the claim that Chinese characters are "well suited" to Asian languages. This latter assertion in particular begins to sound a lot like the wisdom prevalent in the West two or three decades ago about communism being suitable for Asians (just don't bring it here).

Let's pry deeper now into the legacy of Chinese characters by examining their potential impact on thought. We can begin by acknowledging what are believed to be three facts. First, there is no anatomical evidence to suggest that East Asian brains are hard-wired differently than the brains of any other people. My comments, accordingly, apply entirely to the cultural "software" represented by the writing system and to whatever influence it may exert on thought. Second, although language may be a factor in shaping the way people think, it seems certain that other individual and group factors also affect the process to a greater or lesser degree. We saw in Chapter 7 on reading that although users may be inclined to do more or less phonological recoding depending on the amount of phonetic material patently available in the writing, variation among individual users of a given script is probably greater than the difference between any two groups' respective norms (if such can even be defined). The same applies to the psycholinguistic aspects of Chinese character writing: although the system may affect the literate culture as a whole, its effect on individuals within the culture no doubt varies enormously. Finally, it hardly bears mentioning that Western society is in no position today—if it ever was—to boast about its status vis-à-vis the countries of East Asia. If my remarks on the psychological dimensions of character-based writing are unflattering, this only means that the linguistic aspects of culture cannot be the only, or even the determining, elements of a society's progress and well-being.[6]

Nevertheless, there does seem to be an intuition shared by many in East Asia that creativity, in and of itself, has been less valued there than elsewhere in the world. This perception continues to be held by Chinese, Korean, and Japanese intellectuals and government planners, who complain habitually in development symposia and in the national press about a *quantitative* shortage of creative innovation, by comparison with what they believe to be true of "advanced" Western nations. The complaints continue to be heard despite East Asia's wealth, will, access to technology, increased research and development expenditures, peace, universal education, widespread literacy, and a long tradition of respect for intellectual accomplishment. Where could the cause of this perceived disparity be?

Pinning the blame on the culture per se offers one explanation, but it is too facile. Certainly East Asian societies have emphasized obedience and conformity to a degree many Westerners would find intolerable. But then where did that tradition come from? Part of the answer lies in the fact that those people who defined the Confucian norms were society's literate elite, who had a vested interest in maintaining a social structure that preserved their privileges. Having gone to the trouble and expense of acquiring an education in "letters," they meant to preserve the social machinery that rewarded such efforts. To insure that literacy—that is, real access to the leading intellectual paradigms, not just the functional sort needed for shopkeeping and records—remain restricted, they took a very complex writing system and added even more complexities, while suppressing to the extent that they were able popular attempts at simplification. The fact that this may not have been done consciously in all cases had no effect on the outcome.

This explanation implicates Chinese characters, and it is the standard one given by many East Asian and Western advocates of script reform to show how the character writing system has inhibited creativity and progress. The proposition makes sense. Change in any society is not looked on with favor by that society's financial, intellectual, and political elites, unless adopted as a tactic by one group to use against the others. By and large, the elite have no trouble recognizing their common interest in preventing real change—or at least in doing nothing that would encourage it. Innovation of the sort that leads to the creation of new wealth and technical progress generally has its roots elsewhere in the social hierarchy. In the context of the "Chinese character peoples," the linguistic and intellectual tools needed to formulate and direct change were largely separated from the groups predisposed to make change.

Are there other factors working against creativity? I have already suggested a few. Because of the wide gap between character writing and speech, the two norms fail to inform each other as they should. People's linguistic competence is not reinforced, but split, and the ability to create original expression in either medium suffers to that extent. Also, we have seen in Chapter 7 on reading that character script users can get information from a written page as well, and through the same mechanisms, as users of alphabets. Producing the text, however, is another matter entirely. Since people do not think (linguistically) in visual symbols, but rather in sound traces, it is easier to write in a system that, analogically at least, mimics short-term memory coding.

Conversely, when writing in characters, not only is time lost in the mechanical process of getting the code into something visible, the latter offers no informed links to the type of code that we think and produce in. Although we can visualize Chinese characters as a mental exercise, no one actually thinks in them, as evidenced by the many phonetic substitution errors that creep in when drafting a piece in Chinese or even just copying it from one medium to another. Obviously, people can and do write in Chinese character-based scripts. But it is far less natural than writing in a speechlike code, and this unnaturalness is bound to affect creativity to some extent.

There may be other ways the different types of writing systems affect human creativity and thought. Derrick deKerckhove, in a fascinating article on "Alphabetic Literacy and Brain Processes," wondered, "Could the alphabet have acted on our brain as a powerful computer language, determining or emphasizing the solution of some of our perceptual and cognitive processes?" Noting the historical tendency of consonantal alphabets to proceed from right to left, and of fully phonemic (Greek-based) alphabets to read from left to right, deKerckhove proposed that the former type that "depend primarily on feature detection will require less reaction-time from the brain if they are written to the left rather than to the right of the visual field," since they appear in the left visual field first and are lateralized to the brain's right hemisphere, which is best at feature detection (1986:286). Fully alphabetic scripts, however, have less need for "contextualization" and can be processed as sequences. Read from left to right, they reach the right visual field first and are lateralized to the left hemisphere, which, not coincidentally, works best at processing "continguous sequences" (p. 287). DeKerckhove draws the following conclusion:

> Speech finds its place in the left hemisphere, not ontogenetically, but because the left brain's timing processes reflect and accommodate the serial nature of the production and the reception of linguistic sounds. If that is indeed the case, it can also be suggested that the adoption of vocalized alphabets may have more than any other system prompted and *reinforced* reliance of left hemisphere strategies for other aspects of psychological and social information processing. (p. 289, my emphasis)

What is true of consonantal alphabets applies even more to Chinese characters and, I would suggest, to their character-based derivatives *kana* and *hangul*.[7] East Asian writing requires users to break the linguistic code down into syllables, which analytically speaking is no great feat, since the syllable is the most natural unit of linguistic expression. Moving beyond to phonemes and letters is a much greater analytical accomplishment, which is achieved by each individual user of fully alphabetic writing, reinforced through reading, and then driven home each time the user puts pencil to paper or hands on a keyboard.

DeKerckhove believes that this Western "literate bias ... to break down information into parts and to order such parts in a proper sequence" as a concomitant to writing may have "had a reordering effect on the brain and the whole nervous system of literate people" (pp. 290–291). Writing became more precise and flexible and, as a consequence, so did the psychology of its practitioners. Moreover, as the linguistic units moved away from larger meaning-based elements to elements devoid of meaning entirely, the writing system—and, presumably, the users' attendant thought processes—also became more abstract. Meanwhile, the character script in East Asia was forcing (or reinforcing) the opposite mindset on its users. Noting that Westerners "are good at abstract thought and analysis" while Chinese "are satisfied with concrete knowledge," Xu Chang'an suggested similarly that the cause can be found in "the idea-expressive quality of Chinese characters [which] is closely connected with the concrete nature of Chinese thought" (1987:43). While it would be absurd to claim that individual, literate East Asians as a result of using Chinese characters cannot think creatively, abstractly, or deductively, we can maintain that there is nothing in the mechanism of character-based literacy to encourage the analytic mindset.

Are there other ways Chinese characters affect the psychology of their users? Linear analytic thought may also be hindered (not prevented) by peripheral associations drawn from the characters that have no relevance to the concepts being conveyed. The problem occurs on three levels. First, there are the components of the characters. Although users may have difficulty identifying the semantic component or "radical" of a given character and derive little if any useful information about the character from its components' roles as such, practiced users of character scripts have no trouble associating generic meanings with components, irrespective of the rationale for including them in the character. This tendency to associate meanings with components is reinforced in school by the practice of naming components as a pedagogical device to help students discover order—but not sense—within the symbols. Later, having no means to spell characters, users resort to the same trick of identifying a character by naming the generic meanings and locations of its components. Although most or all of these individual "meanings" have nothing to do with the meaning of the whole character, the associations are well known and may register at some level of consciousness. What connections a "dragon" 龍 and "clothing" 衣 have with "inheritance" or "a surprise attack" 襲 (Chinese *xi*) I cannot begin to imagine. But the two components stick out, big as day, and are common enough both as radicals and as individual characters to force some amount of extraneous association. Granted readers learn to ignore most of it, but does the noise ever totally disappear?

The second problem is the characters themselves. I have noted that characters identify morphemes, but I have not sufficiently emphasized the fact that the meanings of morphemes, in Chinese or any other language, drift over time. In alphabetically written languages this drift is not a problem: users are not compelled to associate any one meaning with a given phonetic representation. Not so with Chinese characters. Because of their unique shapes, characters can keep their identity while accumulating over time multiple meanings that may be of interest to specialists but have no relevance to actual users. For example, a popular Chinese-English dictionary lists nine separate meanings for the character 襲 xí above. Nine more are listed for 生 shēng. Now homographs—which is what these characters are or have become—are not unique to Chinese. English and other alphabetically written languages have them in abundance, particularly at the morpheme level. But the crucial difference is that alphabet users are not predisposed by the nature of the writing to link the meanings of different morphemes with the same graphic forms, unlike users of character scripts, who cannot avoid it, even where semantic drift has proceeded so far as to make the practical motivation for the linkage meaningless.

The third type of peripheral association happens at the word level. Because of the characters' unique structures and because they are recognized as meaning-bearing elements, readers may tend to see more or something other than the meaning of the word itself. There is no question that the tendency to identify meanings of individual characters with the overall meaning of the word they represent affects learners, even when the motivation is lost (or contrived to begin with). Hashimoto, in a work co-authored with Suzuki and Yamada, cites several examples of words that he claims misled him as a child, such as 血友病 for "hemophilia" (literally "blood friend illness," a calque of the English term, which because of the more abstract alphabetic representation does not cause a false association) (1987:55). Yamada reports that he first grew interested in the possibility of the character script influencing thought when, after an extended absence from Japan, he returned to find himself having trouble concentrating on the intended meanings of sentences. Yamada noted that the problem was particularly acute when reading materials that presented new or unfamiliar concepts, because the meanings of individual Chinese characters kept getting in the way (1987:98–99).

How and at what depth practiced users are affected by noise at the word level is hard to determine, although there is plenty of anecdotal evidence to support the notion. At a minimum, the emphasis on individual morphemes causes the cluster, that is, the word itself, to be weakened, with the result that users are not focusing on finished concepts. This outcome presents an interesting paradox, the solution to which goes a long way toward understanding the basic flaw with character-based writing and what this flaw may mean for the psychology of its users.

Words are more specific than morphemes. That is, their meanings are more concrete. Morphemes by contrast are necessarily vague and abstract. They achieve specific qualities only when used with other morphemes as components of a word or when they are used specifically (not generically) as words themselves. Since Chinese characters represent morphemes, does this not make the writing system more abstract and predispose its users to abstract thought despite all that I have said to the contrary?

Although the character writing system is abstract in terms of how it treats finished concepts, it is utterly concrete in its treatment of sound. Having only the one unit—the character—at its disposal, the system stands midway between two linguistic poles, linking concepts and sounds through a single mechanism. Given its dual responsibility, it cannot help but fall short in both respects. Unlike most alphabetic writing, which uses two devices—letters, and spelling and word division—to encode the phonetic and semantic parts of the linguistic equation, Chinese characters lump the two separate functions together and do justice to neither. East Asians are not splitting sounds up at the root level, and hence may have less linguistic predisposition to analysis, nor are they putting generic concepts together very well either. To the extent that writing affects the psychology of its users, individually and in their collective cast, it would seem that the "Chinese character peoples" have little to be thankful for and one more compelling reason to seek change.

Change and Chinese Character Culture

I have tried in this book to show that there are no legitimate linguistic reasons why East Asians should regard their character-based writing systems with favor or nostalgia. Of course, rational choices are not the only type people make. Tradition also plays its part in the psychological well-being of individuals and groups, and as a check against hare-brained "rational" schemes that ignore large parts of reality, often resulting in situations worse than what they had promised to rectify. The twentieth century is filled with examples of rational planning run amok, and East Asians more than most peoples have good reason to view plans for wholesale change with skepticism. This applies not only to politics but also to linguistics.

To counter this attachment to tradition manifested in East Asia's most visible and pervasive artifact, writing reform advocates in China, Korea, and Japan have made some excellent arguments, which, to the extent that logic enters into this discussion at all, are very hard to refute. The first of these is attributed to the early-twentieth-century Chinese writer Lu Xun, who turned the tables on opponents of writing reform by pointing out that there will be no culture to preserve if the characters are kept. Lu and many others saw replacement of the character writing system as the key to China's survival. Looking at East Asia today, one might wonder what the fuss was all about, but the final tally is not yet in. Japan's failed "fifth generation" computer project to adapt its obsolete orthography to the demands of modern society is a clear warning that the patch-and-fill approach to dealing with Chinese characters will not work forever.

Three other important arguments were directed at traditionalists by Korean linguist and reformer Choe Hyun-bae (Hannas 1991). Looking at the anatomy of culture, Choe asked what sense it made trying futilely to teach everyone enough Chinese characters to read Korean classics when the goal of cultural transmission could be accomplished more effectively by translating these works into a style accessible to the culture's modern descendants. Looking at East Asia's history and geography, Choe also wondered what the "Chinese character cultural sphere" meant for a country like Korea, whose status was always that of a junior member. Looking ahead, Choe restated what these countries' leaders should regard as obvious: that the future is more important than the past.

Although I recognize the importance of nonlinguistic factors in shaping the linguistic culture of East Asia, the present study has not dwelled on this aspect for two reasons. First, in my view, the whole cultural argument for Chinese characters is bogus. Chinese characters do the same thing culturally that they do linguistically: they straddle the fence between a writing system's two main functions and as a consequence execute neither function properly. Lacking means to convey a language's phonetic structure in detail, Chinese characters prevent individual cultures from expressing and developing their own linguistic resources. At the same time, having no practical means for borrowing foreign words, the characters and syllable-based orthographies that they support make it difficult for the societies using them to tap into the emerging world culture. Whereas alphabetic writing is both local and universal, Sinitic writing is intermediate—phylogenetically, geopolitically, and in terms of the culture it represents—a culture that suppresses national aspirations while inhibiting the growth of a world community.

Chinese characters, in other words, attempt the nearly impossible task of blocking the two dominant political-cultural movements of our time, namely, the erosion of geopolitical blocs and their replacement with a pluralistic, global society. Resisting these powerful social trends indefinitely is more than any cultural artifact can manage, even if its devotees were receiving a high degree of practical utility from it—which they certainly are not. This point leads to the second reason for dismissing the traditionalist argument: it is irrelevant. Change is already happening, and in the long run it makes no difference how much traditionalists whine about it.

Signs of change are abundant. Chinese characters have disappeared or are disappearing as functional parts of the language in two of the four countries that have used them. Vietnamese know as little about the characters as do Americans. The chances of the script being reinstituted in Vietnam for anything more than decorative purposes are zero. Korea's on again–off again use of Chinese characters is a matter of temporary necessity. Given their influence on the shape of the Korean language over centuries, some time and temporizing are needed while phonetic writing conventions are worked out and the language itself can undergo corresponding changes. Although the characters come and go, the outcome is hardly in doubt. Even in China and Japan, the tendency has been toward less—not more—use of Chinese characters. Viewed globally and historically, it is clear that Chinese characters are on their last legs. Linguists dislike them, and most East Asians, in the role of users, seem more than willing to avoid them when alternatives are available.

Moreover, the term "Chinese character" itself has become a misnomer. Although accurate typologically, the term now subsumes two, maybe three separate systems that, owing to different types of reforms, are not transferable even as units. Thus not only have the languages using characters declined in number, the unity that these systems once shared has eroded, for functional purposes almost entirely.[8] Fragmented and in retreat, the "system," as it were, is losing ground, even within those countries still using it, through two different forms of what DeFrancis has called "digraphia" (1984b). The first of these involves the shifting proportion of characters to *kana* or *hangul* in Japan's and South Korea's mixed scripts. Although this proportion waxes and wanes depending on the type of material and spirit of the times, generally speaking post–World War II use of Chinese characters is down in both countries, the result of reforms that were at least partly successful and a flood of phonetic loanwords. Even Chinese, which has no legitimate mechanism for phonetic borrowing, has under the same types of pressure begun to introduce the Roman alphabet directly into the character text (Hansell 1994).

The other type of digraphia, the use of two separate writing systems for different functions, is even more significant. In South Korea and (to a much lesser extent) Japan this phenomenon involves, on one level, using the mixed script for some types of materials and the indigenous phonetic script for others. While technically a form of digraphia, the syllabic, character-inspired shapes of these native phonetic systems do little to help the languages rid themselves of their Chinese character dependencies. Sinitic morphemes are simply written with one syllabary instead of another. Although they may lose their distinctiveness in the transition, context and latent familiarity with the "real" character representation[9] is enough to preserve these units' artificial status as morphemes and the monosyllabic morphology of the language as a whole. The abandoning of Chinese characters itself would cut down on arbitrary neologisms, but only when the syllable boundary preserved by the indigenous orthographies is breached completely will genuine alternatives to the Sinitic paradigm emerge.

True digraphia, therefore, in the East Asian context must refer to the coexistence of character-based traditional writing on the one hand and alphabetic writing on the other, the latter with word (not syllable) division and, where appropriate, some amount of morphophonemic spelling. This situation precisely is taking shape in China and Japan, the two countries where the characters are most thoroughly entrenched. In the face of pressure to absorb international vocabulary, encouraged by new technological venues, and facilitated by English-language bilingualism, the alphabet is taking its place alongside traditional orthographies in more and more applications. As the alphabetic conventions spread, problems associated with their use in specific languages are quietly being worked out. What began as simple notations are becoming alternative orthographies.

Not only is this process painless and far more effective than "positive" reform. It is also harder to undermine. Wholesale writing reforms of the sort done in Korea and spoken about in China and Japan are easy targets for traditionalists to attack in their conceptual phase and during the problematic years when they are first implemented. Suppletion through digraphia is much harder to counter, although it is conceivable that concerted efforts by misguided traditionalists to preserve Chinese characters as part of the dominant orthography could postpone the characters' demise a while longer. My feeling is that many East Asian intellectuals will try to do so, whatever the cost.

This intuition brings us out of the realm of linguistics and into the area of social choice, which is where this study ends. I confess to being ambivalent about what East Asians *should* do with their character writing systems. As a Westerner struggling in a tough new world of international competition, I hope East Asians keep the characters forever; it may be the West's biggest advantage. As a human being, I am appalled by the tragic waste of resources and creativity that Chinese characters cause. As the author of what I have tried to make an objective study, I can only suggest that East Asians consider these facts and draw their own conclusions.

Notes

Chapter 1. Chinese

1. It may be argued that *wén* in the terms *wénhuà* and *wénmíng* refers to "civil" (versus "martial") rather than to "writing" per se. Yet it remains noteworthy that the concept of "civil" in China evolved from that of "writing."

2. Known in Chinese as *wényán,* as opposed to the more speechlike *báihuà* style. Classical or "literary" Chinese is a generic term that encompasses most varieties of premodern character texts written in China, except popular literature and other Buddhist-inspired narratives patterned more closely on the spoken language.

3. For a comprehensive treatment of this subject, presented in the context of an overall theory of writing, see DeFrancis 1989, especially pp. 68–88 and 151–183.

4. An attempt by sinologist Terrien de Lacouperie in 1894 to demonstrate a Bactrian origin for Chinese characters based on the rough similarity of ten pictographic signs is unconvincing, according to Jensen, "since it was a matter of such signs as sun, moon, mountain and so on, in which abbreviated, stylized representations were bound to assume similar forms quite of their own accord" (1970:162).

5. The dynamics of the character-morpheme-syllable relationship in Chinese are discussed later. The usual explanation is that Chinese characters represent morphemes, which in Chinese are usually one syllable long. Ipso facto, they also represent syllables. However, there is good reason to believe that if characters did not obligatorily represent syllables in Chinese, the morphemes that they help define would not necessarily be monosyllabic.

6. Another connection between characters and language involves the use of phonology in reading and writing character texts, which is a function of their relationship to the language's morphemes.

7. Some support for Creel's position comes (unwittingly) from Boodberg's own observation that the words of the language in earliest times were in an "almost unbelievably undifferentiated" state. Boodberg had used internal reconstruction on individual phonetic series to recover alleged protoforms and expressed surprise at the wide range of concepts—including polar opposites—that single morphemes appeared to represent. This situation is precisely what one would expect if, as Creel maintains, characters representing unrelated words are erroneously treated as cognates by virtue of misidentified "phonetic" elements.

8. Liu Fu et al. (*Sòng-Yuán Yílái Súzì Pǔ*, 1930) drew on twelve different types of sources to list some 1,600 simplified characters in use over the preceding nine hundred years (Kaizuka and Ogawa 1981:355).

9. Qian identified eight types of simplified characters: (1) the entire character's shape is reduced; (2) handwritten "grass" characters are used as a model; (3) a part of the original represents the whole; (4) a component of the character is simplified; (5) the old form is resurrected; (6) the phonetic element is replaced by one homophonous; (7) a new form is created; and (8) the entire character is replaced by a simpler one with the same sound.

10. The normal way of phrasing it is "a different form of the same character," which is hard to reconcile with the notion of the character itself being only a form: "a different form of the same form." Yet intuitively the former expression *seems* reasonable. The usage suggests that the term "Chinese character" implies a physical shape *and* its linguistic component.

11. See DeFrancis 1950 for a history of pre-*pinyin* alphabetic writing in China.

Chapter 2. Japanese

1. A full treatment of the relationship of Japanese writing to language can be found in James Unger, *The Fifth Generation Fallacy* (1987). Unger's approach, taking the perspective of computerization, is especially effective in ferreting out many of the system's difficulties that can go unnoticed by humans, whose minds are used to a world filled with contradictions. If you want to know how a system really works, try modeling it on a computer.

2. As Sansom described it, "One hesitates for an epithet to describe a system of writing which is so complex that it needs the aid of another system to explain it. There is no doubt that it provides for some a fascinating field of study, but as a practical instrument it is surely without inferiors" (1928:44).

3. There is no word division in either Japanese or Chinese. Readers determine this as well from context. This feature of character-based writing is treated in detail in later chapters.

4. I became disgusted early on with these convoluted devices to make good Chinese read like bad Japanese and passed my *kambun* exams by treating the texts straightforwardly as classical Chinese. It was the only time in my graduate career that I enjoyed reading the latter. Happiness is relative.

5. According to Miller, use of the word *go* (Chinese *wú*) does not indicate a southern origin for the earlier series. Rather, the word should be understood in a "specialized pejorative T'ang philological sense of 'non-standard' in regard to language" (1967:108).

6. Morohashi (1960) associates *miru* with 217 different Chinese characters!

7. Sansom notes that *kambun* became less like Chinese and more like Japanese under the influence of the colloquial style, eventually abandoning the Chinese word order (1928:60). Habein equates this shift with the rise of the warrior class during the Kamakura period (1185–1333) (1984:55).

8. To accomplish the same thing semantically, the Chinese character 雲 "cloud" would be used with its *kun* reading *kumo* implied.

9. The system evolved; it was not created as such from scratch. Mythology nevertheless attributes one style of *kana*, *hiragana*, to Kūkai (774–835), founder of

the Shingon ("true words") sect of Buddhism, and the other, *katakana,* to Kibi no Mabiki (697–775), an envoy to China.

10. *Hiragana no setsu* (On the Use of *Hiragana*), in *Meiroku zasshi* 7 (1884). Shimizu pointed to parallel examples of homophony in English.

11. In January 1921, the latter reorganized as the Nihon romaji-kai, whose essential program was accepted by the Ministry of Education in 1937 as the national romanization standard.

12. The plan was published in February 1920 by the Ministry of Education under the title "Proposed Modifications to Chinese Characters" *(Kanji seirian).* It included 241 permissible simplified forms.

13. Gottlieb concurs that the primary impetus for the postwar reforms originated with the Japanese themselves: "Background support was provided by the presence of the Americans, whose observations on the difficulty of the existing script system and tentative suggestions that romanization be adopted as Japan's national script galvanized the Japanese into action to counter the perceived threat (never a real possibility) that they might lose their own script if they did not modify the way it was used" (1994:1177).

14. Nationalism was also an important stimulus for reform, inasmuch as Korean reformers were seeking not only to abandon the characters, but also to adopt universal application of *hangul,* a script of their own invention. The general connection between nationalism and writing reform has been established by John DeFrancis (1950) and Choe Hyon-bae (1970).

15. All factions in all three countries enlisted "democracy" in support of their causes. In the People's Republic of China, writing reform was carried out in the name of making education and literacy available to the common folk; those opposing the reforms complained, with some justification, that the new state-enforced standards, decided for all intents by a minority of functionaries, contradicted the very principle of democracy. In South Korea, the same songs were sung by both camps, each claiming to represent the democratic interests. According to Gottlieb, conservatives in postwar Japan "stressed that the decisions of the Council were not taken democratically enough, with sufficient consideration of 'the will of the people,' despite the reformers' counterclaim that the policies were worked out for the sake of that same people and that the conservatives would like to return to the undemocratic prewar writing system" (1994:1186).

16. In Chapter 11 I will argue to the contrary that character-capable word processors will eventually lead to the replacement of the mixed script with fully alphabetic writing.

Chapter 3. Korean

1. Japanese *-n* is treated as a syllabic nasal, not as a syllable-final consonant.

2. Korean syllables used with Sinitic sounds outnumber the Japanese *on* readings marginally: 393 versus 319, according to a count based on Chang Sam-sik 1974 and Nelson 1962. Nam Kwang-u claims a figure of 490 Sino-Korean syllables (1984:324). Korean preserves the richer Middle Chinese phonology, lost in Mandarin, through its *-p, -t, -k* syllable-final consonants. Although Japanese, strictly speaking, has no syllable finals, it kept many of the original endings by using two Japanese syllables to borrow a single Chinese syllable. These two-syllable morphemes are counted among the 319 *on* readings.

3. To be exact, the character-derived *kana* represent mora—short syllables—
not the full range of syllables in the language. Japanese developed gimmicks to
stretch the forty-eight basic *kana* (forty-six are used today) so that all the language's
syllables could be represented, such as two types of diacritics to show different
classes of consonants and doubling or tripling the symbols to accommodate palatalization and long vowels. The particular conventions varied historically.

4. In Japanese, besides representing single syllables, characters represent
whole or large parts of indigenous polysyllabic words as well as Sinitic morphemes
that in the process of being borrowed into Japanese acquired a second syllable to
represent an original final consonant. In the first case, users as speakers are free to
alter their pronunciation of the word without orthographic restraint, because the
representation is holistic. Unlike *kana,* the character makes no demand on how the
word is to be pronounced. In the second case, it is likely that the final syllable (there
are only four) of the bisyllabic Sinitic term is *perceived* by Japanese as what it was
intended to represent—a syllable-final consonant. *Kana,* however, legitimizes these
dummy syllable sounds and prevents the cluster from developing into a more complex syllable of the CVC type.

5. The system for most of its history was known as *ŏnmun* ("vulgar writing"). The word *hangul* first came into use at the end of the nineteenth century.

6. Incredibly, Vietnamese, which uses a romanized alphabet whose letters
appear serially with spaces between each syllable, also had a convention for writing
in Chinese character–like blocks. One or more syllables written with arched, heavily
stylized letters were compressed into a square framework and aligned vertically in
the traditional Chinese manner, looking very much like a line of Chinese characters.
The style has been used with photographs on ancestral altars, apparently to enhance
the dignity of the orthography.

7. Ideology is making the transition harder for the North than it need be.
South Koreans are introducing Western (primarily English) vocabulary into their
language through *hangul* in droves, taking pressure off the Sinitic part of the lexicon
by reducing its size and making its phonological patterns proportionately more distinctive. The North's political philosophy of self-determination eschews Western
loanwords, so that new vocabulary is made up of the remnants of indigenous morphology or, more commonly, the phonetically depleted Sinitic morphemes, all written in *hangul.*

8. The negative side is that, in the absence of any *kun*-like device for authenti-
cating a character's indigenization, the whole corpus of Chinese characters and
vocabulary is theoretically accessible to Koreans, whether or not these terms fill any
genuine need or are phonetically viable.

9. *Idu* has also been called *ito, itu, imun, isŏ,* and *ido.* According to Lee Ki-
mun, it is not certain that any of these designations was in use in Silla times,
although the style itself was (1977:59).

10. In chapter 102 of *Sejong sillok* (Annals of King Sejong's Reign), the original twenty-eight *hangul* symbols are said to have been fashioned by the king personally. Ledyard, after acknowledging some foreign influence, concludes that it was
"elaborated after conscious research and study by a single man" (1966:79). Kontsevicha believes Sejong was personally responsible for the idea of creating an alphabetic transcription of Korean, continuously took part in the elaboration of such a
system, and wrote the introduction to the edict announcing its promulgation. The

actual working out of the system "in all likelihood" was left to other scholars whom Sejong had commissioned (1979:37).

11. In June 1992, North and South Korean linguists agreed on a set of unified "Romanization Rules for Use in Mechanized Writing" following a series of discussions that began in Moscow in 1987. Automated data transfer between the Koreas and with other countries was reported to be a major goal (*Chosŏn ilbo*, June 19, 1992).

12. In 1937, Japan officially adopted a phonemic romanization system called *kunrei-siki*, based on conventions used in the *kana* syllabary. It replaced in Japan the earlier Hepburn system, which was largely phonetic and more easily read by foreigners.

13. The equivalent term in Japanese for Sinitic vocabulary, *kango,* omits the Korean *-ja-* meaning "character," which may illustrate the closer connection between borrowed Chinese words and characters in the minds of Koreans.

14. Sahoe kwahakwŏn ŏn'ŏhak yŏnguso, *Hyŏngmyŏng kwa kŏnsŏlui mugirosŏui minjok'ŏui paljŏne kwanhan Kim Ilsong tongjiui sasang* (Comrade Kim Il-song's Thoughts on the Development of the National Language as a Weapon of Revolution and Construction) (Pyongyang: Sahoe Kwahak Publishing Co., 1970), p. 57.

15. Oeguk Mungyoyuk Tosŏ Publishing Co., Pyongyang, 1972. It contains 269 pages of text and indexes.

16. Hangul hakhoe (Hangul Society) was a private group headquartered in Seoul founded to promote all-*hangul.* Its presidents have included the former head of the Ministry of Education's Textbook Compilation Bureau Choe Hyon-bae and Seoul National University linguistics professor Ho Ung.

Chapter 4. Vietnamese

1. Called *tự-điển* (Mand. *zìdiǎn*), versus word-based Vietnamese dictionaries known as *từ-điển (cídiǎn).*

2. The fact that Sinitic vocabulary can be borrowed at all without Chinese characters serving as a medium should be no surprise to linguists, who recognize interlanguage borrowing as a universal process. Only scholars blinded by their attachment to the characters claim that their loss would complicate the process. "Lost" are the self-created Sinitic nonwords that without characters cannot be borrowed, because there is no agreement among users that they constitute words. This process itself is one more way (among others to be discussed in later chapters) in which phonetic writing helps users decide what the words of their language are (or should be).

3. Hai provides an elaborate etymology of Vietnamese vocabulary, which ranges from unassimilated Chinese to fully indigenous words, with all intermediate possibilities: partly assimilated Sino-Vietnamese vocabulary, Sinitic terms so well adapted that their origins have been mostly forgotten, Sinitic words and expressions rearranged to fit Vietnamese grammar, and other words made up jointly of indigenous and Sinitic roots. The two languages were in contact so long that whatever combinations could come about did come about.

4. DeFrancis gives 1174 as the date classical Chinese was adopted "as the official writing of the state" (1977:13).

5. The texts were read in Sino-Vietnamese, which to the Vietnamese reading

them *was* Chinese. Chinese sounds borrowed with the characters were standardized in Vietnam, as in Korea and Japan. Typically, the borrowing languages changed character pronunciations less over time than the Chinese did themselves.

6. The dictionary was *Bảng Tra Chữ Nôm.* (Hanoi: Ủy Ban Khoa Học Xã Hội Việt Nam, 1976).

7. See in this connection the comments in Chapter 3 on the squarish, syllable-based shapes of Korean *hangul.*

8. The origin of the term *quốc ngữ* (Mand. *guóyǔ*) as it applies to Vietnamese remains uncertain. According to Thompson, "The earliest reference to official use of the system is a circular of 1910 in which the Résident supérieur of Tonkin (northern Viet Nam) required that all public documents be transcribed into *quốc ngữ*" (1987:54). Thompson feels the term may have been adopted as a symbol of Vietnamese unity, much as *guóyǔ* is used by Chinese for the national spoken standard there. DeFrancis believes that the word was first used long ago to distinguish spoken Vietnamese from spoken Chinese, that it was later used to mean *chữ nôm* since it was through the so-called demotic script that the "national language" was first written, and that it finally was applied by extension to Vietnam's romanized script (1977:87).

9. For example, Jensen states that the Vietnamese system "can be regarded as proof that it is in fact possible to reproduce a language of a construction closely related to that of Chinese without question through the Roman alphabetical script" (1970:184). DeFrancis' 1977 book was motivated by a similar insight.

10. I have on my shelf a bilingual Vietnamese-English dictionary recently published by what is probably a U.S. government agency (publishing data are not provided). The dictionary's 971 pages have two columns of entries per page, with up to sixty-five entries per line, for about 125,000 entries. Huge as it is, the dictionary lists the "words" I am looking for perhaps 25 percent of the time. This figure would be much lower for native speakers, who already know most of the genuine vocabulary and need to consult a dictionary less often.

Chapter 5. Representation

1. Chinese characters were not always written as they are today as single units occupying one square of space. Oracle bones and bronze inscriptions show many examples of two or more characters packed into a single area. Conversely, a character's "radical" and "phonetic" components were sometimes separated and placed in two adjacent squares. Both practices seem to have stopped by the early Zhou dynasty (Jiang Shanguo 1987:65), but surface so regularly in the copy sheets of beginning students that one is tempted to see a replay of the system's phylogeny in its acquisition by individuals.

2. See DeFrancis 1984a, pp. 132–136, 161–164, and 1989, pp. 20–21, for the origins of this school of thought and some contemporary examples.

3. "It is the meaningful units of a *language* and not 'naked ideas' which may be taken to serve as the representata of the graphemes of a writing system" (French 1976:105). Sampson likewise concludes that "Chinese writing comes no closer than English or any other 'to signify thoughts directly,' or to express 'things' rather than words" (1985:149).

4. Pulgram, for example, writes "I chose *word* rather than *lexeme* or *morpheme* for logographic writing because . . . a logogram may represent the one or

the other, or more than one unit of either; *word* is, though less precise, a more suitable term for what a logographeme signals in most cases" (1976:12). Pulgram also states that Chinese is logographic because it has "graphemes that represent, by and large, words."

5. For example, Coulmas (1983:240), Chao (1968:102), DeFrancis (1984a: 125–126), French (1976:113), Kratochvil (1968:157), and Sampson (1985:156).

6. Strictly speaking, the final segment of morphemes ending in a consonant is transferred to the *kana* part of the representation, in keeping with the CV structure of the language.

7. That is, the units, not the system itself as it applies to Chinese. DeFrancis argues that the graphic units are systematized—that is, related to one another—by virtue of their shared phonetic base, that base consisting of single-syllable sounds (1995). Ipso facto, the system is a syllabary.

8. The dimensions of the Chinese syllabary seem less preposterous in light of data that show English to have 1,768 graphemes for its forty phonemes, a ratio of 44:1. By contrast, the ratio of characters to syllables in Chinese is only 37:1 in a worst case scenario that counts all of the *Kangxi* dictionary's 48,000 characters against the 1,300 syllables of Mandarin (DeFrancis 1989:289).

9. Eugene Nida argued similarly that "linguistic meaning" be considered part of a morpheme's meaning, mentioning specifically the types of constructions in which the morpheme occurs, its frequency of occurrence, and its productiveness in new combinations (1948:264).

10. Logographic systems do "not capitalize on a structural characteristic of every human language, namely, that the sound forms of the thousands of words in each are all made up of a limited number of distinctive sounds. . . . Viewed exclusively from the point of view of minimizing arbitrariness, the end result of this development would logically be a system where characteristics of the form of the letters would be related in a systematic way to distinctive phonetic features of the individual sound segments" (Klima 1972:62).

Chapter 6. Learning and Literacy

1. Tape recordings of Wu speech provided by a thirty-two-year-old native-speaking informant born and raised in Shanghai are used for the Shanghainese segment of my course on nonstandard Chinese languages. The recordings were criticized by another Wu speaker, also from Shanghai but ten to fifteen years her senior, as "kids' talk" and not "correct" Shanghainese. Incredibly, the same taped specimens elicited bored winces from a third native speaker who had spent all of her nineteen years in that city: "We don't talk that way anymore."

2. Chemical elements are often cited as an example, but the process extends even to some chemical compounds. History, reflecting the aptitude East Asian families have for finding and often creating unique characters to name their progeny, and geography are the worst offenders.

3. Downing suggests that "the burden of memorization in the alphabetic writing system has certainly been underestimated" (1973:149–150). English, strictly speaking, does not use twenty-six symbols. According to Downing, A. J. Ellis "analyzed all the alternative ways of printing and writing the forty or so phonemes of English and found more than 2,000 alternative graphemes" (1845). Nyikos counted 1,768 graphemes in English (1988).

, which is

4. Professional native instructors of Chinese, Japanese, and especially Korean, with advanced degrees in the languages, often forget how to write characters that they are called upon in class to reproduce or that they find themselves committed to writing halfway through a sentence. I long ago stopped being surprised by the phenomenon and wrote it off, like other students, to the difficulty of the system. It is hard to imagine an English teacher having the same problem with spelling—or commanding the same sympathy from students for failing to recollect.

5. Nevertheless, until recently with the advent of on-line programs that allow users to create characters, it was not uncommon to find isolated characters drawn by hand into the text of books printed by reputable publishing houses.

6. According to Wang Fangyu, cursive writing is used for "personal letters, personal signatures, personalized orders, manuscripts, informal records, notes, diaries, invoices, menus, receipts, inter-departmental memoranda, notes that a teacher writes in chalk on blackboards, colophons on paintings and on couplets and inscriptions on most works of art or decorative objects" (1958:xxvi).

7. Or, more accurately, the individual character in context, since many characters have multiple meanings and sounds.

8. In his *Systema phoneticum scripturae Sinicae* (Macao, 1841).

9. W. E. Soothill, *The Student's Four Thousand Character and General Pocket Dictionary* (London, 1942; preface dated 1889).

10. DeFrancis regards it as more or less self-evident that Chinese characters are morphemes (1994, personal communication), but expends considerable effort establishing that the system is, at heart, a syllabary (1984a, 1989). The thrust of my attempt, in contrast, has been to show that the characters by and large either are or represent morphemes and that their connection with syllables is a given. The difference in our respective views, if any, seems to be in what their primary connection with language is, which is another way of asking what the primary aspect of *language* is. If language is viewed as speech, the argument that the characters primarily are a syllabary cannot be questioned. If language is viewed as a set of abstract relations leading to speech, then the characters are primarily morphemes. Either argument is valid depending on one's perspective. The fact that morphemes are as wedded to sound as they are to meaning and that the meaning, in any case, is language-specific establishes the morphemic interpretation within the same linguistic hierarchy, albeit on a different level. The source of these two interpretations, I believe, is the nature of the character unit itself. Unlike alphabets, which use two distinct devices for graphemes and morphemes—letters and rules describing how the letters are to be combined—Chinese seeks to fulfill both functions with just one device—the character. Serving two masters, the unit is interpretable in either of its roles.

11. The same phenomenon, known as the "word superiority effect," applies to English. Experiments show that whole words written alphabetically are recognized more quickly than any individual letter. This phenomenon is discussed in more detail in the following chapter on reading.

12. Interestingly, this same feature—in reverse—has been cited by supporters of the character script in Korean, who complain about the disutility of using an indigenous phrase in *hangul* to translate one Sinitic term.

13. Downing, for example, suggests, "One could claim that very few people achieve full literate proficiency in the English writing system, if that phrase includes the ability to spell from memory any word according to the conventions of English

orthography. Probably, both in China and England it is more appropriate to recognize that literacy learning is a lifetime process" (1973:150).

14. It is interesting to note that Vietnamese writing—an alphabetic script that under the influence of Sinitic morphology and its own history of character use separates each syllable-morpheme as if they were words—engenders the same free-for-all attitude toward word formation. The tradition has outlived the characters or, to put it less politely, the characters continue to hobble the language from the grave.

Chapter 7. Reading

1. Reading speed is usually cited as evidence against phonological recoding; if both reading and speech make use of the same lower mechanisms, how does one account for the ability of most readers to process written text more rapidly than speech? I omit this argument from those listed below because it seems flawed in its assumption that phonological recoding requires the reader to process all items that appear. Recoding, like direct access, could function through a strategy of discrete sampling.

2. Goodman, for example, argues against the "common misconception ... that graphic input is precisely and sequentially recoded as phonological input and then decoded bit by bit. Meaning is cumulative, built up a piece at a time, in this view" (1976b:503). This may or may not be true, but this statement encompasses two entirely different problems.

3. Foss and Hakes write of an "iconic storage system" at the first stage of the reading process (1978:328). Input lasts about one-half second, and its representation "is in terms of lines and angles." Johnson's model likewise allows for intermediate processing of features, resulting in an "Interpretable Perception Representation (Icon)" that is matched to a lexical item (1981:61).

4. Rozin and Gleitman come to the same conclusion: "It is difficult to conceive of a whole-word recognition device that does not identify component letters on the way" (1977:75–76). Johnson sees a role for both letters and clusters of letters, the latter manipulated as single perceptual units (1981:33–35).

5. Banks et al. believe that "the purpose of speech recoding at this stage is to provide short-term memory (STM) with a speech-like representation, to hold for the use of the comprehension process" (1981:140). Conrad's views are similar; he sees short-term memory satisfying "the need to hold on to one or more words, or to a group of words condensed to an idea, while considering the related implication of subsequent words or ideas" and adds that "we use a speech code in reading because it best sustains the necessary STM processes" (1972:236–237). Kleiman also allows use of a phonological code in short-term memory, but only after visual capacity is exhausted: "After the lexical information is accessed via the visual route, the word, with either its associated lexical information or the memory address of this information, is stored in visual temporary storage. Then there is a check to see if this storage buffer is overloaded. If it is, then speech recoding occurs, thereby enabling additional words to be stored" (1975:338). The superiority of auditory over visual short-term memory is supported by recall experiments that show the last several digits of a series remembered more accurately when presented aurally (Studdert-Kennedy 1975:117). By these accounts, inner speech arises as a reflex of short-term memory coding, "a kind of auditory imagery, dependent upon linguistic awareness of the sentence already synthesized, reassuring but by no

means essential to the synthesis" (Mattingly 1972:144), not as an obligatory path toward lexical access.

6. Characters were chosen with and without clear "phonetic" indicators to control against possible influence from this variable. A strong right hemisphere preference was manifested regardless of character type (Tzeng et al. 1979:500).

7. Elman's hypothesis is consistent with the behavior of deep dyslexics with left hemisphere lesions who can read concrete nouns such as "inn" but not abstract function words such as "in" (Hooper and Teresi 1986:225).

8. For right-handed people. The other region specialized for language, Broca's Area, is also on the left in the frontal lobe, adjacent to the motor cortex.

9. Carrol reaches a similar conclusion: "Word recognition depends on a matching of the stimulus with some deep, abstract representation of graphic configuration that is stored in memory. . . . For an educated speaker of Chinese, the internal representation clearly consists of much more than sound and meaning; it has a graphic counterpart. I wonder whether this may not also be the case for literate speakers of alphabetic languages" (1972:107–108).

Chapter 8. Appropriateness to East Asian Languages

1. See, for example, Coulmas 1989:44.

2. Interestingly, many of these three- and four-syllable words came into service in conscious imitation of European-language morphology. There was little, if anything, in the indigenous Sinitic tradition that encouraged multisyllable words.

3. Li Xingjie mentions this in his criticism of the fallacy (1987:29).

4. In *Zhōngguó yǔwén*, February 1953. Cited by Ohara 1989:159.

5. See Mair 1992:5–13 for examples.

6. Excepted are the Ancient Chinese -p, -t, -k endings, analyzed in the Chinese linguistic tradition as an "entering tone" and adapted by the borrowing languages more or less as is (Korean, Vietnamese) or as the initial consonant of a second syllable (Japanese). Vietnamese, also a tonal language, was able to accommodate this Chinese feature.

7. I.e., the character as a whole. Most characters have components that were based etymologically on sound and that play an important role in helping users identify and process the unit.

8. The official figure for China's non-Han population was 67 million in 1982, compared with a Han population of 950 million (Ramsey 1987:164–165). Assuming a present population of 1.2 billion, the non-Han figure rises to 79 million and is probably much higher.

9. Yuan Jiahua (1960), Zhan Bohui (1981), DeFrancis (1984a), Ramsey (1987), and Norman (1988).

10. Figures are from Ramsey (1987:87) and are based on a Han population of 950 million.

11. *Guóyǔ* in Taiwan, and *pǔtōnghuà* ("common speech") in the People's Republic of China. The two are essentially identical, although in practice Taiwan speakers model their speech on the southern standard. Both terms are translated into English as "Mandarin."

12. The support need not be direct. The identification of a character with a unique meaning and a Sinitic sound in any of the languages is enough to establish

its viability in the others where characters are not used, that is, in Vietnam and North Korea.

Chapter 9. The Chimera of Reform

1. Presumably, these figures refer to the number of different characters that appear in a text, as opposed to just the number of characters in a text. There is a difference between recognizing nine of every ten different characters and stumbling over every tenth symbol.

2. A character can be used so often in one narrow field of knowledge as to mask the fact that it almost never appears outside this limited context, that is, is not really a "common use" character.

3. "Iconicity" here means a one-to-one symmetrical alignment between basic units of meaning, sound, and writing.

4. Zhang Zhiyi and Zhang Qingyun, for example, explicitly endorse reduction by elimination of radicals as a means of changing the nature of the script from morphemic to phonographic and concurrently instilling this way of thinking into the people (1980:109).

5. Zhou Youguang gives three reasons for the failure of this "second" batch to catch on: (1) not all specimens had wide, popular use, (2) too many were being changed at once, (3) few Chinese were eager for more "reforms" in the wake of the Cultural Revolution (1987a:416).

6. Zheng Linxi gives 11.2 for two thousand common characters (1957:20). Chen Guangyao cites counts made on two "common use" dictionaries published in 1952 and 1953 for his figures of 11.2 and 11.9 (1955:77). Statistics provided by Bao Qi show the most common one thousand characters using an average of 10.2 strokes, the 1,500 most common averaging 10.8, and the two thousand most common characters raising the average to 11.2; a list of 7,261 characters yields an average of 11.4 strokes (1955b:98). Working with a dictionary of 7,846 characters, Liu Shih-hong found the number of characters per given stroke count increasing regularly to a peak of 704 characters at 12.0 strokes (1969:54–55).

7. Fu Yonghe's figures for the same group of characters are 15.6 reduced to 10.3 strokes (1987:92).

8. The "running script" style, which uses greatly reduced forms, was rejected as too simple. Other popular forms, including many of the so-called off-the-top-of-the-hand characters (shǒutóuzi) endorsed by the mass language movement that began around 1940 in Shanghai, had more strokes than the standard versions.

9. Based on the 313 "Significantly Changed Tōyō Kanji" listed in Nelson's (1962) dictionary. "Significant" is probably an overstatement, since some of these changes differ by one stroke only. In others the stroke count remains constant.

Chapter 10. Language, Speech, and Writing

1. Personal communication, June 25, 1995.

2. According to Amirova, theorists who reject the subordination of writing to speech view the relationship between written and spoken language as (1) two languages, (2) "two forms (or norms) of one and the same language," or (3) "simply as different material that manifests an abstract language system" (1977:5). In

the last case, language must be understood as a "scheme" without substance (p. 13), in which the "plane of expression is variable [and] liable to free substitution" (1985:28). Vachek holds the second view, which regards "the written and spoken norms . . . as parallel quantities that are not subordinate to any higher norm; the connection between them is explained only by the circumstance that they carry out complementary functions in the language collective that uses them" (1967:531). The term *language,* according to Vachek, designates "the sum of both norms." I. F. Vardul' denies the possibility of a single underlying language. In the opinion of Vardul', "That which as a rule remains unchanged in the substitution of one substance for another is not the structure [scheme], but [semantic] information, for the transmission of which language was intended" (1977:56–57). This makes language the substance itself, so if the substance is different, we are dealing with different languages.

3. It is rumored that Charles Hockett, the leading figure in American linguistics before Chomsky, kept a sign in his office stating that if something cannot be measured, it is not science. Bloomfield acknowledged his debt to behaviorism as the foundation of his system.

4. According to Goodman, "The necessary concern for oral language which had been neglected for so long caused many scholars to dismiss written language—without adequate consideration—as a secondary representation of oral language" (1970:105).

5. Needless to say, people establishing the written convention would have no idea what the phonetic conventions were unless they were expressed through speech. The concrete material, however, is only a starting point for analyzing the underlying system of contrasts, which is abstract and not manifested overtly.

6. Defined by Olson as "an agreed upon or presupposed possible world" (1982:155), and by Solntsev as "certain constants of thought activity and facts of consciousness; these are ideas and concepts worked out by collectives of people in their practical activities" (1985:15).

7. The reader is reminded that I am using the term "speech" here as a concrete *expression* of language, not as a synonym for language.

8. Gleitman and Rozin point out that "speech itself does not consist of physically segmental discrete units, but is a continuous, gradually varying event. Examination of the sound pattern that leads to the perception of a phone sequence shows no trace of segmentation. . . . There is no way a physicist looking at such spectrograms could infer segmental components. The segmentation we perceive comes from within the head" (1977:39).

9. Amirova observes that the most important principle of orthography is "to bring morphologically connected words closer than they are made in speech, and to make the morphological relationship more apparent" (1977:117). That is, "written language reflects a morphological division of the language that is spoken and heard" (p. 34).

10. Strictly speaking, the user has to relate the symbol to its semantic context occasionally in Chinese and almost always in Japanese to ascertain which sound (and meaning) is intended, just as in alphabetic scripts.

11. Linguists have elaborated an entire discipline—historical linguistics—to study how languages change over time. Although written texts are scrutinized for evidence of change, the assumption is that the mechanisms for change exist outside

the text itself and are endemic to speech. Writing as a "representation" of speech may give us some idea what the "real" (i.e., spoken) language was like if analyzed in conjunction with contemporary dialects, rhymes, and other data. But the thrust of the enterprise has always been on getting past the written record and its "distortions" in order to reconstruct the "living" language. Few have cared to consider what effect writing itself may have had on the body of rules and relationships that constitute language other than to note in passing the effect of "spelling pronunciations" on sound change or some such peripheral influence.

12. Victor H. Mair, 1994, personal communication. Professor Mair relates cases of young Mandarin speakers who habitually drop or deemphasize syllable-initial consonants, presumably as a sign of group identity. Older Mandarin speakers deplore the trend, and some reportedly find the speech of their own children "incomprehensible."

13. Chinese phonological analysis, which dates from the sixth century, until very recently was based entirely on the syllable. Although initial segment and tones were distinguished, glides, individual vowel phonemes, and final consonants were lumped together as "finals" or "rhymes" with no further analysis.

14. Whereas Chinese talk of "four modernizations," South Koreans refer directly and habitually to catching up with the "advanced countries" *(sŏnjinguk)*.

15. North Korea, with its *chuche* ("self-reliant") state ideology, avoids direct phonetic borrowing of foreign (Western) terms and insofar as is possible uses loan translations, which of necessity are made up largely of Sinitic morphemes.

Chapter 11. Computing with Chinese Characters

1. For example, the parent group of a major Japanese newspaper operates a database service for Japanese-language newspapers and periodicals. Since the language has no word division, an editor must decide beforehand what the keywords are for each and every text. Users, in turn, have to guess whether the parameters of the keyword searches they want to run will match the intuition of the editor. In practice the system is full of snags; not surprisingly, it works best when searching romanized acronyms. Western database managers already have most of their work done for them by the orthographic convention. From the Western user's perspective, the problem is not one of getting insufficient data, but how to build a search so as to avoid getting too much.

2. Even this large number of characters is inadequate for some users. According to Mair, at least one Japanese scholar is concerned that the "restricted" character fonts used with computers is constraining sinological research; he wants a font with thirty thousand or more characters (1995, personal communication).

3. Memory, human or electronic, is taxed enormously in any character-related manipulative application. Photocopiers, facsimile, and other types of image scanners do not process information, they pass it on as such. The two functions are qualitatively different, and it is unreasonable to hope for some technological breakthrough that will put Chinese character text processing on the same footing with alphanumerics.

4. I once knew a man who because of his unusual profession had learned enough Standard Telegraphic Code to speak simple Chinese sentences in numbers. If you asked him, "Nǐ hǎo ma?" (how are you?), he would reply, "2053 1771 1170" or "0008 1170," depending on how he felt. A friend told me years later that

he was last seen waving a sword from atop a government building challenging the police to apprehend him.

5. Kaiho Hiroyuki summarizes the results of experiments that demonstrate that character recognition is affected by users' ability to draw them and that users' appraisal of a character's complexity depends more on stroke count than on the number of lines actually present in the character (1987:67).

6. Feng lists some other tricks used in Chinese phonetic conversion programs to cut down on ambiguity. To input a single character, a two-syllable word containing the target morpheme can be typed, and the computer instructed to input the former or the latter. For compound-syllable words not listed in the computer's dictionary, one can split the word into its constituent morphemes and use the above technique to input the morphemes of the word individually (Feng 1989:23).

7. Wu states that "the provision of tonal information may indeed be counterproductive, as it tends to increase word length, thus slowing down the speed of data entry."

8. In Yin's words, the "standardization of contemporary Chinese will be 'fixed' as its word-bank database is perfected, rather than remaining a mere aspiration" (1991:30).

Chapter 12. Chinese Characters and East Asian Culture

1. *Kanji minzoku no ketsudan* (Hashimoto et al. 1987).

2. Chang Sam-sik's *Tae Han-Han sajŏn* (Seoul, 1974) lists 2,708 twelve-stroke characters in its total stroke index.

3. For example, Liang Shih-ch'iu, ed., *A New Practical Chinese-English Dictionary* (Taipei, 1971).

4. These movements fail because of the impossibility of distinguishing assimilated from unassimilated borrowings. What may be foreign to one group of users is familiar to others who have more formal education or who are well-versed in particular fields. Phonetic intelligibility fails as a criterion of assimilation for the same reason: sounds are strange or familiar according to one's ability to relate these to concepts in one's own repertoire.

5. For example, Japanese *puro,* besides rendering the Western term "pro," also translates "program," "prostitute," "percent," "production," "professional," "proletariat," and sometimes "bromide."

6. Abundant evidence exists, if any were needed, in the historical record and present-day culture of East Asia's intellectual accomplishments. Chinese philosophy is the equal of anything penned in the West. The magnitude of East Asian creativity as expressed in technological innovation has been demonstrated beyond question by scholars such as Joseph Needham and Nathan Sivin. My position here is not that East Asians lack creativity, but that they have achieved their intellectual greatness in spite of the character-based writing system.

7. *Hangul* is more analytical in form because the script does designate letters, although this effect is mitigated by the orthography's grouping of these elements into syllables.

8. Literally as I write this, a Japanese exchange student in my university's linguistics department is taking a Ph.D. reading exam in Chinese. Fluent in Japanese *kanji,* she spent the better part of a year learning enough Chinese grammar to be able to connect the dots on a linguistics-related text, which, given her background

and specialty, should be a straightforward task—right? It turns out that she is up to her ears in the test and will be happy just to pass it. The test is in traditional Chinese characters. When I asked if she wanted to be tested with a People's Republic of China character-based text, she looked at me like I was crazy.

9. Pak's (1968) thesis that total replacement of the characters with an all-*hangul* script would lead to the breakdown of Sinitic morphology is belied by the North Korean practice of deliberately using—even coining—Sinitic terms, expressed in *hangul*, to avoid introducing impure Western terminology, and by the use in Vietnamese of new Sinitic compounds. Linguists and lexicographers in all of the East Asian countries for many decades to come will have no trouble identifying the character source of Sinitic compounds and using this information to form new Sinitic words with correct Sino-indigenous pronunciations, even without active use of the characters in any of the languages.

Bibliography

Aleshina, I. E. 1977. Yazykovaya politika v SRV: protsess normirovaniya termi-
nologii vo v'etnamskom yazyke. In L. B. Nikol'skiy, ed. *Yazykovaya politika v
Afro-Aziatskikh stranakh.* Moscow.

Amirova, T. A. 1977. *K istorii i teorii grafemiki.* Moscow.

———. 1985. *Funktsional'naya vzaimosvyaz' pis'mennogo i zvukovogo yazyka.*
Moscow.

An Pyŏng-hui. 1984. Hanja kyoyuk kwa hanja chŏngch'aek. In Kim Min-su et al.,
Kuk'o wa minjok munhwa. Seoul.

Ao Xiaoping. 1984. Xinxilun yu wenzi gaige. M.A. thesis, East China Normal University, Shanghai.

Banks, William P., Evelyn Oka, and Sherri Shugarman. 1981. Recoding of Printed
Words to Internal Speech: Does Recoding Come before Lexical Access? In
Ovid J. L. Tzeng and Harry Singer, eds., *Perception of Print.* Hillsdale, NJ.

Bao Qi. 1955. Tantan xie hanzi. In *Hanzi de zhengli he jianhua.* Zhongguo yuwen
zazhi she, Beijing.

Barnard, Noel. 1978. The Nature of the Ch'in "Reform of the Script." In David T.
Roy and Tsuen-hsuin Tsien, eds. *Ancient China: Studies in Early Civilization.*
Hong Kong.

Barnes, Dayle. 1988–1989. A Continuity of Constraints on Orthographic Change:
Chen Guangyao and Character Simplification. *Monograph Series* 38:135–166.

Baron, Jonathan, and Ian Thurston. 1973. An Analysis of the Word Superiority
Effect. *Cognitive Psychology* 4:207–228.

Bauer, Robert S. 1994. Sino-Tibetan **kolo* "Wheel." *Sino-Platonic Papers* 47
(August).

Becker, Joseph D. 1983. *"User-Friendly" Design for Japanese Typing.* Xerox Cor-
poration, Palo Alto, CA.

———. 1984. Multilingual Word Processing. *Scientific American* 251.1:96–107.

———. 1985. Typing Chinese, Japanese, and Korean. *Computer* 18.1:27–36.

Berry, Jack. 1977. "The Making of Alphabets" Revisited. In Joshua A. Fishman,
ed., *Advances in the Creation and Revision of Writing Systems.* The Hague.

Blank, Lenore Kim. 1981. Language Policies in South Korea and Their Probable
Impact on Education. Ph.D. dissertation, University of San Francisco.

Bloom, Alfred. 1981. *The Linguistic Shaping of Thought: A Study in the Impact of
Language on Thinking in China and the West.* Hillsdale, NJ.

Bloomfield, Leonard. 1933. *Language*. New York.

Bolinger, Dwight L. 1946. Visual Morphemes. *Language* 22:334–340.

Boodberg, Peter A. 1937. Some Proleptical Remarks on the Evolution of Archaic Chinese. *Harvard Journal of Asiatic Studies* 2:329–372.

———. 1940. "Ideography" or Iconolatry? *T'oung Pao* 35:266–288.

Brewer, William F. 1976. Is Reading a Letter-by-Letter Process? A Discussion of Gough's Paper. In Harry Singer and Robert B. Ruddell, eds., *Theoretical Models and Processes of Reading*. Second edition (revised). Newark, DE.

Brooks, Lee. 1977. Visual Pattern in Fluent Word Identification. In Arthur S. Reber and Don L. Scarborough, eds., *Toward a Psychology of Reading*. Hillsdale, NJ.

Burani, Cristina, Dario Salmaso, and Alfonso Caramazza. 1984. Morphological Structure and Lexical Access. *Visible Language* 18.4:342–352.

Cao Bohan. 1955a. Jingjian hanzi wenti. In *Hanzi de zhengli he jianhua*. Zhongguo yuwen zazhi she, Beijing.

———. 1955b. Hanzi wenzhang jiayong pinyinzi juli. In *Hanzi de zhengli he jianhua*. Zhongguo yuwen zazhi she, Beijing.

Cao Bohan, et al. 1955. Jieshao 'changyong hanzi.' In *Hanzi de zhengli he jianhua*. Zhongguo yuwen zazhi she, Beijing.

Carrol, John B. 1972. The Case for Ideographic Writing. In James F. Kavanagh and Ignatius G. Mattingly, eds., *Language by Ear and by Eye: The Relationship between Speech and Writing*. Cambridge, MA.

———. 1976. The Nature of the Reading Process. In Harry Singer and Robert B. Ruddell, eds., *Theoretical Models and Processes of Reading*. Second edition (revised). Newark, DE.

Chafe, Wallace L. 1970. *Meaning and the Structure of Language*. Chicago.

———. 1982. Integration and Involvement in Speaking, Writing, and Oral Literature. In Deborah Tannen, ed., *Spoken and Written Language: Exploring Orality and Literacy*. Norwood, NJ.

Chang Sam-sik, ed. 1974. *Tae Han-Han sajŏn*. Seoul.

Chang Tsung-tung. 1988. Indo-European Vocabulary in Old Chinese. *Sino-Platonic Papers* 7 (January).

Chao Yuen Ren. 1968. *Language and Symbolic Systems*. Cambridge.

Chen Guangyao. 1955. Tan jingjian hanzi. In *Hanzi de zhengli he jianhua*. Zhongguo yuwen zazhi she, Beijing.

Chen Mingyuan. 1980. Dianzi jisuanji yu hanzi gaige. *Yuwen xiandaihua* 1:56–71.

———. 1981. "Biaozhun xiandai hanzi biao" de dingliang gongzuo. *Yuwen xiandaihua* 5:38–59.

Chen, Virginia Wei-chieh. 1977. Simplified Characters in the PRC, Japan, Singapore and Taiwan. *Journal of the Chinese Language Teachers Association* 12.1:63–75.

Cheng Chin-chuan. 1979. Language Reform in China in the Seventies. *Word* 30.1–2:45–57.

———. 1983. "Constructions in the Chinese Language Reform." Paper presented to the Conference on Linguistic Modernization and Language Planning in Chinese Speaking Communities at the East-West Center, University of Hawai'i, Sept. 7–13.

Cheng Fang. 1981. Yuenan cong shiyong hanzi, nanzi guodu dao shiyong pinyin wenzi de lishi jingyan. *Yuwen xiandaihua* 5:188–198.

Cheng, Robert L. 1978. Taiwanese Morphemes in Search of Chinese Characters. *Journal of Chinese Linguistics* 6.2:306–313.

———. 1981. "Borrowing and Internal Development—Comparison of Taiwanese Words and Their Mandarin Equivalents." Paper presented at the 14th International Conference on Sino-Tibetan Languages and Linguistics, Gainesville, Florida.

Choe Ho-ch'ŏl. 1989. Pukhan ŭi ŏhui chŏngri. In Kim Min-su, ed., *Pukhan ui ŏhak hyŏngmyŏng.* Seoul.

Choe Hyŏn-bae. 1946. *Kŭlja ŭi hyŏngmyŏng.* Seoul.

———. 1970. *Hangŭl man ssŭgi ŭi chujang.* Seoul.

Chomsky, Noam, and Morris Halle. 1968. *The Sound Pattern of English.* New York.

Conrad, R. 1972. Speech and Reading. In James F. Kavanagh and Ignatius G. Mattingly, eds., *Language by Ear and by Eye: The Relationship between Speech and Reading.* Cambridge, MA.

Coulmas, Florian. 1983. Writing and Literacy in China. In Florian Coulmas and Konrad Ehlich, eds., *Writing in Focus.* Berlin.

———. 1989. *The Writing Systems of the World.* Oxford.

Creel, Herrlee Glessner. 1936. On the Nature of Chinese Ideography. *T'oung Pao* 32:85–161.

———. 1938. On the Ideographic Element in Ancient Chinese. *T'oung Pao* 34:265–294.

Cui, Wei. 1985. Evaluation of Chinese Character Keyboards. *Computer* 18.1:54–59.

DeFrancis, John. 1943. The Alphabetization of Chinese. *Journal of the American Oriental Society* 63:225–240.

———. 1950. *Nationalism and Language Reform in China.* Princeton. Reprint New York, 1972.

———. 1977. *Colonialism and Language Policy in Vietnam.* The Hague.

———. 1984a. *The Chinese Language: Fact and Fantasy.* Honolulu.

———. 1984b. Digraphia. *Word* 35.1:59–66.

———. 1985. Homographobia. *Xin Tang* 6:2–16.

———. 1989. *Visible Speech.* Honolulu.

———. 1995. Graphic Indeterminacy in Writing Systems. Draft.

de Kerckhove, Derrick. 1986. Alphabetic Literacy and Brain Processes. *Visible Language* 20.3:274–293.

de Saussure, Ferdinand. 1916/1974. *Cours de linguistique generale.* New York.

Ding Xilin. 1955. Duiyu zhengli hanzi zixing de jidian yijian. In *Hanzi de zhengli he jianhua.* Zhongguo yuwen zazhi she, Beijing.

Diringer, David. 1968. *The Alphabet.* New York.

Downing, John. 1973. Is Literacy Acquisition Easier in Some Languages Than in Others? *Visible Language* 7.2:145–154.

DuPonceau, Peter S. 1838. *A Dissertation on the Nature and Character of the Chinese System of Writing.* Philadelphia.

Ellis, A. J. 1845. *A Plea for Phonotype and Phonography.* Bath.

Elman, Jeffrey L., Kunitoshi Takahashi, and Yusu-hiko Tohsade. 1981. Lateral Asymmetries for the Identification of Concrete and Abstract Kanji. *Neuropsychologia* 19.3:407–412.

Endo, Masaomi, Akinori Shimizu, and Tadao Hori. 1978. Functional Asymmetry of Visual Fields for Japanese Words in *Kana* (Syllable-Based) Writing and

Random Shape Recognition in Japanese Subjects. *Neuropsychologia* 16:291–297.

Endo, Masaomi, Akinori Shimizu, and Ichiro Nakamura, 1981. Laterality Differences in Recognition of Japanese and Hangul Words by Monolinguals and Bilinguals. *Cortex* 17.3:391–399.

Falk, Julia S. 1973. *Linguistics and Language*. Lexington, MA.

Feng Zhiwei. 1989. *Xiandai hanyu he jisuanji*. Beijing.

———. 1992. *Zhongwen xinxi chuli yu hanyu yanjiu*. Beijing.

Forrest, R. A. D. 1948/1973. *The Chinese Language*. London.

Foss, Donald J., and David T. Hakes. 1978. *Psycholinguistics*. Englewood Cliffs, NJ.

Fowler, Carol A. 1981. Some Aspects of Language Perception by Eye: The Beginning Reader. In Ovid J. L. Tzeng and Harry Singer, eds., *Perception of Print*. Hillsdale, NJ.

French, M. A. 1976. Observations on the Chinese Script and the Classification of Writing-Systems. In W. Haas, ed., *Writing without Letters*. Manchester.

Fu Yonghe. 1981. Tantan xiandai hanzi de dingxing gongzuo. *Yuwen xiandaihua* 5:22–32.

———. 1987. Hanzi de zhengli he jianhua. In *Xin shiqi de yuyan wenzi gongzuo*. Quanguo yuyan wenzi gongzuo huiyi mishuchu, Beijing.

Gao Hanping and Yin Binyong. 1983. Yinjie xingshi de bijiao yanjiu. *Yuwen xiandaihua* 6:69–76.

Gelb, I. J. 1962. *A Study of Writing*. Chicago.

Gibson, Eleanor J., and Harry Levin. 1975. *The Psychology of Reading*. Cambridge, MA.

Gleitman, Lila R., and Paul Rozin. 1973a. Teaching Reading by Use of a Syllabary. *Reading Research Quarterly* 8.3:450–474.

———. 1973b. Phoenician Go Home? (A Response to Goodman). *Reading Research Quarterly* 8.3:494–500.

———. 1977. The Structure and Acquisition of Reading I: Relations between Orthographies and the Structure of Language. In Arthur S. Reber and Don L. Scarborough, eds. *Toward a Psychology of Reading*. Hillsdale, NJ.

Glushko, Robert J. 1979. The Organization and Activation of Orthographic Knowledge in Reading Aloud. *Journal of Experimental Psychology: Human Perception and Performance* 5.4:674–691.

Goodman, Kenneth S. 1970. Psycholinguistic Universals in the Reading Process. *Visible Language* 4.2:103–110.

———. 1976a. Behind the Eye: What Happens in Reading. In Harry Singer and Robert B. Ruddell, eds., *Theoretical Models and Processes of Reading*. Second edition (revised). Newark, DE.

———. 1976b. Reading: A Psycholinguistic Guessing Game. In Harry Singer and Robert B. Ruddell, eds., *Theoretical Models and Processes of Reading*. Second edition (revised). Newark, DE.

———. 1982. *Language and Literacy*. Vol. 1: *Process, Theory, Research*. Boston and London.

Gottlieb, Nanette. 1994. Language and Politics: The Reversal of the Postwar Script Reform Policy in Japan. *Journal of Asian Studies* 53.4:1175–1198.

Gough, Philip B. 1976. One Second of Reading. In Harry Singer and Robert B.

Ruddell, eds., *Theoretical Models and Processes of Reading.* Second edition (revised). Newark, DE.

Gunther, Harmut. 1983. The Role of Meaning and Linearity in Reading. In Florian Coulmas and Konrad Ehlich, eds., *Writing in Focus.* Berlin.

Haas, W. 1976. Writing: The Basic Options. In W. Haas, ed., *Writing without Letters.* Manchester.

Habein, Yaeko Sato. 1984. *The History of the Japanese Written Language.* Tokyo.

Hai Pham Van. 1974. *So-luoc Ve Anh-huong Trung-hoa Trong Tieng Viet.* Washington, DC.

Hai Ying. 1980. Kongge he duanheng de zuoyong. *Yuwen xiandaihua* 4:147–155.

Han Rin-kyo. 1975. Kukmin hakkyo e issŏsŏ ŭi hanja kyoyuk ŭi p'ilyosŏng. *Ŏmun yŏngu* 9:464–471.

Hannas, William C. 1991. Korean Views on Writing Reform. *Sino-Platonic Papers* 27 (August):85–94.

Hannas, William C., and Joshua Edelstein. 1994. Renaissance of the Chinese Languages. *Penn Language News* 9:10–13, 19.

Hansell, Mark. 1994. The Sino-Alphabet: The Assimilation of Roman Letters into the Chinese Writing System. *Sino-Platonic Papers* 45 (May).

Hashimoto Mantaro, Suzuki Takao, and Yamada Hisao. 1987. *Kanji minzoku no ketsudan: kanji no mirai ni mukete.* Tokyo.

Hatta, Takeshi. 1977. Recognition of *Kanji* in the Left and Right Visual Fields. *Neuropsychologia* 15:685–688.

———. 1978. Recognition of Japanese *Kanji* and *Hiragana* in the Left and Right Visual Fields. *Japanese Psychological Research* 20.2:51–59.

Havelock, Eric A. 1987. Chinese Characters and the Greek Alphabet. *Sino-Platonic Papers* 5 (December).

Hayashi Oki. 1949. Tōyō kanji jitaihyō ni tsuite. *Kokugo to kokubungaku*, February, pp. 69–73.

Hayashi Oki et al. 1983. Higashi Ajia ni okeru kanji shiyō. *Gengo seikatsu* 378:2–15.

Hink, R. F., K. Kaga, and J. Suzuki. 1980. An Evoked Potential Correlate of Reading Ideographic and Phonetic Japanese Scripts. *Neuropsychologia* 18:454–464.

Hjelmslev, Louis. 1961. *Prolegomena to a Theory of Language.* Madison, WI.

Hirata, K., and R. Osaka. 1969. Tachistoscopic Recognition of Japanese Letter Materials in Left and Right Visual Fields. *Neuropsychologia* 7:179–187.

Hŏ Ung. 1971. Hanja nŭn p'yeji toe'ŏ ya handa. In Hangul Hakhoe, *Hangŭl ch'ŏnyong ŭro ŭi kil.* Seoul.

———. 1974. *Urimal kwa kŭl ŭi naeil ŭl wihayŏ.* Seoul.

Hockett, Charles F. 1947. Problems of Morphemic Analysis. *Language* 23:341–343.

———. 1951. Review of *Nationalism and Language Reform in China. Language* 27:439–445.

———. 1958. *A Course in Modern Linguistics.* New York.

Hodge, Carleton Taylor, 1973. "Hieroglyphs." In *Encyclopedia Britannica* 11:477–480.

Hooper, Judith, and Dick Teresi. 1986. *The Three Pound Universe.* New York.

Horodeck, Richard Alan. 1987. The Role of Sound in Reading and Writing Kanji. Ph.D. dissertation, Cornell University.

Huang Diancheng. 1954. Yuenan caiyong pinyin wenzi de jingyan. In *Pinyin wenzi he hanzi de bijiao*. Zhongguo yuwen zazhi she, Shanghai.

Huang, Jack Kai-tung. 1985. The Input and Output of Chinese and Japanese Characters. *Computer* 18.1:18–26.

Iwada Mari. 1982. Gendai no nihongo ni okeru kanji no kinō. In Maruya Saiichi, ed., *Nihongo no sekai*, vol. 16. Tokyo.

Jakobson, Roman, and Morris Halle. 1956. *Fundamentals of Language*. The Hague.

Jensen, Hans. 1970. *Sign, Symbol and Script*. London.

Jian Bozan. 1957. Wenzi gaige wenti zuotanhui jilu, session III. *Pinyin*, July, 1–29. Reprinted in Peter J. Seybolt and Gregory Kuei-ke Chiang, *Language Reform in China*. New York, 1978.

Jiang Shanguo. 1987. *Hanzixue*. Shanghai.

Jin, Shunde. 1986. *Shanghai Morphotonemics*. Bloomington, IN.

Johnson, Neal F. 1981. Integration Processes in Word Recognition. In Ovid J. L. Tzeng and Harry Singer, eds., *Perception of Print*. Hillsdale, NJ.

Kaiho Hiroyuki. 1987. Nihongo no hyōki kōdō no ninchi shinrigakuteki bunseki. *Nihongogaku* 6:65–71.

Kaizuka Shigeki and Ogawa Kanju. 1981. Chūgoku no kanji. In Maruya Saiichi, ed., *Nihongo no sekai*, vol. 3. Tokyo.

Karlgren, Bernard. 1923. *Sound and Symbol in Chinese*. Oxford.

———. 1926. *Philology and Ancient China*. Oslo.

———. 1949. *The Chinese Language*. New York.

Kato Hiroki. 1979. Nihongo hyōkihō no yūrisei. *Gengo* 8.1:66–71.

Kelly, Kevin. 1994. *Out of Control*. Reading, MA.

Kennedy, George A. 1964. *Selected Works of George A. Kennedy*. Ed. Tien-yi Li. New Haven.

Kim Il-song. 1964. Chosŏn'ŏ rŭl paljŏn sik'igi wihan myŏch'gaji munje e taehayŏ. Reprinted in *Munhwa'ŏ haksŭp* 2 (1968):1–7. Seoul.

———. 1966. Chosŏn'ŏ ui minjokjŏk t'ŭksŏng ŭl olkhge sallyŏnagalte taehayŏ. Reprinted in *Munhwa'ŏ haksŭp* 3 (1969):1–9. Seoul.

Kim Jin-p'yŏng. 1983. The Letter Forms of Han'gul: Its Origin and Process of Transformation. In Korean National Commission for UNESCO, *The Korean Language*. Seoul.

Kim Min-su. 1973. *Kuk'ŏ chŏngch'aek ron*. Seoul.

———, ed. 1989. *Pukhan ŭi ŏhak hyŏngmyŏng*. Seoul.

Kim Min-su et al. 1984. *Kuk'ŏ wa minjok munhwa*. Seoul.

Kleiman, Glenn M. 1975. Speech Recoding in Reading. *Journal of Verbal Learning and Verbal Behavior* 14:323–339.

Klima, Edward S. 1972. How Alphabets Might Reflect Language. In James F. Kavanagh and Ignatius G. Mattingly, eds., *Language by Ear and by Eye: The Relationships between Speech and Reading*. Cambridge, MA.

Ko Yŏng-gun. 1989. Pukhan ŭi ŏn'ŏ chŏngch'aek. In Ko Yŏng-gun, ed., *Pukhan ŭi mal kwa kŭl*. Seoul.

Koestler, Arthur. 1964. *The Act of Creation*. New York.

Kondo Tatsuo. 1977. Ilbon ŭi kuk'ŏ kukja munje kaksŏ. *Ŏmun yŏngu* 18:94–120.

Kontsevicha, L. R. 1979. *Khunmin chonym*. Moscow.

Korchagina, T. I. 1975. Nekotorie voprosy issledovaniya reaktsii yaponskogo yazyka na omonimiyu. *Voprosy yaponskoy filologii* 3:45–52.

————. 1977. Osnovnye istonchniki omonimii v yaponskom yazyke. *Voprosy yaponskoy filologii* 4:42–50.

Koriat, Asher, and Ilia Levy. 1979. Figural Symbolism in Chinese Ideographs. *Journal of Psycholinguistic Research* 8.4:353–365.

Kratochvil, Paul. 1968. *The Chinese Language Today.* London.

Laberge, David. 1972. Beyond Auditory Coding. In James F. Kavanagh and Ignatius G. Mattingly, eds., *Language by Ear and by Eye: The Relationships between Speech and Writing.* Cambridge, MA.

Ledyard, Gary. 1966. The Korean Language Reform of 1446. Ph.D. dissertation, University of California, Berkeley.

Lee Ki-mun. 1977. *Geschichte der koreanische Sprache.* Seoul.

————. 1983. Foundations of Hunmin Chongum. In Korean National Commission for UNESCO, *The Korean Language.* Seoul.

Lee Sang-baek. 1957. *The Origin of the Korean Alphabet According to New Historical Evidence.* Seoul.

Li Dongyi. 1980. Guanyu Yuenan de "nanzi." *Yuwen xiandaihua* 4:242–248.

Li Fang-kuei. 1973. Languages and Dialects of China. *Journal of Chinese Linguistics* 1:1–13.

Li Xingjie. 1987. Tongjiazi de xiaozhang yu zhengcifa de queli. *Yuwen jianshe* 5:22–27.

Liang Shih-ch'iu, ed. 1971. *A New Practical Chinese-English Dictionary.* Taipei.

Lin Lianhe. 1980. Guanyu hanzi tongji tezheng de jige wenti. *Yuwen xiandaihua* 1:135–150.

Liu Shih-hong. 1969. *Chinese Characters and Their Impact on Other Languages of East Asia.* Taipei.

Liu Yongquan. 1991. Difficulties in Chinese Information Processing and Ways to Their Solution. In Victor H. Mair and Yongquan Liu, eds., *Characters and Computers.* Amsterdam.

Logan, Robert K. 1986. *The Alphabet Effect.* New York.

Lu Zhifen. 1955. Zhengli yinshwa ziti de jianyi. In *Hanzi de zhengli he jianhua.* Zhongguo yuwen zazhi she, Beijing.

Mae, Chu-chang, and Donald J. Loritz. 1977. Phonological Encoding of Chinese Ideographs in Short-Term Memory. *Language Learning* 27.2:341–351.

Maevskiy, E. V. 1973. K voprosu o sootnoshenii ustnogo i pis'mennogo variantov yaponskogo yazyka. *Voprosy yaponskoy filologii* 2:60–78.

Mair, Victor. 1990. Old Sinitic *mʸag, Old Persian *magus,* and English "magician." *Early China* 15:27–47.

————. 1991a. What Is a Chinese "Dialect/Topolect"? Reflections on Some Key Sino-English Linguistic Terms. *Sino-Platonic Papers* 31 (September).

————. 1991b. Building the Future of Information Processing in East Asia Demands Facing Linguistic and Technological Reality. In Victor H. Mair and Yongquan Liu, eds., *Characters and Computers.* Amsterdam.

————. 1992. East Asian Round-Trip Words. *Sino-Platonic Papers* 34 (October):5–13.

————. 1994. Buddhism and the Rise of the Written Vernacular in East Asia: The Making of National Languages. *The Journal of Asian Studies* 53.3:707–751.

————. 1995. Mummies of the Tarim Basin. *Archaeology* 48:2 (March/April):28–35.

Marcie, Pierre. 1983. Writing Disorders Associated with Focal Cortical Lesions. In Margaret Martlew, ed., *The Psychology of Written Language*. New York.

Marshall, John C. 1976. Neuropsychological Aspects of Orthographic Representation. In R. J. Wales and Edward Walker, eds., *New Approaches to Language Mechanisms*. Amsterdam, New York, Oxford.

Martin, Helmut. 1982. *Chinesische Sprachplanung*. Bochum.

Martin, Samuel. 1972. Nonalphabetic Writing Systems: Some Observations. In James F. Kavanagh and Ignatius G. Mattingly, eds., *Language by Ear and by Eye: The Relationships between Speech and Reading*. Cambridge, MA.

Martlew, Margaret. 1983a. Problems and Difficulties: Cognitive and Communicative Aspects of Writing. In Margaret Martlew, ed., *The Psychology of Written Language*. New York.

————. 1983b. The Development of Writing: Communication and Cognition. In Florian Coulmas and Konrad Ehlich, eds., *Writing in Focus*. Berlin.

Maruya Saiichi. 1982. Kotoba to moji to seishin to. In Maruya Saiichi, ed., *Nihongo no sekai*, vol. 16. Tokyo.

Matsuda Ryouichi. 1985. Processing Information in Japanese. *Computer* 18.1:37–45.

Matsunaga, Sachiko. 1994. The Linguistic and Psycholinguistic Nature of Kanji. Ph.D. dissertation, University of Hawai'i.

Mattingly, Ignatius G. 1972. Reading, the Linguistic Process, and Linguistic Awareness. In James F. Kavanagh and Ignatius G. Mattingly, eds., *Language by Ear and by Eye: The Relationship between Speech and Reading*. Cambridge, MA.

Miller, Roy A. 1967. *The Japanese Language*. Chicago.

————. 1977. *The Japanese Language in Contemporary Japan*. Washington, D.C.

Morioka Kenji. 1973. Kanji no sōbetsu. *Kokubungaku ronshū* 7. Cited in Maruya Saiichi, ed., *Nihongo no sekai* 16:188 (1982). Tokyo.

Morohashi Tetsuji. 1960. *Dai kanwa jiten*. 13 volumes. Tokyo.

Motsh, B. 1963. K voprosu ob otnoshenii mezhdu ustnyi i pis'mennym yazykom. *Voprosy yazykoznaniya* 1.

Muller, Brigitte. 1975. *Kōyōbun: Ein Beitrag zur japanischen Sprachpolitik seit dem Zweiten Weltkrieg*. Hamburg.

Nakada Norio. 1982. Nihon no kanji. In Maruya Saiichi, ed., *Nihongo no sekai*, vol. 4. Tokyo.

Nam Kwang-u. 1970. *Hyŏndae kuk'ŏ kukja ŭi che munje*. Seoul.

————. 1979. Hanguk ŏmun kyoyuk yŏnguhoe an: sangyong hanja 1,800 ja rŭl hwakjŏnghamyŏnsŏ. *Ŏmun yŏngu* 21:7–13.

————. 1984. Kukhan honyong ron. In Kim Min-su et al., *Kuk'ŏ wa minjok munhwa*. Seoul.

Nelson, Andrew N. 1962. *Japanese-English Character Dictionary*. Second edition (revised). Rutland, VT.

Neverov, S. V. 1977. Yazyk massovoy kommunikatsii—"obshchiy yazyk" sovremennoy yaponii. In L. B. Nikol'skiy, ed., *Yazykovaya politika v Afro-Aziatskikh stranakh*. Moscow.

Nguyen Dinh Hoa. 1959. Chu Nom: The Demotic System of Writing in Vietnam. *Journal of the American Oriental Society* 79:270–274.

————. 1966. *Vietnamese-English Dictionary*. Vermont and Tokyo.

Nida, Eugene. 1948. The Identification of Morphemes. *Language* 24:414–441.

Norman, Jerry. 1988. *Chinese*. Cambridge, MA.

Nyikos, Julius. 1988. A Linguistic Perspective of Illiteracy. In Sheila Embleton, ed., *The Fourteenth LACUS Forum* (1987), 146–163. Lake Bluff, IL.

Oh Chi-ho. 1971. *Kuk'ŏ e taehan chungdaehan ohae*. Seoul.

Ohara Nobukazu. 1989. *Shin kanji no utsurikawari*. Tokyo.

Okazaki Tsunetaro. 1938. *Kanji seigen no kihonteki kenkyū*. Tokyo.

Olson, David R. 1982. What Is Said and What Is Meant in Speech and Writing. *Visible Language* 16.2:151–161.

Ono Susumu. 1982. Kokugo kaikaku no rekishi (senzen). In Maruya Saiichi, ed., *Nihongo no sekai*, vol. 16. Tokyo.

Packard, Jerome L. 1987. Review of Michel Paradis, Hiroko Hagiwara, and Nancy Hildebrandt, *Neurolinguistic Aspects of the Japanese Writing System*. *Brain and Language* 30:381–386.

Pak Chong-so. 1968. *Kuk'ŏ ŭi changnae wa hanja ŭi chae insik*. Seoul.

Paradis, Michel, Hiroko Hagiwara, and Nancy Hildebrandt. 1985. *Neurolinguistic Aspects of the Japanese Writing System*. New York.

Pu Li. 1973. Hanzi jingjian da you kewei. *Renmin ribao*, August 22, 1973. Reprinted in Peter J. Seybolt and Gregory Kuei-ke Chiang, *Language Reform in China*. New York, 1978.

Pulgram, Ernst. 1976. The Typologies of Writing Systems. In W. Haas, ed., *Writing without Letters*. Manchester.

Qian Nairong. 1989. *Shanghai fangyan liyu*. Shanghai.

Ramsey, S. Robert. 1987. *The Languages of China*. Princeton.

Rawski, Evelyn Sakakida. 1979. *Education and Popular Literacy in Ch'ing China*. Ann Arbor.

Read, Charles. 1983. Orthography. In Margaret Martlew, ed., *The Psychology of Written Language*. New York.

Reed, David W. 1970. A Theory of Language, Speech, and Writing. In Mark Lester, ed., *Readings in Applied Transformational Grammar*. New York.

Rozin, Paul. 1978. The Acquisition of Basic Alphabetic Principles: A Structural Approach. In A. Charles Catania and Thomas A. Brigham, eds., *Handbook of Applied Behavior Analysis*. New York.

Rozin, Paul, and Lila R. Gleitman. 1977. The Structure and Acquisition of Reading II: The Reading Process and the Acquisition of the Alphabetic Principle. In Arthur S. Reber and Don L. Scarborough, eds., *Toward a Psychology of Reading*. Hillsdale, NJ.

Rozin, Paul, Susan Poritsky, and Raina Sotsky. 1971. American Children with Reading Problems Can Easily Learn to Read English Represented by Chinese Characters. *Science* 3977:1264–1267.

Ruan Dezhong. 1979. *Taiwanhua Rumen*. Taipei.

Rubenstein, H., S. S. Lewis, and M. A. Rubenstein. 1971. Evidence for Phonemic Recoding in Visual Word Recognition. *Journal of Verbal Learning and Verbal Behavior* 10:645–657.

Saiga Hideo. 1971. Tōyō kanjihyō no mondaiten. In Morioka Kenji, ed., *Tadashii nihongo*, vol. 3. Tokyo.

Sampson, Geoffrey. 1985. *Writing Systems*. London.

Sansom, George. 1928. *An Historical Grammar of Japanese*. London.

Sapir, Edward. 1921/1949. *Language*. New York.

Sasanuma, Sumiko, and O. Fujimura. 1971. Selective Impairment of Phonetic and Non-Phonetic Transcription of Words in Japanese Aphasic Patients: *Kana* vs. *Kanji* in Visual Recognition and Writing. *Cortex* 7:1–18.

Sasanuma, Sumiko, Motonobu Itoh, Kazuko Mori, and Yo Kobayashi. 1977. Tachistoscopic Recognition of *Kana* and *Kanji* Words. *Neuropsychologia* 15:547–553.

Scinto, Leonard F. M. 1986. *Written Language and Psychological Development.* New York.

Seeley, Chris. 1984. The Japanese Script since 1900. *Visible Language* 18.3:267–302.

Serruys, Paul L-M. 1959. *The Chinese Dialects of Han Time According to Fang Yen.* Berkeley.

———. 1962. *Survey of the Chinese Language Reform and the Anti-Illiteracy Movement in Communist China.* Berkeley.

Seybolt, Peter J., and Gregory Kuei-ke Chiang. 1978. *Language Reform in China.* New York.

Shi Xiaoren. 1983. Tan tongyinci he tongyinzi wenti. *Yuwen xiandaihua* 6:53–68.

Shibata Takeshi. 1987. Watashi no mojiron. *Nihongogaku* 6:8–11.

Shimizu, Akinori, and Masaomi Endo. 1981. Tachistoscopic Recognition of *Kana* and *Hangul* Words, Handedness and Shift of Laterality Difference. *Neuropsychologia* 19.5:665–73.

Shtrintsin, A. G. 1972. Ieroglifika i nauchnyy stil' sovremennogo kitayskogo i yaponskogo yazykov. In O. D. Rivkina, ed., *Literatura i kul'tura kitaya.* Moscow.

Sim Kyong-ho. 1989. Pukhan ŭi hanja hanmun kyoyuk. In Ko Yŏng-gun, ed., *Pukhan ŭi mal kwa kŭl.* Seoul.

Smith, Frank. 1983. *Essays into Literacy.* London.

So T'ae-gil. 1989. Pukhan ŭi ŏn'ŏ chŏngch'aek koch'al. In Kim Min-su, ed., *Pukhan ui ŏhak hyŏngmyŏng.* Seoul.

Sokolov, A. N. 1959. K voprosu ob ieroglificheskoy pis'mennost'. In A. A. Pashkovskiy, ed., *Yaponskiy lingvisticheskiy sbornik.* Moscow.

———. 1963. Yavlenie amorfemnosti v yaponskom ieroglificheskom pis'me. In A. G. Ryabkin and E. A. Potseluyevskiy, eds., *Yaponskiy yazyk.* Moscow.

———. 1970. Krizisnyye yavleniya v yaponskom pis'me. *Voprosy yaponskoy filologii* 1:94–106.

———. 1977. Vzglyad na pis'mo s pozitsii teori znakovosti yazyka. *Voprosy yaponskoy filologii* 4:73–80.

———. 1981. Ieroglificheskaya omografiya v sisteme yaponskogo pis'ma. *Voprocy yaponskoy filologii* 5:16–20.

Solntsev, V. M. 1985. Preface to T. A. Amirova, *Funktsional'naya vzaimosvyaz' pis'mennogo i zvukovogo yazyka.* Moscow.

Steinberg, Danny D., and Jun Yamada. 1978–1979a. Are Whole Word Kanji Easier to Learn than Syllable Kana? *Reading Research Quarterly* 14.1:88–99.

———. 1978–1979b. Pigs Will Be Chickens: Reply to Tzeng and Singer. *Reading Research Quarterly* 14.4:668–671.

Stubbs, Michael. 1980. *Language and Literacy: The Sociolinguistics of Reading and Writing.* London.

Studdert-Kennedy, Michael. 1975. From Continuous Signal to Discrete Message:

Syllable to Phoneme. In James F. Kavanagh and James E. Cutting, eds., *The Role of Speech in Language*. Cambridge.

Sugimori Hisahide. 1982. Kokugo kaikaku no rekishi (sengo). In Maruya Saiichi, ed., *Nihongo no sekai*, vol. 16. Tokyo.

Suzuki Takao. 1975. On the Twofold Phonetic Realization of Basic Concepts: In Defense of Chinese Characters in Japanese. In Fred C. C. Peng, ed., *Language in Japanese Society*. Tokyo.

———. 1987. In Hashimoto Mantaro, Suzuki Takao, and Yamada Hisao, *Kanji minzoku no ketsudan: kanji no mirai ni mukete*. Tokyo.

Tao Kun. 1957. Wenzi gaige wenti zuotanhui jilu. *Pinyin*, July, 1–29. Reprinted in Peter J. Seybolt and Gregory Kuei-ke Chiang, *Language Reform in China*. New York, 1978.

Tezuka Akira. 1987. Gengo shikō no wakugumi toshite no moji shisutemu no hyōron. *Nihongogaku* 6:88–103.

Teng, Ssu-yu, and Knight Biggerstaff. 1971. *An Annotated Bibliography of Selected Chinese Reference Works*. Cambridge, MA.

Thompson, Laurence C. 1987. *A Vietnamese Reference Grammar*. Honolulu.

Thompson, Laurence C., and David D. Thomas. 1967. Vietnam. In Thomas Sebeok, ed., *Trends in Linguistics*, 2. The Hague.

Thranhardt, Anne Maria. 1978. *Schriftreform-Diskussion in Japan zwischen 1869 und 1890*. Hamburg.

Tien, Su-O L. 1983. A Psycholinguistic Study of the Reading Process in Chinese, with Comparison to English. Paper presented to the Conference on Linguistic Modernization and Language Planning in Chinese-Speaking Communities, East-West Center, University of Hawai'i, September 7–13, 1983.

Treiman, Rebecca A., Jonathan Baron, and Kenneth Luk. 1981. Speech Recoding in Silent Reading. *Journal of Chinese Linguistics* 9:116–125.

Tsao, Yao-chung, and Tsai-guey Wang. 1983. Information Distribution in Chinese Characters. *Visible Language*. 17.4:357–364.

Twine, Nanette. 1983. Toward Simplicity: Script Reform Movements in the Meiji Period. *Monumenta Nipponica* 38.2:115–132.

Tzeng, Ovid J. L., Daisy L. Hung, Bill Cotton, and William S-Y. Wang. 1979. Visual Lateralisation Effect in Reading Chinese Characters. *Nature* 282:499–501.

Tzeng, Ovid J. L., Daisy L. Hung, and Linda Garro. 1978. Reading the Chinese Characters: An Information Processing View. *Journal of Chinese Linguistics* 6:287–305.

Tzeng, Ovid J. L., Daisy L. Hung, and William S-Y. Wang. 1977. Speech Recoding in Reading Chinese Characters. *Journal of Experimental Psychology: Human Learning and Memory* 3.6:621–630.

Tzeng, Ovid J. L., and Harry Singer. 1978. Failure of Steinberg and Yamada to Demonstrate Superiority of Kanji over Kana for Initial Reading Instruction in Japan. *Reading Research Quarterly* 14.4:661–667.

Uldall, H. J. 1944. Speech and Writing. *Acta Linguistica* 4:11–16.

Unger, J. Marshall. 1987. *The Fifth Generation Fallacy*. New York.

———. 1991. Minimum Specifications for Japanese and Chinese Alphanumeric Workstations. In Victor H. Mair and Yongquan Liu, eds., *Characters and Computers*. Amsterdam.

Vachek, Josef. 1967. *K probleme pis'mennogo yazyka:* Prazhskiy Lingvisticheskiy

Kruzhok. Moscow. Translated from *Zum Problem der geschriebenen Sprache*. Travaux du Cercle linguistique de Prague. 1939.

———. 1989. *Written Language Revisited*. Amsterdam and Philadelphia.

Vardul', I. F. 1977. *Osnovy opisatel'noy lingvistiki*. Moscow.

Venezky, Richard L. 1972. *Language Cognition and Reading*. Madison, WI.

Wang, Fang-yu. 1958. *Introduction to Chinese Cursive Script*. New Haven.

Wang Fengyang. 1980. Hanzi pinlu yu hanzi jianhua. *Yuwen xiandaihua* 3:83–103.

Wen Wu. 1980. Cong Yingwen de tongxingci lai kan hanyu pinyin wenzi de tong-yinci. *Yuwen xiandaihua* 2:120–124.

Wieger, L. 1915. *Chinese Characters*. Reprinted in 1965. New York.

Wrolstad, Merald E. 1976 A Manifesto for Visible Language. *Visible Language* 10.1:5–40.

Wu, Apollo. 1991. Enhanced Hanyu Pinyin Input Accuracy with a Skewed Tone-Indication Approach. In Victor H. Mair and Yongquan Liu, eds., *Characters and Computers*. Amsterdam.

Xie Kai. 1989. Cong fuhaoxue guandian kan yuyan wenzi de guanxi. *Yuwen jianshe* 1:16–20.

Xin Feng. 1989. "Buzhi zhi zheng" youle zhi. *Yuwen jianshe* 1:35–36.

Xu Chang'an. 1987. Hanzi ladinghua shi yitiao lishi Chang He. *Wenzi gaige* 5:42–44.

Yamada Hisao. 1987. In Hashimoto Mantaro, Suzuki Takao, and Yamada Hisao. *Kanji minzoku no ketsudan: kanji no mirai ni mukete*. Tokyo.

Yamada Yoshio. 1967. The Writing System: Historical Research and Modern Development. In Thomas Sebeok, ed., *Trends in Linguistics* 2. The Hague.

Yi Kang-ro. 1969. *Kuk'ŏ kyoyuk ŭi parŭn kil*. Seoul.

Yi Sang-ok. 1989. Pukhan ŭi romaja pyogibŏp. In Ko Yŏng-gun, ed., *Pukhan ŭi mal kwa kŭl*. Seoul.

Yi Sang-un. 1973. Hangul chŏnyong kyoyuk ŭi ch'il tae p'yehae wa kŭ sijŏng-ch'aek. *Ŏmun yŏngu* 2:117–128.

Yi Ul-hwan. 1977. Tong'ŭm'ŏ hyŏnsang. *Ŏmun yŏngu* 15:64–69.

Yi Un-jong. 1989. *Kaejŏnghan hanguk'ŏ match'umbŏp, p'yojun parumbŏp*. Seoul.

Yi Xiwu. 1955. Tongyin jiajie shi jingjian hanzi de yige fangfa. In *Hanzi de zhengli he jianhua*. Zhongguo yuwen zazhi she, Beijing.

Yi Yong-baek. 1974. Hyŏndae inmyŏng chimyŏng e ssŭin hanja yŏngu. *Ŏmun yŏngu* 4:168–177.

———. 1979. Sinmun p'yoje e nat'anan hanja wa kyoyuk hanja kŏmt'o. *Ŏmun yŏngu* 22:195–226.

Yi Yun-p'yo. 1989. Pukhan ŭi hanja kyoyuk e taehayŏ. In Kim Min-su, ed., *Pukhan ui ŏhak hyŏngmyŏng*. Seoul.

Yin Binyong. 1991. Pinyin-to-Chinese Character Computer Conversion Systems and the Realization of Digraphia in China. In Victor H. Mair and Yongquan Liu, eds., *Characters and Computers*. Amsterdam.

Yu Chong-gi. 1975. Kuk'ŏ hanja ŭi soksŭpbŏp. *Ŏmun yŏngu* 7.8:280.

Yu Pong-yong. 1974. Sahoe siljong kwa kyoyuk chŏngch'aek. *Ŏmun yŏngu* 4:152–162.

Yuan Jiahua. 1960. *Hanyu fangyan gaiyao*. Beijing.

Zhan Bohui. 1981. *Xiandai hanyu fangyan*. Hubei.

Zhang Renbiao. 1955. Guanyu "chang yong zi biao" de jige wenti. In *Hanzi de zhengli he jianhua*. Zhongguo yuwen zazhi she, Beijing.

Zhang Yuquan and Li Dongyi. 1980. Hanzi gaige yu wenzi xinxi chuli. *Yuwen xiandaihua* 1:80–90.

Zhang Zhiyi and Zhang Qingyun. 1980. Shi lun yitici de zhengli. *Yuwen xiandaihua* 3:104–113.

Zheng Linxi. 1955. Hanzi tongyin daiyong guilu de chubu yanjiu. In *Hanzi de zhengli he jianhua*. Zhongguo yuwen zazhi she, Beijing.

———. 1957. *Hanzi gaige*. Shanghai.

Zhou Youguang. 1961. *Hanzi gaige gailun*. Beijing.

———. 1978. Xiandai hanzi zhong shengpang de biaoyin gongneng wenti. *Zhongguo yuwen* 3:172–177.

———. 1987a. Chugoku no kanji kaikaku to kanji kyoiku. In Hashimoto Mantaro et al., *Kanji minzoku no ketsudan: kanji no mirai ni mukete*. Tokyo.

———. 1987b. Zhongguo yuci chuli he xiandai hanzixue. *Yuwen jianshe* 5:7–13.

———. 1991. The Family of Chinese Character–Type Scripts. *Sino-Platonic Papers* 28:1–11.

Index

Literacy: 126, 284–285, 287; in Japan, 285–286; in Korea, 286–287; in Vietnam, 78, 83, 90; in the West, 271. See also Chinese characters, and literacy
Liu Fu, 302
Liu Shih-hong, 132, 183, 311
Liu Yongquan, 260
Li Xingjie, 152, 310
Loanwords. See Borrowing
Logographic, 10, 32, 109, 111, 169, 249, 306–307
Lo Lang, 54
Lu Xun, 128, 297
Lu Zhifen, 211
Lu Zhuanzhang, 24

Maejima Hisoka, 39, 249
Maevskiy, E. V., 120
Mair, Victor, 191, 199, 247, 267, 313
Majiribun. See Mixed script
Malaysian, 75
Manchu, 97
Mandarin, 7, 20, 24, 76, 142, 175, 181, 191–201, 203, 224–225, 252–253, 256, 273–274, 303, 310, 313
Manga, 285
Manyōgana, 37
Manyōshu, 37
Marcie, Pierre, 157
Marshall, John C., 161–162, 171
Martin, Helmut, 86, 90, 183
Martin, Samuel, 58, 184
Martlew, Margaret, 241
Marxism-Leninism, 65–66
Mass Education Movement, 210
Matsuda Ryouichi, 136
Mattingly, Ignatius G., 310
May 4 Movement, 20
McCune-Reischauer, 61–62
Meiroku zasshi, 40
Mencken, Henry L., 88
Mental lexicon, 159
Miao-Yao, 199
Miller, Roy A., 34, 38, 47, 145
Min, 7–8, 116, 191–192, 196–198, 200
Missionaries, 39, 84
Mixed script, 26, 38, 249–250, 299
Mongolian, 27, 49, 277
Mon-Khmer, 75
Monno, 39

Monosyllabic, 8, 76–77, 129, 174–178, 181, 184, 201, 203, 209, 212, 217, 253, 255, 275, 299, 301
Mora, 304
Mori Arinori, 40
Morioka Kenji, 149
Morohashi Tetsuji, 302
Morphemes: definition, 101, 112–113, 118–122, 307; in Chinese, 4–5, 13, 15, 32, 36, 112, 127, 129, 178–180, 197, 203, 215; in Japanese, 27, 29–30, 34, 36, 38, 112–113, 216; in Korean, 51, 64; psychological reality, 122, 159; in Vietnamese, 77, 79. See also Chinese characters and morphemes
Morphophonemic, 76, 121, 275, 299
Morse telegraphy, 269, 280
Motsh, B., 237
Muller, Brigitte, 45, 216

Nambu Yoshikazu, 40
Nam Kwang-u, 138, 184, 250, 303
National Language Committee (Korea), 70
National Language Council (Japan), 43–44, 47
National Language Research Committee (Japan), 42–43
National Phonetic Alphabet, 25
Native American languages, 235
Needham, Joseph, 314
Nelson, Andrew, 107, 140, 184
Neurolinguistics, 122
Neverov, S. V., 186
Nguyen Thuyen, 79
Niga, Eugene, 307
Nihon Romaji-kai, 303
Nihon shoki, 32, 34
Nihon-siki, 42
Nishi Amane, 40
Nonhearing, 157, 161, 163
Nyikos, Julius, 307

Oath record style, 55
Ohara Nobukazu, 20
Oh Chi-ho, 145
Okazaki Tsunetaro, 215–216
Okoten, 35
Okurigana, 31, 45–46, 216–217, 273
Olson, David R., 105, 254
Ŏnmun, 63, 304
Ono Susumu, 136